NORTHWESTERN ZEALAND
Pages 112–147

SOUTHERN ZEALAND AND THE ISLANDS
Pages 148–167

COPENHAGEN
Pages 46–107

BORNHOLM
Pages 212–223

Skagen

Frederikshavn

Grenå

Ebeltoft

Århus

Odden Færgehavn

Frederiksværk

Helsingør

Hillerød

Hørsholm

Birkerød

Frederikssund

Holbæk

Copenhagen (København)

Kalundborg

Roskilde

Tåstrup

NORTHWESTERN ZEALAND

Odense

Slagelse

Sorø

Ringsted

Køge

Korsør

SOUTHERN ZEALAND AND THE ISLANDS

FUNEN

Nyborg

Næstved

Faaborg

Svendborg

Rudkøbing

Vordingborg

Stege

Ærøskøbing

Bagenkop

Nakskov

Nykøbing F.

Rødbyhavn

Gedser

Puttgarden

0 km   40

0 miles   20

BORNHOLM

Denmark

Bornholm

DENMARK

EYEWITNESS TRAVEL GUIDES

DENMARK

MONIKA WITKOWSKA
JOANNA HALD

DK

LONDON, NEW YORK,
MELBOURNE, MUNICH AND DELHI
www.dk.com

Produced by Wydawnictwo Wiedza i Życie, Warsaw

SENIOR GRAPHIC DESIGNER Paweł Pasternak
EDITORS Maria Betlejewska, Joanna Egert-Romanowska
AUTHORS Joanna Hald, Marek Pernal, Jakub Sito,
Barbara Sudnik-Wójcikowska, Monika Witkowska

CARTOGRAPHERS Magdalena Polak, Olaf Rodowald,
Jarosław Talacha
PHOTOGRAPHERS Dorota and Mariusz Jarymowiczowie
ILLUSTRATORS Michał Burkiewicz, Paweł Marcza
GRAPHIC DESIGN Paweł Pasternak
DTP Elżbieta Dudzińska

For Dorling Kindersley

TRANSLATOR Magda Hannay
EDITOR Matthew Tanner
SENIOR DTP DESIGNER Jason Little
PRODUCTION CONTROLLER Rita Sinha

Reproduced by Colourscan, Singapore

Printed and bound in China by
Toppan Printing Co. (Shenzhen), Ltd

First published in Great Britain in 2005
by Dorling Kindersley Limited, 80 Strand, London WC2R 0RL

Copyright © 2005 Dorling Kindersley, London
A Penguin Company

A CIP CATALOGUE RECORD IS AVAILABLE FROM THE BRITISH LIBRARY.

ISBN-13 978-1-40531-064-2
ISBN-10 1-40531-064-2

FLOORS ARE REFERRED TO THROUGHOUT IN ACCORDANCE WITH BRITISH
USAGE; IE THE "FIRST FLOOR" IS THE FLOOR ABOVE GROUND LEVEL.

**The information in this
Dorling Kindersley Travel Guide is checked regularly.**
Every effort has been made to ensure that this book is as up-to-date
as possible at the time of going to press. Some details, however,
such as telephone numbers, opening hours, prices, gallery hanging
arrangements and travel information are liable to change. The publishers
cannot accept responsibility for any consequences arising from the
use of this book, nor for any material on third party websites,
and cannot guarantee that any website address in this book
will be a suitable source of travel information. We value the views and
suggestions of our readers very highly. Please write to:
Publisher, DK Eyewitness Travel Guides
Dorling Kindersley, 80 Strand, London WC2R 0RL, Great Britain

◁ **Colourful 18th-century houses and yachts on Nyhavn, Copenhagen**

CONTENTS

Church organ, Copenhagen

INTRODUCING DENMARK

**Amalienborg and Marmorkirken,
Copenhagen, seen from the water**

The Lille Tårn (Little Tower), Frederiksø

Trumpeters' monument standing near Copenhagen's Rådhus

Christiansborg, Copenhagen

HOW TO USE THIS GUIDE

THIS GUIDE WILL HELP you get the most out of a visit to Denmark. The first section, *Introducing Denmark*, provides information about the country's geographic location, its history and culture. The sections devoted to the capital and other large cities, as well as to individual regions, describe the major sights and visitor attractions. Information on accommodation and restaurants can be found in the *Travellers' Needs* section. The *Survival Guide* provides practical tips on everything a visitor may need to know, from money and language to getting around and seeking medical care.

COPENHAGEN

This section has been divided into three parts, each devoted to a separate part of the city. Sights outside the capital's centre are described in the *Further Afield* section. All sights are numbered and plotted on the area map. Detailed information for each sight is given in numerical order.

Sights at a Glance lists the sights in an area by category: churches, museums and art galleries; streets and squares; parks and gardens.

A suggested route for sightseeing is indicated by a dotted red line.

2 Street-by-Street Map
Provides a bird's-eye view of the town centre described in the section.

Pages referring to Copenhagen are marked in red.

A locator map shows where visitors are in relation to other areas of the city.

1 Area Map
For easy reference the sights are numbered and plotted on the area map, as well as on the main map of Copenhagen (see pp104–7).

Star Sights indicate parts of buildings, historic sights, exhibits and monuments that no visitor should miss.

3 Detailed Information
All the major sights of Copenhagen are described individually. Practical information includes addresses, telephone numbers, the most convenient buses and trains, and opening hours.

1 Introduction
This section deals with the landscape, history and character of each region, revealing how it has changed over time, and describing its current attractions.

DENMARK REGION BY REGION
In this guide Denmark is divided into seven regions, each of which has a separate section devoted to it. The most interesting cities, towns, villages and sights worth visiting are marked on each pictorial map.

2 Area Map
The area map shows the main road network and the overall topography of the region. All sights are numbered, and there is also information on public transport and getting around.

Boxes highlight interesting aspects or people associated with a sight.

Each region of Denmark can be found by using the colour code. The colours are explained on the inside front cover.

3 Detailed Information
Towns, villages and major tourist attractions are listed in numerical order, corresponding with the area map. Each entry contains information on important sights.

The Visitors' Checklist provides practical information to help plan your visit.

4 Major Sights
At least two pages are devoted to each major sight. Historic buildings are dissected to reveal their interiors. Major towns and town centres have street maps with the principal sights marked on them.

INTRODUCING DENMARK

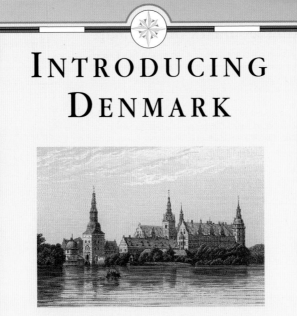

Putting Denmark on the Map

DENMARK IS SITUATED between the North Sea to the west and the Baltic Sea to the southeast. Most of Denmark consists of Jutland, a peninsula that covers 29,766 sq km (11,493 sq miles). The rest of the country consists of some 480 islands, of which the largest are Bornholm, Funen and Zealand. Far to the north, Greenland and the Faroe Islands are self-governing overseas regions of Denmark.

KEY

✈ Airport

⛴ Ferry port

▬ Motorway

▬ Major road

= Other road

–⋅– National border

FAROE ISLANDS *(see p230)*

Streymoy
Borðoy
Eysturoy
Vágar
Thorshavn
Sandoy
Suðuroy

0 km 15
0 miles 15

GREENLAND *(see p226)*

Qaanaaq (Thule)
Qeqertarsuaq (Godhavn)
Tasilaq (Ammassalik)
Nuuk (Godthåb)
Qaqortoq (Julianehåb)

0 km 400
0 miles 400

Skagerrak

Oslo
Larvik
Moss
Kristiansand
Hirtshals
Hjørring
Brønderslev
Egersund
Bergen
Tórshavn
Hanstholm
Aalborg
Limfjorden
Thisted
Nykøbing Mors
Hobro
Nissum Bredning
Lemvig
Skive
Klejtrup Sø
Randers
Struer
Viborg
Gudenå
Nissum Fjord
Holstebro
Storå
Skive Å
Silkeborg
Århus
Herning
Julsø
Ringkøbing
Mossø
Skanderborg
Ringkøbing Fjord
Omme Å
Horsens
Vejle
Varde
Fredericia
Esbjerg
Kolding
Middelfart
Fanø
Ribe
Flådså
Fanø Bugt
Haderslev
Helnæs
Faaborg
Rømø
Åbenrå
Als
Ær
Tønder
Sønderborg
Flensburg

GERMANY

Schleswig

◁ **Chapel of Sankt Anna Kirke in Gudhjem, Bornholm**

EUROPE

CANADA

GREENLAND

RUSSIA

ICELAND

FAROE
ISLANDS

FINLAND

SWEDEN

NORWAY

ESTONIA

LATVIA

LITHUANIA

Copenhagen

BELARUS

0 km   100

0 miles   100

IRELAND

GREAT
BRITAIN

HOLLAND

BELGIUM

GERMANY

POLAND

UKRAINE

MOLDOVIA

CZECH REP.

SLOVAK REP.

Gothenburg

kagen

ederikshavn

Læsø

Aalborg Bugt

Anholt

Lagan

Kattegat

Grenå

Oslo

Ängelholm

15

21

Ebeltoft

Helsingør

Helsingborg

Landskrona

Odden
Færgehavn

Frederiksværk

Arresø

Hørsholm

rhus Bugt

Samsø

Sejerø

Hillerød

Birkerød

Øresund

Frederikssund

Sejerø Bugt

COPENHAGEN
(KØBENHAVN)

Lund

Røsnæs

Holbæk

Roskilde

Tåstrup

Amager

Malmø

E65

Kalundborg

Tissø

23

Køge Bugt

Trelleborg

9

Odense

Slagelse

Sorø

Ringsted

Køge

Baltic
Sea

Rønne

Nyborg

Korsør

E20

Agersø

Næstved

Fakse Bugt

Rostock
Travemünde

Svendborg

Knudshoved
Odde

Smålandsfarvandet

Vordingborg

Møn

Langeland

Stege

inge

Rudkøbing

røskøbing

Falster

Nakskov

Søndersø

Nykøbing F.

Bagenkop

Lolland

Rødbyhavn

Gedser

Kiel
Bay

Kiel

Puttgarden

Rostock

0 km   50

0 miles   50

BORNHOLM (see p212)

158

158

Rønne

38

0 km   10

0 miles   10

A PORTRAIT OF DENMARK

DENMARK IS MOST FAMOUS *for its association with the Vikings and the writer Hans Christian Andersen. It has, of course, far more to offer visitors, including miles of sandy coastline, beautiful countryside and historic buildings. Copenhagen, the country's capital, has a rich cultural life and world-class museums.*

Denmark, the southernmost and most continental of the Scandinavian countries, occupies over 480 islands, of which about 100 are inhabited. It acts as a bridge between mainland Europe and Scandinavia and is linked with the European continent by a narrow stretch of land, in the southern part of the Jutland peninsula, at the border with Germany.

Porcelain doll in traditional costume

Although not part of the Scandinavian peninsula, the Danes are linked with their northern neighbours by ties of common history and culture. There are also linguistic similarities and Danes can easily converse with people from Sweden or Norway.

The country has strong links with two autonomous regions: the Faroe Islands and Greenland, both of which are represented in the Danish parliament. Denmark exercises control over their banking, foreign policy and defence.

Denmark is a low-lying country with wide stretches of cornfields, moors and forests, including Rebild Bakker – Denmark's only national park. In addition, it has vast sand dunes, fjords and long stretches of beach. The country's immaculate towns and villages, with colourful houses adorned with flowers, include many examples of half-timbered design.

Picturesque houses along the bank of Nyhavn, Copenhagen

◁ The "Black Diamond" extension to Det Kongelige Bibliotek (The Royal Library), Copenhagen

Changing of the guards at Amalienborg Slot, Copenhagen

Majestic castles, palaces and historic churches pepper the Danish landscape. There are also many Viking ruins, as well as older remains including ancient dolmens dating from the Stone Age.

Denmark is acknowledged to be a peaceful and liberal country, with a well-organized transport system and a comprehensive system of social welfare. It has enviably low levels of crime and corruption. In rural areas it is not unusual to see stalls by the roadside on which local farmers have left their produce on sale unattended.

Statue of the Little Mermaid – a symbol of Copenhagen

Charming half-timbered house in Rønne, on the island of Bornholm

TRADITIONS AND POLITICS

The national flag – the Danneborg – is the world's oldest and the Danes demonstrate their patriotism by unfurling it during state and family celebrations. According to legend, the flag takes its origin from a banner, bearing a white cross on a red background, which was dropped from heaven to rally the Danish knights during a battle fought in present-day Estonia in the early 13th century.

The Danes are proud of their heritage and in summer many families visit Viking villages in order to sample the lives of their distant ancestors. Most Danes regard the fact that their monarchy is the oldest in the world with pride. The present queen, Margrethe II, has been on the throne since 1972 and is the first female monarch in Denmark since the 14th century. In addition to performing all ceremonial functions, this popular queen is credited with transforming the monarchy into a modern institution.

In political matters, the monarchy's influence is limited by the Danish constitution. The direction of national policy is determined in the Folketinget, the chamber in Christiansborg Slot, Copenhagen, where the country's 179 members of parliament sit. About a dozen parties are represented in parliament. Elections take place every four years and over 90 per cent of those eligible to vote turn out at election time. Most important national issues are decided by popular vote, however. Decisions made in referenda have included the Danes' approval of a constitutional amendment allowing a woman to inherit the throne in 1953 and, in 2000, the rejection of the euro.

View of Egeskov Slot, Funen, surrounded on all sides by water

SOCIETY AND EVERYDAY LIFE

Denmark is largely inhabited by ethnic Danes who are ancestors of the Teutonic tribes that once populated all of Scandinavia.

Harald I (Bluetooth), Denmark's second king, was baptised as a Catholic in 960 and Denmark remained a Catholic country until well into the 16th century. During the 16th century the ideas of the German Protestant reformer Martin Luther won widespread support and Lutheranism became the official religion of Denmark with the accession of Christian III in 1534. Today, about 90 per cent of the population are Protestant, and although the churches remain fairly empty, many Danes subscribe to a tax that supports the Church.

Although Denmark is largely an ethnically homogenous country, relaxed immigration policies introduced in the 1960s helped to establish small communities of foreign nationals from outside Europe. Copenhagen is home to significant numbers of Turks and Palestinians as well as new arrivals from Ethiopia and the former Yugoslavia.

When it comes to bringing up children, many parents continue with their careers after taking parental leave. The progressive welfare system enables most women to return to work, at least part time.

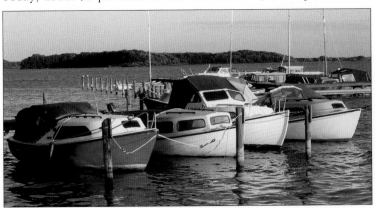
Harbour and sailing boat jetty, Maribo (Lolland)

Denmark's famous liberalism is perhaps best illustrated by "Christiania", a hippy commune that sprang up in 1971. Allowed to remain as a social experiment, it is inhabited by about 900 people seeking an alternative lifestyle.

The Danes are similarly relaxed when it comes to issues such as marriage. The country's divorce rate is one of the highest in Europe and nearly 20 per cent of couples co-habit without ever getting married. Abortion has been available "on demand" since the 1960s.

ECONOMY AND ECOLOGY

The Danish economy is fairly robust and the country has the EU's highest per-capita Gross National Product and a high standard of living.

Denmark was for centuries a land of farmers and fishermen. Today only 5 per cent of the country's population are employed in agriculture. Fishing, however, is still an important sector of the economy. The country is a major exporter of fish and is also known for its dairy and pork products. Other exports include beer, furniture and home electronics.

The Danes attach great importance to environmental issues. The country has an extensive network of alternative energy sources and the state-subsidized power-generating windmills are a common feature of the landscape. These supply over 15 per cent of the country's energy needs. Major investments are also made in the use of solar power and the island of Ærø, south of Funen, has one of Europe's largest solar power stations. All new building projects are scrutinized to minimize the impact on the environment. Danes take great care of their coastline, many resorts have been awarded the blue flag, denoting clean beaches. Recycling domestic waste is normal practice in Denmark, as is the use of environmentally friendly packaging (80 per cent of the country's paper production comes from recycled sources).

Father and son feeding pigeons in one of Copenhagen's open squares

Seaside scenery in Allinge, Bornholm

CULTURE, ART AND DESIGN

Denmark's cultural events range from major music festivals to local parades and concerts. Even smallish towns consider it a point of honour to organize festivals and concerts, putting on anything from classical music to pop and rock.

Oven-smoked fish, a popular delicacy

One of the largest events is the June rock festival in Roskilde, which attracts over 70,000 visitors.

Copenhagen's July jazz festival, held every year since 1978, is one of the top events of its kind in Europe and has attracted top performers including Dizzy Gillespie, Miles Davis and Oscar Peterson.

Denmark has a wide variety of wonderful museums including the Ny Carlsberg Glyptotek *(see pp78–9)* and the Nationalmuseet *(see pp84–5)*, both in Copenhagen, as well as the Arken and Louisiana museums, which are within easy reach of the capital. The Nationalmuseet devotes much of its space to exhibits relating to Danish culture and history but also has world-class collections of Greek, Roman and Egyptian artifacts. Among the Glyptotek's collection are examples of 19th-century European painting, representatives of Denmark's "Golden Age" *(see pp42–3)* and works by major international artists such as Pablo Picasso and Francis Bacon.

Many smaller museums and galleries are spread throughout the country. Some of these are devoted to the life and work of famous

Sculpture from the Holmegård glassworks

Danish individuals such as the composer Carl Nielsen and sculptor Bertel Thorvaldsen. Then there are more unusual museums such as Museum Erotica in Copenhagen *(see p71)* and Roskilde's Viking Ship Museum *(see p137)*.

Among the country's best-known architects and designers are Ole Kirk Christiansen, inventor of Lego, Jørn Utzon, creator of the Sydney Opera House and Arne Jacobsen, a pioneer of Danish modernism famous for his furniture and minimalist tableware. Prominent examples of Danish applied art include jewellery by Georg Jensen and sleek audio and visual equipment by Bang & Olufsen.

Ultra-modern Tycho Brahe Planetarium, Copenhagen

Danish Landscape and Flora

MORE THAN THREE QUARTERS of Denmark is less than 100 m (330 ft) above sea level. Most of its land-forms are of glacial origin, which adds variety to the lowland scenery. Forests, whose wholesale destruction was halted in the 19th century, occupy only a small percentage of the landscape and include commercial forests planted with spruce and fir, and natural forests dominated by beech and oak. Pastures and meadows are also distinctive features of the landscape and most of these are given over to crop cultivation and the rearing of livestock. A large portion of Denmark's highly diversified coastline consists of dunes, marshland and tidal flats.

DANISH FAUNA

Many mammals, including elks and bears, have disappeared in Denmark. What forests remain provide a habitat for deer, marten, wild boar and hare. Excellent nesting grounds are a haven for many birds including geese, storks, swans and sandpipers. The largest wild animal to be found in Denmark is the red deer, while polar bears can still be found in Greenland.

ZEALAND
The island covers an area of 7,000 sq km (2,702 sq miles), and has a diverse land-scape. In its northern section, on the outskirts of Copenhagen, there are fragments of natural forests – all that remains of a vast former wilderness. Elsewhere, the island has lakes, beaches and pasture land.

BORNHOLM
This island, largely composed of volcanic rock, has a mild climate. Its rugged granite cliffs, with stone rubble at their base, rise to over 80 m (262 ft) in height. At its northeastern end the well-preserved deciduous forests grow to the edge of the cliffs. The southern coast has long stretches of white sand beaches.

Seaside Centaury *(Centaurium littorale) is a species associated with salt flats, but can also sometimes be found growing on seaside sands.*

Bird's Eye Primrose *(Primula farinosa) is a rare peat bog species, which in Denmark is found only in isolated clusters.*

Common Wintergreen *(Pyrola minor) has a distinctive rosette of slightly leathery leaves; it grows in forests and deciduous woodlands, on acid soil.*

White Helleborine *(Cephalanthera damaso-nium) is an orchid with creamy-white flowers, and is often found in forests.*

Helleborine *(Epipactis) is found in several different varieties in Denmark. This orchid can be recognized by its labium, which is divided into two parts.*

Wild Strawberry *(Fraga-ria vesca) grows on woodland glades and banks. Its small red berries are sweet and fragrant.*

Five species of seal can be found on the coast of Greenland. The largest of these is the hooded seal, the male of which can weigh up to 400 kg (884 lbs). The Inuit still rely on seals for clothing and food.

The greylag goose is one of Denmark's largest wild geese. Pairs mate for life; some 4,000 pairs are thought to be breeding in Denmark.

The mute swan is Denmark's national bird and can be found in many parks and ponds throughout the country.

White storks, which winter in Africa, can be seen in summer in Denmark's marshes, meadows and pastures.

FUNEN

The island that separates Jutland from Zealand is famous for its scenery and is known as the "garden of Denmark" because it produces much of the country's fruit and vegetables. The terrain in the north of the island eventually levels out into marshland, while in the south it is more hilly.

JUTLAND

Lakes, which occupy about one per cent of Denmark's total area, are clustered mainly in the central part of Jutland. Yding Skovoj, Denmark's highest peak, can also be found here and is 173 m (568 ft) above sea level. Himmelbjerdget is 147 m (482 ft) above sea level and is a famous viewpoint.

Mountain Arnica (Arnica montana), *contrary to its name, is also found growing on lowlands, meadows, pastures and by roads. It is a valuable medicinal plant.*

Field Fleawort (Senecio integrifolius) *is a rare species, found in meadows, grasslands, pastures and woodlands.*

Sea Rocket (Cakile maritima) *is a delicate plant associated solely with Funen's sandy coast.*

Gentian (Gentianella) *is in danger of extinction and is legally protected in Denmark and many other European countries.*

Sea Holly (Eryngium maritimum) *is a typical plant of the seaside dunes and comes in white and grey varieties.*

Cinquefoil (Potentilla) *belongs to the rose family. There are several varieties growing in Denmark with yellow flowers.*

Danish Architecture

D ENMARK'S ARCHITECTURE includes many of the styles found elsewhere in Europe. The country's vernacular architecture includes 17th-century fortress churches and half-timbered houses. The influence of Baroque and Dutch Renaissance dominated the style of palaces built in the 17th and 18th centuries. Denmark's native character re-established itself with Neo-Classicism at the end of the 19th century and this trend has continued with contemporary landmark designs.

Dutch Renaissance Frederiksborg Slot, built mainly in the 17th century

ROMANESQUE ARCHITECTURE

The first Danish churches were built of wood, but they were quickly replaced by Norman structures that were usually constructed of granite. The 10th to 12th centuries marked the arrival of brick and stone Romanesque architecture, exemplified by the churches in Viborg and Ribe. Village churches, such as the one in Hover, Jutland, were usually built as single-aisle structures, with an apse or presbytery. The historic round churches found on Bornholm represent a very distinctive style. These medieval fortress-like buildings were built in the 12th century and were used not only for religious purposes but as places of refuge. Three-storeys high, the top two storeys were used for storage rooms and also provided shelter for the local population in times of danger.

Portal finial in the form of a pediment, with ornamental carvings

The portal tympanum has been decorated with a granite relief depicting the Deposition from the Cross, reminiscent of the reliefs found in the churches of northern Spain.

Ribe Domkirke *is a prime example of a Romanesque cathedral. Built on the site of a wooden structure, this stone building was begun in 1150. One of its most notable features is the "Cat's Head" door on the south side.*

Sankt Bendts Kirke, *Ringsted, was built during the reign of Valdemar I (1152–82) as a tomb for his father, Canute III. Later, more royals were buried here including Valdemar I. Its rich architecture encompasses an imposing edifice with a front tower, a presbytery enclosed with an apse and a mighty transept.*

Round churches were used as shelters during enemy raids.

Nylars' round church on Bornholm, built around 1150

GOTHIC ARCHITECTURE

One of the earliest Gothic buildings in Denmark is Roskilde's Domkirke (Cathedral), founded by Bishop Absalon in 1170. The most prominent example of the mature Gothic is the cathedral church in Odense. The introduction of red brick is an important element of the Danish Gothic style. Other typical features of Gothic architecture are its severe forms, ornate decorations and a façade that features stepped peaks. Many Gothic buildings have whitewashed or polychromatic interiors.

Sankt Knuds Domkirke *in Odense is a magnificent example of pure Gothic church brickwork. Most of the cathedral is 13th-century but the finely detailed gilded altar dates from the early 16th century and is the work of Claus Berg, a master craftsman from Lübeck.*

RENAISSANCE ARCHITECTURE

Danish Renaissance architecture grew out of the church's practice of importing architects for major projects in the late 16th century. Dutch architects and craftsmen were employed by Frederik II, and later by Christian IV in the 17th century, to build grand palaces such as Frederiksborg Slot in Hillerød and Kronberg Slot in Helsingør.

Triton figure from the Neptune fountain at Frederiksborg, by Adrian de Vries (c.1615).

Gables with richly-carved ornaments

Kronborg Slot, a stately castle built in 1585 by Frederik II, and later rebuilt by Christian IV

Jens Bangs Stenhus, Aalborg, is, along with the Børsen (Stock Exchange), Copenhagen, and the quaint streets and crooked houses of Christianshavn, a fine example of town architecture from this period.

BAROQUE ARCHITECTURE

From the mid-17th to mid-18th centuries Baroque in Denmark left its mark mainly on residential architecture. The best examples are Copenhagen's palaces – Charlottenborg and Christiansborg – along with the grand residence in Ledreborg. The main force behind Baroque in Denmark was the architect Nicolai Eigtved. His greatest achievement was the Frederikstad district in Copenhagen, which was built in a French style and intended as a royal quarter.

Audience Room in Frederiksborg Slot with moulded decorations

Fredensborg Slot is a sumptuous early-18th-century castle and was built by Frederik IV to a design by Johann Cornelius Krieger in an Italian Baroque style.

Altar from Vor Frelsers Kirke (Our Saviour's Church), Copenhagen

20TH-CENTURY ARCHITECTURE

In the early part of the 20th century Danish architecture began to reflect a desire for better design in housing and everyday objects, resulting in Modernism and, subsequently, Functionalism. A major result of this trend was the creation of the Design Council at the Association of Architects, in 1907. Characteristics of modern Danish architectural practice are an honest use of materials, clean lines and an abundance of natural light.

Water emphasises the visual link with a ship

The "Black Diamond", an extension of Det Kongelige Bibliotek (The Royal Library), Copenhagen, represents a Neo-Modernist trend that is gaining favour in Denmark.

Arken's Museet for Moderne Kunst (Museum of Modern Art) was designed by the then 25-year-old architect Søren Robert Lund, in metal and white concrete, and is a splendid example of Danish Deconstructivism.

Danish Design

Logo for Danish food chain

Lego® bricks, chairs by Arne Jacobsen, audio-visual equipment by Bang & Olufsen, jewellery by Georg Jensen: all are recognized throughout the world as examples of a Danish aesthetic. Design has a high profile in Denmark and constitutes an important source of revenue for the country, as well as being a major element of the national identity, supported by many institutions. Two good places to learn more about the traditions and history of Danish design are the Kunstindustrimuseet (Museum of Art and Design) and the Danish Design Centre, both of which are in Copenhagen.

Danish glass *is admired throughout the world. The factory in Holmegård was founded in the first half of the 19th century and initially employed workers brought over from Norway.*

Large windows blur the boundary between a room's interior and the outside.

Bang & Olufsen *high-fidelity products have been manufactured since 1925. The beauty of these products resides in the discreet use of the latest technology, which is coupled with audiophile performance.*

Furniture designer Kaare Klint *was fascinated by the possibility of combining ergonomics with traditional furniture design. His designs draw on many sources including pieces from 18th-century England.*

The Bodum company *was founded at the end of World War II by Peter Bodum. His smart and simple kitchen appliances, designed in the 1950s, are produced to this day and still enjoy great popularity.*

LEGO *is the name of the toy company founded in 1932 by Ole Kirk Christiansen. Christiansen started by producing wooden toys and, in 1958, introduced the now familiar plastic building bricks. The well-known brand name is a contraction of the Danish phrase "leg godt" ("play well").*

The Cylinda-Line (1967) series of tableware is one of Arne Jacobsen's best-known creations. It is made of steel which, along with wood and plastic, was one of his preferred materials.

The "Pins" stool (2002), by Hans Sandgren Jacobsen, is an example of modern design that still maintains Danish precision and aesthetics.

Light, open space

Functional, simple furniture

This Lamp by Poul Henningsen, from a series of lamps produced for Louis Poulsen & Co, is the result of a persistent endeavour by the designer to create lamps that give maximum natural light, while eliminating all shadows. He achieved the desired result by employing sets of shaped shades to produce a soft, dispersed light.

Innovative use of material

Danish porcelain, particularly the Flora Danica dinner service (1789), is famous throughout the world. This service is decorated with floral motifs drawn by the botanist Teodor Homskjal, a pupil of Linnaeus.

DESIGN FOR LIVING

Following World War II, Danish architects began to take an interest in the architectural styles of a number of other countries, drawing on many influences to produce open-plan house designs. This trend is, perhaps, best exemplified by houses that architects have built for themselves, such as the home of Jørn Utzon in Hellebæk, erected in 1952.

ARNE JACOBSEN

Born in 1902, Arne Jacobsen is the unquestionable "star" of Danish design. In his youth, Jacobsen was fascinated by the work of the Swiss-born architect Le Corbusier, especially his focus on functionality. As a designer Jacobsen created many well-known pieces including the Ant (1951). This plywood chair could be stacked and was the forerunner of chairs found in schools and cafés all over the world today. The majority of Jacobsen's chair designs, including the Egg and the Swan, are still being produced. He died in 1971.

Danish Art

BOTH PAINTING AND SCULPTURE have an important place in the history of Danish art. Sculpture flourished particularly during the Late Gothic and Mannerist periods, but above all, thanks to the genius of sculptor Bertel Thorvaldsen, during the so-called "Golden Age" in the early 19th century, which saw a flowering of Danish expression. Painting also flourished during this period and the formal portraiture of earlier painters such as Jens Juel began to be replaced with lively depictions of everyday life by artists such as Christoffer Wilhelm Eckersberg and his student Christen Købke.

View from the Loft of the Grain Store at the Bakery in the Citadel (1831), Christen Købke

Wounded Philoctetes (1774–75), Nicolai Abildgaard (Statens Museum for Kunst)

Danish painting came with the founding of the Royal Academy of Fine Arts in 1754. Its alumni included many prominent painters from the period such as Jens Juel and Nicolai Abildgaard, who studied in Rome, from 1772 to 1776.

belief that truth is beauty. He brought back the precision of Neo-Classicism and made it a dominant trait in Danish painting. Portraiture during the "Golden Age" was also of a very high standard. Among the other outstanding artists of the period are Christian Albrecht Jensen and Christen Købke.

OLD MASTERS

THERE ARE many well-preserved medieval works of art in Denmark, including Romanesque paintings and, in the churches of Zealand, the cycles of frescoes dating mainly from the 12th century.

The subsequent centuries were dominated by formal portraiture. Among the most outstanding, and the largest in size, are the oil paintings on display in Rosenborg Slot in Copenhagen, produced after 1615 by Dutch artists including Reinchold Timm and Rembrandt. The artists working for Christian IV, in Kronborg, included the Dutch painter Gerrit van Honthorst, who painted for the court of Denmark between 1635 and 1641. During the reign of Frederik IV the influences of French painting became more pronounced. During the Rococo period a French influence was also present and can be seen in the works of Scandinavians such as Johan Salomon Wahl and Carl Gustaf Pilo. The turning point in the development of

THE "GOLDEN AGE"

THE PERIOD between 1800 and 1850 saw a great surge in creativity. One of the prime movers of the "Golden Age" *(see pp42–3)* was Christoffer Wilhelm Eckersberg, who drew much of his inspiration from the native Danish landscape, as well as from scenes of everyday life. He had studied in Paris where he was taught by Jacques Louis David to see nature for what it was. Eckersberg returned to Denmark, fired with the

MODERN ART

AFTER 1880 Realism and Naturalism ruled supreme in Danish painting. Their most famous exponents was the Skagen School, which placed an emphasis on natural light and its effects. Among the leading members of this school were Peder S. Krøyer and Anna and Michael Ancher. Around 1900, Danish painting came to be dominated by Symbolism. The situation changed just before World War I, when new trends, such as the

Dead Drunk Danes (1960), Asger Jorn

experiments with form by the Expressionists and Cubists, began to challenge existing traditions in art. The ranks of Danish Cubists included Jais Nielsen and Vilhelm Lundstrom. One of the most important phenomena of the 1950s was CoBrA (Copenhagen–Brussels–Amsterdam), a movement that tried to give free expression to the unconscious. One of the movement's founders was the Danish artist Asger Jorn, whose vivid abstract paintings have received international acclaim.

High altar of Roskilde Domkirke, 16th century

SACRED ART

BEFORE TURNING to Protestantism Danish churches were richly decorated. In the 16th century, after the Reformation, many frescoes were painted over, as they were considered to be examples of Catholic flamboyance. Surviving to this day are a few gilded altars dating from the Romanesque period (12th–13th centuries); two of them are still found in their original locations, in Sahl and Stadil churches. Some outstanding altarpieces were created in the Late Gothic period (late 15th and early 16th centuries) by woodcarvers from Lübeck, notably Claus Berg. Berg's work, which includes the main altar in the cathedral in

Odense, is particularly striking. Filled with emotional charge and high in drama, his carving maintains a realism of detail that is typical of work found in southern Germany.

The Renaissance high altar in Roskilde Domkirke was made in Antwerp in 1560. It was originally intended for Gdansk, until it was requisitioned by Danish customs authorities.

The 17th century saw a culmination of the Reformation. At that time large sums of money were spent on building churches and chapels, notably Holmens Kirke in Copenhagen, for which Frederik III ordered a sumptuously decorated altarpiece of raw oak wood.

SEPULCHRAL SCULPTURE

WITH THE PASSING of the medieval era, funereal or sepulchral sculpture began to enjoy success in Denmark. Characteristic of this period are the works of the sculptor and architect Cornelius Floris of Antwerp, who designed the tomb of Christian III (d.1559) in Roskilde Domkirke (Cathedral), west of Copenhagen. It is made of multi-coloured marble and extraordinarily richly ornamented, with an open plan colonnade that contains two statues of the monarch. This is one of Europe's largest royal tombs from this period.

Renaissance tombs and epitaphs of the aristocracy, found in great numbers throughout Denmark, were more modest, and usually limited to a single slab of stone bearing the image of the deceased in a prostrate position, with an inscription. A new type of tombstone appeared in the 17th century. Its main creator was

Tomb of Christian III in Roskilde Domkirke, by Cornelius Floris

Thomas Quellinus of Antwerp. His marble tombs realistically depicted the deceased, and were accompanied by personified images of his virtues.

MODERN SCULPTURE

PRIOR TO the 19th century sculpture was treated in Denmark solely as a means of portraying the monarchy. This art form began to be taken more seriously with the establishment of the Royal Academy, however, and among its early exponents were Johanes Wiedeweilt (d.1802) and Nicolai Dajon (d.1823). Sculpture was only elevated to a high form of art, however, by Bertel Thorvaldsen (d.1844), who created an austere variety of Classicism based on his in-depth studies of classical antiquity while in Rome. After working in southern Europe for many years, Thorvaldsen returned home to a hero's welcome in 1838. He bequeathed many of his finest works to the city of Copenhagen on condition that a museum was established in which to house them (Thorvaldsens Museum *see p85*).

Self-portrait, by Bertel Thorvaldsen

Famous Danes

DENMARK HAS PRODUCED an impressive number of Nobel prize-winners in categories ranging from physics and chemistry to literature. The Nobel Peace Prize was awarded to the Danish pacifist Fredrik Bajer in 1908. The country has also produced many eminent designers *(see pp22–3)* including Arne Jacobsen and Ole Kirk Christiansen, creator of Lego. Among the country's writers are Karen Blixen, author of *Out of Africa* and Hans Christian Andersen whose classic fairy tales have been translated into over 150 languages. Being a sea-faring nation, the country also has its fair share of explorers including Knud Rasmussen and Vitus Jonassen Bering, who discovered the Bering Strait in 1728.

Arne Jacobsen (1902–71) was an outstanding designer and architect, and a pioneer of Danish modernism. His work includes Århus's city hall, ground-breaking industrial designs, such as the famous Egg chair, and a beautiful range of tableware known as Cylinda-Line.

Vitus Jonassen Bering (1681–1741), one of the world's most famous explorers, led a number of expeditions to the Arctic regions. He is credited with discovering Alaska and the strait between it and Russia that bears his name.

Carl Nielsen (1865–1931) is regarded as one of Denmark's most outstanding composers. A museum in Odense is devoted to his life and work.

Hans Christian Andersen (1805–75), the world's most famous creator of fairy tales, was born in Odense. Among his best-known creations are The Ugly Duckling, The Snow Queen *and* The Emperor's New Clothes.

Knud Rasmussen (1879–1933), a polar explorer and ethnographer, organized many expeditions to Greenland and to the arctic regions of North America (he crossed Canada by dog-sleigh, from Baffin Island to the Bering Strait).

Jørn Utzon (b.1918) is best-known as the designer of Australia's Sydney Opera House and his work can be seen all around the world. In Denmark he has designed an innovative housing project at Fredensborg, North Zealand, and, just outside Copenhagen, the light-filled Bagsværd Church.

Karen Blixen (1885–1962) was born in Rungsted. She had a successful career as a writer of short stories and wrote her first novel at the age of 50, under the pseudonym of Isak Dinesen. Her most famous work, Out of Africa, was made into a film in 1985.

Niels Henrik Bohr (1885–1962) is regarded as the father of atomic energy. He was one of the creators of quantum theory and was awarded the Nobel Prize for his model of the hydrogen atom.

Hans Christian Ørsted (1777–1851), born on the island of Langeland, had a profound influence on the development of Danish science and is known for his discovery of electromagnetism.

Søren Kierkegaard (1813–55) is often regarded as one of the forerunners of Existentialism. Most of the philosopher's works, including Either-Or and Fear and Trembling, stress the importance of human choice.

DENMARK THROUGH THE YEAR

DENMARK IS roughly on the same latitude as Moscow and southern Alaska but has a fairly mild climate. The coldest months are January and February, and most events and festivals are scheduled for spring and summer. The Danes like to enjoy themselves, and during the summer holiday season the whole country comes alive, with almost every town having its own festival. Denmark is not a large country yet it hosts many world-class events, including one of the oldest rock-music festivals, in Roskilde, which is attended by many major international acts. The world-famous Copenhagen jazz festival also attracts top performers. As elsewhere in Europe, religious festivals such as Christmas are widely observed and provide an opportunity for people to spend time with their families.

A clown dressed for Copenhagen's carnival

Royal family at the official celebrations of the Queen's birthday

SPRING

SPRING ARRIVES slowly in Denmark, but its advent is welcomed with great celebration around the country. The biggest of the festivals is Copenhagen's Whitsun Carnival, when the streets fill with Danes dressed in colourful costumes to mark the end of the long winter.

MARCH

Aalborg Opera Festival *(1st half of Mar)*, Aalborg. In early March opera lovers congregate to hear some of the world's best performers.
National Film Festival *(late Mar–Apr)*, Copenhagen, Odense, Århus & Aalborg. The biggest international festival in Denmark. Film entries include Scandinavian producers, as well as many world-famous directors.

APRIL

Birthday of Queen Margrethe II *(16 Apr)*, Copenhagen. The Danish queen is very popular and on this day large crowds of loyal Danes congregate outside Amalienborg Slot to sing "Happy Birthday", which is accompanied by the ceremonial changing of the Livgarden (royal guards).
Store Bededag *(4th Friday after Easter)*. Common Prayer Day or Great Prayer Day is a movable Easter feast. Following the introduction of Protestantism to Denmark in the 16th century the church calendar was revised and several feasts were combined into one – the Store Bededag. On this day many Danes eat wheat buns – *varme hveder*.

MAY

Arbejdernes Kampdag *(1 May)*. Rallies are held to mark Labour Day.
Pinsedag. Whitsunday.
Viking Market *(1st weekend in May)*, Ribe. Held at the Viking Museum, this annual event recreates a Viking marketplace complete with displays of Viking crafts.
Copenhagen Marathon *(mid-May)*, Copenhagen. This race attracts amateur and elite runners from many European countries.
Aalborg Carnival *(2nd half of May)*, Aalborg. Four days of spring celebrations including a firework display and a parade.
Ølfestival *(20–22 May)*, Copenhagen. Arranged by the Danish Beer Society, this lively beer festival includes stalls, music and, of course, lots of beer to sample.
Whitsun Carnival *(Whitsun weekend)*, Copenhagen. This three-day event includes a parade, dancing and special activities for children.

Viking Market, Ribe

Average Daily Hours of Sunshine

Hours

10
8
6
4
2
0

Jan Feb Mar Apr May Jun Jul Aug Sep Oct Nov Dec

Hours of Sunshine
Most sunny days occur in late spring and early summer but visitors can also expect some fine weather through until September. November, December and January are generally the cloudiest months.

SUMMER

SUMMER FESTIVITIES begin with Midsummer Eve (23 June) when bonfires are lit on many beaches. Numerous attractions are scheduled for the summer holidays – from local one-day events to major festivals.

Roskilde Festival – one of Denmark's most popular events

JUNE

International Kite Festival *(mid-Jun)*, Fanø.
River Boat Jazz Festival *(mid-Jun)*, Silkeborg. Jazz bands perform all around Silkeborg, some on boats.
International Sand Sculpture Festival *(Spring to Autumn)*, various towns. Competition to build the best sand sculptures.
Sankt Hans Eve *(23 Jun)*. Midsummer Night is celebrated around camp fires.
Roskilde Festival *(late Jun)*, Roskilde. For more than three decades this rock festival has been attracting some of the biggest names in music. Past performers include Bob Dylan, Bob Marley and David Bowie.

JULY

Copenhagen Jazz Festival *(early Jul)*, Copenhagen. For two weeks jazz, blues and fusion blast out of almost every public space in the city.
Århus International Jazz Festival *(mid-Jul)*, Århus. Another opportunity to hear some top-class jazz.
Hans Christian Andersen Plays *(end Jun–early Aug)*, Odense. Andersen's tales are staged in the Hans Christian Andersens Hus garden.

AUGUST

Cultural Harvest. Festivals celebrated in castles and stately homes, including exhibitions and theatre.
International Clown Festival *(mid-Aug)*, Klampenborg. A 10-day meeting of clowns and other performers from around the world.
Hamlet Summer *(mid-Aug)*, Helsingør. Perform-

Jazz Festival, Copenhagen

ances of Shakespeare's *Hamlet* and other works are staged in Kronborg Slot.
International Film Festival *(mid-Aug)*, Odense.
Baltic Sail *(mid-Aug)*, Helsingør. Regatta of traditional and historic sailing boats.
Schubertiade *(mid-Aug)*, Roskilde. Top musicians perform a selection of the works of Franz Schubert.
Copenhagen International Film Festival *(19–28 Aug)*, Copenhagen. Celebration of world cinema.
European Medieval Festival *(end of Aug)*, Horsens. For two days the town is transformed into a 15th-century city.

Historic sailing ships, Baltic Sail, Helsingør

AVERAGE MONTHLY RAINFALL

Rainfall
July is one of the warmest, but also one of the wettest, months. The best time to visit is in late spring, when it is warm and there is very little rain.

AUTUMN

EARLY AUTUMN provides the final opportunity to stage outdoor performances of jazz and theatre. The beginning of October marks a transition between the carefree holiday season and the beginning of the new school year with months of hard work and study ahead. Theatres stage their first-night performances, and cold autumn evenings bring music-lovers into the clubs.

Israels Plads flea market, Copenhagen, in early autumn

SEPTEMBER

Golden Days *(2 weeks in Sep)*, Copenhagen. This bi-annual event celebrates Copenhagen's rich cultural heritage and city life.
Limfjorden Race *(early or mid-Sep)*, Løgstør. Scandinavia's biggest sailing event. Participating vessels include, among others, fishing boats, yachts and square-riggers.
Tourde Gudenå *(mid-Sep)*, various towns. Kayak and canoe contest attracting many participants and spectators.

Father Christmas Parade during Christmas celebrations in Tønder

OCTOBER

Cultural Night *(2nd Fri in Oct)*, Copenhagen. A night when it is possible to visit many exhibitions, museums, castles, theatres and churches, including some buildings that are usually closed to visitors. Events include classical concerts and special theatre shows.
Antiques Fair *(end Oct or early Nov)*, Copenhagen. Antiques and rare coins fair.
Copenhagen Gay and Lesbian Film Festival *(end Oct)*, Copenhagen. International gay and lesbian film festival organized by the Danske Film Institut.

NOVEMBER

Tivoli Christmas *(Nov–Dec)*, Copenhagen. Numerous events for the young and young at heart in Tivoli as Christmas draws closer. Among the attractions are a Christmas market, ice-skating on a frozen artificial lake and the chance of spotting a Christmas pixie.

Copenhagen Irish Festival *(1st half of Nov)*, Copenhagen. Four days of good-natured celebrations including plenty of Irish music.
Tønder – The Christmas Town *(mid-Nov)*, Tønder. A colourful parade featuring a multitude of Father Christmases, accompanied by marching bands, passes along the main street of the town.
Feast of St Morten *(10 Nov)*. St Morten's Evening is often marked by roasting a goose.
Dukketeaterfestival *(mid Nov)*, Silkeborg. International Festival of puppetry.

Street vendor roasting almonds on a Copenhagen pavement

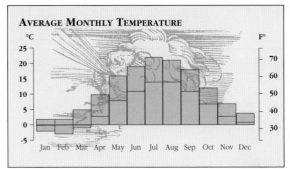

AVERAGE MONTHLY TEMPERATURE

Temperature
Average summer temperatures reach about 20° C (68° F), although temperatures can top 25° C (77° F) from time to time. Winters can be cold with the temperature often dropping below zero, though severe frosts are rare.

WINTER

WINTER IS the quietest time of the year. Little happens and the weather is not conducive to outdoor entertainment. The Christmas period abounds in concerts, however. These are often staged in churches and feature choral ensembles singing psalms and carols. Denmark's streets are beautifully decorated and illuminated at this time and Christmas fairs are held throughout the country, with plenty to eat and drink, and the occasional parade.

DECEMBER

Jul *(24–26 Dec)*. The Danes celebrate Christmas in family circles. As in most of Europe, children play a central role. Danes tend to celebrate on Christmas Eve, decorating the tree the night before Christmas and often hanging it with real candles. The traditional Christmas dinner is also eaten on the 24th and usually consists of roast duck with red cabbage and potatoes. Rice pudding is eaten for dessert; whoever finds the hidden almond gets a prize.

JANUARY

Nytårsdag *(1 Jan)*. New Year's Day witnesses a boisterous welcome to the New Year in Denmark. Many towns stage firework displays, while classical concerts are performed in most major cities.
Winter Jazz Festival *(late Jan or early Feb)*, Copenhagen. Jazz festival, held since 1979.

FEBRUARY

Copenhagen International Fashion Fair *(early Feb)*, Copenhagen. Top Scandinavian and European

Symphony orchestra performing for Aalborg's New Year concert

fashion designers present their latest collections.
Fastelvan *(last Sun before Lent)*. Shrovetide is a time for fun and games. The Danish tradition of "knocking a cat out of the barrel" is still practised by children in fancy-dress. Originally the barrel, hanging from a string, contained a real cat, which was held to be a symbol of evil. Today, the barrel contains sweets, toys and fruit, which eventually fall to the ground.

New Year fireworks in Tivoli, Copenhagen

THE HISTORY OF DENMARK

D ENMARK'S HISTORY HAS *long been associated with the sea. Viking raids on England and elsewhere between the 9th and 11th centuries marked the beginnings of Danish influence and by the late Middle Ages Denmark had a tight grip on trade in the Baltic. The country later lost its position as a world power, but continues to play an important role in the international arena.*

The earliest evidence of human existence to be found in Denmark dates from about 12,000 BC. Between 3900 and 1700 BC the first agricultural settlements began to emerge. Denmark's Bronze Age dates from around 1800 BC and jewellery and cult objects have been unearthed from this period. By about 500 BC iron had largely replaced bronze.

Bronze-Age cult object discovered at Trundholm

UNIFICATION

During the late Iron Age (5th and 6th centuries AD) a Nordic tribe known as Danes began to take control of the Jutland peninsula, forming a social order based around tribal structures.

As a result of the threat from the south presented by the Frankish empire under Charlemagne, these clans began to co-operate as a defensive measure. The Danish strategic position was strengthened in about AD 737 by the building of the Danevirke, a rampart that cut across the Jutland peninsula. This wall, and the forces of Godfred,

king of Jutland, forced Charlemagne to recognize the local Eider River as the Franco-Danish border in AD 811.

After Godfred's death, rivalry between different clans again brought chaos. The first ruler to restore unity was Gorm the Old, the son of a Norwegian chieftain who had conquered the Jutland peninsula in the late 9th century. Gorm's son, Harald I (Bluetooth) took the throne in AD 950 and extended his power base across the rest of Denmark. Harald I's conquest enabled the widespread adoption of Christianity, which not only unified the country but also appeased Denmark's Frankish neighbours.

Increased security gave new impetus to a series of Viking *(see pp34–5)* raids on the British Isles and Ireland. These raids made it possible for Danish kings to win control of England and, for a period, an Anglo-Danish kingdom was formed under Canute I (The Great), who ruled as monarch of Denmark, England and Norway until his death in 1035.

TIMELINE

12,000 BC Earliest evidence of man in Denmark

Cover of a stone urn from the Bronze Age

3900–1700 BC Earliest agricultural settlements

5th–6th century Danes occupy the Jutland peninsula

9th century Danish Viking raids on British Isles and France

737 Building of the Danevirke rampart

Clay pot, 1700–500 BC

811 Army of Charlemagne stopped by Danevirke wall

1018–1035 Reign of Canute I. Unification of Denmark, England and Norway

1013 Sweyn I conquers England

c.985 Harald I (Bluetooth) unites Jutland, the islands and southern Sweden

12,000 BC	4000 BC	500 AD	750	1000	1100

◁ **Danish flag descending from heaven during Valdemar's II campaign in present-day Estonia in 1219**

The Vikings

THE TERM VIKING is generally used to refer to the Scandinavian peoples who journeyed overseas in wooden ships, between AD 800 and 1100, to raid and trade throughout the North and Irish seas and along the rivers of eastern and western Europe. Early Viking raiders targeted monasteries for their wealth and the ferocity of these lightning raids spread terror throughout Christian Europe, giving rise to the image of Vikings as plunderers and rapists. In fact these pagan people were expert sailors and ventured as far as North America where they traded in such items as tusks and pelts.

Ornament
This silver ornament, found in Lindholm Høje in 1952, represents a typical piece of Viking jewellery.

Strong ropes holding the mast

Silver Coin
The Vikings established trade routes to the East and the West. From the 9th century, silver coins, such as this one from the market place of Hedeby, were used as currency.

Sails were made from sheep's wool or flax and were often worth more than the rest of the boat.

Viking Chieftain
In the 19th century a view of Vikings began to take hold, which saw them as barbarians. This portrait by Carl Haag is typical of the common image. Actually they were skilled craftsmen, traders, and hunters.

The bow and stern of a Viking ship had the same shape, enabling it to make a rapid change in direction.

Figurehead
The stems of ships were decorated with figureheads, in the form of a snake or a dragonhead. The loss of a figurehead was believed to be a bad omen.

Keel produced from a trunk of hard oak

VIKING SHIP
Viking warships were usually about 28 m (92 ft) in length. The longest one ever found measured nearly 70 m (230 ft). Along with a 60-strong crew of oarsmen, they could carry as many as 400 people.

KEY

— Viking expeditions

VIKING ARCHITECTURE

Most Viking buildings, which were built of earth, wood and stone, have not survived. The best preserved are the round fortresses erected during the reign of Harald I (Bluetooth), in the late 10th century, at strategic points around Fyrkat (eastern Jutland), Aggersborg (northern Jutland), Trelleborg (Zealand) and Nonnebakken (Funen). These fortified settlements were surrounded by circular embankments 120 m (394 ft) in diameter, 12 m (39.4 ft) wide and rising to a height of 4 m (13 ft).

The Frykat fortress included 16 huge buildings containing domestic quarters, and was probably inhabited by between 800 and 1,000 people. Close to where the fortress stood, there is now a replica Viking farmstead including houses and outbuildings.

Woman Statuette
The independent and self-reliant Viking women ran their homes and farms for many months when their men went out to sea.

This replica longhouse, near Frykat, was built using authentic tools and materials, with knowledge gained from archaeological research.

The ship's planking was made of overlapping planks of oak and joined together with nails. Any gaps between the planks were sealed with tarred wool or fur.

Viking sailing ships had a very shallow draught and could sail in waters less than 1 m (3.3 ft) deep.

Viking Raids
Early raids were carried out only during spring and summer. From about 845, Vikings began wintering at the mouths of foreign rivers, making raids possible throughout the year.

Viking house doors, such as this one in Frederikssund, was heavily built as a defence against intruders as well as the forces of nature.

Valdemar I removing a pagan statute on the coast of Rugia

number of laws which for the time were quite progressive. These changes included the end of imprisonment without just cause (1282) and the establishment of the first supreme court in 1360.

THE MIDDLE AGES

King Canute's son Hardicanute died in 1042 and the Anglo-Danish kingdom disintegrated as the successors of Denmark's eighth monarch, Sweyn II (1047–74), began fighting each other for the throne. As royal supremacy weakened, the power of wealthy landowners and church leaders grew and this early medieval period of Denmark's history is scarred by internal strife and corruption.

This period of unrest came to an end with the succession of Valdemar I (The Great) in 1157. He reunited the country and enacted Denmark's first written laws (the Jutland Code). With help of the powerful Bishop Absalon, he made a series of successful raids against the Wends in eastern Germany. By the time of Valdemar II's succession, Denmark had won control of Meklenburg, Holstein, Lübeck and Estonia, making it one of the greatest powers in northern Europe.

Denmark's pre-eminence ended in 1227 when the country was defeated by its German vassals at the Battle of Bornhøved. As a result, Denmark was forced to give up much of its recently acquired territory and, following the death of Valdemar II in 1241, the Danish monarchy lost much of its power. As a result, successive monarchs were forced into enacting a

THE KALMAR UNION

One of the greatest achievements of King Valdemar IV (1340–75) was to arrange the marriage of his daughter Margrethe to Norway's King Haakon. Margrethe succeeded in forming the Kalmar Union, an alliance uniting Denmark, Norway and Sweden under a common sovereign. The main aim of the union was to counter the dominance of the Hanseatic League, which under the influence of Germany dominated trade in the region.

Queen Margrethe, regent of Denmark and the initiator of the Kalmar Union

TIMELINE

Bronze amulet

1167 Founding of Copenhagen

1227 Denmark defeated at the Battle of Bornhøved

1397 Creation of the Kalmar Union

1361 Conquest of Gotland

1100	1175	1250	1325	14

1157 Reunification of Denmark by Valdemar I (The Great)

1241 Death of Valdemar II

1282 Erik V signs an agreement to create an annual assembly (hof) of feudal lords

1286 Assassination of Erik V

c.1350 Arrival of the bubonic plague in Denmark

Gustav Vasa persuading Lübeck authorities to join in the attack on Christian II

addition to these battles, the major European conflict, the Thirty Years War, took place (1616–48). Denmark was involved from 1625 to 1629 and suffered a disastrous defeat, while Sweden, joining in 1630, gained power and wealth through the conflict. Renewed warring between the two countries ended in 1658 with Denmark losing all of its territories on the Swedish mainland. Two more wars occurred, 1675–79 and 1709–20.

While each country remained free to follow their own policies, they were obliged to fight any wars together and elect a common monarch. In 1397, Margrethe's grand-nephew Erik of Pomerania was crowned king of Denmark, Norway and Sweden.

Initially, a long line of military successes, the introduction of customs duties in the Øresund (Sound) and a growing demand for Danish produce strengthened the country's position. Soon, however, Denmark's domination in the Baltic was challenged by the growing power of Sweden, which sought a greater influence in its own internal affairs. In 1520 the Danish king, Christian II, ruthlessly suppressed an insurrection by what is known as the Stockholm Bloodbath. Three years later, however, Sweden elected its own king, Gustav Vasa, effectively putting an end to the union.

Wooden altar by Abel Schrøder, 1661, in Holmens Kirke, Copenhagen

WARS WITH SWEDEN

Denmark's and Sweden's aims to gain control of Øresund lead to a long series of wars between the two countries during the 16th and 17th centuries. In

TOWARDS ABSOLUTE MONARCHY

The strength of the monarchy had been increased by the introduction of Lutheranism in 1536, which placed the wealth of the Catholic church in the hands of the Crown. The king, however, was still elected by the nobility. Although political power was divided between the Crown and Council, the nobles often had the last say, especially in financial matters. After the defeats of 1658, state coffers were empty and King Fredrik III needed to assert himself and take control. This led to the instatement of absolute monarchy *(see pp38–9)*.

Christian IV, King of Denmark, welcomed in Berlin by the Brandenburg Elector, 1595

Christian II, King of Denmark (1513–23)

1520 Stockholm Bloodbath

1660 Establishment of hereditary monarchy; rise of an absolute monarchy

1658 Treaty of Roskilde. Denmark loses its territories on the Swedish mainland

1665 Denmark begins to establish colonies in the Virgin Islands

1475	1550	1625	1700

1479 Founding of Copenhagen University

1536 Introduction of Lutheranism in Denmark

1523 Termination of the Kalmar Union

Two-crown coin dating from 1618

The Era of Absolute Monarchy

FREDERIK III introduced hereditary monarchy in 1660 in an effort to curtail the power of the nobles of the Council *(see p37)*. In 1665, he took the matter further and passed the Royal Act, which declared the sovereign to be beyond the law and inferior only to God. Five years later Christian V became the first monarch to be crowned under the new system. The people seemed to prefer an almighty king to the old nobility, and kings continued to rule as absolute monarchs until 1848.

Christian III
King Christian III's decision to introduce Lutheranism in 1536 allowed the Crown to seize the assets of the Catholic church and paved the way for a more authoritative monarchy.

Frederik VII
In 1848 Frederik VII renounced absolute power and, with a new constitution, turned Denmark into a democratic country, with guaranteed freedom of speech.

Holmens Kirke, built in 1619 to serve the Royal Navy

Holmens Canal

The Holmens Drawbridge enabled ships to enter the canal.

Academy of Knights
Denmark's elite schools were established by Frederik III. These academies became popular in the 17th century.

Frederiksborg Chapel
The Slotskirken (Palace Chapel) is where Danish kings were crowned from 1670 to 1840.

THE INTRODUCTION OF ABSOLUTISM IN DENMARK

The decision by Frederik III to introduce absolute monarchy in Denmark in 1665 was met with general approval. The ceremonial meeting between the king and the parliament has been immortalized in minute detail in many paintings including examples found in Rosenborg and Frederiksborg.

Corfitz Ulfeldt

Corfitz Ulfeldt, son-in-law of Christian IV, was a typical example of the powerful nobility. After a disagreement with Frederik III, he switched sides and negotiated the Roskilde Treaty on Sweden's behalf in 1658.

Colourful burgher homes were built in the form of narrow-fronted terraced houses.

Børsen (the Stock Exchange)

Numerous inhabitants of the capital attended the celebrations marking the introduction of absolute monarchy.

Boats moored along the canal

The king's troops

Copenhagen (c.1700)

Following the introduction of absolute monarchy the Danish capital's defences were strengthened.

ARCHITECTURE

The period of absolute monarchy brought with it many magnificent buildings. The most opulent examples of the residential architecture of this period include Charlottenborg in Kongens Nytorv, Copenhagen, which was completed in 1683 as a palace for the royal family *(see p69)*. Other outstanding buildings from this period are Ledreborg, a stately home designed by the architect Lauritz de Thurah *(see p135)*, Copenhagen's Børsen (Stock Exchange) and Amalienborg Slot *(see pp56–7)*, which was designed by Nicolai Eigtved, the architect also responsible for Copenhagen's Frederiksstad district.

***Vor Frelsers Kirke** was built in 1696 by Lambert van Haven in Dutch Renaissance style. The spire was added by Lauritz de Thurah in 1752 (see p88).*

***Christian VII's Palace** at Amalienborg has typically opulent Rococo interiors, designed by Nicolai Eigtved and the sculptor Le Clerk.*

Painting by C.A. Lorentzen of the British attack on the Danish fleet, 1801

THE AGE OF REFORM

A peace treaty with Sweden signed in 1720 marked the beginning of the longest war-free period in Denmark's history. The absence of external threats encouraged economic growth and this in turn brought about a period of social change, which became more urgent as the French Revolution gathered pace. Under Frederik VI (1808–39) feudal obligations such as compulsory labour were abolished and large tracts of land were broken up and redistributed to peasants. At the same time landowners were given a role in government and compulsory education was introduced for all children under the age of 14.

THE NAPOLEONIC WARS

The outbreak of the Napoleonic Wars in 1796 eventually brought this period of peace and reform to a halt. Denmark, which derived major benefits from trade, tried to remain neutral in the face of the conflict in Europe but, in 1801, Britain accused Denmark of breaking the British trade embargo and attacked and destroyed the Danish fleet in Øresund. In 1807 the British, fearing the strengthening of a Franco-

Danish alliance, struck again and bombarded Copenhagen for four days, inflicting heavy damage. By the end of the attack much of the city was ablaze and the naval yard was destroyed. The British then sailed away with what remained of the Danish fleet, which included 170 gunboats. In the aftermath of this assault, Denmark joined the continental alliance against Britain and Britain in turn blockaded Danish waters.

The war ended with the signing of the Kiel Peace Treaty in 1814 under the terms of which Denmark lost some 322,000 sq km (124,292 sq miles) of territory, including Norway. The new boundaries left Denmark

Peasants give thanks to Christian VII for abolishing serfdom, painting by C.W. Eckersberg

TIMELINE

1720 End of war with Sweden	**1750** Increase in foreign trade; end of economic crisis	**1807** Bombardment of Copenhagen by Wellington's army
1721 Denmark regains Schleswig		

| 1720 | 1740 | 1760 | 1780 | |

Armchair from the Chinese Room in Amalienborg Slot, Copenhagen

First Danish banknote, dating from 1713 during the reign of Frederik IV

1788 Abolishment of serfdom

1801 British attack Danish fleet

Painting by C.W. Eckersberg depicting bombardment of Copenhagen in 1807

with a mere 58,000 sq km (22,388 sq miles), which included the Duchy of Schleswig, with its Danish-German population, and the Holstein and Lauenburg dukedoms.

The Napoleonic Wars had a catastrophic effect on Denmark. The British blockade led to famine and starvation while territorial losses and wartime destruction resulted in a bankrupt state treasury. Culturally, however, this was the beginning of Denmark's Golden Age (see pp42–3).

Denmark's national emblem, 1774–1820

SCHLESWIG CONFLICT

Events in Europe, including the 1830 July Revolution in France, contributed to the weakening of absolute monarchy. With increasing force, demands were made for the creation of a representative government. Eventually, in 1848, pressure from liberal circles resulted in the enactment of a new constitution, putting an end to absolute monarchy.

The new constitution included the incorporation of the duchies of Schleswig and Holstein as permanent regions of Denmark. With the support of Prussia, the armies of Schleswig and Holstein rose up against the Danish authority. War ensued and ended in 1851 with the defeat of the duchies, but failed to solve the conflict. Trouble erupted again with even greater force, in 1863, when the Danish parliament agreed a new joint constitution for the Kingdom of Denmark and the Duchy of Schleswig. A year later, on the pretext of defending the German populations within the duchies, Prussia and Austria declared war on Denmark. Within months Denmark was defeated and the contested duchies were lost to Prussia and Austria.

The shock of defeat led Denmark to declare its neutrality and concentrate its efforts on rebuilding the economy. Danish agriculture entered a period of rapid growth, assisted by a high demand for grain in Britain, and the railway system was extended to cover much of the country. By the end of the 19th century Denmark had a well-developed economic base that included mature shipbuilding and brewing industries.

Return of Danish soldiers to Copenhagen in 1864, painting by Otto Bache

Denmark's Golden Age

THE PERIOD OF POLITICAL and economic turmoil that occurred during the Napoleonic wars, and the years immediately following them, witnessed an unprecedented flourishing of culture. The leading figures of Denmark's "Golden Age", which lasted throughout the first half of the 19th century, achieved recognition far beyond the borders of Denmark. Among the most prominent are the sculptor Bertel Thorvaldsen, the painter Christoffer Wilhelm Eckersberg and the romantic poet Adam Oehlenschläger. More famous than these, however, are the writer Hans Christian Andersen and the philosopher Søren Kierkegaard.

Market Day
This painting by Paul Fischer depicts Højbro Plads with its opulent houses, which was turned into a market place twice a week.

Interior of a House
The drawing room of a Copenhagen merchant, portrayed in this painting by Wilhelm Marstrand, represents a typical interior of a middle-class home during the 1830s.

Gottlieb Bindesbøll

Martinus Rørbye

Constantin Hansen

Folk Costumes
Women in national costumes would come out on to the streets of Copenhagen on market days.

Parade
Festivals, parades and fairs coloured the lives of Copenhagen's citizens.

H.C. Andersen Telling his Stories
An illustration from one of the earliest editions of Hans Christian Andersen's tales, which are some of the most famous works of children's literature.

Wilhelm Morstrand, Albert Küchler and Dietlev Blunck on a balcony

Jørgen Sonne

H.C. Andersen
Born in humble circumstances in 1805, the popular writer later socialized with the bourgeoisie and at court.

Andersen's Inkpot
As well as writing nearly 200 fairy tales, Andersen also wrote novels, librettos and other works.

ARTISTS OF THE GOLDEN AGE
This painting, entitled *A Group of Danish Artists Visiting Rome* was painted in 1837 by Constantin Hansen. Like many painters of this period, Hansen learnt his craft abroad and returned to Denmark with a fresh perspective.

Søren Kierkegaard
One of the forerunners of Existentialism, Kierkegaard (1813–55) described human life in terms of ethics, aesthetics and religion.

THE GOLDEN AGE IN COPENHAGEN

Following the ravages that befell Copenhagen at the turn of the 18th and 19th centuries, including the 1807 British bombardment *(see p40)*, the city was rebuilt in a new form. Classicism became the dominant architectural style. Christian Frederik Hansen and other Danish architects often drew their inspiration from antiquity. Office buildings, as well as the new bourgeois residences, were adorned with columns, porticoes and tympanums. The most interesting buildings include Thorvaldsens Museum, the Domhuset (Court House) in Nytorv, and the Harsdorff Hus in Kongens Nytorv.

Thorvaldsens Museum *was built in 1848 and approved personally by the sculptor who had bequeathed his work to the city. This building is decorated with friezes by Jørgen Sonne (see p85).*

Vor Frue Kirke *was designed by Christian Frederik Hansen, who got his inspiration from Classical buildings. It had an imposing façade, but no tower until Frederik VI declared that a tower was essential (see p72).*

Stockholm, Copenhagen and Oslo portrayed in a satirical magazine, in 1906

WORLD WAR I

Before World War I Denmark had maintained good relations with both Britain and Germany and with the outbreak of war the Danish government declared its neutrality. This brought considerable benefits to the country's economy, although a third of Denmark's merchant fleet was sunk during the conflict. Also, the war drew attention to the commercial and strategic importance of Denmark's colonies in the West Indies, and the USA bought the Virgin Islands from Denmark in 1917.

Germany's defeat in 1918 revived the old Schleswig-Holstein problem. Under the Treaty of Versailles, the area was divided into two zones and, after a referendum in 1920, the northern part of the former duchy was returned to Denmark. The southern zone remained with Germany.

WORLD WAR II

In September 1939, during Hitler's invasion of Poland, Denmark again confirmed its neutral status. This failed to stop the Third Reich from invading Denmark on 9 April 1940, and after a brief period of resistance by the royal guards at Amalienborg Slot Germany began a "peaceful occupation". Hoping to minimize casualties, the government in Copenhagen decided on a policy of limited co-operation. Opposition among ordinary Danes to this occupation was widespread, however, and in 1943 an increasingly strong resistance movement brought an end to the policy of collaboration. Following a wave of strikes and anti-German demonstrations, the government resigned and was replaced by a German administration.

The Nazis disarmed the Danish army and fleet and began to round up Danish Jews. Fortunately, most were spirited away at night in fishing boats by the Danish Resistance to neutral Sweden.

The final 18 months of the war saw the Danish Freedom Council, an underground movement that

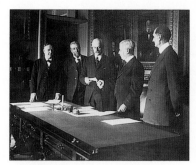

US State Secretary hands the Danish minister a cheque in payment for the Virgin Islands

TIMELINE

1914–18 World War I. Denmark remains neutral

Frederik VIII with his wife, Louise

1940 Denmark occupied by the Third Reich

1944 Iceland becomes a republic

1900   1915   1930   1945

1901 Adoption of democratic parliamentary government

1933 Implementation of first social reform programmes

1949 Denmark becomes a co-founder of NATO

1960 Denmark joins EFTA

1917 Sale of the Virgin Islands to the United States

1920 Schleswig-Holstein referendum

Christian X (1912–47)

Germans on the streets of Copenhagen during World War II

organized the Resistance, become increasingly active. The Danish Resistance, which by 1945 had some 50,000 operatives ready to assist the Allies, did all it could to hamper the German war effort, including blowing up railway lines and sabotaging German-run factories. With the German surrender in 1945, a new government was formed in Denmark, which was composed of Resistance leaders and pre-war politicians.

Margrethe II, Queen of Denmark

POSTWAR DENMARK

Thanks to the activities of the Resistance, Denmark was recognised as a member of the Allied Forces and joined the United Nations in 1945. In 1949 it joined the ranks of NATO. This move marked a departure from a policy of neutrality, which the country had followed since 1864. Denmark's participation in the Marshall Plan enabled the country to thoroughly modernize its industry and agriculture and laid the foundations for postwar prosperity. A new constitution, enacted in 1953, introduced a single-chamber parliament and changed the rules governing female succession to the throne. These new rules were applied in 1972 when Queen Margrethe II ascended the throne following the death of her father, Frederik IX.

Denmark did not participate in the talks which in 1957 resulted in the formation of the European Union, but in 1973, after a referendum, it became the first Scandinavian country to join the EU. Denmark's EU membership has remained a controversial subject with many Danes, however, and 87 per cent of the country voted against the adoption of the euro.

Throughout the 1960s and 70s a series of reforms, including a generous system of social welfare and a virtual lack of censorship, bolstered the country's reputation as a liberal country. In the 70s and 80s Denmark entered a conservative phase with calls for curbs on immigration and tax cuts. However, it is still acknowledged as a tolerant society, with a high standard of living, a strong sense of social conscience and many positive policies towards protecting the environment.

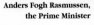

Anders Fogh Rasmussen, the Prime Minister

1972 Queen Margrethe II ascends the throne of Denmark	2002 Copenhagen Summit; negotiations end on the enlargement of the EU	2005 Denmark celebrates the bicentenary of H.C. Andersen
	2000 Denmark rejects adoption of the euro	
1975	**1990**	**2005** · · · **2020**
1973 Denmark joins the European Union	2004 Wedding of the Crown Prince	
1992 Rejection of the Maastricht Treaty, by public referendum	*Marriage of Prince Frederik and Mary Donaldson*	

COPENHAGEN AREA BY AREA

Copenhagen at a Glance

COPENHAGEN'S MAIN ATTRACTIONS include its three royal palaces (Rosenborg, Amalienborg and Christiansborg), as well as numerous museums, churches and monuments, including the much-loved Little Mermaid. There is no shortage of parks. The most famous of these is Tivoli in the heart of the city. The city centre is compact and can easily be explored on foot. Enjoyable alternatives to walking are touring the city on a bicycle or riding one of the waterbuses that run along some of the most interesting canals.

| 0 metres | 200 |
| 0 yards | 200 |

Marmorkirken
The Marble Church is also known as Frederikskirken, after Frederik V who ordered its construction. Its most impressive feature is its vast dome, which visitors may climb with a guide (see p58).

Gefion Springvandet
The biggest fountain in Copenhagen is inspired by a popular Scandinavian myth about the creation of Zealand (see p55).

◁ Royal guards sporting red uniforms and busbies and carrying drums

Livgarden
The royal guards are one of the symbols of Copenhagen. They can be seen in front of Amalienborg Slot, the official residence of Queen Margrethe II (see p57).

Statens Museum for Kunst
The National gallery has a great treasure of European art dating from the 13th to 19th centuries (see pp62–3).

Rådhuspladsen
The city's main square is a good starting point to explore Strøget; it is also the seat of the city hall (see p75).

KEY

🚔	Police
✝	Church
P	Parking
⊠	Post office
M	Metro

NORTH COPENHAGEN

Emblem from a frieze decorating Marmorkirken

THE NORTH OF the city is particularly attractive and includes the famous statue of the Little Mermaid *(Den Lille Havfrue)* and two royal palaces: Amalienborg Slot and Rosenborg Slot. The area also contains several interesting museums of a highly diverse nature – ranging from the Statens Museum for Kunst (Danish National Gallery), through to the Geologisk Museum (Geological Museum) and the Frihedsmuseet (Danish Resistance Museum). Standing close to one another are sacred buildings belonging to three different religions: the Protestant Marmorkirken, the Roman Catholic Sankt Ansgars Kirke and the Russian orthodox Alexander Newsky Kirke. North Copenhagen has masses of greenery. The gardens and waterfalls of Botanisk Have (Botanical Gardens) are well worth exploring, as is the King's Garden (Kongens Have), which surrounds Rosenborg Slot.

SIGHTS AT A GLANCE

Churches
Marmorkirken **8**
Sankt Albans Kirke **3**

Historic Buildings and Monuments
Amalienborg Slot pp56–7 **7**
The Little Mermaid **1**
Gefion Springvandet **4**
Kastellet **2**
Rosenborg Slot pp60–61 **12**

Museums and Galleries
Davids Samling **9**
Frihedsmuseet **5**
Geologisk Museum **14**
Hirschsprungske Samling **15**
Kunstindustrimuseet **6**
Livgardens Historiske Samling **11**
Statens Museum for Kunst pp62–3 **16**

Places of Interest
Botanisk Have **13**
Kongens Have **10**

GETTING AROUND
This part of Copenhagen can be reached by taking the S-tog to Østerport or Nørreport or the metro to Kongens Nytorv and walking from there. Amalienborg is served by buses 1A and 15; Rosenborg by 6A, 26 and 173E.

KEY

▢	Street-by-Street Map *See pp52–3*
🅿	Parking
✝	Church
🚖	Taxi rank

0 m   200
0 yards   200

◁ **Marble Hall with 17th-century stuccowork, Rosenborg Slot**

Street-by-Street: Around Amalienborg Slot

THE MAIN REASON to come to this part of Copenhagen is to visit Amalienborg Slot, the official residence of Queen Margrethe II, which is guarded by soldiers in traditional uniforms. The best time to visit is at noon, when the daily ceremony for the changing of the guard takes place. Frederik V made Amalienborg Slot the focal point of a new, smart district, which he built to mark the 300th anniversary of the Oldenburg dynasty, celebrated in 1748. In honour of the king the district was named Frederiksstaden.

Medicinsk-Historisk Museum, a medical museum, is housed in the former Danish Academy of Surgery and has on display some gruesome human remains as well as an old operating theatre.

Alexander Newsky Kirke is a Russian Orthodox church and was completed in 1883. It was a gift from Tsar Alexander III to mark his marriage to a Danish princess.

★ **Marmorkirken**
Also known as Frederiks-kirken, this church is just west of Amalienborg. Its huge dome rests on 12 pillars and is one of the biggest of its kind in Europe, measuring 31 m (102 ft) across ⑧

KEY

– – – Suggested route

STAR SIGHTS

★ Amalienborg Slot

★ Kunstindustri-museet

★ Marmorkirken

★ **Amalienborg Slot**
Consisting of four almost identical buildings, the palace has been the main residence of the Danish royal family since 1794 ⑦

★ **Kunstindustri-museet**
Looking at the exhibits in this museum of art and design, it is hard to imagine that in the 18th century it served as the city hospital ⑥

LOCATOR MAP
See Street Finder Map 2

NORTH COPENHAGEN

CENTRAL COPENHAGEN

Sankt Ansgars Kirke
stands on the site of a Roman Catholic chapel and was once used by Copenhagen's foreign population. The present building was completed in 1842 and consecrated 23 years later.

Afstøbningssamling, or Royal Cast Collection, has over 2,000 sculpture casts, including a copy of the *Venus de Milo* and copies of statues from the Acropolis.

Amaliehaven
is a modern park, donated to the city by the A.P. Møller shipping company in 1983. The gardens are next to Nyhavn and are a popular place for a walk.

0 m   20
0 yards   20

The Little Mermaid ❶

Langelinie. **Map** 2 F3. 1A, 15, 19.

THE TINY FIGURE of the Little Mermaid (*Den Lille Havfrue*), sitting on a rock and gazing wistfully at the passing ships, is Denmark's best-known monument. The sculpture, commissioned by Carl Jacobsen, head of the Carlsberg brewery, was inspired by the ballet version of *The Little Mermaid*, which in turn was based on Hans Christian Andersen's tale about a mermaid who falls in love with a prince.

The sculptor, Edvard Eriksen (1876–1959), wanted to use as his model Ellen Price, a prima ballerina who had played the part of the mermaid. However, when the dancer learned where the statue was to be located she refused to continue posing and allowed only her face to be used. As a result, it was the sculptor's wife who eventually modelled for the body.

The final bronze cast was placed at the end of the harbour promenade in 1913. Since then, the sculpture has fallen victim to vandals and pranksters on a number of occasions. In 1961 she had her hair painted red. In 1964 her head was cut off; some time later she lost both arms and in 1998 she lost her head once again. Now, moved a little further towards the sea, she enjoys more peace.

One of the buildings inside the Kastellet

Kastellet ❷

Map 2 E3. 33 47 95 00. ⓢ Østerport. 1A, 15,19. ◯ *Only the grounds are open to visitors.*

A FORTRESS WAS first built on this site in 1626 but a Swedish attack in 1658 revealed its numerous weak points and on the orders of Frederik III the defences were rebuilt. The works were completed in 1663. The final structure, known as the Kastellet (Citadel), consisted of a fort in the shape of a five-pointed star surrounded by high embankments and a deep moat. In the 19th century the fortress was partially demolished and rebuilt once more. During World War II it was taken over by the occupying German forces who used it as their headquarters. It is now used by the Danish military, although the grounds and ramparts are open to visitors.

In the 19th century Kastellet served as a prison. The prisoner's cells were built against the church so that the convicts, unseen by the public, could participate in the mass by peering through small viewing holes cut into the walls.

Sankt Albans Kirke ❸

Churchillparken. **Map** 2 E3. 39 62 77 36. 1A, 15, 19.

THIS CHURCH was built in 1887 to serve the city's Anglican community and is named for Saint Alban, a 4th-century Roman soldier who converted to Christianity and suffered a martyr's death.

Situated not far from the

Churchillparken, just south of Kastellet

THE STORY OF THE LITTLE MERMAID

The heroine of Andersen's tale is a young mermaid who lives beneath the waves with her five sisters. The little mermaid rescues a prince from a sinking ship and falls in love with him. Desperate to be with the prince, she is seduced by a wicked sea witch into giving up her beautiful voice in return for legs so that she can go ashore. The price is high and the witch warns the mermaid that should the prince marry another she will die. For a long time the prince adores his new, mute lover but in the end he is forced into marrying a princess from another kingdom. Before the wedding is to take place on board a ship, the mermaid's sisters swim to it and offer her a magic knife. All she need do is stab the prince and she will be free to return to the water. The mermaid cannot bring herself to murder the prince and, as dawn breaks, she dies.

Andersen surrounded by fairytale characters

The Little Mermaid, Copenhagen's most famous landmark

Gefion fountain, along Langelinie promenade in Churchillparken, the elegant Gothic church was a gift from Edward, Prince of Wales, who at the time was vying for the hand of Princess Alexandra, the daughter of Christian IX. They married in 1863 and the prince soon ascended to the throne as Edward VII. The church's interior has attractive stained-glass windows and a miniature copy of Bertel Thorvaldsen's sculpture – *St John the Baptist Praying in the Desert*. Religious services are still held here in English and the congregation often includes visitors to the city.

Gefion Springvandet **4**

Map 2 F4. 🚌 *1A, 15, 19.*

BUILT IN 1908, the Gefion fountain is an impressive work by Anders Bungaard and one of Copenhagen's largest monuments. Its main feature is a statue of the goddess Gefion – a mythical Scandinavian figure. According to legend, the king of Sweden promised to give the goddess as much land as she could plough in one night. Gefion, who took him at his word, turned her four sons into oxen and harnessed them to a plough. By the time the cock crowed she had managed to plough a sizeable chunk of Sweden. She then picked it up and threw it into the sea, and so formed the island of Zealand. The hole left behind became Lake Vänern (whose shape closely resembles that of Zealand).

Danish armoured car in front of the Frihedsmuseet

Frihedsmuseet **5**

Churchillparken. **Map** 2 E4.
📞 *33 13 77 14.* Ⓢ *Østerport.*
🚌 *1A, 15, 19.* 🕐 *May–mid-Sep: 10am–4pm Tue–Sat, 10am–6pm Sun; mid-Sep–Apr: 11am–3pm Tue–Sat, 11am–4pm Sun.* 📷
🅦 *www.frihedsmuseet.dk*

THE ARMOURED car standing in front of the Danish Resistance Museum was built by members of the Danish underground movement and is one of the star attractions of this fascinating museum, which tells the story of Denmark's role during World War II.

Many of the secrets of sabotage are revealed and exhibits include a makeshift printing press, home-made weapons and police reports. Another section is devoted to the evacuation of Denmark's Jewish population, who were spirited away to Sweden by the Resistance.

Photographs of resistance workers killed in action are especially moving, as are letters to family and friends written by those

The goddess Gefion and her oxen, from the Gefion Springvandet

sentenced to be executed by firing squad.

The thorny issue of Denmark's collusion with Germany during World War II is also covered and uniforms from the Danish Freikorps – volunteers who signed up to fight with the German army – are on display.

Kunstindustri-museet **6**

Bredgade 68. **Map** 2 E4.
📞 *33 18 56 56.* Ⓢ *Østerport.*
Ⓜ *Kongens Nytorv.* 🚌 *29.*
Permanent collection 🕐 *noon–4pm daily, noon–6pm Wed.* **Special exhibitions** 🕐 *10am–4pm Tue, Thu–Fri, 10am–6pm Wed, noon–4pm Sat & Sun.* ⬤ *Mon.* 📷
🅦 *www.kunstindustrimuseet.dk*

DESIGNED BY Nicolai Eigtved and erected in the mid-18th century, the buildings that now house the Museum of Art and Design were originally the city hospital; it was here that the philosopher Søren Kierkegaard died in 1855. The hospital was closed in 1919 and today contains one of the largest collections of royal porcelain in Denmark including pieces from the famous *Flora Danica* service *(see p93)*, as well as furniture, Japanese ceramics, silverware and textiles. Exhibits on display range from medieval items to examples of contemporary design.

Nearby, on the same side of the street, is **Sankt Ansgars Kirke**, a Roman Catholic church that has a small exhibition devoted to the history of Danish Catholicism.

Amalienborg Slot 🕖

Balustrade Statues
All the palace statues were renovated in the late 1970s by sculptor Eric Erlandsen with the help of experts from the Statens Museum for Kunst (Danish National Gallery).

A MALIENBORG WAS BUILT on the orders of King Frederik V and completed in 1760 to a design by Nicolai Eigtved. The first buildings erected around an octagonal square were meant as residences for four wealthy families. However, when Christiansborg Slot burned down in 1794, the homeless royal family moved to Amalienborg. Parts of the living quarters are now on public display and include the private rooms of previous monarchs, paintings and all manner of family mementos, from pipes and slippers to priceless Fabergé treasures.

Gallery
The palace gallery has a beautiful ceiling and is the work of Fossatti. The French architect Nicolas-Henri Jardin designed the furniture.

Fireplace Room
The tiled stove standing in this room comes from a factory in Lübeck. The silver wall lining was a present from Ludwig XV to an important high court official named Count Moltke.

★ Entrance Hall
The entrance hall has been renovated to appear as it would have done when the palace was first built. Its decorations have been recreated according to period designs. The statue of Andromeda was reforged from the original cast.

★ Knights' Chamber
This elegant room is an example of the artistry of Nicolai Eigtved and is the most beautiful Rococo chamber in Denmark.

VISITORS' CHECKLIST

Amalienborg Museum, Christian VIII's Palace, Amalienborg Plads. 33 12 21 86. ⑤ Nørreport. 1A, 15, 19. ◯ May–Oct: 10am–4pm; Nov–Apr: 11am–4pm Tue–Sun.

The royal guards, sporting bearskin hats, stand watch, day and night, in front of the palace.

Clock
This grandfather clock is one of many objects on display in the palace that were once used by the Danish royal family.

Changing of the Guard
The usual attire of the Livgarden (royal guards) consists of a navy blue jacket and blue trousers. On major state occasions the guards wear red jackets.

ROYAL RESIDENCE

The name Amalienborg actually refers to an earlier palace, built in 1669 by Frederik III for his young bride Sophie Amalie. The present palace consists of four buildings grouped round a courtyard, collectively known as Amalienborg Slot, which is in the heart of Frederiksstaden. The equestrian statue of Frederick V in the middle of the complex is the work of French sculptor Jacques Saly who spent 30 years working on it. The statue reputedly cost as much as the entire complex.

KEY

- ☐ Christian IX's Palace
- ☐ Christian VII's Palace
- ☐ Christian VIII's Palace
- ☐ Frederik VIII's Palace

STAR SIGHTS

★ **Entrance Hall**

★ **Knights' Chamber**

Marmorkirken ❽

Frederiksgade 4. **Map** 2 D4.
🄲 *33 15 01 44.* ▦ *1A, 15, 19, 26.*
Church 🄾 *10am–6:30pm Mon,
Tue, Thu, 10am–6pm Wed,
noon–5pm Fri, Sun.* **Dome** 🄾
*Sep–mid-Jun: 1pm, 3pm Sat & Sun;
mid-Jun–Aug: 1pm, 3pm daily.* 🆓
Ⓦ *www.marmorkirken.dk*

T HE VAST DOME of the
Baroque Frederikskirken,
also known as Marmorkirken
or the Marble Church, leads
many visitors to suspect that
its architect, Nikolai Eigtved,
based his design on St Peter's
Basilica in Rome. The church
was named for Frederik V
who wanted to celebrate the
fact that his family had ruled
Denmark for 300 years by
building a new
district in
Copenhagen –
Frederiksstaden –
with the church as its
focal point.
When work
began, in 1749,
it was assumed
that the church would be
constructed of marble
imported from Norway
(hence its alternative name).
However, it quickly became
apparent that the cost of such
a venture would exceed the
financial resources of the
treasury and in 1770 work
was abandoned.

A century later the building
was completed using local
Danish marble. The most
obvious feature of the church
is its dome – one of the
largest in Europe. Visitors can
climb the 260 steps to enjoy
wonderful city views from the
top of the bell tower.

Inside the church are frescoes
by Danish artists. On the
outside, the building has
statues of Danish saints.

Davids Samling ❾

Kronprinsessegade 30–32. **Map** 2 D5.
🄲 *33 73 49 49.* Ⓢ Ⓜ *Nørreport.*
▦ *1A, 19, 42, 43, 350S.* 🄾 *1–4pm
Tue, Thu–Sun, 10am–4pm Wed.*
Ⓦ *www.davidmus.dk*

T HE MUSEUM'S founder,
Christian Ludvig David
(1878–1960), was a lawyer
who donated his collection to
the state in 1945. The main
museum building is 19th
century and, like others on
this street, has a characteristic
L-shaped floor plan. David's
family had lived
there since 1810,
although he did
not personally take
possession of it until
1917. In 1968 the
state donated the
adjacent house,
helping to
accommodate the museum's
growing collection.

The museum is best known
for its collection of Islamic
art, which includes items
from Spain, Persia, India and
elsewhere. Among the many
treasures, some of which date
back to the 6th century, are
ceramics, silks, jewellery and
ancient daggers inlaid with
jewels. The museum also
houses a small collection of
European art, as well as
examples of 18th-century
English, French and German
furniture and Danish silver
dating from the 17th and
18th centuries.

*17th-century bronze vessel
from India, Davids Samling*

Kongens Have ❿

Map 1 C5. 🄾 *6am–dusk.*

T HE KING'S GARDEN was
established by Christian IV
in 1606 and is Copenhagen's
oldest park, retaining most of
its original layout. In the 17th
century the gardens supplied
the royal court with fresh
fruit, vegetables and roses to
adorn the royal apartments.

Today, the shady gardens,
criss-crossed by paths and
with numerous benches, are
one of the favourite places for
Copenhagen's citizens to walk
and relax. Here, visitors can
also find one of the capital's
most famous monuments.
Unveiled in 1877, it is a statue
of Hans Christian Andersen
enchanting a group of
children with some of his
fairy tales.

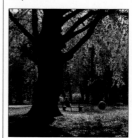

**Leafy Kongens Have surrounding
Rosenborg Slot**

Livgardens Historiske Samling ⓫

Gothersgade 100. **Map** 1 B5.
🄲 *45 99 40 00.* Ⓢ Ⓜ *Nørreport.*
▦ *14, 42, 43, 184, 185.*
🄾 *Oct–Apr: 11am–3pm Sun;
May–Sep: 11am–3pm Tue, Sun.*
Ⓦ *www.hok.dk/lg*

T HE LIVGARDEN or royal
guards, dressed in
colourful uniforms and
sporting furry busbies, are
one of the symbols of
Copenhagen. Many people
come to watch them during
the daily ceremony for the
changing of the guard in front
of Amalienborg Slot, but even
their daily marches between
Rosenborg and Amalienborg
palaces are a popular sight.

Circular grand nave of Marmorkirken, decorated with wall paintings

Vast palm house, built in 1874, in Copenhagen's Botanisk Have

The museum is housed in a cluster of 200-year-old barracks and contains background information on the guards' history. Examples of their uniforms are on display along with weapons, paintings, documents, and musical instruments played by the guardsmen.

Rosenborg Slot ⑫

See pp60–61.

Botanisk Have ⑬

Gothersgade 128. **Map** 1 B4.
📞 35 32 22 40. 🚌 6A, 26,184,185.
Ⓢ Ⓜ Nørreport. ◯ May–Sep:
8:30am–6pm daily; Oct–Apr:
8:30am–4pm Tue–Sun.

THE 20,000 species of plants gathered in the Botanical Gardens include native Danish plants, as well as some highly exotic ones collected from around the world. The garden was established in 1872, on the grounds of old town fortifications. Bulwarks have been turned into rockeries, and the moat that once surrounded the fortified walls is now a lake filled with water and marsh plants.

The gardens themselves have much to offer. There is a small forest, waterfalls and greenhouses, one of which contains over 1,000 varieties of cactus. Elsewhere, it is possible to see coffee, tea, avocados, papaya and

pineapples growing. A special attraction is the steamy palm-house, with huge palms and a roof-top walkway.

Geologisk Museum ⑭

Øster Voldgade 5–7. **Map** 1 B4.
📞 35 32 23 45. Ⓢ Ⓜ Nørreport.
🚌 6A, 126,184,185.
◯ 1–4pm Tue–Sun.

STANDING CLOSE TO THE eastern end of Botanisk Have, the Geological Museum opened in 1893 and occupies an Italian Renaissance-style building. Its carved stone decorations include rosettes, columns and arches.

The earliest museum exhibits are the meteorites on display in the courtyard. The biggest of these was found in Greenland in 1963 and, at 20 tonnes (17.86 tons), is the sixth largest in the world. On the ground and first floors are glass cabinets filled with minerals and fossils including the imprint of a jellyfish made over 150 million years ago. Elsewhere, there is an exhibition devoted to volcanoes, displays relating to the history of man and collections of dinosaur bones.

A separate section is devoted to oil and gas exploration and provides an overview of Denmark's geology. Colourful stones and rock crystals are on sale in the museum shop.

Hirschsprungske Samling ⑮

Stockholmsgade 20. **Map** 1 C3.
📞 35 42 03 36. Ⓢ Østerport.
🚌 6A, 26, 42,43. ◯ 11am–4pm
Thu–Mon, 11am–9pm Wed.
W www.hirschprung.dk

THIS GALLERY, one of Copenhagen's best, owes its existence to the art patronage of Heinrich Hirschsprung (1836–1908), a Danish tobacco baron who supported many Danish artists. The Hirschsprung collection has been on public display since 1911 and is housed in a Neo-Classical building on the outskirts of Østre Anlæg park.

The collection includes works by prominent Danish artists from the 19th and 20th centuries such as Eckersberg, Købke, Bendz, Hansen, Anna and Michael Ancher, Johannes Larsen and Peder S. Krøyer. Among the works on display is a portrait of Hirschsprung himself, smoking a cigar, which was painted by Krøyer.

One of the exhibition rooms displaying the Hirschsprungske collection

Rosenborg Slot ⑫

THIS ROYAL PALACE is one of Copenhagen's most visited attractions and contains thousands of royal objects including paintings, trinkets, furniture and a small armoury. Most impressive of all is the underground treasury containing the crown jewels and other royal regalia. The exquisite Dutch-Renaissance brick palace was erected in 1606, on the orders of Christian IV, to serve as a summer residence. It was used by successive monarchs until the early 18th century when Frederik IV built a more spacious palace at Fredensborg. In the early 19th century Rosenborg was opened to the public as a museum.

Marble Hall
The hall's Baroque décor was at the request of Frederik III. The Italian decorator Francesco Bruno gave the ceilings new stuccowork and clad the walls with imitation marble.

The spire-topped towers were converted from bays

★ Long Hall
17th-century tapestries decorate the walls of the hall, which also contains a collection of 18th-century silver furniture including three silver lions that once guarded the king's throne.

Tower Stairway
Equestrian paintings, portraits, and a series of 17th-century floral water colours by Maria Merian are hung on the walls.

"The Rose"
The ceiling paintings and gilded wall linings found here were brought from Frederiksborg in the 19th century. The 18th-century chandelier was made in England.

STAR SIGHTS

★ **Long Hall**

★ **Treasury**

★ **Treasury**
The underground treasury rooms house the royal jewels, including the Crown of the Absolute Monarch which weighs 2.89 kg (6.4 lbs).

VISITORS' CHECKLIST

Øster Voldgade 4A. **Map** 1 C4.
📞 33 15 32 86. Ⓢ Ⓜ Nørreport.
🚌 6A, 26, 150S, 173E, 184, 185.
🕐 Jan–Apr: 11am–2pm; May: 10am–4pm; Jun–Aug: 10am–5pm; Sep: 10am–4pm; Oct: 11am–3pm; Nov–Dec: 11am–2pm. ● Mon. ♿

The Main Tower was originally shorter and was raised in the 1620s.

Mirror Cabinet
The mirrored room on the first floor dates from 1714 and was the fancy of Frederik IV, who had a connecting bedroom placed next door. It is the only room of its kind in Europe.

The third floor
was completed in 1634 and was designed to provide space for the magnificent, long banqueting hall.

Chinese Drawing Room
This room was used by Sophie Hedevig, sister of Frederik IV. Some of its most distinctive items are the Chinese-style chairs, a guitar encrusted with ivory and tortoiseshell and bearing the princess's monogram, a 17th-century Japanese porcelain jug and an ebony table.

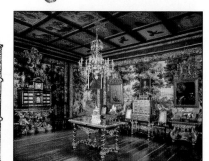

Royal Chamber of Frederik IV
The table standing at the centre of the room was given to Frederik IV in 1709 by the Grand Duke of Tuscany. The magnificent rock crystal chandelier was probably made in Vienna.

Statens Museum for Kunst ⑯

THE DANISH NATIONAL GALLERY houses one of the country's great collections of European art. Danish painters are especially well represented and include artists from the "Golden Age", such as Christoffer Wilhelm Eckersberg, and Skagen artists Anna and Michael Ancher. There are also works by Old Masters like Bruegel, Rubens and Rembrandt as well as masterpieces by 20th-century giants such as Matisse and Picasso, and contemporary installation art. Children have their own gallery and an inspiring workshop.

2nd floor

The New Wing, a striking Modernist structure by Anna Maria Indrio, opened in 1998 and is linked to the old building by a glass-roofed atrium.

Boys Bathing in Skagen, Summer Evening *(1899)*
The painting by Peder S. Krøyer is typical of the Skagen School in that it depicts an everyday scene from Danish life and perfectly captures the country's crisp light.

Girl with a Fruit Basket (c.1827)
The picture is one of many works in the museum by Constantin Hansen; one of the most famous Danish painters from Denmark's "Golden Age".

STAR EXHIBITS

★ Christ as the Suffering Redeemer

★ Portrait of Madame Matisse

★ **Portrait of Madame Matisse *(1905)***
This portrait by Henri Matisse combines some of the most typical elements of Fauvism including simple lines and sharply contrasting colours.

Main entrance (temporary entrance in the New Wing until autumn 2006)

Ground floor

★ Christ as the Suffering Redeemer *(1495–1500)*
The Italian artist Andrea Mantegna's depiction of the garments of Christ is reminiscent of many of Donatello's sculptures.

VISITORS' CHECKLIST

Sølvegade 48. **Map** 1 C4.
📞 33 74 84 94. Ⓢ Østerport.
Ⓜ Nørreport. 🚌 5A, 6A, 26, 42, 43, 150S, 173E, 184, 185, 350S.
⭕ 10am–5pm Tue & Thu–Sun, 10am–8pm Wed 🎫 (free on Wed). 🌐 www.smk.dk

The Last Supper *(1909)*
Emil Nolde, a well-known representative of German Expressionism, has often pursued religious themes in his art.

The Strife of Lent Against Carnival *(1540–69)*
This detail from a painting by Bruegel is typical of his earthy moralizing.

GALLERY GUIDE
During fireproofing of the old building, a temporary entrance is at the New Wing, which hosts Highlights, an eclectic selection of the gallery's collection, until autumn 2006. A temporary exhibition of modern art is in X-Rummet, while Sculpture Street features Danish sculpture. When the old building is reopened, temporary exhibitions will be on the ground floor and the permanent collection will be on display on the first floor and in the New Wing.

1st floor

The Judgement of Solomon *(c.1620)*
This painting by Rubens, depicting a brutal Old Testament scene, is one of several works by the artist included in the museum's vast collection.

Library

KEY

⬜	Permanent collection
⬜	X–Rummet
⬜	Children's Art Museum
⬜	Sculpture Street
⬜	Highlights (until 2006)
⬜	Temporary exhibitions

CENTRAL COPENHAGEN

THE STRØGET, A CHAIN of five pedestrianized streets, links the city's two main squares, Kongens Nytorv and Rådhuspladsen. Shops and restaurants line the promenade, which bustles with activity well into the night. Equally busy is Nyhavn, the city's canal district, where the streets are lined with café terraces and restored 18th-century houses. Central Copenhagen's many museums include the Ny Carlsberg Glyptotek, housing one of the world's best collections of

Façade detail, Latin Quarter

painting and sculpture, and the rather more frivolous Museum Erotica and Guinness World Records Museum. On a fine day it is well worth visiting the famous Tivoli pleasure gardens. The Latin Quarter, located around the old university, has some pleasant traffic-free streets, such as Fiolstræde, which is packed with second-hand bookshops. A climb up the spiral walkway of the 17th-century Rundetårn (Round Tower) is rewarded by magnificent views over the city.

SIGHTS AT A GLANCE

Churches
Helligåndskirken **9**
Sankt Petri Kirke **15**
Vor Frue Kirke **16**

Museums and Galleries
Guinness World Records Museum **6**
Københavns Ravmuseum **2**
Museum Erotica **10**
Musikhistorisk Museum and Carl Claudius Samling **12**
Nikolaj, Copenhagen Contemporary Art Centre **7**
Ny Carlsberg Glyptotek pp78–9 **22**
Ripley's Believe It Or Not! **18**

Streets and Squares
Gråbrødretorv **13**
Højbro Plads **8**
Kongens Nytorv **3**
Nyhavn **1**
Nytorv **17**
Rådhuspladsen **20**

Historic Buildings
Charlottenborg Slot **4**
Det Kongelige Teater **5**
Rådhus pp74–5 **19**
Rundetårn **11**
Universitet **14**

Gardens
Tivoli pp76–7 **21**

GETTING AROUND
Kongens Nytorv is served by metro and buses 1A, 15, 19, 26, 350S. The main transport terminal is Rådhuspladsen, served by buses 2A, 5A, 6A, 10, 12, 14, 26, 29, 33, 67, 68, 69, 173E, 250S.

KEY

	Street-by-Street Map *See pp66–7*
P	Parking
✝	Church
⊠	Post office
M	Metro

◁ **The picturesque Moorish façade of Restaurant Nimb in Tivoli**

Street-by-Street: Around Kongens Nytorv

D̲URING THE LATE 17th century, Kongens Nytorv (King's New Square) was laid out to link the medieval parts of the city with its newer districts. Today, it is Copenhagen's biggest square and makes an excellent starting point for exploring the city. To the southeast it joins the picturesque Nyhavn district where historic ships belonging to the National-museet's collection can be admired from a canalside café. It also marks the beginning of Strøget, which has plenty of restaurants and bars as well as specialist shops and boutiques to tempt visitors.

Hotel d'Angleterre is one of the oldest and most exclusive hotels in Scandinavia *(see p68)* and has entertained many celebrities visiting Denmark.

Guinness World Records Museum
The museum collection includes numerous curios, including a figure of the world's tallest man (2.72m/8 ft 11 inches) ❻

0 m   30
0 yards   30

Nikolaj
This former church has been used as a cultural centre since the early 20th century and was the venue for "happenings" in the 1960s. It is currently an exhibition gallery and concert hall ❼

KEY

--- --- ---   Suggested route

Magasin du Nord is more than 100 years old and is one of the biggest and most exclusive department stores in Scandinavia.

★ Kongens Nytorv
Built in 1680 by Christian V, whose huge equestrian statue is at its centre, Kongens Nytorv is one of Copenhagen's most elegant squares and contains some of the city's finest buildings ❸

An anchor
from a 19th-century sailing vessel has been transformed into a monument to the victims of World War II.

KONGENS NYTORV

LOCATOR MAP
See Street Finder Map 4

Charlottenborg Slot
This is the oldest building in Kongens Nytorv, and is used by Det Kongelige Kunstakademi (The Royal Academy of Fine Arts) ❹

★ Nyhavn
The northern side of the canal is lined with colourful houses, many of which were once brothels frequented by sailors after months at sea ❶

Pleasure boat rides
along the 17th-century canal are one of the main visitor attractions. It has became a tradition that each year old sailing ships arriving in Copenhagen moor alongside Nyhavn.

NYHAVN

HEIBERGSGADE

HERLUF TROLLES GADE

TORDENSKJOLDSGADE

★ Det Kongelige Teater
This 19th-century building houses a prominent theatre, staging both drama and ballet ❺

STAR SIGHTS

★ Det Kongelige Teater

★ Kongens Nytorv

★ Nyhavn

Nyhavn, lined with bars, restaurants and cafés

Nyhavn ❶

Map 4 E1.

Lined on both sides with colourful houses, this 300-m (328-yard) long canal, known as the New Harbour, was dug by soldiers between 1671 and 1673 and was intended to enable ships loaded with merchandise to sail into the centre of Copenhagen. Today, stylish yachts are moored at many of the quays and, amid them, a 19th-century lightship, which is now used as a restaurant.

When Hans Christian Andersen lived here the area north of the canal was a notorious red-light district with a seedy reputation thanks to the cheap bars, rough-and-ready hotels, tattoo parlours and numerous brothels. Since then Nyhavn

has smartened up a great deal (though a few tattoo parlours still remain) and is now one of the city's best-known districts. The boozy joints packed with sailors are long gone and have been replaced with bars, cafés and restaurants targeting a more prosperous clientele. The place is especially popular on warm summer evenings and many of the restaurants and bars can get extremely busy. The huge anchor found at the Kongens Nytorv end of the canal once belonged to *Fyen*, a 19th-century frigate, and has been used to commemorate Danish sailors who lost their lives during World War II.

Københavns Ravmuseet ❷

Kongens Nytorv 2. **Map** 4 D1.
C *33 11 67 00.* **M** *Kongens Nytorv.*
🚌 *1A, 15, 19, 26, 350S.* **◯** *mid-Sep–mid-May: 10am–6pm daily; mid-May–mid-Sep: 10am–8pm daily.* **🅦** *www.houseofamber.com*

The private Amber Museum at the Kongens Nytorv end of Nyhaven is devoted to "Nordic Gold". On display are numerous specimens of this 30–50-million-year-old petrified tree resin, some of which contain fossilized insects such as flies, mosquitoes and termites. The exhibition boasts the biggest piece of amber found in the Baltic Sea, which was fished out of the water off the coast of Sweden in 1969. It weighs an impressive 8.886 kg (19.64 lbs) – most amber pieces rarely exceed 10 g (0.35 ounces). Another of the exhibits, displayed in a glass cabinet, is an amber sailing ship made in Gdansk. The exhibition occupies the upper floors of the historic building, which dates from the late 17th century. The ground floor is taken up with a shop where a range of amber products can be purchased including jewellery and knick-knacks.

An exhibit from the Amber Museum

Kongens Nytorv ❸

Map 4 D1.

King's new square was created over 300 years ago. This is one of Copenhagen's central points and the site of Det Kongelige Teater (The Royal Theatre) and Charlottenborg Slot. As well as marking the end of Nyhavn, it is also a good starting point for exploring Strøget, Copenhagen's famous walkway, which is lined with shops and restaurants.

At the centre of this oval square is an equestrian statue of Christian V, on whose orders the square was built.

Hotel d'Angleterre's Romantic Origins

In the mid-18th century Jean Marchal, a young hairdresser and make-up artist travelling with a troupe of actors, arrived in Copenhagen. Jean decided to settle in town and took the job of valet to Count Conrad Danneskiold Laurvig. At a reception, to which he accompanied the count, he met Maria Coppy, daughter of the court chef. They married in 1755 and, exploiting the culinary talents of Maria, opened a restaurant with a handful of bedrooms for passing travellers. Unfortunately neither lived long enough to fully enjoy the fruits of their enterprise. Their small hotel has survived and thrived, having undergone a great many changes including the addition of a hundred or so rooms. It now receives some of the world's most distinguished figures.

Hotel d'Angleterre

Equestrian statue of Christian V in Kongens Nytorv

The original sculpture was made in 1688 by a French artist. Unfortunately, with time, the heavy lead monument, which depicts Christian V as a sombre Roman general, began to sink, distorting the proportions of the figure. In 1946 the monument was recast in bronze.

Each June graduates gather in the square to dance around the statue as part of a traditional matriculation ceremony. In winter the square becomes an ice rink (skates are available for hire). Kongens Nytorv was once filled with elm trees, planted in the 19th century. Sadly, these fell prey to disease in 1998 and the square has since been replanted.

Charlottenborg Slot ❹

Nyhavn 2. **Map** 4 D1. ☎ 33 13 40 22. ◻ 10am–7pm Wed, 10am–5pm Thu–Tue. Ⓜ Kongens Nytorv. 🚌 1A, 15, 19, 26, 350S. ♿ 🆆 www.charlottenborg-art.dk

THIS BAROQUE PALACE was built between 1672 and 1683 for Queen Charlotte Amalie (wife of Christian V), and was named after her. In the mid-18th century King Frederik V handed over the palace to the newly-created Royal Academy of Fine Arts, and it is now filled with faculty and students. The building is also sometimes used as a venue for temporary art exhibitions, at which times its doors are opened to the public.

Det Kongelige Teater ❺

Tordenskjoldsgade 7. **Map** 4 D1. ☎ 33 69 69 33. FAX 33 69 69 19. 🆆 www.kgl-teater.dk

ANYONE VISITING the area around Kongens Nytorv is usually struck by the sight of the Royal Theatre, a vast Neo-Renaissance building that has been the main venue in Denmark since it was founded in 1748. The present building, which occupies the original site, dates from 1872. For many years, this theatre set itself apart by putting on ballet, opera and threatre in the same space. The complex includes two theatres – Gamle (old) Scene and Nye (new) Scene. Since the opening of Operaen, the striking new opera house, across the harbour from Amalienborg Slot

One of Charlottenborg's portals

in January 2005 (*see p89*), Det Kongelige Teater only hosts ballet and theatre.

The statues at the front of the theatre celebrate two distinguished Danes who made contributions to the development of theatre and the arts. One is the playwright Ludvig Holberg, often hailed as the father of Danish theatre, the other is the poet Adam Oehlenschläger.

Guinness World Records Museum ❻

Østergade 16. **Map** 4 D1. ☎ 33 32 31 31. Ⓜ Kongens Nytorv. 🚌 1A, 15, 19, 26, 350A. ◻ 2 Jan–9 May & mid-Sep–Dec: 10am–6pm Sun–Thu, 10am–2pm Fri & Sat; mid-May–mid-Sep: 10am–8pm daily; Jun–Aug: 9:30am–10:30pm daily. ● 24–25 Dec, 31 Dec, 1 Jan. ♿ 🆆 www.guinness.dk

VISITORS TO the Guinness World Records Museum are welcomed at the entrance by a replica of the world's tallest man. Inside is a collection of the biggest, smallest, fastest, heaviest, longest and shortest, as well as a number of rooms in which visitors can try to beat a world record or experience how it feels to drive a car at 500 km/h (311 mph). A film showing how people from all over the world have trained for their record-breaking attempts can also be seen.

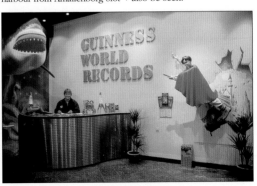

Entrance to the Guinness World Records Museum

Café situated in the former Sankt Nikolaj Kirke

Nikolaj, Copenhagen Contemporary Art Centre ❼

Nikolaj Plads. **Map** 3 C1.
☎ *33 93 16 26.* Ⓢ *Nørreport.*
Ⓜ *Kongens Nytorv.* 🚌 *1A, 15, 19, 26, 350S.* 🕐 *noon–5pm daily.*
📷 *(free on Wed).*
🌐 *www.nikolaj-ccac.dk*

T HIS UNIQUE exhibition space, housed in a renovated 16th-century church, focuses on Danish and international modern art.

The first art exhibitions were held here in 1957 but the art centre really came to prominence in the 1960s when it was used by Fluxus, an important international group of avant-garde artists, that staged a number of innovative "Fluxus-performances" here. Some unique works remain from this period including a "juke box" by Fluxus organiser

Knud Petersen, which has since been developed to contain more than 22 hours of experimental music, sound poetry, and the latest in audio art. The "Crying Space" by Eric Andersen is filled with tear-inducing objects and suggestions on the wall. Eleven hollow stones are there to collect visitors' tears.

As well as these permanent exhibits, Nikolaj puts on a number of temporary shows including an annual art exhibition for children.

Højbro Plads ❽

Map 3 C1.

T HIS COBBLED SQUARE is one of the most enchanting places in Copenhagen. Although at first glance it looks like a single large unit, it is in fact divided into Højbro Plads and Amagertorv.

Højbro Plads contains a vast monument to Bishop Absalon, who from his horse points out towards Christiansborg Slot on the other side of the canal. In Amagertorv, the former city market, is a 19th-century fountain with three birds about to take flight. It is named Storkespringvandet (The Stork Fountain) though the birds are actually herons.

The northern section of Amargertorv has an interesting twin-gabled house, built in

1616, in the style of the Dutch Renaissance. It is one of the city's oldest buildings and houses the Royal Copenhagen Porcelain Shop. Adjacent to it is the showroom of Georg Jensen, which specializes in upmarket silverware. A small museum is devoted to the work of Jensen and contains some of his early pieces.

Portal of Helligåndskirken – one of Copenhagen's oldest churches

Helligåndskirken ❾

Niels Hemmingsensgade 5.
Map 3 C1. ☎ *33 15 41 44.*
🕐 *Noon–4pm Mon–Fri.*

D ATING ORIGINALLY from the early 15th century when it was an Augustinian monastery, the "Church of the Holy Spirit was built on an even earlier religious site, founded in 1238. The church, which is one of the oldest in Copenhagen, acquired its towers in the late 16th century and its sandstone portal, originally intended for the Børsen (Stock Exchange), early in the 17th century. The building was ravaged by one of the city's great fires in 1728, and has been largely rebuilt, although some original 14th-century walls in the right-hand wing can still be seen. Now surrounded by a park, the church still holds religious services. It is also used for art shows and exhibitions, which provide an occasion to admire its magnificent vaults supported by granite columns.

In the churchyard is a memorial to Danish victims of the Nazi concentration camps.

STRØGET

The word "Strøget" ("stripe") cannot be found on any of the plates bearing street names; nevertheless all those who know the city are familiar with it. Copenhagen's main walkway runs east to west. It is made up of five interconnected streets: Østergade, Amagertorv, Vimmelskaftet, Nygade and Frederiksberggade. Pedestrianized in 1962, it has since become one of the town's favourite strolling grounds. Shops range from exclusive boutiques and second-hand clothes outlets to cafés and restaurants offering food from all parts of the world. There are also some pretty churches and squares and a handful of museums. Every day (when the Queen is in residence), at about 11:45am, the Livgarden or royal guards march along Østergade, heading for Amalienborg Slot for the changing of the guards.

Tourist train running along Strøget

Museum Erotica ⓾

Købmagergade 24. **Map** 3 C1.
☎ 33 12 03 11. ◯ May–Sep:
10am–11pm daily; Oct–Apr:
11am–8pm Sun–Thu, 10am–10pm
Fri–Sat. 📷 ⓦ www.museumerotica.dk

COPENHAGEN's adults-only Museum Erotica was founded by Ole Ege, the son of the one-time chief of police, and offers an in depth history of pornography, from Roman, Hindu and Japanese erotic art to chastity belts, sex toys and covers of *Playboy* magazine. A whole room is devoted to Marilyn Monroe and exhibits include a cocktail dress that she once wore, which was bought in 1999 at a New York auction. Elsewhere, display boards describing the sexual tastes of other famous people make interesting reading. Visitors can, for example, learn more than they probably ever wanted to know about the attitudes to sex of, among others, Jean-Jacques Rousseau, Toulouse-Lautrec, Charlie Chaplin, Hans Christian Andersen, Adolf Hitler, Karl Marx and Cleopatra (who is alleged to have had over one thousand romantic liaisons).

There are displays relating to virtually every conceivable genre of pornography and some people may find a visit to the museum distasteful. On the top floor are banks of televisions screening non-stop hardcore porn while a new "Shock Room" has recently been added to the attractions.

Entrance to Museum Erotica, enticing passers-by with its lights

Rundetårn's cobbled spiral ramp winding to its top

Rundetårn ⓫

Købmagergade 52A. **Map** 3 C1.
☎ 33 73 03 73. ◯ Jun–Aug:
10am–8pm Mon–Sat, noon–5pm
Sun; Sep–May: 10am–5pm Mon–Sat,
noon–5pm Sun. 📷
ⓦ www.rundetaarn.dk

THE ROUND TOWER, 35 m (115 ft) tall and 15 m (49 ft) in diameter, provides an excellent vantage point from which to view Copenhagen. Access to the top is via a cobbled spiral ramp, 209 m (686 ft) long, which winds seven and a half times around to the top. Over the years the Rundetårn has been damaged by several fires and part of the observatory was rebuilt in the 18th century.

Rundetårn was erected on the orders of Christian IV, and was originally intended as an observatory for the nearby university. It is still used by the university, making it the oldest working observatory of its kind in Europe.

In 1642, during the tower's opening ceremony, Christian IV is said to have ridden his horse up the spiralling pathway to the very top. Later on, in 1716, the Tsar of Russia, Peter the Great, allegedly repeated this stunt during a visit to Copenhagen and was followed by his wife Tsarina Catherine II, who, as legend would have it, climbed to the top in a coach drawn by six horses.

The modern-day equivalent of such antics is an annual bicycle race; the winner is the person who cycles to the top and back again in the fastest time, without dismounting or falling off.

Musikhistorisk Museum og Carl Claudius Samling ⓬

Åbenrå 30. **Map** 3 C1. ☎ 33 11 27 26. ◯ 2 May–30 Sep: 1–3:50pm Mon–Wed, Fri–Sun; Oct–Apr: 1–3:50pm Sat–Sun. 📷 Guided tours by appointment.
ⓦ www.musikhistoriskmuseum.dk

COPENHAGEN's Museum of Musical Instruments occupies three 18th-century buildings situated in the Latin Quarter. The ground floor is used for temporary exhibitions, while the upper floors house a permanent exhibition. The collection has been pieced together over the last hundred years and is divided into two sections – the Middle Ages to the 1900s and the 20th century. A huge variety of instruments from Europe, Asia and Africa is on display, including folk instruments and such rarities as one of Danish composer Carl Nielsen's pianos and a zither that once belonged to Frederik IX. The museum is also used as a venue for numerous music events including recitals of chamber music and jazz concerts.

Traditional 19th-century Swedish violin

Outdoor restaurant tables in Gråbrødretorv

Gråbrødretorv ⓑ

Map 3 C1. 🚌 *5A, 14.*

THIS CHARMING, cobblestone square is filled with music from buskers in summer when the restaurant tables spill out into the street. It is an excellent place in which to stop for a lunch. The square dates back to 1238, and its name refers to the so-called Grey Brothers, Franciscan monks who built the city's first monastery here. A great fire in 1728 destroyed the surrounding buildings; the present buildings date mainly from the early 18th century.

Universitet ⓒ

Vor Frue Plads. **Map** 3 B1. Ⓢ Ⓜ *Nørreport.* 🚌 *5A, 6A, 14, 42, 43, 150S, 173E, 184, 185, 350S.* 🅦 *www.ku.dk/english*

THE COBBLED Vor Frue Plads and its surrounding university buildings are the heart of the so-called Latin Quarter (Latin was once spoken here). Despite the fact that the university was founded by Christian I in 1479, the buildings that now stand in Vor Frue Plads date from the 19th century. They house only a handful of faculties including law; the remaining departments and staff have moved to the main campus, on the island of Amager, east of Copenhagen.

The vast, Neo-Classical university building stands opposite Vor Frue Kirke. It has an impressive entrance hall decorated with frescoes depicting scenes from Greek mythology, which are the work of Constantin Hansen. Adjacent to the university building is the 19th-century university library. On the library's main staircase is a glass cabinet containing fragments from a cannon ball that was fired during the British bombardment in 1807. The ball struck the library and ironically hit a book entitled *The Defender of Peace*. A number of second-hand bookshops are located along Fiolstræde, which runs up to the Universitet.

Sankt Petri Kirke ⓒ

Sankt Peders Stæde 2. **Map** 3 B1. 📞 *33 93 38 76.* Ⓢ Ⓜ *Nørreport.* 🚌 *5A, 6A, 14, 42, 43, 173E, 150S, 350S.* 🕐 *Mar–Nov: 11am–3pm Tue–Sat.* 🎟 📷 *11am Thu & Sat .* 🅦 *www.sankt-petri.dk*

SAINT Peter's church has been the main church for Copenhagen's German community since 1586. It dates from 1450 but suffered serious damage in the course of a series of fires and the British bombardment of 1807. However, many of the bricks used in the building work are from the original structure. Particularly noteworthy is the "burial" chapel containing

Statue of Christ from the high altar in Vor Frue Kirke

numerous tombs and epitaphs, mainly from the 19th century. There are also some interesting tablets commemorating the dead which can be seen on the church's outside wall.

Vor Frue Kirke ⓒ

Nørregade 8. **Map** 3 B1. 📞 *33 37 65 40 .* Ⓢ Ⓜ *Nørreport.* 🚌 *5A, 6A, 14, 42, 43, 150S, 173E, 184, 185, 350S.* 🕐 *8am–5pm Mon–Sat, 8am–7pm Sun.* 🅦 *www.koebenhavnsdomkirke.dk*

COPENHAGEN'S cathedral, Vor Frue Kirke (Church of Our Lady), has a somewhat sombre look and is the third consecutive church to be built on this site. The first, a small 12th-century Gothic church, was consumed by fire in 1728, while the next one was destroyed by British bombs in 1807 (the tower presented an excellent target for the artillery). The present structure dates from 1820 and was designed by Christian Frederik Hansen. Its interior is a veritable art gallery, full of sculptures by the prominent Danish sculptor Bertel Thorvaldsen *(see p85)*. Standing on both sides are marble statues of the 12 apostles; the central section of the altar has a kneeling angel and a vast figure of Christ – one of the artist's most

The imposing Neo-Classical façade of the Universitet

Interior of Vor Frue Kirke, with statues by Bertel Thordvaldsen

famous masterpieces. Thorvaldsen is also the creator of the relief depicting St John the Baptist, seen at the entrance to the cathedral. During Sunday mass it is sometimes possible to see Queen Margrethe II among the congregation. In the past she used to occupy a special box. Now, however, not wishing to distance herself from her subjects, the Danish monarch sits in the pews.

Nytorv ⓱

Map 3 B1.

ALTHOUGH NYTORV looks like one big square, it is in fact made up of two separate areas – Gammeltorv (Old Square) and Nytorv (New Square) which are separated by the Nygade section of the Strøget walkway. To the northwest of Strøget, Gammeltorv was a busy market place in the 14th century and therefore has the longest trading tradition in Copenhgen. Today, it is dominated by a small fruit and vegetable market along with stalls selling jewellery and all kinds of handicrafts.

Standing at the centre of the square is Caritas Springvandet (The Charity Fountain), which dates from 1609. This Renaissance treasure is the work of Statius Otto, and depicts a pregnant woman carrying one child in her arms and leading another by the hand – a symbol of charity and mercy. Water flows from the woman's breasts and also from the urinating boy at her

feet (the holes were blocked with lead for reasons of decency in the 19th century). The fountain was comissioned by Christian IV to draw the public's attention to his charitable virtues. At one time it supplied the city's inhabitants with water brought along wooden pipes from a lake 5 km (3 miles) north of Copenhagen.

Nytorv was established in 1606 and for a long time was used by the authorities as a place of execution. The squares were joined together and given their present form soon after the city hall was destroyed by fire in 1795. The outline of the city hall can still be seen in Nytorv's pavement.

The striking Neo-Classical Domhuset, or Court House, with its six large columns, on the south side of Nytorv was completed in 1815 to a design by Christian Frederik Hansen, the Danish architect who worked on rebuilding the town after a fire in 1795. The materials used in the rebuilding work included those taken from the ruined Christiansborg Slot, and the resulting building is redolent of an ancient temple. The building was first used as the city hall, becoming the fifth seat of the town's authorities. In the early 20th century the city hall was moved to the Rådhus. The inscription seen on the front of the Domhuset refers to more recent

function as a court house and quotes the opening words of the Jutland Code of 1241: "With law the land shall be built".

Ripley's Believe It Or Not! ⓲

Rådhuspladsen 57. **Map** 3 B2. 33 32 31 31. 2A, 5A, 6A, 10, 12, 14, 26, 29, 33, 67, 68, 69, 173E, 250S. Jan–mid-Jun & Sep–Dec: 10am–6pm Sun–Thur, 10am–8pm Fri–Sat; mid-Jun–Aug: 9:30am–10:30pm daily. 1 Jan, 24, 25 & 31 Dec. www.ripleys.dk

THIS MUSEUM is part of an American chain that is based on an idea of Robert L. Ripley, a radio presenter, comic book writer and adventurer, who dreamt up a freakshow in the early 20th century to stun and amaze his American audience.

The museum may well prove popular with children. Many strange exhibits are on display, some of which were collected by Ripley himself. Here, visitors can marvel at a man who eats bicycles or a doll covered in 7,000 buttons, wince at a collection of medieval torture instruments and shrunken voodoo heads, and be astounded by various freaks of nature including a fish covered in fur and a two-headed cow.

Nytorv, a colourful and bustling square

Rådhus ⑲

THE RED-BRICK RÅDHUS (City Hall), which opened in 1905, was designed by the Danish architect Martin Nyrop (1849–1921), who was inspired by Italian buildings but also employed some elements of Danish medieval architecture. Its large main hall, sometimes used for exhibitions and official events, is decorated with statues of Nyrop as well as three other prominent Danes – Bertel Thorvaldsen, H.C. Andersen and Niels Bohr.

Though it is an official building, the Rådhus is open to visitors. It is well worth climbing the 298 stairs to the top of the 105-m (344-ft) tower to reach the city's highest viewpoint.

Ceilings

The Rådhus rooms and chambers are full of details and architectural flourishes such as intricate brickwork, mosaics and decorated ceilings.

Copenhagen's Emblem

This has changed little since the 13th century. It consists of three castle towers, symbolically drawn waves of the Øresund and images of the sun and moon.

National flag of Denmark

★ Main Hall

This vast, rectangular hall on the first floor is flanked by cloisters and topped with a glazed roof. It has Italianate wall decorations and a number of sculptures.

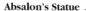

Absalon's Statue

Standing above the main entrance is a gilded statue of Bishop Absalon, the 12th-century founder of Copenhagen.

Main entrance

★ World Clock

Jens Olsen spent 27 years building this clock. Its extraordinary mechanism was set in motion in 1955. One of its many functions is to provide a calendar for the next 570,000 years.

Clock Tower
The peals from the tower's bells are heard throughout the streets of Copenhagen and are also transmitted by radio across the whole of Denmark.

Staircase
The stately rooms on the top floors are reached by graceful stairs with marble balustrades.

Rådhuspladsen ⑳

Map 3 A2 & B2. **Ⓢ** Central Station. **🚌** 2A, 5A, 6A, 10, 12, 14, 26, 29, 33, 67, 68, 69, 173E, 250S.

THIS OPEN SPACE is the second biggest square in the Danish capital (after Kongens Nytorv). City Hall Square was established in the second half of the 19th century, following the dismantling of the western gate that stood on this site, and the levelling of the defensive embankments. Soon afterwards it was decided to build the present city hall, providing further impetus to the development of the surrounding area. The square has been pedestrianized since 1994 and is popular with shoppers and sightseers. It is also a gathering point on New Year's Eve.

A number of monuments in Rådhuspladsen are worthy of note. Standing immediately by the entrance to the city hall is the Dragon's Leap Fountain, erected in 1923. A little to one side, by Rådhus's tower, is a tall column, unveiled in 1914, featuring two bronze figures of Vikings blowing bronze horns. Close by, in Hans Christian Andersens Boulevard, is a sitting figure of Andersen, facing Tivoli gardens. Another curiosity is an unusual barometer hanging on a building that is covered with advertisements, located at the corner of Vesterbrogade and H.C. Andersens Boulevard. It includes a figure of a girl, who in fine weather rides a bicycle. When it rains she opens her umbrella. A nearby thermometer gives a reading of the daily temperature.

The Rådhus with its red brick elevations

STAR SIGHTS

★ **Main Hall**

★ **World Clock**

Tivoli ㉔

WHEN TIVOLI first opened in 1843 it had only two attractions: a carousel with horses and a roller coaster. Today Tivoli is an altogether grander affair. Part amusement park, part cultural venue, part wonderland, it is one of the most famous places in Denmark and much loved by the Danes themselves, who regard it as one of their national treasures. Situated in the heart of the city, this large garden is planted with almost one thousand trees and blooms with 400,000 flowers during the summer. At night, when it is lit by myriad coloured bulbs, it is a truly breathtaking sight.

The Ferry Inn
Scenically located next to the jetty, this is one of 30 restaurants in Tivoli.

Frigate
The huge ship, known as St George's Frigate III, *is a floating restaurant, and is moored on Tivoli's picturesque lake – the remains of a former moat.*

Pantomime Theatre
Pantomime in Denmark dates back to the early 19th century. The Chinese-style pavilion hosts regular performances and is the oldest building in Tivoli gardens.

Main Entrance
The main gate, in Vesterbrogade, was built in 1896. Standing nearby is a statue of George Carstensen, the designer of Tivoli.

STAR SIGHTS

★ **Pagoda**

★ **Restaurant Nimb**

★ Pagoda

The tower, built in the style of a Chinese pagoda, houses a restaurant that has been here since its construction in 1900; it specializes in Chinese cuisine.

VISITORS' CHECKLIST

Vesterbrogade 3. **Map** 3 A2.
☎ 33 15 10 01. ⑤ Central.
🚌 1A, 2A, 5A, 6A, 10, 15, 26, 30, 40, 47, 65E, 250S. ◻ mid-Jun–mid-Aug: 11am–midnight Sun–Thu, 10am–1am Fri–Sat; mid-Aug–mid-Sep: 11am–11pm Sun–Wed, 11am–midnight Thu & Sat. 🦽 ⓦ www.tivoligardens.com

Concert Hall

Tivoli's pastel-coloured indoor concert hall was built in 1956. Concerts range from musicals to symphonies. Elsewhere in the park, every kind of music is performed from classical to pop.

Amusements

Rides and other amusements are scattered throughout the park. Two of the most popular are the mountain train and the "drop".

TIVOLI GARDEN GUARD

A group of boys dressed in smart uniforms and marching to the beat of drums is a frequent sight when strolling along the park's avenues on weekends. According to promoters of the gardens, "the Queen has her own guards and the Tivoli has its own". Made up of about 100 boys, aged between 8 and 16, the Tivoli Garden Guard is smartly dressed in red jackets and busbies and covers some 300 km (186 miles) a year. The marching band was founded in 1844 and is one of Tivoli's four orchestras, the other three being the Symphony Orchestra, the Tivoli Big Band and the Tivoli Promenade Orchestra.

Garden Guard marching through Tivoli

★ Restaurant Nimb

The perspex bubble fountain in front of this Moorish-style restaurant was inspired by the work of Niels Bohr.

Ny Carlsberg Glyptotek ㉒

THIS WORLD-CLASS art museum boasts over 10,000 treasures including Ancient Egyptian art, Greek and Roman sculptures and a huge collection of Etruscan artifacts. It also exhibits a wealth of Danish paintings and sculptures from the era known as the Golden Age *(see pp42–3)* and exquisite works by French Impressionist masters such as Degas and Renoir. It has grown from the fine collection of sculptures *(glyptotek)* donated by Carl Jacobsen, founder of the Carlsberg Brewery, and the museum now consists of three architecturally different buildings, the first one built in 1897 and the latest added in 1996.

Alabaster Relief
This 9th-century BC relief depicting the Assyrian King Assurnasirpal II is part of the multifaceted collection representing the Middle East.

★ **Ancient Egyptian Art**
The outstanding collection of Egyptian art ranges from delicate vases to monumental statues, such as this granite figure of Ramses II from the 2nd millennium BC.

Danish Sculpture
Sculptures representing the great artistic flourishing of Denmark's Golden Age include works such as Jens Adolph Jerichau's Penelope *(1840s), as well as many pieces by Bertel Thorvaldsen.*

STAR FEATURES
★ **Ancient Egyptian Art**
★ **Head of Satyr**
★ **The Kiss**

★ **The Kiss**
This famous pair of lovers is one of 35 works by Auguste Rodin, which constitutes the largest collection of the artist's works anywhere outside France.

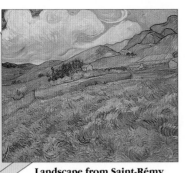

VISITORS' CHECKLIST

Dantes Plads 7. **Map** 3 B3.
33 41 81 41. 10am–4pm
Tue–Sun. (free Wed & Sun).
2A, 33, 69, 173E, 250S.
Until 2006 the museum is undergoing restoration, during which
only parts of the building will be
open; phone or check website
for latest information.
www.glyptoteket.dk.

Landscape from Saint-Rémy
*Along with this picture painted by
Vincent van Gogh during his stay in
a psychiatric hospital in 1889, the
museum has numerous works by
many of the Impressionists and Post-
Impressionists, including Gauguin,
Toulouse-Lautrec, Monet and Degas.*

2nd floor

The Little Dancer
*The statue of a 14-year-
old dancer dates from
1880 and is one of the most
famous sculptures
to be produced by
Edgar Degas.*

★ Head of Satyr
This beautiful painted terracotta Head of
Satyr *is part of the Etruscan collection,
which includes vases, bronze sculptures
and stone sarcophagi dating from the
8th to the 2nd century BC.*

1st floor

WINTER GARDEN

This green oasis of palm trees, planted
under a glass dome, was included in
the original design as a way of
attracting visitors who might not
normally be interested in art. It has
always provided a pleasant place in
which to stroll
during a visit.
Many visitors are
drawn to the *Water
Mother* sculpture
by Kai Nielsen.
Unveiled in 1920, it
depicts a naked
woman reclining in
a small pool,
surrounded by a
group of babies.
The Winter Garden
is also used as a
concert venue.

GALLERY LAYOUT
*The Glyptotek's layout is in a
state of transformation at
present, with some of its best
works on display in the
"Compact Glyptotek" in the
Larsen building (until December
2005). Renovation works will
bring improved access as
well as new arrangements
of the collections.*

KEY

- Dahlerup Building (1897)
- Kampmann Building (1906)
- Central Hall
- Winter Garden
- Larsen Building (1996)

Ground
floor

SOUTH COPENHAGEN

CRISS-CROSSED by canals and waterways, this part of Copenhagen contains two areas that are about as different from each other as it is possible to be. The islet of Slotsholmen is dominated by Christianborg Slot, standing on the site of a fort built by Bishop Absalon in the 12th century, when there was nothing here but a tiny fishing village. The area flourished and in 1443 København, or "merchant's port", was made the Danish capital. Many historical sights are situated here.

Across the water is Christianshavn where the "free state of Christiania",

Dragon's tails on Børsen's spire

an alternative community, has been in existence since the 1970s. Both Christianshavn and nearby Holmen are undergoing a period of redevelopment and the area is becoming one of Copenhagen's more fashionable districts. The city's striking new opera house has taken centre stage with its location on Dokøen, an islet that was once used as a naval base.

Waterbus tours provide an enjoyable way of getting to know the area. Alternatively, a bicycle can be useful for exploring the many nooks and crannies of Christianshavn.

SIGHTS AT A GLANCE

Churches
Vor Frelsers Kirke **9**

Museums
Nationalmuseet pp84–5 **1**
Orlogsmuseet **10**
Thorvaldsens Museum **2**
Tøjhusmuseet **6**

Historic Buildings
Børsen **5**
Christiansborg Slot pp86–7 **4**
Det Kongelige Bibliotek **7**
Folketing **3**

Places of Interest
Christiania **11**
Christianshavn **8**
Operaen **12**

KEY

▨	Street-by-Street Map See pp82–3
P	Parking
✚	Church
▣	Police
M	Metro
⊠	Post office

GETTING AROUND

Christiansborg and Børsen can be reached by metro (getting off at Kongens Nytorv), and also by buses 1A, 2A, 15, 26 and 29. Christianshavn also has metro links with the rest of the city. Buses 2A, 19, 66 and 350S stop close to Christiania. Waterbuses depart from Nyhavn.

0 m	300
0 yards	300

◁ **Three-storey organ, with a bust of Christian V, in the 17th-century Vor Frelsers Kirke**

Street-by-Street: Around Christiansborg Slot

CHRISTIANSBORG SLOT, with its adjoining palace buildings including the palace church, former royal coach house and royal stables, as well as Tøjhusmuseet, Det Kongelige Bibliotek and Børsen, are all situated on the islet of Slotsholmen. The palace derives its name from a castle that was built on this site in 1167 by Bishop Absalon. Opposite the palace, on the other side to the canal, is the Nationalmuseet, which has many exhibits relating to the history of Copenhagen and the rest of Denmark.

Thordvaldsens Museum
The collection confirms the genius of the Danish sculptor, whose tomb can be found in the museum courtyard ❷

★ **Nationalmuseet**
This museum was founded in 1807, though its origins date back to 1650 when Frederik II established his own private collection ❶

VINDEBROGADE

FR. HOLMS KANAL

NY VESTERGADE

TØJHUSGADE

NY KONGENSGADE

FR. HOLMS KANAL

0 m   50
0 yards   50

BRYGHUSGADE

CHRISTIA
BRYGGE

Tøjhusmuseet
Visitors interested in militaria will enjoy the huge array of arms and armour in this museum ❻

STAR SIGHTS

★ **Christiansborg Slot**

★ **Nationalmuseet**

★ Christiansborg Slot

Although this has not been the home of the royal family for more than 200 years, the palace rooms are still used for grand occasions, such as state banquets attended by Queen Margrethe II ④

LOCATOR MAP
See Street Finder Maps 3 & 4

KEY

- - - Suggested route

Folketing

The Danish parliament building is open to visitors during the summer, when its members are on vacation ③

BØRSGADE

SLOTSHOLMSGADE

BØRSGADE

CHRISTIANS BRYGGE

Børsen

The former Stock Exchange, with its spire sculpted in the form of entwined dragon tails, represents an outstanding example of 17th-century public architecture ⑤

Det Kongelige Bibliotek

The library's "Black Diamond" extension, utilizing black glass and granite imported from Zimbabwe, is one of the capital's most innovative buildings ⑦

Nationalmuseet ●

EXHIBITS IN THIS prestigious museum include many items relating to Denmark's history as well as artifacts from all over the world. It is worth allocating several hours for a visit. Among the vast array on display are Inuit costumes and tools, Viking weapons, priceless Egyptian jewellery and Stone-Age tools. There is a good children's section, where kids will enjoy trying on armour or "camping out" in a Bedouin tent. All exhibits are labelled in English.

Antiquities
Greek pottery, Etruscan jewellery and Egyptian mummies are on display in the Egyptian and Classical section.

★ Inuit Culture
Included in the ethnographic section are rooms devoted to the Inuit containing many costumes, including a suit made of bird feathers, as well as traditional kayaks and harpoons.

3rd floor

Ethnography
Items from around the world include exhibits from Africa, India and Japan. One room is devoted to world music.

1st floor

Main entrance

KEY

☐	Pre-history (1300 BC–AD 1050)
☐	Middle Ages & Renaissance (1050–1660)
☐	Tales of Denmark (1660–2000)
☐	Ethnography
☐	History of the Museum
☐	Royal Collection of Coins
☐	Ethnographic Treasures
☐	Near East & Antiquities
☐	Children's Museum

Helmet
This Bronze Age helmet, in the museum's pre-history department, dates from the 9th century BC and was found at Viksø on Zealand.

Gallery Guide

The collection is spread over four floors with pre-history on the ground floor. The medieval department shares the first floor with Ethnography, which continues on the second floor with a exhibits relating to the Inuit. A section designed to appeal to children aged between four and 12 is in the basement.

2nd floor

★ Guldhorn
The pre-history section contains, among other exhibits, fragments of golden horns forged around 400 BC.

Ground floor

Star Sights

★ Guldhorn

★ Inuit Culture

Thorvaldsens Museum ❷

Bertel Thorvaldsen Plads 2.
Map 3 C2. ■ 33 32 15 32.
Ⓢ Central. Ⓜ Nørreport, Kongens
Nytorv. 🚍 1A, 2A, 15, 26, 29.
⭘ 10am–5pm Tue–Sun.
🔲 free on Wed.
Ⓦ www.thorvaldsensmuseum.dk

Located behind the palace church (Christiansborg Slotskirke), Thorvaldsens Museum was the first art museum in Denmark and opened in 1848. The Danish sculptor Bertel Thorvaldsen (1770–1844) lived and worked in Rome for more than 40 years, but towards the end of his life he bequeathed all his works and his collection of paintings to his native Copenhagen. The collection is placed in Christianborg's old Coach House. The building is worth a visit in its own right, with a frieze on the outside by Jørgen Sonne and mosaic floors within.

Despite the fact that he worked on some of his pieces for 25 years, Thorvaldsen's output is staggering and includes sculptures based on classical mythology, busts of well-known contemporaries such as Byron, monumental studies of Christ and a number of self-portraits. The museum also displays Thorvaldsen's drawings and sketches and includes items from his private collection of paintings and Egyptian and Roman artifacts.

Vaulted ceiling and decorative floor in Thorvaldsens Museum

Folketing ❸

Christiansborg. **Map** 3 C2.
🗓 Jun–Sep: daily.

The folktinget is the Danish parliamentary chamber. Seating for the 179 members is arranged in a semi-circle with "left wing" MPs positioned on the left and "right wing" MPs on the right. The civil servants' offices occupy the largest section of the palace. Separate offices are used by Queen Margrethe II, whose duties include chairing weekly meetings of the State Council and presiding over the annual state opening of parliament in early October.

Christiansborg Slot ❹

See pp86–7.

Børsen ❺

Slotsholmsgade. **Map** 4 D2.
⭘ to visitors.

Copenhagen's former Stock Exchange was built between 1590 and 1640 on the orders of Christian IV, to a design by Lorentz and Hans van Steenwinckel. Today, the building houses the city's Chamber of Commerce and is not open to the public, but its stunning Renaissance façade, copper roofs, numerous gables and unusual spire have

Dragon tails forming Børsen's tower

made it one of Copenhagen's best-known sights. Its sleek 54-m (177-ft) spire, carved to resemble the entwined tails of four dragons, is a city landmark. Topping the spire are three crowns representing Denmark, Sweden and Norway. Trade in goods continued at Børsen until 1857, when it was purchased by a private association of wholesalers who pledged to maintain the historic building.

Christiansborg Slot ❹

CHRISTIANSBORG IS less than 100 years old but stands on the site of three former buildings. A 12th-century fortress built by Bishop Absalon was torn down by Christian IV to build the first Christiansborg Slot. Christian VI replaced this building with one of the grandest palaces in Europe, which burnt down in 1794 forcing the royal family to move to Amalienborg. A new palace was not completed until 1828. This, in its turn, was damaged by fire in 1884. Work was completed on the present building in 1928.

★ Throne Room
As in every royal palace, the Throne Room is one of the grandest rooms in Christiansborg. However, Queen Margrethe II is famous for her "common touch" and has apparently never sat on this magnificent royal seat.

Velvet Room
Completed in 1924, this room is noteworthy for its grand marble portals, reliefs and luxurious velvet wall linings.

Decorative Vase
This 18th-century vase can be found in the "Swedish Gallery", one of the many state rooms in the palace. It was a gift to Queen Juliane Marie Braunschweig-Wolfenbüttel, second wife of monarch Frederik V.

The Dining Room
is decorated with portraits of Danish kings and contains two crystal chandeliers.

★ Great Hall
The 17 tapestries on display here were commissioned for the 50th birthday of Queen Margrethe II. They were made by Bjørn Nørgaard and depict key events from Denmark's history.

STAR SIGHTS
★ Basement Ruins
★ Great Hall
★ Throne Room

Tower Hall
Copenhagen's tallest tower is 106 m (348 ft) high and topped with a 5-m (16-ft) crown. The tower's interior has a series of paintings created by Joakim Skovgaard depicting scenes from Danish folk tales.

VISITORS' CHECKLIST

Christiansborg Slotsplads. **Map** 3 C2. (33 92 64 92. 🚌 1A, 2A, 15, 26, 29. **Reception Rooms** ◯ Apr–Sep: noon, 2pm (Danish), 3pm (English) Tue–Sun; May–Oct: noon, 2pm (Dan), 11am, 1pm, 3pm (Eng) daily. 🎦 tours only. 🕍 **Ruins** ◯ Apr–Sep: 10am–4pm Tue–Sun. 🕍 W www.ses.dk/christiansborg

★ Basement Ruins
The foundations of previous structures were unearthed during work on the present building and include parts of Bishop Absalon's castle.

Library
A small portion of the vast royal collection is housed here. The remaining volumes are kept at Det Kongelige Bibliotek (see p88).

Alexander Hall
Bertel Thorvaldsen's frieze depicting Alexander the Great entering Babylon is displayed in this hall.

Tøjhusmuseet ❻

Tøjhusgade 3. **Map** 3 C2.
🕿 33 11 60 37. 🚌 1A, 2A, 15, 26, 29, 650S. 🕐 noon–4pm Tue–Sun. ♿
Ⓦ www.thm.dk

THE ROYAL Danish Arsenal was built between 1598 and 1604 and was one of the earliest of Christian IV's building projects. When completed, the 163-m (535-ft) long complex was one of the largest buildings in Europe and was capable of equipping an entire army. In 1611 the building was extended to include a harbour pool, which was situated next door in what are today the Library Gardens. The building now serves as a museum. Its collection covers the history of artillery from the invention of gunpowder up to the present day (exhibits include artillery guns as well as firearms). Suits of armour and military uniforms are also on display.

Det Kongelige Bibliotek ❼

Christians Brygge, entrance from Søren Kierkegaards Plads. **Map** 4 D2.
🕿 33 47 47 47. 🚌 48. 🕐 10am–9pm Mon–Sat. ♿ Ⓦ www.kb.dk

THE ROYAL LIBRARY is an excellent example of how to merge two very different architectural forms. The original library building is

Gate leading to the old section of Det Kongelige Bibliotek

19th century. The Neo-Classical building's courtyard has been transformed into a garden and contains a statue of the Danish philosopher and theologian Søren Kierkegaard. Next to the old building is the ultra-modern new library, linked by a special passage to its historic predecessor. Nicknamed the "Black Diamond" because of its angular black glass-and-granite exterior, the extension houses library and exhibition areas, the National Photography Museum, a concert hall and a restaurant and café. It is worth stepping inside, if only to see the vast ceiling mural by Per Kirkeby.

Cannon from the Tøjhusmuseet collection

Christianshavn ❽

Map 4 D & 4 E.

THIS DISTRICT, which is sometimes referred to as "Little Amsterdam" because of its many canals, can be explored on foot, by bicycle or by hopping aboard a waterbus. Built in the first half of the 17th century by Christian IV, Christianshavn was originally intended both as a fortified city and a naval base. The area was the site of the first boatyards established in Copenhagen, as well as the warehouses belonging to major shipping lines. It is also where most sailors and boatyard workers lived. Until recently, Christianshavn was known only as the site of the "free state of Christiania" and was considered to be unattractive, poor and neglected. Lately, however, Christianshavn, together with nearby Holmen, has blossomed thanks to a sustained programme of urban redevelopment. Former run-down warehouses have been transformed into trendy restaurants, cafés, company offices and smart apartments, which are favoured by artists and young professionals.

Vor Frelsers Kirke ❾

Sankt Annæ Gade 29. **Map** 4 E2.
🕿 32 57 27 98. Ⓜ Christianshavn.
🚌 2A, 19, 48, 350S. 🕐 Apr–Aug: 11am–4:30pm Mon–Sat, noon–4:30pm Sun; Sep–Mar:11am–3.30pm daily. **Tower** Apr–Oct: during church opening hours. ♿
Ⓦ www.vorfrelserskirke.dk

OUR SAVIOUR'S CHURCH is most famous for its extraordinary spire, completed in 1752, and accessible via a spiral staircase that runs around the

Yachting marina and houses built out over the water, in Christianshavn

exterior. Be warned – it takes considerable stamina to climb all 400 steps, not to mention a good head for heights. This is Copenhagen's second-highest panoramic viewpoint and the reward for the climb is a fabulous view of the city from 90 m (295 ft) up.

The spire's creator was the architect Lauritz de Thurah, who struck upon the idea of a spiral staircase while visiting the church of Sant'Ivo alla Sapienza in Rome. Legend has it that Thurah was so obsessed by his work that when it was alleged that his encircling staircase wound up the wrong way he committed suicide by leaping from the top of the tower. The truth is more prosaic, however, as the architect died in his own bed, poor and destitute, seven years after completing the tower. The tall tale was nevertheless made into a movie by the Danish director Nils Vest in 1997.

The church itself is also worth visiting. It was built in 1696, to a design by Lambert von Haven. Inside, a Baroque altar by the Swede Nicodemus Tessin is adorned with cherubs. The huge three-storey organ dates from 1698. It has over 4,000 pipes and is supported by two giant elephants.

Spiral stairs of Vor Frelsers Kirke's tower

Orlogsmuseet ⓾

Overgaden oven Vandet 58. **Map** 4 E2. 🛈 *33 11 60 37.* Ⓜ *Christianhavn.* 🚌 *2A, 19, 66, 350S.* ⭘ *noon–4pm Tue–Sun.* 📷 Ⓦ *www.orlogsmuseet.dk*

THE ROYAL Danish Naval Museum's building dates from 1780 and was once a sailors' hospital. Among its exhibits are navigation instruments, ships' lights, figureheads that were once

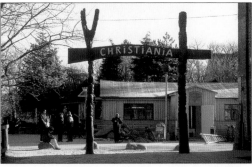

Entrance to Christiania – a district promising an alternative lifestyle

fixed to the bows of windjammers, and uniforms. A collection of over 300 model ships includes one that dates back to 1687.

Christiania ⓫

Map 4 D3 & E3. Ⓜ *Christianhavn.* 🚌 *2A, 19, 66, 350S.* 🎟 *3pm Sat & Sun (meeting point in Prinsessegade).* 📷 Ⓦ *www.christiania.org*

THE "free state of Christiania" has been in existence since 13 November 1971, when a group of squatters took over some deserted military barracks to the east of Christianshavn and established a commune. The authorities initially tried to force the squatters to leave but as the community's numbers swelled the government decided to treat the community as a "social experiment". Today it has about 900 residents.

The community has its own schools, infrastructure and system of government, which are financed in part by the proceeds of its cafés and restaurants and the sale of locally-made handicrafts.

Christiania was initially linked with hippy drug culture and cannabis was openly sold and smoked here until the trade was outlawed in 2004.

Operaen ⓬

Ekvipagemestervej 10. **Map** 2 F5. 🛈 *33 69 69 69.* 🚌 *66.* ⭘ *10am–midnight Mon–Sat, 10am–8pm Sun.* 📷 Ⓦ *www.operahus.dk*

THE STUNNING new Copenhagen Opera House opened in January 2005 on the island of Holmen in Copenhagen Harbour. For over a century the Danish Royal Opera shared a space with the Danish ballet and theatre companies at Det Kongelige Teater. The new auditorium was designed by the prominent Danish architect Henning Larsen whose works include the Ny Carlsberg Glyptotek extension and the Danish Design Centre. The modern building is clad in German limestone and covers 35,000 sq m (376,000 sq ft). It includes an 1,800-seat auditorium as well as a second, smaller stage.

Striking façade of Copenhagen's new opera house

FURTHER AFIELD

HERE IS PLENTY to see outside the city centre. Some attractions, such as the Tycho Brahe Planetarium, are within walking distance. Others, like the Carlsberg Brewery, Zoological Garden, or Assistens Kirkegård can be reached by bus. Sights even further afield are served by a network of modern suburban trains.

Tuborg brewery sign

A visit to one or more of these places provides an alternative to the bustle of inner-city Copenhagen.

Dragør, a charming and prosperous village close to Danmarks Akvarium, has a patch of surrounding woodland that is perfect for gentle walks, as is the pleasantly green enclave around Frederiksberg Slot. And, thanks to the bridge and tunnel that spans the Øresund (Sound), the long sandy beach and fine parks of Malmö in Sweden are only half an hour away. The bridge is a marvel of modern engineering and can be admired from Dragør's small harbour.

SIGHTS AT A GLANCE

Historic Buildings
Frederiksberg Slot ❹

Places of Interest
Amager ⓬
Carlsberg Brewery ❷
Danmarks Akvarium ❾
Dragør ⓭
Experimentarium ❽
Royal Copenhagen ❺
Tycho Brahe Planetarium ❶
Øresund Bridge ⓫

Parks and Gardens
Charlottenlund ❿
Zoologisk Have ❸

Museums
Arken Museum For Modern Kunst ⓮

Churches
Grundtvigs Kirke ❼

Cemeteries
Assistens Kirkegård ❻

KEY

   City centre

   Greater Copenhagen

🚇 Railway station

✈ Airport

═ Motorway

▬ Major road

═ Other road

OUTSIDE COPENHAGEN'S CITY CENTRE

◁ **Decorative lamps on Dronning Louises Bro (Queen Louise Bridge) east of the city centre**

Tycho Brahe Planetarium in the shape of a bevelled cylinder

Tycho Brahe Planetarium ●

Gl. Kongevej 10. **C** *33 12 12 24.* **Ⓢ** *Vesterport.* **Ⓜ** *Forum.* 🚌 *14, 15 831.* **○** *10:30am–8:30pm daily.* 📷 **W** *www.tycho.dk*

COPENHAGEN'S planetarium is the largest of its kind in western Europe and is named after Tycho Brahe (1546–1601), the renowned Danish astronomer. Brahe is credited with the discovery of a new star in the constellation of Cassiopeia, in 1572, and with making important advances in our knowledge of planetary motion. One of the reasons his work is so impressive is that he made these advances before the invention of the telescope.

The planetarium opened in 1989 in a cylindrical building designed by Knud Munk. Built from sand-coloured brick, it appears at its most attractive when viewed from across the small lake, which was created in the late 18th century by damming the local river. The street in which the planetarium is located is the Old Royal Route (Gammel Kongevej), which was once travelled by royal processions heading for Frederiksberg Slot.

The planetarium houses a small astronomical collection that includes antique telescopes and studies of the night sky. A number of films are screened in the planetarium's huge IMAX cinema including one on the wonders of space travel.

Carlsberg Brewery ●

Museum *Valby Langgade 1.* **C** *33 21 01 12.* **○** *10am–3pm Mon–Fri.* **Ⓢ** *Valby.* 🚌 *6A, 18, 26, 832.* **Carlsberg Visitors Center** *Gamle Carlsberg Vej 11.* **C** *33 27 13 14.* **○** *10am–4pm Tue–Sun.* ● *national holidays.* **W** *www.carlsberg.com*

CARLSBERG WAS founded in 1847 by Jacob Christian, whose father had worked at the king's brewery in Copenhagen. Jacob Christian chose this site on Valby Hill (now Frederiksberg Hill) because of the quality of the water nearby, and named his company Carlsberg (Carl's Hill) after his son. By the late 19th century the business had an international reputation. In 1882 Carl founded his own brewery, Ny Carlsberg (New Carlsberg), while his father's brewery was named Gamle

East entrance gate to the Carlsberg Brewery

Carlsberg (Old Carlsberg). In 1906 the two combined.

This site no longer produces lager but has an information centre where visitors can learn about the manufacturing process and sample the beer. Jutland horses, once used to distribute the beer on carts, are still kept in the stables.

A museum recounts the brewery's history and has a section on the company's charitable work, which has led, among other things, to the foundation of Ny Carlsberg Glyptotek *(see pp78–9).*

Along the same street are some examples of industrial architecture including the Elephant Gate. Built in 1901, it consists of four 5-m (16-ft) high elephants made of granite shipped from Bornholm. A short distance further on is the current state-of-the-art Carlsberg plant where vast fermentation tanks produce about 10 billion bottles of lager a year.

Giraffes in the city zoo, near Frederiksberg Have

Zoologisk Have ●

Roskildevej 32. **C** *72 20 02 00.* **Ⓢ** *Valby.* **Ⓜ** *Frederiksberg.* 🚌 *4A, 6A, 26, 832.* **○** *Jan–Feb, Nov–Dec: 9am–4pm daily; Mar: 9am–4pm Mon–Fri, 9am–5pm Sat & Sun; Apr–May, Sep: 9am–5pm Mon–Fri, 9am–6pm Sat & Sun; Jun–Aug: 9am–6pm daily; Oct: 9am–5pm daily.* **W** *www.zoo.dk*

COPENHAGEN'S zoological garden was established close to Frederiksberg Slot in 1859, making it one of Europe's oldest zoos. Although not large by international standards, the zoo has a good

Frederiksberg Slot, headquarters of the Danish Military Academy

record of breeding in captivity. A wide selection of animals are kept here including giraffes, polar bears, elephants and lions. A tropical section houses butterflies and birds as well as some crocodiles. An additional attraction is the 42-m (138-ft) high wooden observation tower, built in 1905, which affords views as far as the coast of Sweden.

Frederiksberg Slot ➍

Roskildevej 28. **M** Frederiksberg. **🚌** 4A, 6A, 14, 15. **Palace ●** to visitors. **Garden ○** 7am–sunset daily.

BUILT BETWEEN 1700 and 1735 this palace was the summer residence of Frederik IV who used it to entertain visitors including, in 1716, the Tsar of Russia, Peter the Great. The king is said to have enjoyed sailing along the park canals, while Copenhagen's inhabitants lined the banks and cheered.

The palace was designed in the Italian style by the architect Ernst Brandenburger following the king's visit to Italy. During the reign of Christian IV the building was enlarged with two additional wings, giving it its present horseshoe shape.

Since 1869 Frederiksberg Slot has been used by the Danish Military Academy. Having its origins in the Cadets' Corp established by Frederik IV in 1713, the school's emblem still bears the king's monogram. The school is not open to the public, though visitors are free to explore the grounds. The palace gardens, known as Frederiksberg Have, were laid out in a French symmetrical style in the early 18th century. Later on they were transformed into a romantic

rambling English park, criss-crossed with a network of canals and tree-lined paths, and dotted with statues and park benches.

Frederiksberg Slot stands on top of a hill and, for the people of Copenhagen, marks a notional boundary of the city. In the 18th century, when it was built, the palace stood outside the city limits and, even today, many locals refer to this area of Copenhagen east of the hill as the "village".

Royal Copenhagen ➎

Søndre Fasanvej 5. **[** 38 14 92 97. **M** Frederiksberg. **🚌** 4A, 14, 15. **○** 9am–3pm Mon–Fri; **□** 9am–5pm Mon–Fri, 9am–2pm Sat. **●** public holidays, 1 May, 5 Jun, 24 Dec, 1 Jan. **W** www.royalcopenhagen.com

THE ROYAL Copenhagen Porcelain Manufactory was founded by Christian VII in 1775 in order to supply the royal court with exquisite tableware worthy of a

monarch. One of the first designs was a pattern known as Blue Fluted, which has since become a trademark of the company. To decorate a single plate in this distinctive blue-and-white pattern takes nearly 1,200 individual brush strokes. *Flora Danica*, however, is the more well known design, based on an ornate 1,800-piece dinner service that was created in the 18th century.

Production now takes place elsewhere and the factory is used as a visitor centre, providing an opportunity to learn about the manufacturing process. A display includes historical pieces and one of the factory's oldest kilns. Royal Copenhagen is famous throughout the world and its products are especially popular with collectors in the USA and Japan. A wide variety of items are on sale in the centre's shop.

Decorating a plate at Royal Copenhagen

FLORA DANICA

This dinner service, decorated with floral designs copied from the *Flora Danica* encyclopedia of plants, was ordered in 1790 by Christian VII. The set was intended as a present for Catherine II of Russia. However, during the 12 years when the first *Flora Danica* was in production the Tsarina died, and the king decided to keep the set for himself. It was used for the first time in 1803 during a reception to celebrate the king's 37th birthday. Over 1,500 of the original 1,802 pieces have survived and are now in the possession of Queen Margrethe II. Copies of individual items are made to order and the methods of production hardly differ from those employed over 200 years ago. The pieces are hand-painted by artists who train for over 10 years to master the exquisite flower paintings. This kind of quality is expensive – a plate costs about 5,000 Dkr.

An example of *Flora Danica* tableware

Assistens Kirkegård, both a park and a cemetery

Assistens Kirkegård ⑥

Kapelvej 2. **C** 33 79 60 23.
(S) M Nørreport. **▥** 5A, 6A, 350S.
◯ Jan–Feb, Nov–Dec: 8am–4pm
daily; Mar–Apr, Sep–Oct: 8am–6pm
daily; May–Aug: 8am–8pm daily.
W www.kbh-kirkegaarde.kk.dk

IN 1760 Copenhagen's graveyards were too small to accommodate victims of a plague that was assailing the city at this time. The plague first struck in 1711 and claimed 23,000 lives in all, reducing the city's population by a third. Assistens Kirkegård was established to supplement the existing provisions for burials.

Initially the cemetery was used only for burying the poor but, from the late 18th century, burial plots at Assistens came into fashion. The list of famous people who are buried here include Søren Kierkegaard, Niels Bohr and Hans Christian Andersen, as well as the artists Christoffer Wilhelm Eckersberg and Christian Købke.

The cemetery is also a pleasant park, and popular with many locals. Visitors are as likely to see buskers, joggers, cyclists and sunbathers as people tending the graves.

Grundtvigs Kirke ⑦

På Bjerget 14B. **C** 35 81 54 42.
(S) Emdrup. **▥** 6A, 42, 43, 69.
◯ Nov–Mar: 9am–4pm Mon–Sat,
noon–1pm Sun; Apr–Oct: 9am–
4:45pm Mon–Sat, noon–4pm Sun.
W www.gruntvigskirke.dk

THIS UNUSUAL yellow brick church, remarkable not only for its size but also its highly original shape, was designed in 1913 by P.V. Jensen Klint. Standing almost 49 m (161 ft) high, it ranks as one of Denmark's largest churches and is designed in a Danish Modernist style. It was built between 1921 and 1940 on Bisperbjerg, the highest hill in Copenhagen, and financed by public donations to honour the memory of Nicolai Frederik Severin Grundtvig (1783–1872) – a prominent clergyman, theologist and philosopher. In addition to his social work, this remarkably versatile man found time to write books and treatises, and composed some 1,500 hymns, many of which are sung to this day in Danish churches. For over 10 years Grundtvig was a member of the Danish Parliament, and in 1861 became an honorary bishop of the Danish Church.

The charismatic clergyman became famous in his country as the founder of the Danish Folkehøjskole (People's High School), a system that enabled those from the lower ranks of society to gain access to education. The shape of the church building symbolizes this sphere of his activities, being reminiscent of a typical Danish village church. On the other hand, the top of the tower is designed to resemble a church organ and alludes to the many religious hymns written by Grundtvig.

Hands-on fun for kids at Experimentarium

Experimenta-rium ⑧

Tuborg Havnevej 7. **C** 39 27 33 33.
(S) Hellerup or Svanemøllen. **▥** 1A,
14, 21, 166, 169, 179. **◯** 9:30am–
5pm Mon, Wed–Fri, 9am–9pm Tue,
11am–5pm Sat & Sun. **◑** 23–25
Dec, 31 Dec, 1 Nov. **▨**
W www.experimentarium.dk

THE MAIN IDEA behind this innovative science centre, in the Hellerup district of Copenhagen, is to bring science to life through hands-on exploration. Almost all the exhibits are interactive; there are about 300 experiments that can be independently performed by anyone.

The display area is huge and, not surprisingly, the place is hugely popular with children who run about trying out all the exhibits. Adults, too, will find much of interest, whether it be testing the latest in virtual technology, programming robots or experiencing an

Front elevation of Grundtvigs Kirke, inspired by small village churches

Some of the many aquatic creatures to be found at Danmarks Akvarium

earthquake of 5.5 degrees on the Richter scale.

At every point, children are confronted with exhibits and puzzles to fire their curiosity, and tested with such imponderable questions as "Are there green rabbits?" and "Can you lift yourself?". Kids can try their hand at guiding a cargo vessel into harbour, test their emotions, check their hearing from the lowest to the highest frequencies, and learn how ice-dancers' hands affect the speed of their pirouettes. Environmental issues are high on the agenda and topics include how winds develop, what kind of climate can be expected in 100 years' time by simulating various concentrations of carbon dioxide emissions into the atmosphere, and methods of water conservation.

The Kids' Pavillion is a separate section where younger visitors between 3 and 6 years old can experiment with magnetism, build a house using a crane, hear what their voice sounds like backwards and decide whether the sounds of bird song or rain should fill a colourful section known as the "Poppy Wood".

All the exhibits are labelled in Danish and English, and there are numerous lectures and special exhibitions staged throughout the year.

Danmarks Akvarium ❾

Charlottenlund. ☎ 39 62 32 83. 🚌 14, 166. ⏰ Sep–Oct: 10am–4pm daily; Feb–Apr: 10am–5pm daily; May–Sep: 10am–6pm daily. 🅿 🔤 www.danmarks-akvarium.dk

COPENHAGEN'S aquarium is located in the grounds of Charlottenlund Slot and was founded in 1939.

Although it is not as large as the Nordsø-museet in Hirtshals *(see p200)*, it is one of the oldest establishments of its kind in Scandinavia and still plays a major role in conservation, research and education, and is also a popular visitor attraction.

It contains more than 90 glass tanks, the largest holding 85,000 litres (18,700 gallons) of water. The tanks are populated by over 300 species of fish from all over the world including sharks and sharp-teethed piranha. Among the other aquatic wildlife are a giant octopus, crocodiles and an electric eel (capable of producing up to 2,000 volts), as well as turtles, sponges, lobsters and many hundreds of brightly coloured tropical fish.

One of the most recent arrivals is a young caretta turtle (an endangered species from the Caribbean) that was found washed up on one of Denmark's beaches on a frosty December morning in 1999.

Dried seahorse, Danmarks Akvarium

Charlottenlund ❿

🚌 14, 166. Ⓢ Charlottenlund St. Palace ⬤ to visitors. Gardens ⬜

A ROYAL RESIDENCE has stood on this site since 1690 but the present palace was built between 1731 and 1733 on the orders of Princess Charlotte Amalie. The princess, who remained single all her life, liked the place so much that it was soon named after her.

The building was remodelled in the 19th century, when its Baroque character gave way to a Renaissance style. A number of other Danish royals have enjoyed staying here including Frederik VIII and his wife, Princess Louise, who remained here until her death in 1926. The couple are commemorated by an obelisk at the rear of the building.

The palace is now used by the Danish Institute for Fisheries, but it is still possible to stroll in its surrounding gardens. The appearance of the park, with its pruned conifers and pleasant avenues, dates from the 1990s, though marked pathways and ponds remain from the 17th century. The vegetable garden dates from 1826 and once grew herbs and produce for the palace kitchen. There are a number of ancient trees in the grounds, notably two larches that stand at the rear of the palace and are considered to be the oldest of their kind in Denmark.

Charlottenlund Slot, surrounded by parkland

Øresund Bridge ⑪

*Cost of one-way ticket: motorcycle –
125 Dkr; car up to 6 m (20 ft) – 230
Dkr, car with trailer – 320 Dkr, bus up
to 9 m (29.5 ft) long – 520 Dkr, large
bus – 1,075 Dkr; no bicycles allowed;
toll and passport control points are
located on the Swedish side.* 🏛
W www.oeresundsbroen.com

Wind turbines rising from the seabed east of Amager

In 2000, when Queen
Margrethe II and King Carl
XVI of Sweden jointly
snipped the ribbon at the
opening ceremony of the
Øresund Bridge, it was
the first time that the
Scandinavian peninsula had
been connected to mainland
Europe since the Ice Age.
Now, thanks to the bridge,
the delights of Malmö, the
largest city in southern
Sweden, are only 35 minutes
away from Copenhagen.

The bridge is the second
longest fixed-link bridge in
the world. The entire crossing
is 16 km (10 miles) long and
consists of (from the Danish
side): a 430-m (1,411-ft) long
artificial peninsula, a tunnel
measuring over 3.5 km (2.2
miles) and running 10 m (33
ft) below the water, a 4-km
(2-mile) long artificial island
and a 7,845-m (25,738-ft) long
cable-stayed bridge. From
either side of the sound, the
sight of the structure, with its
huge 204-m (670-ft) high
pylons, is truly impressive.

The bridge is a marvel of
modern engineering. It has a
two-level structure; the top is
for motor traffic, the bottom
for rail. At its highest point
the bridge is suspended 57 m

(187 ft) above the water. At
the tunnel entrance, on both
sides, are light filters designed
to allow drivers to adjust to
the dimmer conditions. About
one thousand sensors are
installed along the route as
part of a fire alarm system,
while over 220 CCTV cameras
operate round the clock.

The idea of linking Danish
Zealand with Swedish Skåne
(Skania) first emerged some
130 years ago, but it was only
in the 1930s that realistic
projects concerning a bridge
began to take shape. The
agreement between the two
countries to build the link
was signed in 1991, and two
years later work commenced.
The bridge has proved to be
popular and over 20,000 rail
passengers and 10,000 cars
make the crossing every day.

The Øresund region's
economy has been boosted
by the crossing, and it is
becoming one of northern
Europe's largest commercial
centres. The bridge also forms
part of a new, annual marathon
run, the first of which took
place in June 2000, before the
official opening.

Amager ⑫

*3 km (2 miles) southeast of
Copenhagen city centre.*

For a great number of
visitors arriving by plane,
the island of Amager is the
starting point of their
exploration of Denmark.
Lying a short way southeast of
Copenhagen's city centre,
Amager is the site of
Copenhagen's international
airport. It is also a place much
appreciated by young people
seeking inexpensive overnight
accommodation – the island
has the largest youth hostel in
the city, offering 520 beds.

The north end of Amager is
virtually in the centre of
Copenhagen and from there it
is possible to get to the area
around Christiansborg. The
south end is entirely different
in character with farms and
small fishing harbours
including the picturesque
village of Dragør. Amager's
beaches, known as the
Amager Strand, are on the
east side of the island and are
the nearest area of coast to
the centre of Copenhagen.

Øresund Bridge linking Denmark and Sweden

The shoreline is mostly pebbly although there is the occasional patch of sand. The Strand is popular during summer as the shallow water and grassy areas for picnics and games make it ideal for families with children. Another attraction of Amager Strand is the Helgoland swimming pool complex. Since 1929 this has been the headquarters of an association known as "Cold Shock" whose members favour winter sea bathing.

Amager is a good point from which to admire the Øresund Bridge and the huge wind turbines that are situated 2 km (1 mile) east of the island's northern tip.

Dragør ⑬

12 km (7 miles) southeast of Copenhagen. **Museum** Havnepladsen 2. 📞 32 53 41 06. ⭘ May–Sep: noon–4pm daily. 🅰️ 🆆 www.dragoer-information.dk

Cutters moored in Dragør's harbour

T HIS PICTURESQUE town to the southeast of Amager was until recently known only as the place to catch a ferry for Limhamn, on the Swedish side of the Øresund (Sound). The opening of a bridge brought about the closing of this route, and Dragør has since become a destination for those wishing to escape the hustle of central Copenhagen.

An exhibit from Dragør's museum

As far back as the Middle Ages, Dragør was a major centre for the Baltic herring trade. Later on, its inhabitants profited by piloting the boats that sailed across the Øresund. Many houses in Dragør still have distinctive observation towers, known as "Kikkenborg". The biggest of these stands by Lodshuset, a building that houses the local pilot service headquarters, which was established in 1684. Surprisingly, for a long time Dragør had no proper harbour and the boats were simply dragged ashore. The word "dragør" means a sandy

or pebbly strip of land up which the boats were hauled. It was not until 1520 that Dutch settlers, inhabiting nearby Store Magleby, built a proper harbour. Once built, it developed fast and by the 19th century it was the third-largest port in Denmark (after Copenhagen and Helsingør), receiving large sailing ships. Today these maritime traditions are kept alive by a pleasant marina overlooking nearby Sweden and the stunning bridge.

The town is a pleasant place for a stroll with cobbled streets and pretty 18th-century yellow walled houses decorated with flowers. The local museum, housed in the old town hall building and a 17th-century harbour warehouse, has a collection of items devoted to Dragør's rich maritime past.

Arken Museum For Moderne Kunst ⑭

20 km (12 miles) south of Copenhagen city centre. Ishøj, Skovvej 100. 📞 43 54 02 22. Ⓢ to Ishøj and from there 🚌 128. ⭘ 10am–5pm Tue, Thu–Sun, 10am–9pm Wed. 🅰️ 🆆 www.arken.dk

L OCATED A stone's throw from the beach, Arken Museum For Moderne Kunst (Arken Museum of Modern Art) is housed in a building designed by Søren Robert Lund and is intended to resemble a marooned ship.

The exhibition area occupies 9,200 sq m (99,000 sq ft), constituting one third of the available space. The museum's permanent collection is comprised mostly of Danish and Nordic art created after 1945 with an emphasis on installations, sculpture and graphic art. Many of the works on display are by Danish artists such as Asger Jørn and Per Kirkeby. Much of the collection consists of major installations, such as Palestinian-born Mona Hatoum's *Sous tension* (a huge wooden table surrounded by electrified kitchen utensils) and Olafur Eliasson's *Quadrible light ventilator mobile* (a mobile comprised of a light and four electric fans).

The building has proved to be as controversial as much of the work inside. Designed by Lund when he was 25 years old and studying at the Det Kongelige Kunstakademi (The Royal Academy of Fine Arts), it has an interior which follows few conventional rules. Its similarity to a ship is apparent not only from the external shape, but also when looking at details that include fake "rivets" and stairs resembling a companionway.

Bold outline of Arken Museum For Moderne Kunst

SHOPPING IN COPENHAGEN

FOR YEARS Copenhagen has been the commercial centre not only of Denmark, but also of an entire region that includes Zealand and, on the Swedish side, Skåne (Skania). In recent years, since the opening of the link with Sweden, more and more people have arrived here not only to sightsee but also to shop. The number of retail outlets has risen, and the city has became a major

Sign for a toyshop

centre for trade. Nevertheless, shopping in Copenhagen is still a pleasurable experience, with many of the most interesting stores concentrated in just a few areas. Strøget has some of the city's best, with a wide variety of independent shops selling everything from designer clothes to antiques. Dozens of picturesque squares and cafés provide shoppers with the chance to take a break.

WHAT TO BUY

DENMARK IS, of course, the home of applied design, and visitors searching for homewares are spoilt for choice by the vast array of ingenious, smart, unusual and extravagant items on offer. The Danes like to dress smartly without spending a fortune, so it is worth checking out the end-of-season sales for good quality clothes and footwear at bargain prices. All of the high-profile international designer designer labels are available. In Strøget almost anything can be bought, from small souvenirs to a luxurious coat. The pedestrian precinct is full of brand stores run by fashion designers and household goods manufacturers. One entire building is filled with Bodum household products for instance, while the Royal Copenhagen Porcelain's show-room has a huge range of crockery.

OPENING HOURS

IT IS NOT worth trying to shop in Denmark for anything other than foodstuffs before 10:30am. Early in the week shops close at around 5:30pm, although many stores remain open on Fridays until 8 or 9pm. On Saturdays some shops close at 2pm, but the majority stay open until 4 or 5pm. Most shops and shopping centres are closed on Sundays in Denmark; there are however several "trading Sundays" throughout the year.

A large shopping centre at Malmö, across the road bridge in Sweden, has many shops open on Sunday.

HOW TO PAY

THE COUNTRY'S currency is the Danish krone (Dkr). Some shops also accept the Swedish krone and the euro, although the rate of exchange

Flea market in one of Copenhagen's picturesque squares

applied in such cases may not be advantageous. A few of the smaller shops may expect payment in cash but the vast majority of outlets accept credit cards. The prices quoted always include VAT and excise tax.

DEPARTMENT STORES

ONE OF COPENHAGEN'S most popular department stores is **Magasin du Nord**. As well as clothes, cosmetics and luxury household goods it sells books, jewellery, and delicious chocolate and foodstuffs. Also popular is **Illum** on Strøget, which has several floors selling high-quality goods with the added advantage of a roof-top café. Copenhagen has several shopping malls with shops, cafés, restaurants and even cinemas. One of the best is **Fisketorvet**, located to the south of Copenhagen, which

Interior of a shop selling Bodum products

Magasin du Nord, one of Copenhagen's best-known department stores

is built on the site of an old fishing market. It is also worth taking a trip out to **Field's**, Denmark's latest shopping centre, which is situated a little way southwest of the city.

JEWELLERY

DANISH JEWELLERY has a reputation for fine design and attention to detail. Copenhagen's most famous jewellery shop is **Georg Jensen**, a renowned silversmiths which also sells cutlery, watches and other household goods. In 2004, on the occasion of its hundredth anniversary, this prestigious firm launched a smart new collection. Slightly cheaper but equally good is **Janina**

Smykker, which sells a reasonably-priced range of silver and gold jewellery.

DOMESTIC DESIGN

DENMARK IS justly famous for combining attractive design with functionality. Most of its best-known brands have their own shops in the city centre. **Bodum Hus**, for example, offers virtually everything that may be required in the kitchen from glassware and coffee-making paraphernalia to colourful vases and litter bins. **Illums Bolighus** sells stylish furniture, lighting and interior decor products, as does the **BoKoncept** furniture store, with everything from sleek shelving and office products

to sumptuous rugs and sofas. The **Louis Poulsen** show-room offers a crash course in Danish minimalism and has on display a bewildering array of designer lighting solutions. Audiophiles should head for the **Bang & Olufsen** showroom, which has special listening rooms where customers can appreciate the quality of the audio products.

GLASS AND PORCELAIN

GLASSWARE AND porcelain are expensive in Denmark, but no one should let this put them off visiting shops such as **Holmegård** or **Royal Copenhagen Porcelain**, if only to admire the displays. Damaged and discontinued items can be bought at lower prices.

A colourful flower market on Copenhagen's Strøget

DIRECTORY	**Illum** Østergade 52. **Map** 3 C1. 📞 33 14 40 02. 🕐 10am–7pm Mon– Thu, 10am–8pm Fri, 10am–5pm Sat. 🌐 www.illum.dk	**DOMESTIC DESIGN** **Bang & Olufsen** Østergade 3–5. **Map** 3 C1. 🕐 10am–5:30pm Mon–Thu, 10am–6pm Fri, 10am–2pm Sat. 🌐 www.bang-olufsen.com	**Louis Poulsen** Nyhavn 11. **Map** 4 D1. 🕐 1–4pm Mon–Fri. 🌐 www.louis-poulsen.dk

ENTERTAINMENT IN COPENHAGEN

COPENHAGEN HAS A flourishing cultural life. The club scene ranges from small café-style venues to major night spots where the latest techno and urban beats can be heard. When planning a trip, visitors may wish to include a visit to the opera, theatre or ballet. It is now possible to check programmes and times and book tickets well in advance of a visit by using the Internet.

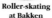

Roller-skating at Bakken

Many kinds of music are on offer in the city ranging from classical concerts given by top rank musicians to local bands and DJs in clubs, and street entertainers. Copenhagen is a child-friendly place and there is plenty to entertain young visitors, from the thrills and spills on offer at Tivoli's amusement park to interactive fun at some of the country's top museums and galleries.

Ballet performance at Det Kongelige Teater

OPERA AND BALLET

COPENHAGEN IS famous for its high artistic standards and **Det Kongelige Teater** (The Royal Theatre) is much valued by the Danes. It has two main spaces which, between them, stage world-class performances of ballet and drama. Its opera performances take place at the striking new Operaen *(see p89)*, which opened in January 2005. **Den Anden Opera** (The Other Opera) was founded in 1995 and is supported by the Ministry of Cultural Affairs. It stages experimental opera.

Nyt Dansk Danseteater concentrates on daring experiments in choreography. It was founded in 1981 and is a leading contemporary dance company, with an international reputation, attracting choreographers and dancers from all over the world.

CINEMA

THERE ARE more than 30 cinemas in and around Copenhagen, ranging from art-house cinemas to modern multiplexes where the latest blockbusters are screened. Almost universally, Danish cinemas are clean with good quality sound systems and comfortable seating. Two of the best art-house cinemas are **Empire Bio** and **Cinemateket**, the latter attached to the Danish Film Institute. **CinemaxX** and the **Palladium** are well-known "big screen" cinemas.

All films in Denmark are generally shown in their original language versions, with Danish subtitles.

MUSIC

MOST KINDS of music are on offer in Copenhagen. Those who enjoy classical music will be thrilled by

concerts given in **Tivoli**'s concert hall, as well as by the regular concerts staged by Danish Radio from concert rooms in the Frederiksberg district. The **Copenhagen JazzHouse** is the country's top jazz venue. Blues music flourishes at **Mojo**, a little venue which claims to have a live act 365 days a year while **Stengade 30** is a good place to go for popular music, ranging from punk and hip-hop to rock and reggae. Music evenings are free in many clubs and the performers range from professional musicians to amateurs bands.

BOOKING TICKETS

TICKETS TO artistic and sporting events – with the exception of cinemas – are booked and bought through **Billetnet**. Tickets to some events can be booked and paid for by credit card, and then collected at any time. Popular

Jazz band playing in a Copenhagen bar

events should be booked well in advance. Cinema tickets tend to be cheaper for morning and weekday performances; these can be booked at *www.biobooking.dk.*

NIGHT LIFE

COPENHAGEN's nightlife starts late and changes fast. To find out about the latest clubs, check the websites listed below.

GAY AND LESBIAN VENUES

THE CITY has plenty of entertainment on offer for lesbians and gays, including the annual **Copenhagen Gay and Lesbian Film Festival** in October. **PAN Disco** is the oldest gay club in the city. It offers

three-floors of up-beat disco and attracts many straight people. **Oscar** is a café and bar serving good food. **Jailhouse Cph** is a popular bar with an upstairs restaurant – the food is served by waiters in police uniform. The **Men's Bar** is a favourite of the leather-clad contingent.

CHILDREN'S ENTERTAINMENT

NO CHILD visiting Copenhagen should miss **Tivoli** (*see pp66–7*), which has enough amusements to keep even the most demanding youngster happy. **Bakken**, in the suburbs, claims to be the oldest amusement park in the country and has over 100 rides. **Zoologisk Have** (*see pp92–3*) is the city's main zoo,

Cirkusbygningen, a former circus that is now a concert venue

with a mini-zoo for toddlers. Several interesting museums in or near Strøget appeal to children including **Ripley's Believe It or Not!** (*see p73*) and **Guinness World Records Museum** (*see p69*). Top of the list is **Experimentarium** (*see pp94–5*), a science-based museum with plenty of hands-on fun.

Advertising pillar in Copenhagen

STREET FINDER

THE MAP REFERENCES given for all of Copenhagen's sights, hotels, restaurants, bars, shops and entertainment venues included in this guide refer to the maps in this section. All major sights, famous historic buildings, museums, galleries, railway, bus, metro and suburban train stations have been marked on the map. Other features are indicated by symbols explained in the key below. The names of streets and squares contained on the map are given in Danish. The word "gade" translates as street; "plads" means square, "allé" translates as avenue and "have" means park or garden.

KEY TO COPENHAGEN STREET FINDER

▪ Major sight	🅿 Parking	═ Railway line
▪ Place of interest	ℹ Tourist information	▬ Pedestrianized street
▪ Other building	✚ A&E hospital	
Ⓜ Metro station	Police station	
Ⓢ S–tog station	Church	
Ⓢ Regional train station	Synagogue	**SCALE OF MAPS 1–4**
Central Station	⊠ Post office	

SCALE OF MAPS 1–4

0 m   200

0 yards   200

1:11 500

Street Finder Index

DENMARK
REGION BY
REGION

Denmark at a Glance

Denmark has a host of attractions for visitors. Small rural farms, rolling fields of wheat, lush woodlands and fine beaches are just some of the things that make the country especially popular with nature lovers. Those favouring outdoor activities will enjoy the many trails and cycle routes. Many of these are themed and are designed to take in some of the country's best historic churches, castles and palaces. For sightseers, there are Neolithic ruins, Viking remains and medieval villages to explore, while the various delights on offer at amusement parks such as Bakken or LEGOLAND® will not be lost on children.

NORTHERN JUTLAND
(See pp196–211)

SOUTHERN AND CENTRAL JUTLAND
(See pp178–195)

Northern Jutland *has some beautiful beaches, as well as fine buildings such as Voergard Slot. The works on display in the Skagens Museum perfectly capture the shimmering Nordic light found in this part of the country.*

Southern Jutland *is famous for towns such as Ribe, which survived flood and fire, and retains some of the best-preserved medieval architecture in Denmark. The level to which the waters of the Ribe Å River rose during a flood in 1634 are marked on a wooden column.*

Funen *has been nicknamed the "Garden of Denmark". The charm of this island resides mainly in its scenery, which includes flower-filled fields and meadows, ancient castles and half-timbered houses.*

◁ **Neo-Classical sculpture adorning Frederiksborg Slot's façade**

Bornholm *is sometimes described as "Scandinavia in a nutshell" because it combines many typically Scandinavian features, such as rocky shores, picturesque villages and peaceful forests.*

BORNHOLM
(See pp212–223)

Northwestern Zealand *is known for its royal castles and palaces. Among these is the magnificent Kronborg Slot on the Oresund coast, which was used by William Shakespeare as the setting for* Hamlet. *The castle now contains a museum.*

NORTHWESTERN ZEALAND
(See pp112–147)

Copenhagen *is Denmark's capital and its largest city. It has many sights, both modern and old, including the magnificent Marmorkirken, which offers splendid views from its grand dome. (See pages 46–107).*

NEN
168–177)

SOUTHERN
ZEALAND AND
THE ISLANDS
(See pp148–167)

Southern Zealand *is a mix of farmland, woodland and glorious coastal scenery. There is much to see, including a 1,000-year-old Viking fortress at Trelleborg and the 12th-century Sankt Bendts Kirke, which is the oldest brick church in Denmark.*

| 0 km | 30 |
| 0 miles | 30 |

NORTHWESTERN ZEALAND

*Z*EALAND IS THE LARGEST *of the Danish islands and has an area of 7,500 sq km (2,895 sq miles). On its eastern shore lies Copenhagen* (see pp46–107) – *the country's capital city as well as its cultural and commercial centre. Away from the city, there is much to enjoy, from mighty castles and historic towns to sandy beaches, rural villages and beautiful countryside.*

The island's scenery is typical of the lowland regions. Idyllic meadow scenery is broken here and there by beech forests and coastal fjords that cut deep into the land. Much of the region's wildlife can be seen around Arresø, Denmark's largest lake.

Most of the port towns were once Viking settlements. A reconstructed 10th–11th-century Viking camp can be visited in Trelleborg, while Viking ships can be seen at Roskilde's Viking Ship Museum. A visit to the Lejre Forsøgcentre, an experimental camp where Danish families volunteer to spend a week living in an Iron Age village, provides a glimpse into the past, as do the Viking plays staged at Frederikssund.

Northwestern Zealand has played an important part in the history of Denmark. Lejre was one of the first centres of Danish administration; later on this function was assumed by Roskilde, which in 1020 became a bishopric and the capital of Denmark. This lasted until 1443 when the role of the country's capital was taken over by Copenhagen. Traditionally, this area has been favoured by wealthy Danes and some of the most impressive royal castles can be found here including Kronborg, Fredensborg and Frederiksborg. In addition, there is a variety of more modest establishments worthy of a visit, such as Ermitagen, a royal hunting lodge a short way west of Klampenborg.

Hundested's popular beach

◁ **Neptune's Fountain, Frederiksborg Slot, symbolizing Denmark's power in the 17th century**

Exploring Northwestern Zealand

MOST VISITORS TO ZEALAND never stray beyond the limits of Copenhagen. There are, however, many other parts of the island that are well worth exploring. The list of sacral buildings includes Roskilde Domkirke (Cathedral) and Vor Frue Kirke, in Kalundborg, a 12th-century church with five spires. The region also has several areas that are conducive to carefree holidays. The northern shores, washed by Kattegat's waters, are famous for their beautiful sandy beaches, while the forests, criss-crossed with a network of trails, are perfect for cyclists and hikers.

SEE ALSO

• **Where to Stay** pp243–5.

• **Where to Eat** pp267–9.

A statue of Esbern Snare, 12th-century founder of Kalundborg

GETTING AROUND

Denmark's capital, served by Copenhagen International Airport, is a good starting point for exploring Zealand. Central Station in Copenhagen is the island's main railway hub. Northwestern Zealand has a well-developed network of motorways and major roads, which make getting around by car straightforward.

ODSHERRED
35
21

Sejerø

Sejerø Bugt

RØSNÆS
32

Saltbæk Vig

KALUNDBORG
31

23

22

Tissø

DRAGSHOLM
34

SVINNINGE
33

NØR
JERNLØSE MØL

JYDERUP

Amoseå

STENLII

255

22

E20

TRELLEBORG
30

SLAGELSE

STORE
BÆLT
29

TÅRNBORG
27

28 KORSØR

Odense

22

250

265

Næst

Næstved

The tall spires of Roskilde Domkirke

KEY

▬	Motorway
▬	Major road
▬	Scenic route
═	Other road
=	River
⚜	Viewpoint

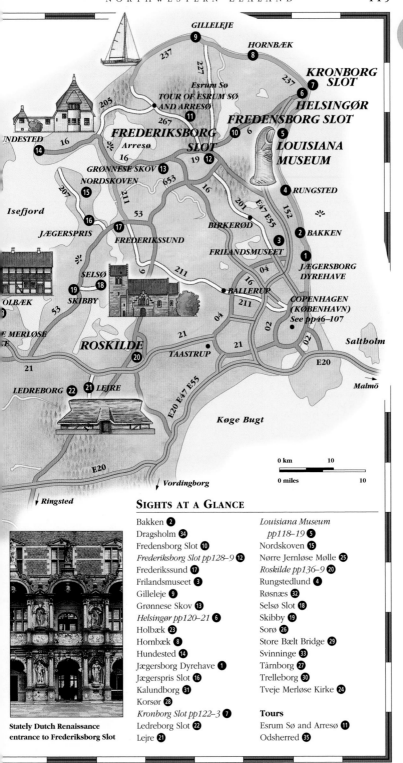

GILLELEJE **9**

HORNBÆK **8**

KRONBORG SLOT 7

Esrum Sø
TOUR OF ESRUM SØ AND ARRESØ 11

HELSINGØR 6

FREDENSBORG SLOT 5

FREDERIKSBORG SLOT 10 12 19

LOUISIANA MUSEUM

JNDESTED **14**   *Arresø* **16**

GRØNNESE SKOV 13

NORDSKOVEN 15

4 RUNGSTED

Isefjord

16

17

BIRKERØD
3

2 BAKKEN

JÆGERSPRIS

FREDERIKSSUND

FRILANDSMUSEET

1

JÆGERSBORG DYREHAVE

SELSØ 18

19
SKIBBY

BALLERUP

COPENHAGEN (KØBENHAVN)
See pp46–107

OLBÆK

Saltholm

E MERLØSE
E

ROSKILDE 20

TAASTRUP

21

E20

Malmö

LEDREBORG 22 21 LEJRE

Køge Bugt

0 km   10
0 miles   10

E20

Vordingborg

Ringsted

SIGHTS AT A GLANCE

Stately Dutch Renaissance entrance to Frederiksborg Slot

Jægersborg Dyrehave ❶

Road map F4. 🚉 🚌

THE BEECH forests and parkland covering an area between the motorway that runs from Copenhagen towards Helsingør and the shore of the Øresund (Sound) is one of the favourite places for weekend forays out of Copenhagen. This area, which is criss-crossed with paths and cycle routes, was established as a royal hunting ground in 1669. The park still supports a herd of some 2,000 deer. A good vantage point from which to look out for them is the Ermitagen hunting lodge at the centre of the park, which was built in 1736 for Christian VI.

Among the park's other attractions are some 600-year-old oak trees, Kirsten Pils Kilde (a holy spring which was a pilgrimage destination in the 16th century) and, nearby, Bellevue (one of the area's best beaches). Horse-drawn carriages offer rides through the park and there is also a golf course and a horse racing track just to the south of Bakken.

Ermitagen hunting lodge

Bakken ❷

Road map F4. 🚋 *39 63 73 00.*
🕐 *Apr–Aug: 2pm–midnight Mon–Fri, 1pm–midnight Sat; noon–midnight Sun, public holidays and Jul.* 🌐 W www.bakken.dk

BAKKEN WAS founded in 1583 and is probably the world's oldest amusement

One of the many rides to be enjoyed at Bakken

park. Located just a short way out of Copenhagen, it is on the edge of a former royal hunting ground that is now the Jægersborg Dyrehave deer park.

The present amusement park has 100 or so rides, including roller-coasters and merry-go-rounds, as well as circus shows and a cabaret-style revue. There are 40 cafés and restaurants on site, although in keeping with Danish tradition people can bring their own supplies for a picnic. Entrance to the park is free though rides must be paid for. Profits from Bakken help to support the deer park.

Frilandsmuseet ❸

Road map F4. 🚉 🚌 *33 13 44 11.*
🕐 *Apr–Sep: 10am–5pm Tue–Sun; Oct: 10am–4pm Tue–Sun.* 🌐 W www.frilandsmuseet.dk

THIS OPEN-AIR museum was founded in 1897 and contains virtually every kind of Danish country dwelling imaginable. It was originally situated near Rosenberg Slot in Copenhagen but was relocated here in 1901 and is now run as part of the Nationalmuseet. Over 100 buildings are arranged into 40 groups and include many examples of rural architecture from cottages to grand manor houses, many of which are furnished and decorated in keeping with the period in which they were built. Visitors should allow a day to look round the collection, which includes fishermen's

cottages, windmills, peasant huts, a post mill (still with working sails) and a smithy (kitted out with irons and a hearth). Many of the museum's staff dress in traditional costume and demonstrate such fading arts as turning clay pots and weaving cloth. The admission price also includes entry to Brede Værk, a textile mill which closed in 1956 and is now preserved as an industrial village complete with cottages, a school and the owner's country house.

A meticulously reconstructed house interior, Frilandsmuseet

Rungstedlund ❹

Road map F4. 2960 Rungsted Kyst. 🚉 🚌 🚋 *45 57 10 57.*
🕐 *May–Sep: 10am–5pm Tue–Sun; Oct–Apr: 1–4pm Wed–Fri, 11am–4pm Sat–Sun.* 🌐 W www.karen-blixen.dk

MADE FAMOUS by Karen Blixen, author of *Out of Africa*, Rungstedlund is the author's birthplace and was where she grew up and wrote most of her works under the pen name Isak Dinesen.

Karen Blixen's house was built around 1500 and was first used as an inn. In 1879 her father bought the property. It is now maintained by a foundation established by the writer, and in 1991 was converted into a museum devoted to Blixen's life and work. The rooms remain little changed from the period when she lived here, and manuscripts, photographs and personal belongings are on display. Blixen's grave is in the surrounding park.

Karen Blixen

KAREN BLIXEN WAS born in 1885. The most colourful period in the Danish writer's life was her stay in Africa. Blixen left for Kenya at the age of 28 with her Swedish husband, Baron Bror von Blixen-Finecke, to establish a coffee plantation. While in Kenya she wrote *Seven Gothic Tales*, a collection of stories that launched her career. Safari expeditions, the raptures and miseries of her affairs, the breakdown of her marriage and the eventual failure of the plantation are all themes of her best-known work, *Out of Africa*, which established her reputation. The author returned to Rungsted in 1931 and lived here until her death in 1962. Among Blixen's other famous stories is *Babette's Feast*, which was made into a film in 1987.

Karen Blixen's House
Only part of the original house is still standing; two wings burned down when Blixen was 13 years old.

African Room
Displayed in the room are Masai shields and spears as well as other mementos brought back from Africa.

Blixen's Grave
The park behind the house contains a beech tree, with a modest gravestone underneath. This is the final resting place of Karen Blixen, who died at the age of 77.

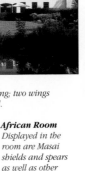

Karen Blixen
Despite suffering from cancer Blixen wrote right up to her death. Towards the end, unable to write herself, she dictated her thoughts to her secretary.

The Film Version
The screen version of Out of Africa *stars Robert Redford and Meryl Streep. It was directed by Sydney Pollack (above) and departs markedly from the novel.*

DEN AFRIKANSKE FARM

KAREN BLIXEN

Out of Africa
Out of Africa *was first published in 1937. It was originally written by the author in English and then translated by Blixen herself into Danish. The cover seen here is of the rare first Danish edition.*

Louisiana Museum **❺**

THIS STRIKING MUSEUM was established in 1958 to house a collection of modern Danish art. The museum's remit has expanded considerably since then and the collection now includes modern American and European paintings, graphic art and photography. The location and architecture are equally impressive. Light-filled galleries form a semi-circle round a 19th-century villa and open out onto a tranquil park filled with sculpture and offering stunning views of the Øresund. Among the many artists represented here are Giacometti, Henry Moore, Picasso and Warhol.

★ Big Thumb (1968)
The French artist Cesar Baldaccini was fascinated by the shape of his thumb. This bronze image is 185 cm (73 inches) high.

Le Déjeuner sur l'Herbe (1961)
Picasso's painting is in homage to a famous work by Edouard Manet painted nearly 100 years earlier.

Sculpture garden

GALLERY GUIDE
Single-storey galleries are connected by a corridor to the south wing and underground galleries. Works are on rotation apart from a room devoted to Giacometti. A children's wing has workshops, art materials and computers to keep kids amused.

Exit

Main entrance

★ Vénus de Meudon (1956)
This work by the French sculptor and painter Jean Arp depicts a woman's body reduced to its simplest form.

Eyes (1997)
This sculpture at the entrance to the museum is a reminder of French-born Louise Bourgeois' exhibition, which took place here in 2003.

KEY

	Exhibition space
	Cinema
	Giacometti collection
	Children's wing

Concert hall

VISITORS' CHECKLIST

Road map F4.
Humlebæk Gl. Standvej 13.
49 19 07 19.
10am–5pm Mon–Tue &
Thu–Sun, 10am–10pm Wed.
www.louisiana.dk

Café
Works on display in the museum's airy café include pieces by the Danish designer Arne Jacobsen.

Marilyn Monroe (1967)
Obsessed by the legendary actress's suicide in 1962, Andy Warhol set about immortalizing the film star by endlessly duplicating her image, using a silk-screen process to transfer the picture onto canvas.

The Graphics Wing, opened in 1991, was built underground to protect its displays from daylight.

Semi-reclining Figure No. 5 (1969–70)
In his image of the semi-reclining woman, split into two parts, Henry Moore intended to blend the female figure with the landscape.

Ground floor

★ South Wing
The south wing was added in 1982 and is half buried in the hillside. It houses the museum's permanent art collection, including several installations.

STAR EXHIBITS

★ **Big Thumb**

★ **South Wing**

★ **Vénus de Meudon**

Helsingør ⑥

HELSINGØR OWES its prosperity to its location on the sound that links the North Sea with the Baltic. The town was a centre of international shipping during the 1400s, when Erik of Pomerania levied a tax on every ship passing through its local waters. In 1857 the dues were abolished, causing a temporary economic decline in the town's fortunes. This downturn was reversed in 1864 with the opening of a railway line and ferry services to Sweden. Today, most people visit Helsingør to see Kronborg Slot (*see pp122–3*), a late-16th century castle that was used by William Shakespeare as the setting for *Hamlet*.

Exploring Helsingør

When sightseeing in Helsingør it is a good idea to start with a visit to the Carmelite Monastery and the Municipal Museum, and then continue with a walk along Biergegade promenade, turning occasionally into side streets (Stengade in particular). Further south is the tourist information centre in Havnepladsen and, a little further on, the ferry terminal.

Gothic cloisters surrounding the Karmeliterklosteret's courtyard

⛪ Karmeliterklosteret Sankt Mariæ Kirke

Sankt Anna Gade 38. **C** *49 21 17 74.* ◻ *mid-May–mid-Sep: 10am–3pm daily; mid-Sep–mid-May: 10am–2pm daily.* 🖼
This Gothic building once belonged to the Carmelites and was erected in the second half of the 15th century. It is considered to be one of the best-preserved medieval monasteries anywhere in Scandinavia and was described by H.C. Andersen as "one of the most beautiful spots in Denmark".

Among its many features are the chapterhouse with its barrel vault and the "Bird Room" decorated with ornithological frescoes. Christian II's mistress, Dyveke, who died in 1517, is believed to be buried in the grounds.

🏛 Helsingør Bymuseum

Sankt Anna Gade 36. **C** *49 28 18 00.* ◻ *noon–4pm daily.* 🖼
The building that currently houses the town museum was erected by friars from the neighbouring monastery, who used it as a hospital for sailors arriving at the local harbour. Some of the instruments once used by the friars for brain surgery in the hospital are on display together with other exhibits relating to the town's past including a model of Kronborg Slot as it was in 1801. Visitors to the museum can also learn about the origin of the region's name: Øresund refers to the levy demanded by Erik of Pomerania which translates as "Penny Sound" ("øre" is the Danish penny, and "sund" means "sound").

Old apothecary on display in the town museum

♜ Axeltorv

Helsingør's main square has a number of restaurants and bars. On Wednesday and Saturday mornings there is a colourful local market here that sells flowers, vegetables, fresh fish, handicrafts, cheese and souvenirs.

The statue in the centre depicts Erik of Pomerania – the Polish king and nephew of Margrethe I who occupied the throne of Denmark between 1397 and 1439. Following the break-up of the Kalmar Union and his subsequent dethronement in 1439 in favour of Christoffer III of Bavaria, the ex-monarch moved to the Swedish island of Gotland. Here, he began to occupy himself with piracy and is sometimes referred to as "the last Baltic Viking".

In his old age Erik returned to Pomerania and is buried in the Polish town of Darlowo. One legend has it that Darlowo's castle still contains hidden treasure plundered from Denmark.

Monument to Erik of Pomerania in Axeltorv

⌗ Stengade

Helsingør's medieval quarter includes Stengade, a pedestrianized street that is linked by various alleyways to Axeltorv. Many of the colourful half-timbered houses once belonged to merchants and ferrymen and date from the 17th and 18th centuries. Oderns Gård, at Stengade No. 66, was built in 1459.

Statue of the Virgin Mary, Skt Olai's Kirke

🛉 Sankt Olai Kirke

Sankt Anna Gade 12. 🔗 49 21 04 43. ○ May–Jul: 10am–4pm Mon–Sat; Sep–Apr: 10am–2pm daily. 🌐
This building was consecrated around 1200 and served for centuries as a parish church. It was elevated to the rank of cathedral in 1961. Numerous elaborate epitaphs can be seen commemorating the many rich merchants and distinguished citizens of Helsingør who are buried here. The church's present-day appearance dates from 16th-century modifications when it also acquired its current furnishings. Among its most precious possessions are a 15th-century Gothic crucifix, a Renaissance pulpit (1568) and a carved wooden altar. The church was restored in 2001.

♠ Marienlyst Slot

Marienlyst Allé 32.
🔗 49 28 27 91.
○ noon–5pm daily. 🌐
The first palace built here dates from 1587 and was used by Frederik II. The present Neo-Classical manor house is the result of extensive remodelling work carried out between 1759 and 1763 by the French architect Nicolas-Henri Jardin, who was asked to adapt the place to the needs of the widowed queen Juliana Maria. The building now serves as a museum with a collection that includes paintings and silverware. Part of the building is also used as a hotel. The surrounding garden contains a mound known as Hamlet's Tomb from which there is a view of the sound.

VISITORS' CHECKLIST

Road Map F4. 🏠 40,000.
🚉 🛈 Havnepladsen 3, 49 21 13 33. 🚢 Baltic Sail (mid-Aug), jazz festival (Aug).
@ info@helsingorturist.dk
W www.helsingorturist.dk

♠ Øresundakvariet

Strandpromenaden 5. 🔗 35 32 18 70. ○ Jun–Aug: 10am–5pm daily; Sep–May: noon–4pm Mon–Fri, 10am–4pm Sat & Sun. 🌐
W www.oresundsakvariet.ku.dk
As well as a colourful collection of tropical fish, Helsingør's aquarium contains many species taken from the waters of the Øresund (Sound) including Baltic jellyfish and seahorses.

Three-storey Neo-Classical Marienlyst Slot

HELSINGØR TOWN CENTRE

Axeltorv ③
Helsingør Bymuseum ②
Karmeliterklosteret ①
Kronborg Slot ⑥
Sankt Olai's Kirke ⑤
Stengade ④

0 m 150
0 yards 150

KEY

🛈	Tourist information
🛉	Church
P	Parking
🚉	Railway station
⚓	Ferry terminal

KRONBORG SLOT
(See pp122–123)

Kronborg Slot ❼

Hamlet's "Castle of Elsinore" was originally built by Erik of Pomerania in the early 15th century. It was remodelled by Frederik II and later by Christian IV but still retains an eerie quality that makes it perfect for the many productions of Shakespeare's play performed here. Among the most impressive rooms are the 62-m (203-ft) Great Hall, the King's Chamber, which has a ceiling painted by the Dutch artist Gerrit van Honthorst, and the "Lille Sal" containing 16th-century silk tapestries by the Flemish painter Hans Knieper. The castle was added to UNESCO's World Heritage List in 2000.

Maritime Museum
Established in 1915 the museum's collection has exhibits relating to the Danish fleet and overseas trade; also on show are the remains of the original 15th-century fortress.

Trumpeter's Tower

Viking Chief
The dungeons contain a sleeping statue of Holger Danske, a Viking chief. According to legend he will wake up should Denmark find itself in peril.

★ Great Hall
Once the longest hall in northern Europe, it was completed in 1582 and is decorated with paintings from Rosenborg Slot. The chandeliers date from the 17th century.

STAR SIGHTS

★ **Chapel**

★ **Great Hall**

★ **"Lille Sal"**

HAMLET

Shakespeare probably never visited Kronborg, but it is here that he set one of his best-known plays. The prototype for the fictional Danish prince was Amlet, a Viking king whose story is recounted by the 12th-century Danish chronicler Saxo Grammaticus in his *Historia Danica* (Danish History). Shakespeare may have encountered this classic tale of murder and revenge via Francois de Belleforest's *Histoires Tragiques* (Tragic Histories), published in 1570. A festival is held in the castle each year during which *Hamlet* and other works by Shakespeare are performed.

King's Tower
Built during 1584-85 it was also known as the "Turner's Tower" as one of its rooms housed Frederik II's turnery containing lathes.

VISITORS' CHECKLIST

Road map F4. Kronborgvej, DK 3000, Helsingør. ▌ *49 21 30 78.* **FAX** *49 21 30 52.* ◯ *May–Sep:10:30am–5pm daily; Jun & Oct: 11am–4pm Tue–Sun; Nov–Mar: 11am–3pm Tue–Sun.* 🖼 **Maritime Museum** ◯ *Same as castle.* 🖼 �W www.kronborg.dk

★ **"Lille Sal"**
The "small room" has seven tapestries depicting Danish kings with verses describing their various achievements.

The North Wing was completed in 1585. Its western section contained the castle offices.

The Queen's Chambers at the corner of the north wing had direct access to the chapel, via the east wing.

Royal Chambers
These rooms contain ornate ceiling decorations and marble fireplaces. At one time the walls would have been lined with gold-embossed leather.

The Pigeon Tower
housed birds that were used for sending important royal messages.

★ **Chapel**
The chapel has a beautiful altar, oak benches with intricately carved ends, a royal balcony and an organ dating from the early 18th century.

Clean sandy beaches of Hornbæk

Hornbæk ❽

Road map F4. 🚉 🚌 🛈 *Vestre Stejlebakke 2A, 49 70 47 47.*

THE NORTHERN shore of Zealand is famous for its pleasant sandy beaches, clean water and the small town of Hornbæk, which has for years been a favoured resort. A large number of visitors come from Copenhagen, many of whom have built holiday homes here. In summer the resort fills with holiday-makers enjoying a variety of outdoor pursuits, including sailing.

Former Cistercian monastery buildings

ENVIRONS:
Esrum, situated southwest of Hornbæk, is famous mainly for its Cistercian monastery. Founded in 1151, it was regarded as one of the most important monasteries in Denmark during the Middle Ages. Its prominence was acknowledged even by the monarchy: in 1374 Queen Helvig, wife of Valdemar IV, was buried here. Even the fires that plagued the establishment (in 1194 and 1204) did not prevent the monastery from becoming one of the largest buildings in Scandinavia. During the Lutheran Reformation in the 16th century much of the church was demolished and the materials were used to build Kronborg Slot *(see pp122–3)*. What remained of the buildings passed into the hands of the monarch and the premises were used first as a hunting base and later as warehouses before being turned into army barracks. In the 20th century they were used as offices, as a post office and then as an orphanage. During World War II they became an air-raid shelter and a fireproof store for valuable documents brought here from the National Archives, and for the Royal Library collection. This chequered history came to an end when a descision was reached to renovate the ancient walls and in 1997 the former monastery opened to visitors. Its main building now houses an exhibition devoted to the Cistercian order while the vaults have been transformed into a café. Also open to visitors is the herb garden, where medicinal plants are grown and used, as they once were when the monastery flourished. Some of the plants are used to produce a flavoured beverage, which is on sale in the shop.

Not far from the monastery is **Esrum Møllegard**, a 400-year old mill. The mill was first used to grind grain, and later to generate electricity. Today, it houses a centre for environmental awareness.

Gilleleje ❾

Road map F4. 🚶 6,000. 🚉
🛈 *Hovedgade 6F, 48 30 01 74.*
ⓦ www.gilleleje.info

THE NORTHERNMOST town in Zealand is also one of the oldest Danish fishing ports and contains the island's largest harbour. From historical records it has been established that the local inhabitants were engaged in fishing here as early as the mid-14th century. Today, Gilleleje is an attractive town with thatched houses, a busy harbour-side fishing auction and a colourful main street that has been turned into a promenade. Rising above the fisherman's cottages is the church – Sønændenesk Kirke. During the German occupation locals used the church as a hiding place for Danish Jews who were then smuggled into neutral Sweden aboard fishing boats under cover of darkness.

Other places of interest include **Gilleleje Museum**, devoted to the town's history, and **Fiskerhuset** an old fisherman's house, which illustrates the realities of everyday life for a mid-19th century fishing family. A coastal trail from the town centre leads east to the Nakkehoved Østre Fyr lighthouse. Built in 1772, this is one of a very few coal-fuelled lighthouses in the world to have survived to this day. This historic building is now open to visitors.

Nakkehoved Østre Fyr, a coal-fired lighthouse near Gilleleje

Fishing boats in Gilleleje's harbour

ENVIRONS: Nearby Græsted, some 8 km (5 miles) south of Gilleleje, has an amusement park – **Nordsjællands Sommerpark** – which has an aqua park as well as paintball and mini golf. In summer refurbished steam and diesel trains run between Gilleleje and Græsted and also to Hornbæk.

🏛 Gilleleje Museum
Rostgårdsvej 2 . 📞 48 30 16 31.
📷 includes a visit to the lighthouse.

🏛 Fiskerhuset
Gilleleje Hovedgade 49 .
📞 48 30 16 31. 📷

♣ Nordsjællands Sommerpark
Kirkevej 43, 3230 Græsted.
📞 48 71 41 41. 📷 admission free for children up to 90 cm (3 ft) in height.
🔲 www.sommerpark.dk

Fredensborg Slot ❿

Road map F4. 📞 33 40 31 87.
🕐 10am–noon daily; Jul: 1–4:30pm daily. 📷 every 15 min (duration about 35 min). 📷 free entry to the gardens all year round, from sunrise to sunset.

FREDERIK IV decided to build Fredensborg Castle in order to commemorate the 1720 peace treaty concluded between Denmark and Sweden at the end of the Nordic Wars (Fredensborg means "Town of Peace"). The building was originally used as a hunting lodge. Nowadays

the castle is one of the main residences of the Danish royal family and is often used to receive VIPs from all over the world. According to tradition, guests who spend the night at the palace must sign their name on a glass pane using a diamond pen.

The original design was modelled on French and Italian castles and the long list of contributors who influenced its final shape includes renowned architects such as Niels Eigtved, Lauritz de Thurah and Caspar Frederik Harsdorf. The present-day complex consists of 28 separate buildings. At its centre is the Dome Hall (Kuppelsalen), surmounted by a dome crowned with a lantern. The magnificent room is encircled by a gallery, which divides the hall into two levels. It is used for formal royal family occasions and also for entertaining special guests.

One of the most interesting rooms in the palace is Havesalon, or the Garden Room, which features a wide door leading to the castle

Fredensborg's gardens decorated with numerous statues

gardens. Its ceiling is decorated with a painting by Henrik Krock depicting Denmark and Norway begging the Olympian gods for help against Sweden.

Fredensborg Slot's ornate Chinese Dining Room (Kinesisk Spisesalon) is another notable room. It is decorated in yellow and red and houses a collection of Chinese porcelain.

The palace garden was established in the 1760s, and contains a lane decorated with a sculpted group of 70 figures, created by J.G. Grund, of fishermen and farmers from Norway and the Faroe Islands. Plants sensitive to cold, including a 250-year-old myrtle shrub, are kept in a greenhouse built in 1995.

Fredensborg Slot, used as a residence by the Danish royal family

A Tour Around Esrum Sø and Arresø ⓫

THESE BEAUTIFUL LAKES are the two largest in Denmark and attract a great many visitors, especially in summer. Gribskov, on the west bank of Esrum Sø, is a forested area where marked paths and bicycle trails lead through thick clusters of ancient beech and spruce trees. Arresø, to the east of Esrum Sø, is Denmark's largest lake and reaches depths of 22 m (72 ft). Ospreys and cormorants can occasionally be spotted diving for fish. As well as being perfect for anglers, bathers and enthusiastic sailors, a tour around the area takes in lush farmland, ancient church ruins, picturesque towns and historic medieval villages.

Ramløse ③
Situated on Arresø's north bank *(above)*, the town's most interesting feature is its Dutch-style windmill (1909) that can be seen working on traditional "Mill Days".

Asserbo ②
Scenic ruins surrounded by a wind-blown forest are all that remains of this former fortress, built in 1663 on the orders of Bishop Absalon.

Frederiksværk ①
Frederiksværk, built alongside a canal, is Denmark's oldest industrial town. A museum in a former gunpowder factory has exhibits on the town's industrial past.

Æbelhof Kloster ⑩
This 12th-century Augustinian abbey was once a hospital. Today, as well as viewing the ruins, visitors can examine the museum's collection of surgical instruments.

Helsinge

Arresø

HUNDSTED

Tulstrup

COPEN

Esrum ⑤
The restored buildings of this former Cistertian monastery house a museum devoted to the community that lived here, giving visitors an idea of the monk's day-to-day life.

TIPS FOR DRIVERS

*Length: about 100 km (62 miles). **Stopping-off points:** There is a large choice of restaurants and accommodation in Fredensborg.*
W www.visitdenmark.com
W www.visit copenhagen.com

Annisse Nord ④
Annisse Nord is a sleepy village but was strategically important for the surrounding area in medieval times; at that time numerous watchtowers were erected along the fjord.

Fredensborg Slot ⑥
The castle gardens are arranged in a Baroque style and are open to the public all year round *(see p125)*.

Fredensborg ⑦
This historic town has a long tradition of hunting and holds regular demonstrations of falconry.

Gribskov ⑨
Growing along the undulating western shoreline of Esrum Sø, Gribskov is the second largest forest in the country.

KEY

▦	Suggested route
▦	Scenic route
═	Other road
═	River, lake
�☆	Viewpoint

Nødebo ⑧
The tiny village of Nødebo is on the banks of Esrum Sø *(left)* and surrounded by Gribskov. The pretty village church is decorated with 15th-century frescoes.

0 km · · · · · 2
0 miles · · · · · 2

Frederiksborg Slot ⑫

THE FIRST ROYAL RESIDENCE was constructed on this site by Frederik II in 1560. A fire in 1859 destroyed most of the castle, which may well have remained a ruin were it not for Carlsberg boss J.C. Jacobsen who restored the building and helped found a national history museum. The museum now takes up 80 or so of the palace rooms. Jacobsen also donated many of his own paintings which, along with others, are arranged chronologically to chart Denmark's history. Period furnishings and some magnificent architecture help to conjure up a feel for the country's past.

★ Slotskirken
From 1671 until 1840 the castle chapel was used to crown Denmark's monarchs. Its ebony altar dates from 1606 and is the work of Jakob Mores, a German goldsmith.

★ Riddersalen
The Knights' Hall has a carved wooden ceiling. The gilded ornaments, a 19th-century black marble fireplace and intricate tapestries add to the splendour.

Audienssalen
The Audience Room was built in 1688. Among the paintings lining the walls is a portrait of a proud-looking Christian V, depicted as a Roman emperor surrounded by his children.

Chapel Portal
The oak door, set within a sandstone portal in the shape of a triumphal arch, survived from the fire of 1859 and looks as it would have done in Christian IV's day.

STAR SIGHTS

★ Riddersalen

★ Slotskirken

VISITORS' CHECKLIST

Road map F4. 3400 Hillerød, Slotsgade 1. ☎ 48 26 04 39. ☐ Apr–Oct: 10am–5pm daily; Nov–Mar: 11am–3pm daily. ☐ **Gardens** ☐ Daily (May–Aug: 10am–9pm; Sep–Oct: 10am–7pm; Nov–Feb: 10am–4pm; Mar–Apr: 10am–7pm). ☐ www.frederiksborgmuseet.dk

Queen Sophie's Room
During the reign of Christian IV this room was used by the king's mother. When the palace became a museum it was hung with paintings associated with Frederik III.

The Royal Wing has a gallery of statues symbolizing the influence of planets on human life and is an excellent example of Dutch Mannerism.

Room 42
This example of overblown Baroque is typical of the taste associated with Denmark's era of absolute monarchy (see pp38–9). The bed with silk draperies was made in France in 1724.

Gardens
The castle gardens were established in the 1720s and restored in 1996. The carefully trimmed shrubs create a symmetrical pattern typical of a Baroque garden.

Room 46
All of the items in this room, such as this ornate wall clock, are in perfect accord with the colours and Rococo excess of the overall design.

Grønnese Skov ⑬

Road map F4.

THE ANCIENT forest of Grønnese Skov is about 5 km (3 miles) east of Hundested, on the shores of Roskilde Fjord. Archaeological excavations indicate that during the Neolithic era this area was one of the more important sites of early culture in Zealand and the site now attracts thousands of visitors every year.

One of the most important relics of Denmark's Neolithic past is an extraordinary burial chamber known as a dolmen. It is one of many such tombs in Denmark and consists of a huge flat stone resting on three chunky pillars. The dolmen is referred to locally as Karlsstenen ("Karl's Stone") and is one of the biggest and best preserved of its type anywhere in Denmark. It must be reached on foot but the forest car park is only a short distance away.

Prehistoric Karlsstenen, Grønnese Skov

Hundested ⑭

Road map E4. 🚍 ℹ️ Nørregade 22, 47 93 77 88.
🌐 www.hundested-turist.dk

THIS SMALL TOWN lies on a slender peninsula. Its name translates literally as "dog's place" and derives from a species of local seal commonly known as a sea dog because of its canine-like barking. The main reason to come to Hundested is to take a look around **Knud Rasmussens Hus**, which is situated on a high cliff close to Spodsbjerg lighthouse. The house was built in 1907 by the intrepid Arctic explorer, Knud Rasmussen, and now houses a museum devoted to his life and travels. Close by is a monument to him erected in 1936 made of stones brought over from Greenland.

ENVIRONS: A short way northeast is **Kikhavn**, the oldest fishing village on the Halsnæs peninsula, which dates back to the 13th century. In the 18th century there were many small farms here, some of which were partly destroyed by a storm in 1793. A handful of these have now been reconstructed to form an open-air museum. Kikhaven is also the starting point of a footpath, **Halsnæsstien**,

Knud Rasmussen's house, now a popular museum

that links the shores of Isefjord and Kattegat.

Another place worth visiting is **Lynæs**, just south of Hundested. The local church, built in 1901 from huge granite blocks, serves as a navigational guide for returning fishermen. A monument standing by the church commemorates those who lost their lives at sea.

🏛 **Knud Rasmussens Hus**
📞 47 93 71 61. 🕐 Apr–Oct: 11am–4pm. 📷

Kongeegen, believed to be the oldest living oak tree in Europe

Nordskoven ⑮

Road map F4.

THE PENINSULA that separates Roskilde Fjord from Isefjord contains one of Denmark's most beautiful beech forests. The forest has two sections, known as Fællesskoven and Studehaven. Running between them is a 15-km (9-mile) long bicycle trail with

KNUD RASMUSSEN

Knud Rasmussen was born in 1879. Half Inuit himself, Rasmussen was fascinated by Inuit culture and language and resolved to become a polar explorer at an early age. He took part in his first scientific expedition in 1900 and soon began organizing them himself. In 1910, together with Peter Freuchen, he founded the Thule settlement in the north of Greenland. Between 1921 and 1924 Rasmussen completed a grand expedition from Greenland to the Bering Straight, covering 18,000 km (11,185 miles) by dog-sleigh. From each of his expeditions the explorer brought back many artifacts; most of these are now in the Nationalmuseet in Copenhagen (see pp84–5). In the course of his seventh expedition Rasmussen fell seriously ill. He died in 1933, aged 54.

The explorer's house, full of reminders of his expeditions

Statue of a deer in front of Jægerspris Slot

Frederikssund ⓱

Road map F4. 🏃 *17,000.* 🚏
ℹ️ *Havnegade 5A, 47 31 06 85.*
🎭 *Viking Festival (mid-Jun–late Jul).*
🌐 *www.frederikssund-tourist.dk*

THIS TOWN WAS founded in 1655 on the orders of Frederik III. The choice of site was not accidental, as it overlooks the narrowest part of the Roskilde Fjord and was used for many years by boats crossing to the other side.

In the town centre is the **J.F. Willumsens Museum**. Willumsen (1863–1958), a prominent Danish Symbolist painter, donated his paintings, sculptures and drawings to Frederikssund on condition that a suitable building be erected to display them. The museum also contains works by other artists that were collected by Willumsen.

Frederikssund is primarily known, however, for its reconstructed **Viking Village**. The village is open to visitors all year round but the best time to visit is during the summer Viking Festival. Its most popular events are the evening Viking plays that feature 200 actors and end with a grand banquet. A popular summer excursion is to take a cruise aboard the *Harald Blåtand*, a river boat named after the Viking chieftain Harald I (Bluetooth).

🏛 **J.F. Willumsens Museum**
📞 *47 31 07 73.*
🕙 *10am–5pm daily.* 🎫

views over Roskilde Fjord. At its highest point, called Frederikshøj, is a hunting pavilion built by Frederik VII in 1875. A number of ancient trees can be found in the forest including three famous oaks: Kongeegen, Storkeegen and Snoegen, which have inspired many artists. Kongeegen, the most ancient of the three trees, is believed to be 1,500–1,900 years old. In 1973 its last bough broke away, leaving only the vast trunk, which has a circumference of 14 m (46 ft).

Jægerspris Slot ⓰

Road map F4. ℹ️ *Jægerspris Slot, Parkvej 1, 47 53 10 04.*
🕙 *Apr–Oct: 11am–3pm Tue–Sun.* 🎫
Park 🕙 *all year round.*

THIS MEDIEVAL castle, situated about 6 km (4 miles) west of Frederikssund, has been used by Danish royalty since the early 14th century and is now open to the public. The first royal building, known as Abrahamstrup, still exists although it has been swallowed by the north wing of the present complex. A life-size statue of a deer standing before the entrance to the castle is by Adelgund Vogt, a pupil of Bertel Thorvaldsen.

In the mid-19th century Frederik VII made the palace his summer residence. After his death in 1863 the monarch's widow, Countess Danner, turned part of the palace into a refuge for poor and unwanted girls. The centre became the first children's home in Denmark. A special exhibition illustrates the often austere way of life in an early 20th-century Danish orphanage.

Much of the house still retains its royal character, however, and visitors can take a look at magnificent rooms arranged by Frederik VII. There is also an exhibition of archaeological finds reflecting one of Frederik VII's abiding passions.

The gardens stretching to the rear of the castle include Zealand's largest collection of rhododendrons; standing among them are 54 obelisks with busts of famous Danish personages. The tomb of countess Danner is also in the castle gardens.

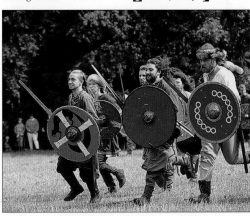

Danes dressed as Vikings during Frederikssund's summer festival

Selsø Slot, built in 1578

Selsø Slot ⑱

Road map F4. ℹ️ Selsøvej, 4050 Skibby, 47 52 01 71. ⭕ May–Jun: 1pm–4pm Sat & Sun; end-Jun–early Aug & mid Oct: 11am–4pm daily; Aug–Oct: 1pm–4pm daily. 📷 🆆 www.selsoe.dk

THIS PROPERTY'S history dates back to the 12th century. According to records, Bishop Absalon became interested in the site in about 1170 and by 1228 a sumptuous residence had been built here.

The present castle was built in 1578. It was reworked in 1734 and much of its original Renaissance style was replaced with Baroque details. The castle is now a museum and gives visitors an idea of what aristocratic life was like in the 1800s. The castle's stern, simple exterior hides a richer interior, including the "Grand Ballroom". With original marble panels and a decorated ceiling, it is used as a venue for classical music concerts. Wine-tasting sessions are held in the castle vaults. The castle church has an altarpiece dating from 1605.

The property owes much of its charm to its location by Selsø lake. A bird reserve established in the gardens is one of the best places for birdwatching in Denmark. A viewing tower standing in the garden was built specifically for this purpose.

Skibby ⑲

Road map F4. 🚌 ℹ️ Havngade, 47 31 06 85. 🆆 www.skibby-tourist.dk

THE MAIN TOWN of the peninsula between Roskilde Fjord and Isefjord, Skibby is known mainly for its early 12th-century church, which is decorated with some well-preserved frescoes. The oldest of these were found in 1855 in the Romanesque apses and date from the second half of the 12th century. Similar decorations can be found in other churches in the district, including some at nearby Dråby. In 1650 a manuscript, known as the *Skibby Chronicle*, was found buried behind the altar. The work, written in Latin, recounts the history of Denmark between 1046 and 1534.

It is uncertain why the chronicle was found here. Its style points to the authorship of Paul Helgsen, a Carmelite monk and orator. Helgsen was a native of Helsingør, however, and since the work is unfinished, its discovery has provoked debate as to the fate of its author. Skibby's other claim to fame is as the location of Scandinavia's first nudist swimming pool.

ENVIRONS: A short way northeast of Skibby, in the town of Skuldelev, is a **toy museum** with a collection of over 4,000 dolls. Also on display are stuffed toys, model trains, toy cars, toy soldiers and mechanical toys.

Roskilde ⑳

See pp136–9.

Trying out a dugout canoe at Lejre's Stone Age village

Lejre ㉑

Road map F4. **Open-air museum** Slangealleen 2, 4320 Lejre. 📞 46 48 08 78. ⭕ May & Jun: 10am–4pm Tue–Fri; end Jun–mid-Aug: 10am–5pm daily; mid-Aug–end Sep: 10am–5pm Tue–Fri, 10am–5pm Sat & Sun. 📷 🆆 www.lejre-center.dk

A RECONSTRUCTED VILLAGE that takes visitors back to the Iron Age is the main attraction of Lejre, which is situated 8 km (5 miles) to the southwest of Roskilde. In summer Lejre Forsøgcenter is populated by volunteer Danish families who, in the

Dråby Kirke, situated near Skibby

◁ **Frederiksborg Slot and its surrounding gardens seen from the lake**

Ledreborg Slot, surrounded by beautiful, well-kept gardens

name of research, dress in prehistoric furs and skins, use traditional tools and carry out all-but-forgotten chores such as chopping firewood and making clay pots.

The village is popular with children, especially in summer, when it is possible for them to take part in a variety of activities including archery, dying clothes and paddling a dugout canoe. The centre also has a 19th-century cottage farm that recreates the lives of Danish farmers of that period.

Research has established that Lejre was one of the earliest centres of government in Denmark. Legend has it that it was the seat of a Stone-Age king named Skjoldungs, although the building shown to visitors, once home of the supposed sovereign, is a recreation built in the 18th century. It is quite likely, however, that the nearby grave-mound dates from the Stone Age period.

Ledreborg Slot ㉒

Road map F4. Ledreborg Slot, 4320 Lejre. 46 48 00 38.
mid-Jun–Aug: 11am–5pm daily.
Park all year round.

ELEGANT ON THE outside and opulent on the inside, Ledreborg Slot is one of the foremost examples of Baroque architecture in northern Europe. It was built in 1739 on the orders of Count Johan Ludvig Holstein. The interior has changed little since that time and contains antique furniture, gilded

mirrors, wall paintings, tapestries and massive candelabras. One of the most interesting rooms is the banqueting hall, designed by the renowned royal architect Nicolai Eigtved. In 1745 this exclusive residence acquired a chapel, which until 1899 served as a parish church.

The gardens that surround the castle are a pleasant place to explore. The well-kept, neatly trimmed hedges make this place one of the most enchanting Baroque gardens in Scandinavia. There is also a maze, created from trimmed shrubs, which can be a source of much merriment.

Holbæk ㉓

Road map F4. 30,000.
Jernbaneplads 3, 59 43 11 31.
www.holbaek-info.dk

AN IMPORTANT PORT, Holbæk is also the the main commercial town for the area. It serves as a good starting point for people wishing to visit Øro island, which lies a

mere 7 km (4 miles) away. The area has several bicycle trails and Holbæk is also popular with cyclists, who set off from here.

Holbæk was granted municipal privileges in the late 13th century, making it one of the oldest of Zealand's towns. At that time it was the site of a dynamic Dominican monastery, although the oldest surviving remains are these of a Franciscan monastery, which is located next to the Neo-Gothic Sankt Nicolaj Kirke in the medieval part of the town.

Not far from this church is **Holbæk Museum**, which consists of a dozen or so period houses dating from 1660 to 1867. Their interiors include typical items and furnishings from rural and urban dwellings of the 17th and 18th centuries. There is also a reconstructed grocery shop. A café, toy shop and pottery exhibition complete the attractions. The tiny market square between the houses is a venue for numerous events staged during summer months, which often feature people dressed in period costumes.

Holbæk has some good local parks, such as Bysøparken, which has a charming fountain, and Østre Anlæg, where entire families of plump ducks can be seen waddling along the lanes and pecking about on the lawns.

🏛 Holbæk Museum
Klosterstræde 18. 59 43 23 53.
10am–4pm Tue–Fri, noon–4pm Sat & Sun. www.holbmus.dk

Period interior in Holbæk Museum

Roskilde ⑳

FOUNDED IN THE 10th century by the Vikings, Roskilde was Denmark's first capital. In AD 980 Harald I (Bluetooth) built Zealand's first church here, making the town an important religious centre and from the 11th century it was a bishopric. In the Middle Ages Roskilde had a population of 10,000 and was one of the largest towns in northern Europe. When Erik of Pomerania moved the capital, the town lost much of its status but it flourishes today as a market centre for the region and is popular with visitors in summer who come to see the historic Viking ships and the ancient cathedral.

Exploring Roskilde

All of the town's attractions are within easy reach. The most prestigious streets, lined with shops and cafés, are Skomagergade and Algade. The Vikingeskibsmuseet (Viking Ship Museum) is by the harbour.

⛪ Roskilde Domkirke

See pp138–9.

Fountain in front of the town hall in Stændertorvet

♜ Stændertorvet

This small square situated by the town's main promenade has for centuries been the heart of Roskilde. In the Middle Ages it was the site of fairs. Sankt Laurence, a Romanesque church, was demolished in the mid-16th century to provide more space for the growing market. A few remaining parts of the church can be seen today including the tower, which now adorns the town hall (built in 1884) and what remains of the church foundations. The foundations are open to the public and

are in the town hall's vaults. In the square is a monument depicting, among others, Roar, the legendary father of Roskilde, who established Roskilde as homage to the two pagan gods, Thor and Odyn.

♞ Bishop's Palace

Stændertorvet 3.
☎ 46 32 14 70.
🕐 noon–4pm Tue–Sun. 🖼

Built in 1733 by the Danish architect Laurits de Thurah, this yellow Baroque palace is the former seat of Roskilde's bishops. It is linked to the neighbouring cathedral by the Arch of Absalon. The palace rooms contain two museums. The Museum of Contemporary Art has a permanent collection and also organizes numerous temporary exhibitions of Danish and foreign artists. The Palace Collections has 18th- and 19th-century paintings on display as well as works of art from other periods that were collected by a number of wealthy Roskilde families such as the Bruuns and the Borchs.

🏛 Roskilde Museum

Sankt Ols Gade 18. ☎ 46 31 65 00.
🕐 11am–4pm daily. 🖼
🌐 www.roskildemuseum.dk

The municipal museum in Roskilde is an excellent place for anyone interested in the town's history. Its collection – including documents,

photographs, archaeological finds and works of art – explains the region's past, from the Stone Age up to the present day (which is aptly symbolized by a display devoted to the prestigious rock festival organized every year in Roskilde since 1971). The museum also includes a building in Ringstedgade, named Brødrene Luetzhøfts Købmandsgård, which is simply a shop furnished in a manner typical of a century or so ago, where potash soap and dried cod can be purchased.

♜ Roskilde Kloster

Sankt Pederstræde 8.
☎ 46 35 02 19. 🕐 Jul: 2–3:30pm; Jan–Jun, Aug–Dec: 9am–9pm.
🖼 🖼
🌐 www.roskilde kloster.dk

In the Middle Ages Roskilde had about 20 churches and monasteries, not counting the cathedral. Their sacral functions ceased as the Reformation swept through the country in 1536.

This brick-built monastery, which stands in its own grounds, was built in 1560 and, in 1699, became Denmark's first refuge for unmarried mothers from well-to-do families. It has some fine interiors including a chapel and banqueting hall.

Hussar's uniform, Roskilde Museum

Brick monastery buildings of Roskilde Kloster

🌿 Kirkegård

The former cemetery, where prominent and wealthy citizens of the town were buried during the Middle Ages, is now used as a park and is located near the railway station. The station was built in 1847 to serve the Copenhagen–Roskilde line and is one of the oldest train stations in Denmark.

Roskilde Jars commemorating the city's 1,000th anniversary

🏛 Hestetorvet

The main landmark of the market square, used in medieval times for horse trading, are the three 5-m (16-ft) tall jars. These were put in place in 1998 as part of the town's millennium

celebrations. Engraved on one of the jars are verses from a poem written by Henrik Nordbrandt, dedicated to Roskilde and to Margrethe I. The jar's creator, Peter Brandes, intended them to symbolize life and death.

🏛 Vikingeskibsmuseet

Vindeboder 12.
📞 46 30 02 00.
🕙 10am–5pm daily. ♿
🌐 www.vikingeskibsmuseet.dk

About 1,000 years ago the boats now exhibited at the Viking Ship Museum were filled with stones and sunk in the fjord in order to block the passage of enemy ships. In 1962 five of the vessels were recovered. Although they had been underwater for so long, they are in remarkably good condition and give a good indication of Viking boat-building skills. The largest of them is a 30-m (98-ft) long warship, which could carry a crew of 70 to 80 Vikings. The best preserved is a 14-m (46-ft) long merchant ship, which sailed around the Baltic and Danish sounds. The other

VISITORS' CHECKLIST

Road map F4. 🏘 50,000. 🚆
ℹ️ Gullandsstræde 15,
46 31 65 65.
🎸 Roskilde Rock Festival (late Jun–early Jul).
@ info@destination-roskilde.dk
🌐 www.visitroskilde.com

ships are a deep-sea trader, a longship and a ferry. The museum also has an exhibition devoted to the Vikings and a working boatyard, where replicas of old Viking ships, including those in the museum, are built using traditional methods and materials. In summer it is possible to sail on a replica ship on the Roskilde Fjord. The museum also has a pleasant café.

Historic boat at Vikingeskibsmuseet

ROSKILDE TOWN CENTRE

0 m   200
0 yards   200

KEY

ℹ️ Tourist information
🏛 Church
🅿 Parking
✉ Post office
🚆 Railway station

Roskilde Domkirke

THE TWIN TOWERS of this magnificent brick cathedral, begun in the 12th century on the orders of Bishop Absalon, are a landmark of Roskilde. The cathedral is an organic mix of styles. For centuries it was used as the burial site of Danish monarchs, 38 of whom are interred here. The remains of Harald I (Bluetooth), a 10th-century Viking king, are said to be inside one of the columns to the side of the main altar. In view of its historic value the cathedral has been declared a UNESCO World Heritage Site.

★ Christian IV's Chapel
Christian IV supervised the construction of his own final resting place. The grand chapel contains a painting of the king in combat and a bronze statue by Bertel Thorvaldsen.

The South Tower has a unique clock with tiny moving figures including one of St Jørgen chasing a dragon.

St Bridgit's Chapel
As well as a wall painting of the four Fathers of the Church, the chapel contains various statues including St Christopher and Pope Lucius.

The storm bell is the oldest medieval bell in Denmark.

Main entrance

Pulpit
The pulpit was ordered by Christian IV in 1610. Its ornate carvings in marble, alabaster and sandstone were made by Hans Brokman of Copenhagen.

The Royal Column indicates the height of several Danish kings. Christian I is recorded as 2.06 m (6 ft 9 inches), although his skeleton is 1.88 m (6 ft 2 inches).

Stalls
Set near the altar these wooden pews are beautiful examples of Gothic carving.

VISITORS' CHECKLIST

Domkirkestræde 10.
☎ 46 35 16 24. ☐ Apr–Sep:
9am–4:45pm Mon–Fri, 9am–noon
Sat, 12:30–4:45pm Sun;
Oct–Mar: 10am–3:45pm
Tue–Sat, 12:30–3:45pm Sun. ☒
Ⓦ www.roskildedomkirke.dk

Margrethe's Spire replaced a tower destroyed by fire in 1968.

★ **Altarpiece**
The altar, depicting scenes from the life of Christ, was produced in Antwerp in the 1500s. It is here quite by chance, having been confiscated while on board a ship bound for Gdansk.

Chapter House contains a crucifix made from two bells that melted in the 1968 fire.

★ **Sarcophagus of Margrethe I**
The sarcophagus bearing an alabaster effigy of Margrethe I as a young girl is considered to be the most beautiful sculpture in the cathedral.

Interior
The cathedral has been rebuilt several times, acquiring features typical of the styles that were currently in fashion. The last major works were carried out following a fire in 1968.

STAR SIGHTS

★ **Altarpiece**

★ **Christian IV's Chapel**

★ **Sarcophagus of Margrethe I**

Tveje Merløse Kirke ㉔

Road map E4. 🚂 Holbæk, Jernbaneplads 3, 59 43 11 31.

BEING A MINIATURE version of Roskilde's original 12th-century cathedral, the church in Tveje Merløse is one of the most interesting Romanesque sacral buildings in Denmark. Its most distinctive features are the two almost identical square towers. The history of the site as a place of worship is believed to date back to the Viking era; some records suggest it was used for worship even earlier than this, in the 3rd century.

The church's interior has an altarpiece by Joakim Skovgaard. At one time the church contained some colourful 13th-century frescoes, depicting among other things, the devil and the motif of God's Majesty, which is a typical medieval theme found particularly in the region of Øresund. These were removed when the church was being restored and are now on display in Copenhagen's Nationalmuseet (*see pp84–5*). A small cemetery is in the church grounds.

Nørre Jernløse Mølle ㉕

Road map E4.
Windmill ☐ May–Oct: every 1st and 3rd Sun of the month, 2–4pm.

THE SMALL VILLAGE of Nørre Jernløse, located some 25 km (16 miles) west of Roskilde, has a 12th-century church containing 16th-century frescoes. The town is best known, however, for its 19th-century windmill, which is set on an sturdy octagonal base surrounded by a distinctive gallery.

The Dutch-style windmill was built in 1893 in Nørrevold, near Copenhagen, where it was known as Sankt Peders Mølle. When financial difficulties forced its owners to sell the mill it was bought by Niels Peter Rasmussen, a miller, who dismantled it and transported it in pieces on a horse cart to Jernløse, 70 km (43 miles) away. In 1899 the windmill was bought by Ole Martin Nielsen, whose family used and maintained it for the next 60 years. Finally, in 1979 the windmill was handed over to the parish of Jernløse.

Built on a stone base, the

Nørre Jernløse mill has a timber structure with a shingled roof crowned with a wooden, onion-shaped cupola. Its sails were once cloth covered and could be operated directly from the gallery. The mill, which is no longer used to grind flour, now has an information centre where visitors can familiarize themselves with the windmill's history and learn a little about early methods of flour production.

Well in front of the monastery in Sorø

Sorø ㉖

Road map E5. 🏘 7,000.
🚂 Storgade 15, 57 82 10 12.
🌐 www.set-soroe.dk

LOCATED ON THE banks of the Tuel and Sorø lakes, Sorø is one of the most beautiful towns in Zealand. In 1140 Bishop Absalon, the founder of Copenhagen, began to build a monastery here. When it was complete the Klosterkirke was the largest building of its kind in Scandinavia and one of the first brick structures ever to be built in Denmark. This 70-m (230-ft) long Romanesque-Gothic church contains the remains of Bishop Absalon in a tomb at the rear of the main altar. The church also contains the sarcophagi of Christian II, Valdemar IV and Oluf III. In 1412 Queen Margrethe I was buried here, but subsequently her remains were transferred to Roskilde Domkirke (*see pp138–9*).

A small museum is devoted to the church and to Bishop Absalon. Included in the

Dutch-style windmill in Nørre Jernløse

collection is the bishop's gold sapphire ring and a 6-m (20-ft) tall crucifix, which was made by Claus Berg and brought to the church in 1527.

Sorø is perhaps best known for its Akademiet, which is set in a picturesque spot on the shores of Lake Sorø. This famous establishment, dedicated to the education of the sons of the nobility, was founded in 1623 by Christian IV in the monastery buildings left empty as a consequence of the Reformation. The Akademiet is surrounded by a park which contains a monument depicting the writer Ludwig Holberg who bequeathed his considerable fortune and library to the school after his death in 1754. The school still operates though it is no longer reserved only for the country's nobility.

ENVIRONS: Tystrup-Bavelse is a national wildlife reserve established near Sorø in the 1960s. The forests contain many prehistoric grave-mounds, including **Kellerøddysen**, Denmark's largest megalithic stone formation, which is over 120 m (394 ft) in length. The reserve's two connected freshwater lakes attract a variety of birdlife and more than 20,000 water birds winter here. **Bjernede**, near Sorø, has the only surviving round church in Zealand. Constructed of stone and brick, it is quite unlike Bornholm's round churches *(see p217)* and was built in 1160 by Sune Ebbeson, a provincial governor to Valdemar I (The Great).

Distinct white exterior of the 13th-century church in Tårnborg

Bjernede Rundkirke – the only round church in Zealand

Tårnborg ②⑦

Road map E5.

THIS ANCIENT parish on the shores of Korsør bay, with the rising outline of a white 13th-century church, was once occupied by a castle and settlement. Tårnborg appeared as a place name for the first time in a royal land survey completed in the first half of the 13th century, though it is likely that a stronghold existed at least one hundred years prior to this and, together with Nyborg and Sprogø, controlled the passage across the Store Bælt *(see pp142–3)*. From the 13th century it was also a major centre of commerce and in the 14th century Tårnborg forged links with neighbouring estates, helping to intensify foreign trade. The castle was demolished in the 15th century following a financial crisis.

Recent archaeological excavations suggest that Tårnborg's original stronghold measured about 30 m (98 ft) in diameter, with an 8-m (26-ft) high tower at its centre.

Korsør ②⑧

Road map E5. 🚗 20,000. 🚂
ℹ️ *Nygade 7, 58 35 02 11.*
🌐 *www.visitkorsoer.dk*

THE EARLIEST records of this town date from 1241. The most prominent building in Korsør is a 13th-century fortress (Korsør Fæstning), which played a crucial role in the town gaining control of the Store Bælt. In 1658 the constantly enlarged fortress was captured by the Swedes, but returned to Danish control a year later. Its 25-m (82-ft) high tower now houses the **Korsør By-og Overfarts-museum** (Town and Ferry Service Museum), which has a collection that includes models of ships that once sailed across the Store Bælt.

Clusters of historic buildings, mainly from the 18th century, can be seen in the environs of Algade, Slottensgade and Gavnegade. The Rococo mansion at No. 25 Algade dates from 1761 and was built by Rasmus Langeland, a shipowner. It was originally used as an inn for sailors who were waiting for the right conditions to cross the Store Bælt. Its front is adorned with allegories of the four seasons of the year. Inside is a small art museum displaying, among other things, sculptures by Harald Isenstein who died in 1980.

🏛 **Kørsør By-og Overfartsmuseum**
Søbatteriet 7. 📞 *58 37 47 55.*
🕐 *Apr–Dec: 11am–4pm daily.* ♿

Ancient cannons outside Korsør Fæstning (Fortress)

Store Bælt Bridge ㉙

UNTIL RECENTLY the only way of travelling to Zealand was by air or ferry across the Store Bælt (Great Belt). In 1998, after 12 years of construction work, the two biggest Danish islands – Zealand and Funen – were joined together. The link consists of two bridges with an artificial island in between. The journey time between Zealand and Funen has now been cut to 10 minutes. Of the two bridges, the Østbro (Eastern) suspension bridge presents a more impressive sight. Situated on the approach to the bridge, on the outskirts of Korsør, is the Storebælt Udstillingscenter (Great Belt Centre), which has an exhibition devoted to the crossing and to the local natural environment.

VISITORS' CHECKLIST

Road map E5. **☏** *70 15 10 15*
🖅 **Ⓦ** www.storebaelt.dk.
**Storebælt Bro og Naturcen-
ter ☏** *58 35 01 00.* ☐ *Apr–Jun,
Sep, second half of Oct: 10am–
5pm daily; Jul–Aug: 10am–7pm
daily; 1st half of Oct: 10am–5pm
Mon, Sat, Sun.* 🖅

These pylons, at 254 m (833 ft), are the highest man-made structures in Scandinavia.

85-m (279 ft) long cables

Bridges
The Østbro is 7 km (4.4 miles) long and carries cars (trains run in a tunnel). The Vestbro is 6.6 km (4.1 miles) long and carries cars and trains.

The bridge is 48.2 m (158 ft) wide.

Sprogø
This small man-made island in the middle of the Store Bælt is the junction where the Østbro motorway and the railway track meet.

THE STORE BÆLT

Slagelse
Trelleborg
Langeskov
Tårnborg Kirke
Korsør
Nyborg
Fuglebje
Skælskør

KEY

═══ Motorway

═══ Major road

─── Other road

Agersø

0 km   15

0 miles   15

Tunnel
An 8-km (5-mile) long rail tunnel, measuring 7.7 m (25 ft) in diameter, descends 75 m (246 ft) below the surface. It is the second largest underwater tunnel in Europe.

A display of Viking archery in Trelleborg

Trelleborg ③⓪

Road map E5. 7 km (4 miles) east of Slagelse. **Tower** Trelleborg Allé 4.
☐ *Apr–Oct: 10am–5pm Sat–Thu.*
● *Fri & Nov–Mar.* 🎫
W *www.vikingeborg.dk*

THE BEST-PRESERVED of Denmark's Viking fortresses was founded in the 10th century by Harald I (Bluetooth). At the height of its power it was manned by an estimated force of 1,000 warriors. Of the reconstructed buildings, the longhouse is the most impressive. It is built of rough oak beams and furnished with benches that were used by the Vikings for sleeping on.

Originally, there were 16 buildings in the main section of the fortress. Outside the fortress was a small cemetery, where archaeologists have counted about 150 graves.

In summer visitors can participate in fun and games. Some of the staff are dressed in Viking costume and are on hand to demonstrate such workaday jobs as grinding corn and sharpening tools. Daily workshops provide children with the opportunity to try their hand at archery and even dress up as Vikings.

A small museum exhibits finds excavated from the grounds such as jewellery and pottery. It also screens a 20-minute film about the history of Trelleborg.

Kalundborg ③①

Road map E4. 🏛 *20,000.* 🚉
ℹ *Volden 12, 59 51 09 15.*
Museum ☐ *May–Aug: 11am–4pm Tue–Sun; Sep–Apr: 11am–4pm Sat & Sun.* 🎫
W *www.kalundborg-turistbureau.dk*

KALUNDBORG is one of Zealand's oldest towns and was populated by the Vikings as early as the 9th century. The town was also once used as a base by pirates but in 1168 a castle was built here and control of the fjord's waters was assumed by the crown.

The ruins in Volden square are all that remains of the castle. Its builder was Esbern Snare, the brother of Bishop Absalon. Snare was also the creator of the well-preserved 12th-century Vor Frue Kirke (Church of Our Lady), which has five octagonal towers and a Byzantine design based on a Greek crucifix.

Kalundborg's medieval quarter surrounds the church and includes cobbled streets and 16th-century buildings. One of these now houses the town museum. Most of the exhibits are devoted to local history and include a collection of costumes and the skeletons of two beheaded Vikings. Standing in the museum courtyard is a model of Kalundborg, providing a view of the town's 17th-century layout.

Røsnæs ③②

Road map D4. ℹ *Kalundborg.*

THE RØSNÆS peninsula, as well as the Asnæs peninsula that flanks the Kalundborg Fjord on the other side, were created by a continental glacier some 20,000 years ago. In the Middle Ages the Røsnæs peninsula, which thrusts into the Store Bælt, was covered with thick forest, making it one of the favourite areas for royal hunting trips. One hunt, in 1231, organized at the request of Valdemar the Victorious, ended in a bitter tragedy when a stray arrow killed the king's son (who was also named Valdemar).

The peninsula's tip is the westernmost point of Zealand and is marked by a lighthouse erected in 1845. The light from its lantern, mounted 25 m (82 ft) above sea level, can be seen up to 40 km (25 miles) away. A short way before the lighthouse, in the village of Ulstrup, is a Dutch-style windmill built in 1894. It was still being used in the 1950s to grind flour but is now purely a visitor attraction.

At the base of the Asnæs peninsula is Lerchenborg Slot, a Baroque castle built in 1753 by General Christian Lerche. H.C. Andersen stayed here in 1862 and some of the rooms contain items relating to the famous writer.

The unusual five-towered church in Kalundborg

Svinninge ③③

Road map E4. 🚉 🏚 *Hovedgaden 7,*
59 21 60 09.

THE MAIN REASON people
come to this town, located
at the base of the Odsherred
peninsula, is to visit its model
electric railway, which is one
of the longest in Europe.
Svinninge Modeljernbane
is housed in a building
measuring 8 m by 14 m (26 ft
by 46 ft) and contains over
550 model railway coaches
and nearly 90 locomotives. All
of the rolling stock, as well as
the convincing recon-
structions of many Danish
stations (including Svinninge,
Hilbæk, Lisebro, Hjortholm
and Egaa), are built to a scale
of 1:87. The creators of this
extraordinary display have
meticulously and painstakingly
recreated entire railway routes,
including the link from
Holbæk to Oxneholm.

The model railway was
originally a private affair and
was opened to the public
after it was donated to the
town by its original creator.
The building of this
impressive display involved a
great deal of work by many
people including model
makers, carpenters, joiners
and electricians. More than
80 m (262 ft) of cable were
laid in order to supply current
to over 2 km (1.3 miles) of
track. Even today, the display
continues to grow with new
sections of track and locomotives being added yearly.

🏛 **Svinninge
Modeljernbane**
Hovedgaden 7, 4520 Svinninge.
📞 *59 21 60 09.* ⏰ *end Apr–end Oct:
9am–4pm.* ♿ 🌐 *www.svmjk.dk*

Section of the model railway in Svinninge

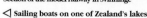
◁ **Sailing boats on one of Zealand's lakes**

Dragsholm Slot, seen from the courtyard

Dragsholm ③④

Road map E4. Dragsholm Allé, 4534
Hørve. 📞 *59 65 33 00.* ✉ *tours
only: Jun–early Aug: four daily tours
in English (check for exact times).* ♿
🌐 *www.dragsholm-slot.dk*

THE CASTLE in Dragsholm
was once a fortress and
later on a royal residence. It is
now used as a luxurious hotel
and restaurant, but has lost
none of its historical
grandeur.

Situated on the
shores of Nekselø
bay, at the foot of
Zealand's third
highest hill –
Vejrhøj (121 m/397
ft above sea level) –
Dragsholm Slot is
one of Denmark's
oldest and biggest
castles. Its origins
date back to the 12th and 13th
centuries, when Roskilde's
bishops decided to build
themselves a seat, which
would also serve as a military
fortress. They occupied it
until 1536 at which point the
bishopric was moved to
Copenhagen. Dragsholm was
then taken over
by the king who
transformed it into
a palace. Following
a war with Sweden
in the mid-17th
century the castle
was converted into
a prison. The
dungeon's most
famous inmate was
Lord James von
Bothwell, the
husband of Mary
Queen of Scots, who

**Heraldic arms from
Dragsholm Slot**

had sought sanctuary in
Denmark after Mary's
downfall. Intead he was
imprisoned and languished
here for five years. He
eventually went mad and
died in 1578. His tomb is in
the castle chapel.

In the second half of the
17th century, during another
war with Sweden, the castle
was badly damaged.
Extensive rebuilding work
began in 1694 and
gave the building its
present distinct
Baroque aspect. At
that time the owners
of the castle were
Christian Adeler and
his wife Henriette
Margrete von Lente.
The castle remained
in the hands of the
family until 1932.
Since 1937 the
property has been owned
by the Bøttger family, who
run it as a hotel and
restaurant. The 1-m (3-ft)
thick walls, high ceilings and
sumptuously decorated
interiors enhance the historic
aura of the place. The most
interesting rooms include the
magnificent Banqueting Hall
(Riddersalen) and Hunting
Room (Jagtværelset).

The castle and its moat are
surrounded by a large
expanse of parkland that
contains, among other plants,
a collection of rhododendrons.
Like all great castles,
Dragsholm is reputed to be
haunted. The three ghosts
that are most frequently
spotted are the White Lady,
the Grey Lady and, of course,
Lord von Bothwell.

Odsherred ㉟

SURROUNDED BY THE waters of the Kattegat, Isefjord and Serejø bay, the Odsherred peninsula is one of the most popular holiday destinations in Denmark, visited annually by sun-seekers and water sports enthusiasts. Its wide sandy beaches, the lure of the sea and the varied landscape also make this region popular with artists, some of whom have established galleries here.

Sjælland Sommerland ③
This amusement park provides a good day out for families with children. Among the many attractions are a mini train, a roller coaster and giant water slides ending in splash pools.

Havnebjen ⑤
Cutters in the harbour and the aroma from the local smokehouses make this fishing village a memorable place.

Lumsaas Mølle ④
This recently restored mill dates from the 19th century and is open to the public. Flour ground on site can still be bought.

Højby Sø ②
The banks of this small lake are inhabited by a wide variety of birds. The lake is also popular with anglers.

Gniben ⑥
The narrow strip of land stretching westwards has wide sandy beaches and is excellent for sunbathing. Gniben, situated furthest to the west, affords magnificent views of the sea.

Overby • Ebbeløkke • Klint • Tengslemark • Nyrup • Stenstrup • Gudmindrup • VIG

0 km 2
0 miles 2

Højby ①
The interior of the local church is decorated with frescoes depicting, among others, Sankt Jørgen.

TIPS FOR DRIVERS

Length of route: 50 km (31 miles). **Tourist information:** Nykøbing SJ: Svanestræde 9, 59 91 08 88. Asnæs: Høve Stræde 1, 59 65 08 05.
@ ot@odsherred-info.dk
W www.odsherred.com

KEY

▬▬ Suggested route
▬▬ Scenic route
══ Other road
⚡ Viewpoint

SOUTHERN ZEALAND
AND THE ISLANDS

T HE LOWLANDS OF SOUTHERN ZEALAND *are characterized by cultivated fields and beautiful lakes. Many visitors see only Vordingborg and Køge, two towns that have played a significant part in Denmark's history, but the islands of Lolland, Falster and Møn to the south are attractive holiday destinations and offer miles of sandy beaches, woodland and awe-inspiring views of coastal cliffs.*

Southern Zealand (Sjælland) is an important region for the Danes. Vordingborg was the capital of the Valdemar dynasty and in the 12th century was used by Bishop Absalon as a staging post for his military expeditions to eastern Germany. The market town of Ringsted, in central Zealand, was for many years the venue of the *landsting*, a regional government assembly that formed the basis of the present-day parliament. In 1677, Køge Bay was the scene of a major naval engagement in which the Danish Admiral Niels Juel became a national hero when he dealt a crushing blow to the Swedish fleet.

The islands to the south of Zealand are more rural in character. Lolland is Denmark's third biggest island (1,243 sq km/480 sq miles) and also its flattest (at its highest point it is a mere 22 m/72 ft above sea level). The island has some pretty beaches and is popular with hikers in summer. Falster is only slightly smaller and is visited mainly for its wide beaches. Møn is the smallest of the islands and the hardest to reach. The journey is worth it, however, as Møn has rustic scenery, spectacular white cliffs, good beaches and some interesting sights including Neolithic burial places and a number of medieval churches containing some spectacular frescoes.

Ducks near the shore of Sondersø, Maribo

◁ **Spectacular chalk cliffs of Møns Klint**

Exploring Southern Zealand and the Islands

THE LARGEST TOWN in southern Zealand is Næstved, which has a number of historic buildings. However, Køge, Ringsted and Vordingborg have more to offer in the way of outstanding buildings. This part of Denmark is particularly attractive to families as it has a slow pace and child-friendly attractions such as BonBon-Land, Knuthenborg Safari Park on Lolland and, on Falster, a recreated medieval village. A number of museums are also popular with children including Ålholm's Automobile Museum. Falster benefits from some of Denmark's best beaches; Lolland has a popular resort complex.

Odense

Slagelse

Korsør

Agersø

SUS

GLUM

Tystrup Sø

● *FUGLEBJE*

22

265

GAV.

S M Å L A N D S F A R V A N D E T

KNUDSHOVE
ODD

Brick-built Holsted Kirke, Næstved

Femø

Fejø

GETTING AROUND

Getting from southern Zealand to Falster and Lolland presents few problems thanks to the toll-free bridges. The main arterial road – the E47 motorway – runs from Copenhagen via southern Zealand to Falster and Rødbyhavn on Lolland. Most places are easily accessible from Copenhagen by train except for Møn, which has no railway.

289

9

9

NAKSKOV **14** 291 *SAFARI PARK* **13**

● *SØLLESTED*

MARIBO **12**

SAKSKØBI

Lolland 275

E47

LALANDIA
15

29

TÅGERUP **16**

KEY

▬	Motorway
▬	Major road
▬	Scenic route
=	Other road
=	River
ᘛ	Viewpoint

SEE ALSO

- **Where to Stay** pp245–6.
- **Where to Eat** pp269–70.

• **Where to Stay** pp245–6.
• **Where to Eat** pp269–70.

0 km   10

0 miles   10

Neolithic burial site on the
Knudshoved Odde peninsula

SIGHTS AT A GLANCE

Vaulted interior of Sankt Bendts Kirke, Ringsted

Ringsted ❶

Road map E5. 🏘 18,000. 🚉
ℹ️ Sankt Bendtsgade 6, 57 62 66 00.
🌐 www.met-2000.dk

OWING TO ITS location at the crossroads of two trading routes, Ringsted was once an important market town. It was the venue for regional government assemblies – the *landsting* – which took decisions and passed laws on major national issues. The three stones standing in the market square were used hundreds of years ago by members of the *landsting*.

Ringsted gained notoriety in 1131 when Knud (Canute) Laward, duke of southern Zealand, was murdered in the neighbouring woods by his jealous cousin Magnus. The monarch is buried in Ringsted's Sankt Bendts Kirke (St Benedict's Church) along with a number of other Danish kings and queens. Sankt Bendts Kirke was erected in 1170 and is believed to be the oldest brick church in Scandinavia. Its main altarpiece dates from 1699; its baptismal font is believed to be 12th century and was for a time used as a flower pot in a local garden until it was discovered quite by chance. The magnificent frescoes were painted in about 1300 and include a series depicting Erik IV (known as Ploughpenny for his tax on ploughs).

In the 17th century it was decided to open some of the coffins. The items found in them are now on display in one of the chapels. The Dagmar Cross, dating from about AD 1000, is a copy. The original cross is on display in the Nationalmuseet in Copenhagen (*see pp84–5*). The famous cross once belonged to Queen Dagmar, the first wife of Valdemar II. Depicted on its enamelled surface is a beautiful figure of Christ with his arms outstretched. On the other side of the cross Christ is pictured with the Virgin Mary flanked by John the Baptist, St John and St Basil.

Fantasy World ❷

Road map E5. **Directions:** from E20 motorway take exit 36 and then follow the signs. ☎ 57 61 19 30.
🕙 mid-Feb, Jun–Aug, Oct–Dec: 10am–5pm daily. 🅿️
🌐 www.fantasy-world.dk

SITUATED ON THE outskirts of Ringsted, Fantasy World is an excellent place for families travelling with children. It is packed with a huge number of animatronic figures that are arranged in a series of colourful dioramas. One section has fairytale creatures inhabiting well-known scenes from the stories of Hans Christian Andersen. Elsewhere, children can see models of tigers and guitar-playing chimpanzees in a jungle setting while a walk through an eerie forest brings visitors face to face with trolls and snickering goblins.

Suså ❸

Road map E5.

AT NEARLY 90 km (56 miles) along, Suså is one of Denmark's longest rivers. From its source near the town of Rønnede it flows through two lakes, Tystrup Sø and Bavelse Sø, to end its journey in the waters of Karrebæk bay, near Næstved. The picturesque surroundings, idyllic scenery and lazy, slow-flowing current make the river particularly popular with canoeists. Canoe trips are usually taken over the final stretch of the river, where a canoe or a kayak can be hired for an hour or two. River traffic gets quite busy in summer and many large family groups enjoy picnicking along the river banks.

It is easy to combine canoeing with a bit of sightseeing. Quite close to the river's source, in Rønnede, is a beautiful rhododendron park. Near Haslev are two magnificent properties. Gissefeldt Slot, completed in 1575, is one of the finest Renaissance castles in northern Europe and is surrounded by gardens containing about 400 species of trees and shrubs. The castle was often visited by Hans Christian Andersen – it was here that he got his idea for *The Ugly Duckling*. Bregentved Slot, on the outskirts of Haslev, is a little newer than Gissefeldt. Its oldest wing dates from 1650; it was substantially modified in the late 1880s.

Suså – Zealand's longest river

Glass production in Holmegård Glassværk

Glumsø ❹

Road map E5.

G LUMSØ is a good base from which to embark upon a canoeing trip along the Suså. Located about 10 km (6 miles) south of Ringsted, its other main attraction is the **Dansk Cykel & Knallert Museum** (Museum of Bicycles and Motorbikes), which has a huge collection of two- and three-wheeled transportation, from vintage cycles to trendy modern scooters. Some bikes can even be ridden by visitors.

ENVIRONS: Some 5 km (3 miles) south of Glumsø, on the banks of the Suså, is **Skelby**. The main point of interest here is Gunderslev Kirke, a 12th-century church. Its sumptuously furnished interior was paid for by the former owners of the nearby Gunderslevholm estate.

🏛 Dansk Cykel & Knallert Museum
Sorøvej 8. 📞 57 64 77 94.
🕐 May–Oct: 11am–5pm Sat & Sun.
📷 🌐 www.dckm.dk/cykelmuseum

Fensmark ❺

Road map E5. **Glassworks** Glasvær-kesvej 1. 📞 55 54 50 00. 📷 mid-Jun–mid-Sep: eight tours daily; mid-Sep–mid-Jun: four tours daily.

A POPULAR stopping-off point for tours, Fensmark is located 13 km (8 miles) south of Næstved. Most people head straight for the famous Holmegård Glassværk (Glassworks) factory, which was founded in 1825. This is Denmark's main manufacturer of top-quality glassware and it is possible to see delicate glass objects of all shapes and colour being produced by skilled glass blowers, learn about the history of glassmaking and take a look at some early pieces that have been produced by the factory.

The factory has its own shop which has a good selection of its glass products on sale. Many are "seconds" and bargains are easy to come by. During peak season the famous "glass band", which plays tunes on instruments made of glass, can sometimes be heard performing.

Glass product from the Fensmark factory

BonBon-Land ❻

Road map E5. Holme-Ostrup, Gart-nervej 2. 📞 55 53 07 00. 🕐 mid-May–mid-Jun & early Aug–early Sep: 9:30am–5pm daily; mid-Jun–early Aug: 9:30am–8pm daily; early Sep–mid-Oct: 9:30am–5:30pm daily. 📷 children up to 90 cm (3 ft) tall are admitted free.
🌐 www.bonbonland.dk

T HIS AMUSEMENT park attracts large numbers of visitors in summer. The entrance fee covers all the 100 or so attractions. In addition, children are given a free cap to take home as a souvenir. The greatest thrill is undoubtedly provided by a ride on the giant roller coaster, which races along at speeds up to 70 km/h (43 mph) and rises to a height of 22 m (72 ft) before hurtling back down again. A similar surge of adrenaline can be felt when dropping from the 35-m (115-ft) high tower. Gentler amusement can be had on the park's merry-go-rounds or mini racetracks. The queues lengthen for the water slides when the temperature rises as do those for a raft trip down some white-water rapids. As well as the rides, BonBon-Land has circus performances, magic shows, trained sea lions, a rodeo and daily concerts. It won't win any prizes for high culture but it is a great day out for families with children.

Children's attractions in BonBon-Land

Næstved ⓐ

Road map E5. 🚶 *50,000.* 🚉
ℹ️ *Havnegade 1, 55 72 11 22.*
🌐 *www.visitnaestved.com*

SOUTHERN Zealand's largest town, Næstved has been an important centre of trade since medieval times. The 15th-century town hall in Axeltorv, the main square, is one of the oldest in Denmark. The town has two Gothic churches. The 14th-century frescoes in Sankt Peder Kirke (St Peter's Church) depict Valdemar IV and his wife Helveg kneeling in prayer. Sankt Mortens is 13th century and has a beautiful altarpiece that was completed in 1667.

Among the town's other notable buildings are Konpagnihuset, a half-timbered Guild House (1493) and Apostelhuset (Apostles' House), built in the early 16th century. Its name derives from the figures of Christ and his 12 disciples placed between the windows.

Næstved's oldest building, however, is Helligåndhuset (House of the Holy Spirit), which dates from the 14th century and was used as a hospital and almshouse. It now houses **Næstved Museum** with displays of local handicraft (pottery, silverware and glassware) and an interesting collection of medieval and contemporary woodcarvings. The Løveapoteket (Pharmacy), on Axeltorv, dates back to 1640 – a herb garden is situated in the courtyard. Munkebakken

Former Benedictine abbey in Næstved

English-style castle garden in Gavnø

Park (a short way from Axeltorv) contains statues of seven monks which have been carved out of tree trunks.

🏛 **Næstved Museum**
Ringstedgade 4. 📞 *55 77 08 11.*
🕐 *10am–4pm Tue–Sun.*

Gavnø ⓑ

Road map E5. 📞 *55 70 02 00.*
🕐 *May: 10am–5pm daily; Jun–Aug: 10am–4pm daily.* 🅿️
🌐 *www.gavnoe.dk*

LOCATED A LITTLE way from Næstved and linked to it by road, this tiny island was used by pirates in the 13th century. In the 14th century Queen Margrethe I established a convent here.

According to legend, the convent was the scene of a tragic love affair in the 16th century between Count Henrik Hog and Ida Baggsen. The boy's father, who disapproved of the girl, sent his son on a European tour, while Ida was forced to enter the convent. When the boy returned, the lovers resumed their affair. The couple were discovered: the nuns punished the girl by burying her alive; the count narrowly escaped death and was whisked abroad.

The remains of the convent include a chapel dating from 1401. After the Reformation the convent become a privately-owned manor house. The current building is 18th century and is constructed on the ruins of the convent. It owes its Rococo appearance to the Reedtz-Tholt family, who took control of the place in 1755. The pride of the house is its art collection, which includes over 2,000 paintings. It is regarded as one of the most important private collections in Scandinavia.

The grounds themselves look their best in spring when there are displays of flowers made from over half a million plants, including tulips, hyacinths and crocuses. The gardens also have a butterfly house containing specimens imported from the Far East.

Vordingborg ⓒ

Road map F6. 🚶 *20,000.* 🚉
ℹ️ *Algade 96, 55 34 11 11.*

VORDINGBORG is on the strait between Zealand and Falster that leads to the Baltic, and was once Denmark's most important town. It was the royal residence of Valdemar I (The Great) who came to the throne in 1157 and built a castle here, ushering in a period of relative peace in the country's history. In 1241 Valdemar II sanctioned the Jutland Code in Vordingborg, which gave

Denmark its first written laws. Subsequent monarchs from the Valdemar dynasty also took a liking to the castle and enlarged it over the years. The final length of its defensive wall was 800 m (2,625 ft) and its imposing appearance was emphasized by nine mighty towers.

Most of the towers are now in ruins except for the 14th-century Gåsetårnet (Goose Tower). This 36-m (118-ft) high tower has walls that are 3.5 m (11.5 ft) thick in places. Its name dates back to 1368 when Valdemar IV placed a golden goose on top of the tower in order to express his belief that the Hanseatic League's declaration of war was no more threatening than the cackling of geese. Though it has been modified (the conical roof was added in 1871), Gåsetårnet is important as the only intact building to remain from the Valdemar era. The building opposite the tower now houses the **Sydsjællands Museum**, which has displays on the castle's history and on southern Zealand in general. Immediately behind the museum is a botanical garden.

Algade is Vordingborg's main street and has been pedestrianized. It leads to Vor Frue Kirke (Church of Our Lady), a 15th-century church which contains a Baroque altarpiece dating from 1642.

The 14th-century Gåsetårnet in Vordingborg

🏛 **Tower & Sydsjællands Museum**

🕐 *10am–4pm Tue–Fri, 1pm–4pm Sat & Sun.* 🌐 *www.aabne-samlinger.dk/sydsjaellands*

Knudshoved Odde ⑩

Road map E5. *The peninsula can be reached by car, from Oreby.* 🚫

THE NARROW strip of the Knudshoved Odde peninsula is 20 km (12 miles) long and only 1 km (half a mile) at its widest point. The peninsula is owned by the Rosenfeldt Estate, which has managed to preserve the unique landscape. There are no towns or villages here and the only road is closed to motor traffic after about 10 km (6 miles). This inaccessibility makes it popular with people who come to sit on the seashore, gather blackberries and explore the woods (which can be reached by foot from the car park halfway along the peninsula where the trail begins). The wood's marked walking trails are not taxing and range from a short stroll to one that is a just under 4 km (2 miles).

Until quite recently another local attraction was a herd of buffalo, which was imported from America by the Rosenfeldt family. The animals inhabited the top end of the peninsula, where they enjoyed a considerable degree of freedom. After a number of incidents it was finally decided that the herd caused too much damage and the buffalo have since been removed.

The peninsula is also known for its Neolithic burial mounds. One of these historic graves, which was dug about 5,500 years ago, can be seen close to the car park. Excavations have established that its ancient occupant was provided with all possible necessities for the after-life, including plenty of food and drink.

Sakskøbing ⑪

Road map E6. Lolland. 🏠 *9,400.* ℹ️ *Torvegade 4, 54 70 56 30 (Jun–Sep).*

ONE OF Lolland's oldest settlements, Sakskøbing has few historic remains other than a Romanesque church (13th century). However, in view of the town's location on the E47, the main road linking Zealand to Falster and Lolland, it is a popular stopping-off point. The town's most striking feature is a water tower that resembles a smiling face. A distinctive landmark in the market square is the monument erected in 1939 for the Polish men and women who worked in the local fields. The town's links with Poland date back to the end of the 19th century when many Poles came here in search of work. Many settled permanently on the island and some local Catholic churches still celebrate mass in Polish.

Monument to Polish workers in Sakskøbing

Shores of the Knudshoved Odde peninsula

Safari Park ⑬

KNUTHENBORG Safari Park provides visitors with the chance to see such exotic creatures as zebras, camels, antelopes and giraffes. The parkland itself has been in the hands of the same family since the 17th century. It was landscaped in an English style in the 19th century and the first animals were transported by ship from Kenya in 1969. Today there are about 1,000 animals. The park's botanical garden contains many rare trees and shrubs.

Bandholmporten

0 m   250

0 yards   250

Knuthenborg

Skovridergo

★ Knuthenborg
The house is surrounded by English-style parkland and was designed by Edward Milner. It bears clear signs of a Victorian influence. The main buidling is still inhabited by the Knuth family.

Tiger Reserve

★ Tiger Reserve
The pride of the park are the Siberian tigers, the largest of all tigers. They enjoy bathing, which is unusual for cats. The deep marks visible on the trees have been left by the tigers' sharp claws.

Statue of the Park's Founder
Eggert Christoffer Knuth (1838–74) was a great 19th-century expolorer. He brought back seeds and cuttings from his many voyages abroad. Many of these were cultivated and some are still growing in the park.

STAR SIGHTS
★ **Knuthenborg**
★ **Tiger Reserve**

Zebras
The zebras are allowed to roam freely and mingle with other animals in the park. They can run at speeds of up to 60 km/h (40 mph) when startled.

Småland
This tot-sized park contains a number of rides for "mini adventurers" including a train and a merry-go-round. Older children can also have fun climbing rope bridges or floating on the lake in a plastic hippopotamus.

Flinthuset

Swan Lake

Deer Park

Children's Zoo

Limpopo House

Savanna

Småland

Safari Grill

Giraffes
The giraffe can grow up to 5.5 m (18 ft) in height. The park's giraffes can sometimes be seen bending, with legs wide apart, to drink water.

Maglemer-porten

Llamas
Along with donkeys, goats and camels, llamas are some of the park's more docile inhabitants and can be seen grazing near the main entrance.

Half-timbered houses in Maribo

Maribo ⑫

Road map E6. Lolland. 🏛 5,500.
🚉 ℹ️ *Torvet, Det Gamle Rådhus, 54
78 04 96.* 🌐 *www.lolland-falster.dk*

SITUATED ON the northern
shore of Søndersø, a large
inland lake, Maribo is
Lolland's commercial centre.
The town was founded in
1416 by Erik of Pomerania
and soon acquired a Gothic
cathedral. All that remains of
an original convent and
monastery complex are the
cathedral's bells (that toll six
times a day) and a gallery
where the nuns used to pray.
The convent was dissolved
following the Reformation.

The cathedral is located a
short way from Torvet, the
town's main square, which
contains a 19th-century Neo-
Classical town hall. Around
the square are several 18th-
century half-timbered houses.

Maribo has two museums,
with a joint admission fee.
The **Lolland-Falster
Stiftsmuseum** has a
collection of church art and
displays relating to Polish
workers. The **Stortrøms
Kunstmuseum** has some
local history displays as well
as a collection of regional art.

Frilandsmuseet, a short
way south of Maribo, is
an open-air museum where
there are a number of period
cottages, as well as other
buildings including a
windmill and a smithy.

🏛 **Lolland-Falster
Stiftsmuseum & Stortrøms
Kunstmuseum**
📞 *54 78 11 01.* ⏲ *noon–4pm
Tue–Sun.* 📷
🏛 **Frilandsmuseet**
📞 *54 78 11 01.* ⏲ *May–Aug:
10am–5pm; Sep–Oct: until 4pm.* 📷

Safari Park ⑬

See pp156–7.

Nakskov ⑭

Road map E6. Lolland.
🏛 16,000. ℹ️ *Axeltorv 3,
54 92 21 72.*

NAKSKOV'S origins
date back to the
13th century. A
reminder of its medieval past
is the tower of Sankt Nikolai
Kirke (Church), which rises
above the old quarter. The
oldest of Nakskov's houses is
Dronningens Pakhus, a
quayside warehouse that was
built in 1590 and Den Gamle
Smedie, a smithy where
visitors can see a blacksmith
working with 200-year-old
tools. The town's greatest
attraction, however, is **U-359**,
a Soviet submarine built
during the Cold War.
Launched in 1953 the
76-m (249-ft) long submarine
was able to descend to a
depth of 300 m (984 ft) and
carried a crew of 58. The
historic vessel sailed under
the Russian flag until 1989,
when it was bought by the
Danes. The sub's claustrophic
atmosphere is intensified by
the piped commands issued
by the captain, which
accompany the sound of
alarm bells and the sonar's
constant "ping".

Most of Denmark's sugar
beet is grown on Lolland and

**Russian U-359 submarine moored
in Nakskov harbour**

Denmark's Sugar Museum
tells the story of the crop and
the Polish immigrants who
arrrived to work in the fields.

ENVIRONS: Købelevhaven,
about 6 km (4 miles) north of
Nakskov, is a botanical
garden. Established in 1975, it
has a large rhododendron
collection, a Japanese garden
and some rare magnolia and
Asian trees.

🏛 **U-359**
📞 *54 95 20 16.* ⏲ *Jan–May: 10am–
4pm; May–Oct: 10am–6pm.* 📷
🏛 **Denmark's Sugar
Museum**
📞 *54 92 14 95.* ⏲ *Jan–May:
1–4pm Sun; May–Dec: 1–4pm
Tue–Sun.* 📷

**Palm trees enliven Lalandia's food
and drink area**

Lalandia ⑮

Road map E6. Lolland. 🚉
ℹ️ *Rødby, Lalandiacentret 1, 54 61
06 00.* 📷 🌐 *www.lalandia.dk*

MANY FAMILIES come to
Lalandia – Denmark's
largest holiday centre – for a
short break. The resort is on
the southern coast of Lolland
and offers numerous attractions
to visitors. The local beach
competes for children's
attention with the aquapark
where swimming pools and
slides are surrounded by
artificial lakes and tropical
vegetation. Regardless of the
outside temperature the water
in the pools never falls below
28° C (82° F). For sports
enthusiasts, there are tennis
courts, a golf course, mini-golf,
and, in the case of bad
weather, a vast leisure complex
that includes a gymnasium,
bowling alleys, amusement
arcades and indoor tennis.

Display in Polakkasernen, Tågerup

Visitors to Lalandia can stay in apartments that can sleep up to eight people. All of the apartments have their own bathrooms and kitchens. There are also numerous restaurants and bars spread around the holiday complex.

Tågerup ⑯

Road map E6. Lolland. 🚌

THE MAIN attraction of Tågerup, a small village situated a short way south of Maribo, is its Romanesque-Gothic church, which contains some fine 15th-century frescoes. At the entrance to the church is a runic stone. Many visitors are surprised to find a building displaying the Polish flag. This is **Polakkasernen**, or the Polish Barracks, and contains documents, fragments of diaries and various items left by Polish immigrants who from 1893 began arriving in Lolland in great numbers. Many Poles were on the move for political reasons as the Soviet Union had taken control of Poland. There were also economic reasons, however, and immigrants arrived from Poland between 1870 and 1920 in a bid to escape a feudal system that gave them few legal rights. Once they arrived most Poles found employment as labourers in the local sugar-beet fields.

A short way from Polakkasernen is **Lungholm**, an early 15th-century residence. Unfortunately, the house itself is not open to the public but a section of the English-style garden that surrounds it can be viewed without restrictions.

🏛 **Polakkasernen**
Højbygårsvej 34. 🕿 54 82 04 01.
◯ Easter, Whitsun, Jul–Aug: 2–4pm Tue–Sun. 🈺

♣ **Lungholm**
Rødbyvej 24. 🕿 54 60 02 53.
Garden ◯ dawn until dusk.

Ålholm ⑰

Road map E6. Lolland.
W www.aalholm.dk

ÅLHOLM SLOT (Castle) is on the outskirts of Nysted and dates from the 12th century. It was crown property for many years and the rooms contain many royal furnishings. In 1332 Christian II was held prisoner in the dungeons here on the orders of his half-brother. The castle is now in private hands. Unfortunately it is not open to the public.

Not far from the castle is the **Ålholm Automobile Museum**. This is the largest museum of its kind in northern Europe and has a collection of over 200 vehicles; the oldest of the cars on display date from the 19th century. Its exhibits also include a vintage airplane and a model railway.

🏛 **Ålholm Automobile Museum**
Ålholm Parkvej 17. 🕿 54 87 19 11.
◯ Jun–Aug: 10am–5pm daily; May, Sep–Oct: 10am–4pm Sat & Sun (daily mid-Oct). 🈺

Nysted ⑱

Road map E6. Lolland. 🏃 6,000. 🚌
🛈 Strandvejen 18A, 54 87 19 85.
W www.nysted-turistforening.dk

THIS SMALL harbour town situated on the Rødsand bay was founded in the 13th century. Nysted's main historic monuments are a large Gothic church dating from the early 14th century, and a much later 17th-century tower. There are also a number of half-timbered houses and a water tower, which now serves as a viewpoint. In Nysted it is possible to tour a local candle factory, Svane Lys, where visitors can not only see some of the factory's products, but also try their hand at making their own candles.

ENVIRONS: About 3 km (2 miles) north of Nysted is **Kettinge**, a small village which has an old Dutch windmill and a church containing some magnificent frescoes.

Ålholm Slot seen from the water

Woman dressed in period costume at Middelaldercentret

Middelalder-centret ⑲

Road map F6. Lolland. **ℹ** *Sundby, Ved Hamborgskoven 2, 54 86 19 34.* ⬤ *May–Sep: 10am–4pm daily.* 🅰
🆆 www.middelaldercentret.dk

LOLLAND'S Middle Ages Centre is a recreated medieval settlement and provides an insight into what life was like in the 14th century. Crafts and games from medieval times are displayed and explained by staff wearing costumes from the period while the local inn serves a range of "medieval" food. A replica sailing ship lies in the harbour and a huge wooden catapult is ready for firing. Jousting tournaments are a regular feature in summer and visitors can also try their hand at archery. A marked walking trail in the nearby forest explains medieval customs and includes a site where charcoal is made.

Along the walk, visitors are warned about woodland spirits and are invited to throw a ghost-repelling stick at an appropriate spot – just in case.

The centre can easily be reached from Nykøbing F by crossing the bridge that connects Lolland and Falster.

Nykøbing F ⑳

Road map F6. Falster. **🏃** *25,000.*
🚉 🚌 **ℹ** *Østergågade 7, 54 85 13 03.* 🆆 www.tinf.dk

FALSTER'S LARGEST town and capital city was a busy commercial centre in medieval times and was granted municipal status in the early 13th century by Valdemar II. In order to distinguish it from two other Danish towns of the same name, this Nykøbing is followed by the letter F (standing for Falster).

Nykøbing F's main historic sight is a 15th-century brick church, which once formed part of a Franciscan monastery. Its richly decorated interior includes an eye-catching series of portraits of Queen Sophie (wife of Frederik II) together with her family, which were commissioned in 1627. Another notable sight is the half-timbered Czarens Hus (Tsar's House), which is one of the oldest buildings in town. In 1716 the Russian Tsar, Peter the Great, stopped here on his way to Copenhagen. Today, the building is used as a restaurant *(see p270)* and also houses a local history museum – **Museet Falsters Minder**. Among the museum's exhibits are some reconstructed interiors including an 18th-century peasant cottage and a traditional 19th-century burgher's house.

The most panoramic view of Nybøking F is from the early 20th-century yellow water tower. **Nykøbing F Zoo** is a little way east of the train station and has a variety of animals including deer, monkeys and goats.

🏛 **Museet Falsters Minder**
⬤ *11am–10pm Mon–Sat.* 🅰
🦌 **Nykøbing F Zoo**
⬤ *Jun–Aug: 9am–8pm daily; Sep–May: 9am–4pm daily.* 🅰

Eskilstrup ㉑

Road map F6. Falster. 🚉 🚌

Statue of a bear in Nykøbing F

THIS SMALL town is situated a short distance from the E47 motorway and has two unusual museums. The **Traktor-museum** is housed in a multi-storey brick building and contains over 200 tractors and engines dating from 1880 to 1960. Alongside a wide selection of vintage Fiats, Fords, Volvos and Fergusons are rare Czechoslovakian and Romanian tractors. The oldest

Nykøbing F, as seen from the river
◁ **Evening horse ride along the beach**

Beautiful white beaches around Marielyst

tractor in the museum is American and was built in 1917. There is also a steam traction engine built in England in 1889. Until 1925 it was still being used as a threshing machine. A number of small pedal-tractors are provided for the amusement of children.

About 3 km (2 miles) from the town centre is the **Krokodille Zoo**. This is the largest collection of crocodiles in Europe and includes all but four species of these sharp-toothed reptiles. The smallest among them is the dwarf cayman, which grows up to 159 cm (62 inches) in length. The zoo's giant Nile crocodile is called Samson and is currently the largest crocodile in Scandinavia.

As well as the crocodiles, the zoo also contains other species including a green anaconda (the world's largest snake) and turtles. A percentage of the admission price is donated to an international programme of research and protection associated with crocodiles living in the wild.

🏛 Traktormuseum
Nørregade 17B. **📞** 54 43 70 07.
◐ May–Jun, Sep: 10am–4pm
Tue–Sun; Jul–Aug: 10am–5pm daily.
🌐 www.traktormuseum.dk
✕ Krokodille Zoo
Ovstrupvej 9. **📞** 54 45 42 42.
◐ mid-Jun–mid-Aug: 10am–5pm daily; mid-Aug–Oct: noon–5pm Tue–Sun; Nov, Feb–mid-Jun: noon–4pm Tue, Sun. **🌐**
🌐 www.krokodillezoo.dk

Marielyst ㉒

Road map F6. Falster. **🚌 ℹ** Marielyst Strandpark 3, 54 13 62 98.
🌐 www.marielyst.org

SITUATED ON the eastern end of the island, Marielyst gets its revenue mainly from summer visitors and is one of the foremost holiday resorts in Denmark. One of the main attractions is the fine white sand beach, which is a good length and easily accessible. It also benefits from clean and fairly shallow waters. The dunes running parallel to the coastline are an additional attraction and are fringed by an ancient beech forest. Marielyst's centre has plenty of shops, restaurants and bars. Along with camp sites, pensions and hotels the town also has about 6,000 summer cottages.

Competing with the beach for visitors' time is **Marielyst Familiepark**, where holiday-

makers can bathe in pools, ride skateboards and shoot it out with paintball guns.

ENVIRONS: Just south of Marielyst is the **Bøtø Nor bird sanctuary** where a variety of birds can be spotted including cranes, ospreys and plovers.

🌸 Marielyst Familiepark
Godthåbs Allé 7. **📞** 54 13 68 86.
◐ mid-May–Jun, Aug: 10am–6pm daily; Jul: 10am–7pm. **🌐**
🌐 www.marielystfamiliepark.dk

Væggerløse ㉓

Road map F6. Falster. **🚌**

THE SMALL TOWN of Væggerløse, situated a little way south of Nykøbing F, has an 18th-century windmill, which now houses a glass-blowing workshop. Another nearby attraction is the **Sports Car Museum**. Road signs direct drivers to a private farmstead where one of the buildings houses a collection of motor cars. Although not as large as the car museum found at Ålholm Slot near Nysted on Lolland (see p159), it is nevertheless worth visiting. Among the 65 vehicles on display are a 1917 Adler (which was once capable of reaching the giddy speed of 35 km/h/22 mph), as well as a Jaguar (which could travel as fast as 240 km/h/149 mph).

🏛 Sports Car Museum
Stovby Tværvej 11. **📞** 54 17 75 89.
◐ 10am–5pm daily. **🌐**

Marielyst Familiepark, an excellent place for families with children

Frescoes in Fanefjord Kirke, painted in the mid-15th century

Fanefjord Kirke ㉔

Road map F6. Fanefjordvej, Falster.
☐ *Apr–Sep: 7am–4pm; Oct–Mar: 8am–4pm.*

THE SMALL CHURCH of Fanefjord stands on top of an isolated hillock surrounded by green fields. It provides an excellent viewpoint and from here it is possible to look out over the Baltic, Zealand and the island of Bogø. The Gothic church derives its name from the Fan fjord bay, whose waters come close to the building. The fjord was in turn named after Queen Fane, wife of King Grøn Jæger.

Built about 1250, the church was at that time far too big for the needs of the 300 or so parishioners, but its builders took into account worshippers from ships anchoring in the bay as this was a busy harbour in the Middle Ages. According to records it was probably here that Bishop Absalon gathered his fleet before embarking on his raids against the Wends in eastern Germany.

Fanefjord Kirke is famous in Denmark for its frescoes. The oldest of them date from around 1350 and include an image of St Christopher carrying the infant Jesus. The later paintings date from the mid-15th century and include frescoes painted by the Elmelunde master, an artist about whom virtually nothing is known. His mark, which looks like a man with long

rabbit-like ears, can be seen on one of the ribs in the northeastern vault. A collection of votive ships hangs in the church. The oldest is a frigate hanging above the entrance which commemorates a tragic shipwreck off the north coast of Møn in which three children lost their lives.

Kong Asgers Høj ㉕

Road map F6. Møn.

KING ASGERS mounds, located in a farmer's field near the village of Røddinge, are all that remain of Denmark's largest passage grave.

The Stone Age corridor consists of an 8-m (26-ft) long underground passage that leads to a large chamber, 10 m (33 ft) long by 2 m (6.5 ft) wide. It is dark inside, so it is wise to take a torch.

Corridor leading to the burial chamber of Kong Asgers Høj

ENVIRONS: A short way south of Kong Asgers Høj stands yet another burial mound – the **Klekkende Høj**, which has two entrances placed side by side. The chamber is 7 m (23 ft) long. The mound has recently been restored and is now illuminated.

At the south end of Møn is **Grønjægers Høj**, another highly unusual tomb that is thought to be about 4,000 years old. The burial site is one of the largest dolmens in Denmark and is constructed of 134 weighty stones arranged in an oval shape. According to one legend the site is the final resting place of Queen Fane and her husband, Grøn Jæger who ruled this part of the island in the late Stone Age.

Chalk crags of Møns Klint, rising from the waters of the Baltic

Møns Klint ㉖

Road map F6. Møn.

THE WHITE CHALK cliffs soaring above the Baltic are one of Møn's main attractions. The cliffs are about 70 million years old and are formed mostly of calcareous shells. Stretching over a distance of about 7 km (4 miles), the crags reach 128 m (420 ft) in height to form a striking landscape. The highest point is near Dronningestolen (Queen's Throne). At one time these cliffs were mined for chalk but are now a legally protected zone.

The coastline can be admired from one of the

many viewpoints on top of the cliffs. After a cliff-top hike many people head inland to explore Klinteskoven (Klint Forest), where about 20 types of orchid can be seen flowering from May to August.

Klintholm Havn is a port south of the cliffs. In the 19th century it was a private estate and later taken over by the local authorities. Small pleasure boats leave for 2-hour cruises from here and are a good way to take in the stunning coastal scenery.

One of Stege's quieter shopping streets

Liselund Slot ㉗

Road map F6. Møn. **Palace**
■ *May–Sep: 10:30am, 11am, 1:30pm & 2pm.* ■ *free admission to the park.* Ⓦ *www.liselundslot.dk*

THE DIMINUTIVE palace of Liselund was once crown property. A subsequent owner gave the building its present name in honour of his wife. The house is set in a large park and its whitewashed walls are reflected in the waters of a small lake. The fairytale atmosphere is enhanced by the immaculate thatch on the building's roof (locals joke that this is the world's only thatched-roof palace). The house may be visited only as part of a guided tour. Liselund Ny Slot (New Castle), a 19th-century building in the midst of the estate, is now a hotel and restaurant.

Sun dial at Liselund Slot

Elmelunde ㉘

Road map F6. Møn. ▦
Churches in Emelunde and Keldby
◻ *May–Sep: 8am–5pm daily; Oct–Apr: 8am–4pm daily.*

ALONG WITH its famous cliffs, Møn boasts a number of churches with highly original frescoes. One of them can be visited in Elmelunde; another in Keldby, a little to the west. The church in Elmelunde is one of the oldest stone churches in Denmark and was built in about 1075. The frescoes date from the 14th and 15th centuries and were whitewashed during the Reformation. Ironically this only served to preserve the paintings from fading. They were restored in the 20th century under the guidance of Copenhagen's Nationalmuseet (National Museum).

The frescoes depict scenes from the Old and New Testaments and include images of Christ and the saints as well as lively portrayals of demons and the flames of hell. Most of them are attributed to one artist, known simply as the Elmelunde Master. The paintings served to explain biblical stories to illiterate peasants and are characterized by their quirky static figures with blank faces devoid of any emotion. More

Medieval fresco in Stege Kirke

frescoes can be seen in Keldby Kirke, which also has a sumptuously carved 16th-century pulpit.

Stege ㉙

Road map F6. Møn. ▦ *4,000.*
▦ ⓘ *Storegade 2, 55 86 04 00.*
Ⓦ *www.visitmoen.dk*

MØN'S commercial centre, Stege grew up around a castle built in the 12th century and reached the height of its power during the Middle Ages, when it prospered thanks to a lucrative herring industry. A reminder of those days is Mølleporten (Mill Gate), which spans the main street of the town and once served as Stege's principal entrance. Ramparts belonging to the fortress walls are another medieval relic. **Empiregården**, Stege's museum, is a short way from Mølleporten and has local history exhibits.

Stege Kirke is in the town centre. This Romanesque church was built by Jakob Sunesen, who ruled Møn in the 13th century. Its ceiling frescoes were painted over during the Reformation and exposed again in the 19th century.

🏛 **Empiregården**
Storegade 75. 🄲 *55 81 40 67.* ◻ *Nov–Apr: 10am–4pm Tue–Sun; May–Oct: 10am–4pm daily.* ▩

Nyord island's meadows, with marshland beyond

Nyord ③⓪

Road map F5.

UNTIL QUITE recently the only way to reach the small island of Nyord was by boat. A bridge, built in 1986, now links Nyord with Møn and has made the island increasingly popular with visitors. Nevertheless, both the island and the pretty hamlet of the same name have changed little since the 19th century. Nyord is particularly favoured by bird-watchers – its salt marshes attract masses of birds, especially during spring and autumn, when the island is used as a stopping-off place for winged migrants. The most numerous among them include arctic terns, curlews and swans. The birds can be viewed from an observation tower near the bridge.

Fakse ③①

Road map F5.
i Postvej 3, Fakse Ladeplads, 56 71 60 34. **W** www.faksekysten.dk

REFERENCES TO Fakse can be found in late 13th-century records when it was an important area for limestone mining. Today the town is best known for its local brewery, Faxe Bryggeri, which produces over 130 million litres (28.6 million gallons) of beer each year.

The town's most historic building is the 15th-century Gothic church, which has a number of wall paintings dating from around 1500. **Fakse Geologiske Museum** has a collection of over 500 types of fossils including some 63 million-year-old remains of plants and animals

found in the Fakse Kalkbrud quarry about 2 km (1 mile) outside the town.

🏛 Fakse Geologiske Museum
Højerup Bygade 38, 4660 Store Heddinge. **C** 56 50 28 06.
O May–Sep: 11am–5pm Tue–Sun; Jul, Easter and mid-Oct: 11am–5pm daily. 🅰

Fakse's brewery, producing millions of gallons of beer a year

Stevns Klint ③②

Road map F5. **i** Rødvig, Havnevej 21, 56 50 64 64.
W www.stevnsinfo.dk

ALTHOUGH DENMARK'S most famous cliffs are found on Møn, the limestone peninsula of Stevns Klint is almost as impressive. The section between Rødvig, a small fishing port, and Gjorslev where there is a 15th-century Gothic castle is the most picturesque, especially when the sun glints against the white chalk surface.

The area was for centuries known for its limestone quarries, which supplied building material for the first castle built by Bishop

Absalon in Copenhagen; this castle became the nucleus of the royal residence, which in later times was given the name of Christiansborg Slot *(see pp86–7)*. Large-scale limestone quarrying was abandoned in the 1940s.

The strip of coastal cliffs is about 15 km (9 miles) long, with the highest peaks rising to about 41 m (135 ft). The best viewpoint can be found next to the old church of Højerup (Højerup Kirke). Legend has it that this 13th-century edifice, built close to the cliff's edge, moves inland each Christmas Eve by the length of a cockerel's jump.

Another local myth recounts a story about a king of the cliffs who lives in a cave in a crag south of the church. The king of the cliffs failed, however, to save the church from the destructive forces of nature. Over the years, due to constant erosion, the sea has advanced closer and closer towards the church and in 1928 the presbytery collapsed and crashed into the water.

A short distance from the church is the small town of Højerup. Here, the **Stevns Museum** has a local-history collection that includes recreated workshops, Stone-Age tools, antique toys and a collection of fire-fighting equipment from the past including pumps and fire engines. There is also an exhibition dealing with the geology of the local cliffs.

Limestone cliffs of Stevns Klint on Zealand's east coast

ENVIRONS: A few kilometres inland is the region's main town, **Store Heddinge**, which has one of Zealand's best Romanesque churches. The 12th-century church is made from limestone excavated in the nearby quarries. Its octagonal shape probably made it easier to defend.

🏛 Stevns Museum
Højerup Bygade 38, 4660 Store Heddinge. 56 50 28 06.
☐ May, Jun, Aug, Sep: 11am–5pm Tue–Sun; Jul: 11am–5pm daily. 🖼

Vallø Slot, a moated 16th-century castle

Vallø Slot ㉝

Road map F5. **Castle** ● to visitors.
Stables 56 26 74 62. ☐ mid-May–Aug: 11am–4pm Tue–Sun. 🖼
Garden 8am–sunset daily.

THE SECLUDED castle of Vallø is one of the most impressive Renaissance buildings in Denmark. As early as the 15th century the islet was surrounded by a moat and featured a complex of defensive buildings. The castle owes its present shape to the influence of two enterprising sisters, Mette and Birgitte Rosenkrantz, who in the 16th century owned the surrounding land. The sisters divided the estate in equal shares between themselves – the east part was managed by Birgitte, while the western section belonged to Mette.

In 1737 the castle was taken over by a trust that provided a home for unmarried daughters of noble birth during their later years.

The castle is closed to visitors. The large park is open, however, as is the former stable block, which houses a museum containing a mix of agricultural implements and equestrian accessories.

Køge ㉞

Road map F5. 🏚 40,000. 🚊 🚌
🛈 Vestergade 1, 56 65 58 00.
🌐 www.visitkoege.com

ONE OF Denmark's best-preserved medieval towns, Køge was granted a municipal charter in 1288 and grew quickly thanks to its large natural harbour at the mouth of a navigable river. Køge Bay entered the annals of Danish history in 1677 when the Danish fleet, led by Admiral Niels Juel, crushed a Swedish armada heading for Copenhagen. The battle and the victorious Admiral Juel are commemorated by a 9-m (30-ft) tall obelisk standing by the harbour.

The heart of the town is its market square, which contains a monument to Frederik VI. The town hall standing in the cobbled square is the longest-serving public building of its kind in Denmark. The cobbled streets leading from the market square are lined with half-timbered houses for which Køge is famous. The most interesting street in this

Kirkestræde 10, now serving as a children's nursery

respect is Kirkestræde. The small house at No. 20, with only two windows, is the oldest half-timbered house in Denmark; the beam under its front door gives the year of construction as 1527.

Another impressive historic building is Sankt Nicolai Kirke, which dates from 1324. Its tower served for many years as a lighthouse and is now used as a viewpoint.

Køge Museum is located along Nørregade and occupies two early-17th-century buildings. Its exhibits include old photographs, historic furniture, costumes and, serving as a reminder of the town's bloody past, the local executioner's sword.

🏛 Køge Museum
Nørregade 4. 56 63 42 42.
☐ Jun–Aug: 10am–5pm daily; Sep–May: 2–5pm Mon–Fri, 1–5pm Sat & Sun. 🖼

THE ARISTOCRATIC LADIES OF THE CASTLE

In 1737, Vallø's owner, Queen Sophie Magdalene, donated the castle to the Royal Vallø Foundation. From then on the castle become a home for unmarried women from noble families. The famously religious queen ensured the typically cloistral character of the place and promoted a lifestyle true to Christian principles. Initially it housed 12 women, some of whom were as young as 15. The convent was run by a prioress of high birth, and the mother superior was also descended from an aristocratic family. The male staff, an administrator, doctor and servants, lived opposite the castle. Some unmarried ladies still reside in Vallø Slot.

The imposing twin towers of Vallø Slot

FUNEN

UNEN (FYN IN DANISH) *is Denmark's second largest island and occupies an area of about 3,000 sq km (1,158 sq miles). It has some of Denmark's best scenery including wide, sandy beaches, steep cliffs and lush pasture land and orchards. A number of neighbouring islands are considered to be part of Funen including Ærø and Tåsinge, which are themselves popular destinations.*

Funen is separated from Zealand by the Store Bælt (Great Belt) and from Jutland by the Lille Bælt (Little Belt). Nearly half of Funen's inhabitants live in Odense, which is the island's capital, a lively cultural centre and the birthplace of Hans Christian Andersen. Aside from Odense there are no large towns on Funen and the island is sometimes described as the "garden of Denmark" because of the large amount of produce that grows in its fertile soil.

Thanks to the fact that the island has escaped most of Denmark's wars with other nations, Funen has an exceptionally high number of well-preserved historic buildings and palaces. The best-known of these is Egeskov Slot, a Renaissance castle encircled by a moat.

The relatively small distances, gently rolling landscape and the many interesting places to visit, make Funen an ideal area for cycling trips. The south-western part of the island features a range of wooded hills. The highest of these, rising to 126 m (413 ft), are found near the town of Faaborg. Central Funen is mostly flat and only becomes slightly undulated in the northeastern region. The south has most of the island's harbours and towns, while the northern and western parts are sparsely populated.

An archipelago of southern islets includes Langeland, Ærø and Tåsinge as well as a number of tiny islands inhabited only by birds. This area is popular with Danish yachtsmen and it is possible to explore the archipelago by joining an organized cruise on board a wooden sailing ship. Some of the islands can be reached by ferry.

The imposing façade of Egeskov Slot, one of Denmark's finest castles

◁ Cultivated fields typical of Funen's coastal region

Exploring Funen

THE UNIVERSITY TOWN of Odense lies at the heart of Funen. In contrast to the rest of the island, it is a busy place and Denmark's third largest city. Throughout the centuries the Danish aristocracy were keen to build their opulent residences on the island and Funen has over 120 beautifully preserved mansions, castles and palaces. The most impressive of them are Egeskov Slot and, on Tåsinge, Valdemars Slot. Funen's coastline is 12,000 km (7,457 miles) long and has some beautiful beaches. The loveliest island under Funen's administration is Ærø, a picturesque place with tiny villages and ancient farms.

Den Gamle Gaard, a merchant's house in Faaborg

KEY

▀▀▀	Motorway
▀▀	Major road
▀▀	Scenic route
—	Other road
=	River
☼	Viewpoint

SIGHTS AT A GLANCE

Assens ❶
Egeskov Slot ❻
Faaborg ❼
Hindsholm ❹
Kerteminde ❸
Langeland ❿
Marstal ⓫
Nyborg ❺
Odense pp174–5 ❷
Svendborg ❽
Tåsinge ❾
Ærøskøbing ⓬

Traditional wooden boat moored in Svendborg harbour

162

HINDSHOLM 4

OTTERUP

ODENSE FJORD

KERTEMINDE 3

315

165

STORE BÆLT

ODENSE 2

Odenseå

LANGESKOV

E 20

165

NYBORG 5

København

43

9

RINGE

323

8

163

Arreskov Sø

43

EGESKOV SLOT 6

44

9

8

ÅBORG

Avernakø

Drejø

SVENDBORG 8

TÅSINGE 9

9

RUDKØBING

LANGELAND 10

Strynø

305

12 **ÆRØSKØBING**

Ærø

11 **MARSTAL**

305

MARSTAL BUGT

Imposing turrets and high walls of Egeskov Slot

GETTING AROUND

Funen is linked to Jutland and Zealand by two bridges. There is a frequent rail service from Copenhagen. The island's main transport artery is the E20 motorway running from east to west (a railway line runs roughly parallel to this).

The most important roads that lead from Odense towards other major towns are the No. 9 road to Svendborg, and the No. 43 to Faaborg. Ferries sail to Ærø, while Langeland can be reached via a bridge.

SEE ALSO

• **Where to Stay** pp247–8.

• **Where to Eat** pp270–71.

Quiet yacht marina in Assens

Assens ❶

Road map C5. 🏛 *15,000.* 🚌
🛈 *Damgade 22, 64 71 20 31.*
🆆 www.visit-vestfyn.dk

SITUATED ON THE shores of the Store Bælt (Great Belt), Assens was for centuries a busy harbour for ferries on the route between Funen and Jutland. Following the construction of a bridge across the strait, far north of the town, it lost its importance. Assens contains numerous historic buildings including 18th- and 19th-century merchants' houses, as well as the 15th-century Vor Frue Kirke (Church of Our Lady).

The best-known citizen of Assens was Peter Willemoes (1783–1808), a war hero who, in 1801, fought against Admiral Nelson during the Napoleonic Wars and distinguished himself during Nelson's bombardment of Copenhagen. Willemoes' birthplace, **Willemoes-gården**, now houses a museum of cultural history. A monument to Willemoes has been erected near the harbour. The small house by the monument was once used as a sailors' kitchen.

A short way from Willemoesgården is the Ernsts Samlinger exhibition in the house of a local silversmith, Frederik Ernst, which has Denmark's largest collection of antique silver and glass.

🏛 **Willemoesgården**
Østergade 36. ☐ *May–Sep, Easter & mid-Oct: 10am–4pm.* ● *Mon.* 🅰

Odense ❷

See pp174–5.

Kerteminde ❸

Road map D5. 🏛 *5,500.* 🚌
🛈 *Strandgade 1B, 65 32 11 21.*
🆆 www.kerteminde-turist.dk

MUCH OF THIS pretty seaside town is clustered around the 15th-century Sankt Laurentius Kirke (Church). One of the town's main attractions is **Fjord& Bælt**, a recently built sea-life centre. A 50-m long tunnel with large windows allows visitors to walk beneath the fjord and enjoy the underwater view. The famous Danish painter Johannes Larsen (1867–1961) once lived in Kerteminde and the **Johannes Larsen Museum** contains many of his paintings.

ENVIRONS: 4 km (2 miles) southwest of Kerteminde is the **Ladbyskibet**, a 22-m (72-ft) long Viking ship that dates from the 10th century and was used as the tomb of a Viking chieftain.

Statue of St Laurentius, in Kerteminde

🛶 **Fjord&Bælt**
Margrethes Plads 1.
📞 *65 32 42 00.* ☐ *Feb–Jun: 10am–4pm Mon–Fri, 10am–5pm Sat & Sun ; Jul–8 Aug: 10am–6pm daily; 9 Aug–Nov: 10am–4pm Mon–Fri, 10am–5pm Sat & Sun.* ● *Jan, Dec.* 🅰
🆆 www.fjord-baelt.dk
🏛 **Johannes Larsen Museum**
Møllebakken. 📞 *65 32 37 27.*
☐ *Jun–Aug: 10am–5pm daily; Mar–May, Sep & Oct: 10am–4pm Tue–Sun; Nov–Feb: 11am–4pm Tue–Sun.* 🅰

Hindsholm ❹

Road map D5. 🚌

RISING AT THE far end of the Hindsholm peninsula is 25-m (82-ft) high cliffs, which provide a splendid view over the coast and the island of Samsø. A little way inland is Marhøj knoll, a 2nd-century BC underground burial chamber.

The small town of Viby, north of Assens, has a 19th-century windmill and an Early-Gothic church. According to legend, Marsk Stig, a hero of Danish folklore, was buried here in 1293. Before setting off for war, Marks Stig is said to have left his wife in the care of the king, Erik Klipping. The king took the notion of "care" somewhat too far and when the knight returned he killed the king and was outlawed. Even his funeral had to be held in secrecy.

Crops growing on the Hindsholm peninsula

Royal painting and suits of armour in the Knights' Hall, Nyborg Slot

Nyborg ❺

Road map D5. 🏯 *15,000.* 🚉 🚌
ℹ️ *Torvet 9, 65 31 02 80.*
🔗 www.nyborgturist.dk

THE CASTLE OF **Nyborg Slot** was built in the early 13th century by Valdemar I as part of the fortifications that guarded the Store Bælt. For nearly 200 years the castle was the scene of the Danehof assemblies (an early form of Danish parliament). The castle was also the venue of the signing, in 1282, of a charter that laid down the duties of the king. Over the centuries the castle gradually fell into ruin and it was only after World War I that it was restored and turned into a museum. A number of rooms are open to the public incuding the royal chambers and the Danehof room. The castle ramparts and moat are now a park.

During July and August, on Tuesdays at about 7pm, the Tappenstreg regiment marches through the streets of Nyborg. This regiment upholds an 18th-century tradition of checking whether all the town's entertainment venues have closed on time.

ENVIRONS: In Knudshoved, about 5 km (3 miles) from Nyborg, is the **Store Bælt Centre**, devoted to the history of constructing the link between Funen and Zealand (*see p142*).

⚓ **Nyborg Slot**
Slotsgade 11. 🎫 *65 31 02 07.*
🕐 *end Mar–May & Sep: 10am–3pm daily, Jun & Aug: 10am–4pm daily; Jul: 10am–5pm daily.* 📷

Egeskov Slot ❻

Road map D5. Kværndrup.
🎫 *62 27 10 16.* 🕐 *May, Sep, Oct: 10am–5pm; Jun, Aug: 10am–6pm; Jul: 10am–8pm.* 📷
🔗 www.egeskov.dk

THIS MAGNIFICENT castle was built in the mid-16th century and is one of Denmark's best known sights. Egeskov means "oak forest" and the castle was built in the middle of a pond on a foundation of oak trees. The interior has some grand rooms containing antique furniture and paintings, and a hall of hunting trophies that include elephant tusks and tiger heads.

Much of the grounds were laid out in the 18th century and include a garden adorned with fountains, and a herb garden. A bamboo maze and a vintage car museum are also in the grounds.

Coat of arms from Egeskov Slot

Faaborg ❼

Road map D5. 🏯 *8,000.* 🚌
ℹ️ *Banegårdspladsen 2A, 62 61 07 07.* 🔗 www.visitfaaborg.dk

FAABORG IS A picturesque place with cobbled streets and half-timbered houses. The market square contains the town's most famous monument, produced by the Danish painter and sculptor Kai Nielsen in the early 20th century. Its main figure is Ymer, a giant who according to Nordic mythology was killed by Odin.

The view from the 15-m (49-ft) tall Klokketårnet (Clock Tower) embraces the bay. The tower is all that remains of a medieval town.

Den Gamle Gaard is a wealthy merchant's house that dates from 1725. Its rooms have been arranged to illustrate the life of a 19th-century merchant.

Faaborg Museum, designed by Carl Petersen, has a number of works by Danish artists such as Peter Hansen and Johannes Larsen.

🏛 **Den Gamle Gaard**
Holkegade 1. 🎫 *62 61 33 38.* 🕐 *Apr–mid-May: 11am–3pm Sat & Sun; mid-May–mid-Sep: 10:30am–4:30pm daily; mid-Sep–end Oct: 11am–3pm daily.* 📷
🏛 **Faaborg Museum**
Grønnegade 75. 🎫 *62 61 06 45.* 🕐 *Nov–Mar: 11am–3pm Tue–Sun; Apr–Oct: 10am–4pm daily.* 📷
🔗 www.faaborgmuseum.dk

Collection of Danish art in Faaborg Museum

Odense ❷

The city's coat of arms

ONE OF THE oldest cities in Denmark, Odense derives its name from the Nordic god Odin who was worshipped by the Vikings. In medieval times it was an important centre of trade and from the 12th century on it was a major pilgrimage destination. Since the 19th century, when a canal was built linking Odense with the sea, the city has been a major port. Odense has a rich cultural life and plenty to see including a cathedral and a museum devoted to the city's most famous son, Hans Christian Andersen.

16th-century cathedral altarpiece by Claus Berg

Exploring Odense

Most attractions lie within the boundaries of the medieval district. Getting around is made easy by the Odense Eventyrpas (Adventure Pass), which entitles the holder to free travel, free admission to museums and cut-price tickets for boat cruises.

⊞ Brandts Klædefabrik
Brandts Passage 37–43.
Danmarks Mediemuseum 📞 66 12 10 20. ◯ Jul–Aug: 10am–5pm daily; Sep–Jun: 10am–5pm Tue–Sun. 📷
Museet for Fotokunst 📞 66 13 78 16. ◯ same as above. 📷
Galeria Tidens Samling 📞 65 91 19 42. ◯ same as above. 📷
For more than fifty years Brandt's textile factory was the biggest company in Odense. After its closure in 1977 it stood empty for a number of years until it was renovated and transformed into a cultural centre. Today it houses museums, a cinema, art galleries, shops, restaurants and cafés. The latest addition is the **Danmarks Mediemuseum**, which has displays on the history of print production and the latest electronic media. The **Museet**

for **Fotokunst** exhibits works by Danish and international photographers, while **Galeria Tidens Samling** has exhibits relating to the operation of the former factory.

Childhood home of Hans Christian Andersen

⊞ H.C. Andersens Barndomshjem
Munkemøllestræde 3–5. 📞 66 14 88 14. ◯ mid-Jun–Aug: 10am–4pm; Sep–mid-Jun: 11am–3pm. 📷
🅦 www.odmus.dk
The Andersen family moved to this small house close to the cathedral when Hans was two years old. Andersen lived here until the age of 14. The museum has only a few rooms, furnished with basic period household objects, but manages to conjure up what life was like for a poor Danish family in the early 19th century.

🔒 Sankt Knuds Kirke
Flakhaven. 📞 66 12 03 92. ◯ Apr–Oct: 9am–5pm Mon–Sat, noon–3pm Sun; Sep–Mar: 10am–4pm Mon–Sat, noon–3pm Sun. 🅦 www.odense-domkirke.dk
Odense cathedral is named after Canute (Knud) II, who ruled Denmark from 1080–86. His

skeleton is on display in a glass case in the basement.
The present cathedral is one of Denmark's most beautiful examples of Gothic architecture. It stands on the site of an earlier Romanesque structure, which was destroyed by fire in 1248. The cathedral's ornate gilded altar is a 16th-century masterpiece by Claus Berg of Lübeck. The triptych is 5 m (16 ft) high and includes nearly 300 intricately carved figures.

♜ Flakhaven
Flakhaven derives its name from an old Danish word meaning an area surrounded by meadows and gardens. For centuries the square was used as a market venue and attracted merchants and farmers from all over Funen. The main building standing in the square is the Rådhus (city hall), which has a west wing dating from the 19th century. The remainder of the building is 20th century. Guided tours are available and include access to the Wedding Room, the Town Council Chamber and a wall commemorating citizens who have made outstanding contributions to the city's history. Flakhaven contains a statue of Frederik VII as well as an abstract metal sculpture made by Robert Jacobson to celebrate the 1,000th anniversary of Odense in 1988.

⊞ Fyns Kunstmuseum
Jernbanegade 13. 📞 66 14 88 14. ◯ 10am–4pm Tue–Sun. 📷
This art museum has the largest collection of Danish art in Denmark outside Copenhagen. The Classicist building is adorned on the outside with a frieze depicting scenes from Danish

Art gallery in Brandts Klædefabrik

history and mythology. The interior is crammed with paintings, etchings and sculptures by Danish artists from all periods. One section contains works by local Funen artists.

🏛 H. C. Andersens Hus

Bangs Boder 29. 📞 66 14 88 14. ⏰ mid-Jun–Aug: 10am–4pm; Sep–mid-Jun: 11am–3pm. 🏷
🌐 www.odmus.dk

Denmark's most famous writer was born in this house in 1805. It is now a museum and has recently undergone a substantial metamorphosis; it was greatly extended and modernized to celebrate the 200th anniversary of Andersen's birth. The exhibition includes a recreation of the author's study and numerous items belonging to Andersen including his notes and letters. There is even an old rope – apparently Andersen was terrified by the thought of a fire and carried this with him wherever he went in readiness for an emergency evacuation. Hanging on one of the walls is a world map

Bust from Fyns Kunstmuseum

indicating the countries in which Andersen's tales have been published in translation. A special collection includes copies of his works in 120 languages.

Close to the museum is Fyrtøjet, a children's cultural centre based on Andersen's stories.

🏛 Carl Nielsen Museet

Claus Bergs Gade 11. 📞 66 14 88 14. ⏰ Jun–Aug: 10am–4pm Tue–Fri, noon–4pm Sun; Sep–May: noon–4pm Thu–Sun. 🏷

This museum, devoted to the famous Danish composer Carl Nielsen (1865–1931), was opened in 1988 to celebrate

the town's millennium. The exhibits, donated by the descendents of the composer, are all associated with Nielsen, who is mainly known for his operas, symphonies and violin concertos. In addition to handwritten scores of the artist's compositions, the collection includes Nielsen's piano and works by his wife, the sculptor Anne Marie Brodersen.

City hall façade, crowned with an allegorical statue of Justice

ODENSE CITY CENTRE

Brandts Klædefabrik ①
Carl Nielsen Museet ⑦
Flakhaven ④
Fyns Kunstmuseum ⑤
H. C. Andersens Barndomshjem ②
H. C. Andersens Hus ⑥
Sankt Knud's Kirke ③

0 m   200
0 yards   200

KEY

ℹ Tourist information
🏛 Church
🅿 Parking
✉ Post office

Svendborg ⑧

Road map D5. 🏃 *30,000.* 🚗 🚌
ℹ️ *Centrumpladsen 4, 62 21 09 80.*
🎿 *Fyn Rundt Regattas (Jul).*
🌐 www.sydfyn.dk

FUNEN'S SECOND largest town, Svendborg is a busy port and has strong links with shipbuilding. In the 19th century its boatyards produced 50 per cent of all vessels sailing under the Danish flag.

Most of Svendborg's sights are within easy reach of Torvet, the market square. Closest to hand is the 13th-century Vor Frue Kirke, which has a carillon consisting of 27 bells. Sankt Nicolai Kirke is slightly older, though also 13th century. A short distance west of Vor Frue Kirke is **Anne Hvides Gård**, a half-timbered building dating from 1560. This is now a local history museum and exhibits locally produced ceramics and glass. Contemporary art is on display at **SAK Kunstbygningen** (SAK Art Exhibitions), which also exhibits works by the Danish sculptor Kai Nielsen (1882–1924) who was born in Svendborg. Other museums in town include a toy museum and a natural history museum. The latter is full of stuffed animals and skeletons including the bones of a whale that was washed ashore in 1955.

🏛 **Anne Hvides Gård**
Fruestræde 3. 📞 *62 21 02 61.*
◻️ *Jun–Aug: 10am–5pm daily.* 🅿️
🏛 **SAK Kunstbygningen**
Vestergade 27. 📞 *62 22 44 70.*
◻️ *11am–4pm Tue–Sat.* 🅿️

Kattesund, a scenic alley in Svendborg

An elegant apartment in Valdemars Slot, Tåsinge

Tåsinge ⑨

Road map D6. 🏃 *2,500.* 🚌

THE ISLAND of Tåsinge is linked by bridge to Funen and Langeland. The major local attraction is **Valdemars Slot**, which was built by Christian IV for his favourite son Valdemar and completed in 1644. Unfortunately the prince had only a short while to enjoy the estate as he was killed in battle in 1656.

The castle's architect was Hans van Steenwinckel, who was also responsible for building Rosenborg Slot in Copenhagen *(see pp60–61).* In 1670s the king gave the castle to Admiral Niels Juel in recognition of his successful command of the Danish fleet during the Battle of Køge Bay. The castle has remained in the hands of the Juel family ever since. A number of rooms are open to the public including the royal apartments, the reception rooms and the kitchens. In the attic there is a collection of items including trophies brought from African safaris. The domestic quarters, arranged around a lake, house a couple of small museums.

ENVIRONS: Close to the castle, while heading for Svendborg, is the fishing port of **Troense**. Its most attractive street, Grønnegade, is lined with pretty half-timbered houses. The Søfartsmuseet (Marine Museum) is housed in an 18th-century village school. Along with marine paintings and model ships it also displays

products brought back by merchant ships from China.

♣ **Valdemars Slot**
Troense. 📞 *62 22 61 06.* ◻️ *May–Jun, Aug: 10am–5pm; Jul: 10am–6pm; Sep: 10am–5pm Tue–Sun.* 🅿️

Statue of Hans Christian Ørsted in Rudkøbing

Langeland ⑩

Road map D6. 🚢 🚌
ℹ️ *Rudkøbing Torvet 5, 62 51 35 05.*

LANGELAND IS positioned off the southeast coast of Funen and can be reached by bridge or from Lolland by ferry. The island has a number of good beaches and marked cycling paths. Windmills are dotted here and there, along with quaint hamlets and farms.

Rudkøbing is the capital and the island's only sizeable town. Its most famous citizen was Hans Christian Ørsted (1777–1851), a physicist who made major advances in the field of electromagnetism. The house in which the scientist was born is known as **Det Gamle Apotek** (The Old Pharmacy) and has been arranged to recreate an 18th-century pharmacist's shop. In front of it stands a statue of Ørsted. From here it is only a short distance to the market square, which contains a 19th-century town hall and a much older church with an inscription giving its year of founding as 1105.

Langelands Museum is devoted mostly to local history and includes archaeological finds.

About 10 km (6 miles) north of Rudkøbing is **Tranekær**, whose main attraction is Tranekær Slot, a pink-coloured castle that dates from around 1200. The castle is closed to visitors but the grounds can be toured. Part of the estate now serves as a botanical garden which has a number of rare trees including some Californian sequoias. An open-air gallery exhibits sculptures and installations by artists from a number of of countries including Denmark, Germany and the USA.

🏛 **Det Gamle Apotek**
Brogade 15, Rudkøbing.
📞 63 51 10 10. ⏲ *by appointment only (contact Langelands Museum).* 🅿️

🏛 **Langelands Museum**
Jens Winthersvej, Rudkøbing.
📞 63 51 10 10. ⏲ *10am–4pm Mon–Thu, 10am–1pm Fri.*
🅦 www.langelandsmuseum.dk

Colourful façade of Tranekær Slot, Langeland

Small boats on Aerøskøbing's harbour

Marstal ⓫

Road map D6. Ærø. 🏘 *3,000.* ⛴
🚏 🛈 *Havnegade 5, 62 52 13 00.*
⏲ *mid-Jun–Aug: 9am–3:30pm Mon–Sat.*

MARSTAL IS the largest town on the island of Ærø. Its history has long been associated with the sea and in the 18th century it was a busy port with about 300 ships arriving here every year. The **Søfartmuseum** (Maritime Museum) occupies four buildings near the harbour and contains many items connected with the sea including model schooners and seafaring paintings.

The dependence of the local population on the sea is apparent in the local church on Kirkestræde, which was built in 1738. Its altarpiece depicts Christ calming the rough waves. Hanging in the church are several votive sailing ships, and in the church cemetery are the gravestones of sailors. The church clock was created by Jens Olsen, who also produced the World Clock in the Rådhus in Copenhagen (*see p74*).

Exhibit from Marstal's Søfartmuseum

🏛 **Søfartmuseum**
Prinsensgade 1. 📞 62 53 23 31.
⏲ *Oct–Apr: 10am–4pm Tue–Fri, 10am–3pm Sat; May, Sep: 10am–4pm daily; Jun, Jul: 9am–5pm daily.* 🅿️

Ærøskøbing ⓬

Road map D6. Ærø. 🏘 *1,500.* ⛴
🚏 🛈 *Vestergade 1, 62 52 13 00.*

MANY OF THE 17th-century houses lining the cobbled streets are a reminder of a time when Ærøskøbing was a prosperous merchant town. The oldest house dates from 1645 and can be found at Søndergade 36. The town's most picturesque dwelling is Dukkehuset (Dolls' House) at Smedegade 37. Also in Smedegade is **Flaske-Peters Samling**, a museum devoted to the work of Peter Jacobsen, who first went to sea at the age of 16. Known as "Bottle Peter", Jacobsen created about 1,700 ships-in-a-bottle before he died in 1960. Also kept in the museum is a cross made by the sailor for his own grave. **Ærø Museum** has displays on the history of the island and its inhabitants, including a collection of 19th-century paintings.

🏛 **Flaske-Peters Samling**
Smedegade 22.
📞 62 52 29 51.
⏲ *mid-Oct–mid-Mar: 1pm–3pm Tue–Fri, 10am–noon Sat & Sun; mid-Mar–mid-Jun: 10am–4pm daily; mid-Jun–early Aug: 10am–5pm daily; mid-Aug–mid-Oct: 10am–4pm daily.* 🅿️

🏛 **Ærø Museum**
Brogade 3–5. 📞 62 52 29 50.
⏲ *mid-Jun–Aug: 10am–4pm Tue–Sun; Sep–mid-Jun: 10am–1pm Tue–Sun.* 🅿️

SOUTHERN AND CENTRAL JUTLAND

A S WELL AS THE *scenic lowlands and undulating hills and meadows found on the eastern side of central Jutland, this region has much to recommend it. Attractions include beautifully preserved medieval towns, traditional hamlets, parks, castles and ancient Viking burial grounds. In addition, no one travelling with children should miss a trip to LEGOLAND®.*

Jutland derives its name from the Jutes, a German tribe that once inhabited this peninsula. When the Vikings, who occupied the islands to the east, began to encroach on this territory the mixing of the two tribes gave rise to the Danes as a distinct people.

Following Denmark's defeat during the Schleswig Wars in 1864, Jutland was occupied by Prussia, and subsequently, as part of Schleswig, remained under German control. It was not until a plebiscite in 1920 that it once more became part of the kingdom of Denmark. After the final resolution of this Danish-German border dispute, many German families remained on the Danish side. The expatriate minority is still active in the region and German speakers have their own newspaper.

The region has also been shaped by Dutch settlers and the lowland scenery is here and there enlivened by Dutch windmills, while some fields are bisected by canals. The Dutch influence can also be seen in many of the houses in this region, some of which are decorated with distinctive Dutch wall tiles.

The top attraction of this region is LEGOLAND®, where millions of Ole Kirk Christensen's famous plastic bricks are used to create Denmark's best-known amusement park.

Carved Viking figures and replica Viking ship in Vejle Fjord

◁ Farmhouses set amid the undulating fields of Jutland

Exploring Southern and Central Jutland

JUTLAND IS THE ONLY part of Denmark that is not an island. The bottom section of the peninsula is cut across by a 69-km (43-mile) long national border with Germany and ties with this country remain close. The most popular attraction of southern and central Jutland is LEGOLAND®. Close to this theme park is the town of Jelling, which is famous for its ancient burial mounds. This region is rich in towns with long histories, of which Ribe is the oldest and best preserved. Århus is Denmark's second city and is famous for its nightlife, while Esbjerg has some good museums.

GETTING AROUND

Esbjerg's harbour handles international ferry traffic; the town's airport handles flights from the UK and Norway. The quickest route to Jutland from Copenhagen is the E20, running through Funen. This joins with the E45 that runs along the eastern coast of the peninsula, from Germany to Århus and further north. It is also possible to take a ferry from Funen to Als and from there join up with Jutland's southern section. Jutland is almost three times larger than the rest of Denmark put together and distances between towns can be significant.

SEE ALSO

- *Where to Stay* pp248–51.
- *Where to Eat* pp272–5.

Restored cutter in front of Esbjerg's maritime museum

Anholt

Aalborg

16

DJURSLAND

● *GRENÅ*

15

EBELTOFT

❶

ÅRHUS

❷

❸

ILKEBORG
AKE DISTRICT

MOESGÅRD

Århus Bugt

Samsø

❹
HORSENS

Endelave

FREDERICIA

❷⓪

Odense

Als

405

❶⑦

SØNDERBORG

**Ramparts around the town of
Fredericia in central Jutland**

| 0 km | 20 |
| 0 miles | 20 |

KEY

▬ Motorway

▬ Major road

▬ Scenic route

═ Other road

═ River

☼ Viewpoint

SIGHTS AT A GLANCE

The 15th-century Koldinghus in Kolding

Fregatten Jylland in Ebeltoft, now serving as a museum

Ebeltoft ❶

Road map D3. 🏃 *5,000.* 🚌
ℹ️ *Strandvejen 2, 86 34 14 00.*

BOASTING THE smallest *rådhus* (town hall) in Denmark, Ebeltoft is over 700 years old. Many of the town's cobbled streets have been pedestrianized including Adelgade, which is lined with half-timbered houses. Ebeltoft Kirke dates from 1301 and contains a font that is even older as well as some 16th-century frescoes.

In the harbour is **Fregatten Jylland**, a 19th-century sailing ship that was used as a royal vessel. The displays on board give an idea of the conditions endured by the 430-strong crew, which are in stark contrast to those found in the royal apartments.

The nearby **Glasmuseet** has many glass items on display. The exhibits include works of art by international artists as well as more everyday glass items.

Bell from Fregatten Jylland

🏛 Fregatten Jylland
Strandvejen 4. 🎫 *86 34 10 99.*
⭕ *Jan–Mar, Nov–Dec: 10am–4pm daily; Apr–Jun, Sep–Oct: 10am–5pm daily; Jul–Aug: 10am–7pm daily.* 📷
🏛 Glasmuseet
Strandvejen 8. 🎫 *86 34 17 99.*
⭕ *Jan–Jun, Aug–Sep: 10am–5pm daily; July: 10am–7pm daily.* 📷
ⓦ *www.glasmuseet.dk*

Århus ❷

See pp184–5.

Moesgård ❸

Road map D4. *5 km (3 miles) south of Århus.*

THE MAIN attraction of this small town is the **Moesgård Museum**, housed in an 18th-century manor house. Its star exhibit is Graubelle Man who was discovered in 1952 in a bog by peat gatherers from Graubelle. The mummified body was found about 30 km (19 miles) from Moesgård and had been preserved thanks to a combination of acids and iron in the soil. He is believed to have been about 40 years old when he died in 80 BC. A slash across his throat indicates that he may have been murdered.

The museum also has a collection of runic stones, a reconstructed Viking church and weapons including swords and axes. A trail leading from the museum to the beach passes by reconstructed dolmens and homesteads that represent various historic periods. Each year in late July, Moesgård becomes the venue for a lively Viking festival.

🏛 Moesgård Museum
Moesgård Allé 20. 🎫 *89 42 11 00.*
⭕ *Apr–Sep: 10am–5pm daily; Oct–Mar: 10am–4pm Tue–Sun.* 📷

Lichtenberg Palace, Horsens, now used as a hotel

Horsens ❹

Road map C4. *38 km (24 miles) south of Århus.* 🏃 *50,000.* 🚗 🚌
ℹ️ *Søndergade 26, 75 60 21 20.*
🎭 *Medieval Festival (late Aug).*
ⓦ *www.visithorsens.dk*

HORSENS IS the birthplace of Vitus Bering (1681–1741), the explorer who discovered Alaska and the straits that separate it from Siberia (the straits were subsequently named after him). The guns from Bering's ship now stand in the town's main park. Mementos from Bering's expeditions are on display in **Horsens Museum**.

The Danish Romanesque Vor Frelsers Kirke (Our Saviour's Church) is 13th century. Nearby, Lichtenberg Palace was used by the Tsar's family after they fled Russia.

If possible, it is best to visit Horsens during its Medieval Festival, held in August, when armoured knights engage in deadly combat and robed wizards and witches cast spells on unruly children.

🏛 Horsens Museum
Sundvej 1A. 🎫 *76 29 23 50.*
⭕ *Jul–Aug: 10am–4pm daily; Sep–Jun: 11am–4pm Tue–Sun.* 📷

Reconstructed burial chamber at Moesgård Museum

Charming harbour on one of Søhøjlandet's lakes

Silkeborg Lake District ❺

Road map C4.

THE STRETCH between Silkeborg and Skanderborg and the area slightly to the north of it is a land of lakes and hills known as Søhøjlandet. It is here that visitors will find Jutland's largest lake – the Mossø, as well as Denmark's longest river, the Gudenå (158 km/ 98 miles). The Lake District also has some of the country's highest peaks. In summer it is a favourite destination for canoeists and cyclists, as well as hikers, all of whom make the most of the lakeland scenery.

Labyrinthia Park is one of the area's main attractions. It has many kinds of mazes and provides a fun way for the whole family to get lost. Gjern has a vintage car museum (with about 70 models, the oldest dating from the early 20th century), while Tange Sø boasts **Elmuseet**, an electricity museum situated next to the country's largest power station.

Other places worth visiting include the church in Veng which was built around 1100. It is thought to be the oldest monastery in Denmark.

Standing on the shores of Mossø are the ruins of the Øm monastery, which can be explored by visiting the attached **Monastic Museum of Denmark**. At one time this was the largest of the dozen or so local monasteries and the entire estate belonged to a Cistercian order, which included nearly 400 farms.

Silkeborg ❻

Road map C4. 🏠 45,000. 🚊 🚌
ℹ️ Åhavevej 21/2A, 86 82 19 11.
🎷 Jazz Festival (Jun), Country Music Festival (Aug). 🌐 www.silkeborg.com

SILKEBORG OWES much of its past prosperity to the paper factory, built in 1846, that was at one time powered by the local river.

Silkeborg's **Culture Museum** occupies a residential house built in 1767. Most visitors head straight for the remains of the Tollund Man. Only the head of the mummified Iron-Age body is genuine as the body decomposed once it was dug up.

Tollund Man

In summer a 19th-century paddle steamer travels the 15 km (9 miles) to Himmelbjerget (Sky Mountain), one of the area's most visited spots. On top of the 147-m (482-ft) hill is a 25-m (82-ft) high tower that affords magnificent views of the lakeland scenery.

🏛 **Silkeborg Museum**
Hovedgårdsvej 7. 📞 86 82 14 99.
⏰ Oct–Apr: noon–4pm Sat & Sun; May–Sep: 10am–7pm daily. 🅿️

Herning ❼

Road map C4. 🏠 30,000. 🚊 🚌
ℹ️ Torvet 8, 96 27 22 22.

THE TOWN OF Herning was established in the late 19th century following the arrival of the railway. The **Herning Kunstmuseum** (Art Museum), exhibits works by artists such as Asger Jorn and Carl-Henning Pedersen. Another of the town's attractions, the **Danmarks Fotomuseum**, has a large collection of cameras and some imaginative displays including some holograms and a panorama of Copenhagen. **Herning Museum** has displays on the history and archaeology of the region.

🏛 **Herning Kunstmuseum**
Birk Centerpark 3.
📞 97 12 10 33.
⏰ Jan–Jun, Aug–Dec: 10am–5pm Tue–Fri, noon–5pm Sat & Sun (from 10am May & Jun); Jul: 10am–5pm daily. 🅿️

🏛 **Danmarks Fotomuseum**
Museumsgade 28. 📞 97 22 53 22.
⏰ Jan–Jun, Aug–Dec: noon–4:30pm Tue–Sun; Jul: 11am–4:30pm daily. 🅿️

🏛 **Herning Museum**
Museumsgade 32. 📞 97 12 32 66.
⏰ 10am–4:30pm Tue–Fri, 11am–4:30pm Sat & Sun. 🅿️

One of Herning's tranquil streets

Århus ❷

D ENMARK'S SECOND largest city dates back to Viking times, when a small settlement was established here. It was originally named Aros, meaning "at the mouth of the river", and due to its location on Jutland's eastern coast it became a major seaport. After the Reformation Århus grew into an important trading centre. Many merchants' houses were built as a result, and the 19th century saw the development of the harbour. The founding of a university in 1928 led to an expansion of culture and today Århus has some fine museums, as well as lively cafés and bars.

Town panorama from the Rådhus tower

Exploring Århus

Most of the town's attractions are concentrated within a small area; the only site located some distance away is Den Gamle By. Sightseeing is made easier by the Århus Pass, which gives free admission to museums, a guided tour of the Rådhus (city hall) and free use of public transport.

♫ Musikhuset

Thomas Jensens Allé 2. ⬛ 89 40 40 40. ◯ 11am–9pm daily.
Ⓦ www.musikhusetaarhus.dk
The city's concert hall opened in 1982 and is one of Denmark's foremost cultural centres. The glass-fronted building is home to several prestigious music and theatre organizations, including a symphony orchestra, the Filuren Children's Theatre and the Danish Institute of Electroacoustic Music. The building is worth visiting if only to see its vast glazed hall planted with palm trees. Regular weekend events include free concerts of classical, jazz and rock music. The centre has its own café, which often has concerts, and

a restaurant, the Richter, named after Johan Richter, the main architect of the building.

♠ Rådhus

Rådhuspladsen. ⬛ 89 40 20 00.
The modern city hall was designed by Arne Jacobsen and Erik Møller and completed in 1947. The building is a prime example of Danish Modernism. It is clad on the outside with dark Norwegian marble and topped with a rectangular clock tower, which affords a

The Rådhus with its strikingly Modernist clock tower

good view of the city. The interior has a lighter feel with spacious rooms featuring wooden and brass furnishings. The large council chamber and Civic Room are worth seeking out. The floral designs in the latter are by Albert Naur who, while working during the Nazi occupation, incorporated a series of Allied insignia into his designs. *The Human Society*, a vast mural over the Rådhus entrance, is by Hagedorn Olsen.

🏛 Vikingemuseet

Sankt Clemens Torv. ⬛ 89 42 11 00.
◯ 10am–4pm Mon–Wed, Fri, 10am–5:30pm Thu.
Situated in the basement of the Nordea Bank next to the cathedral is a museum devoted to the Viking era. The prime exhibit is a section of archaeological excavation that was conducted in Clemens Torv. Fragments of the original Viking ramparts, discovered in 1964, are on display along with items dating from 900 to 1400 including a skeleton, a reconstructed house, wood-working tools and pottery. Similar discoveries at nearby Store Torv have confirmed the importance of Århus as a major centre of Viking culture on the Jutland peninsula.

🔒 Domkirke

Bispetorv. ⬛ 86 20 54 00.
◯ Oct–Apr: 10am–3pm Mon–Fri; May–Sep: 9:30am–4pm daily.
Århus's main place of worship is at the heart of the city's oldest district. The cathedral was built in 1201 but destroyed by fire in the 14th century. It was rebuilt in the late 15th century in a Gothic style and enlarged and extended by 20 m (66 ft). It is easily Denmark's longest cathedral with a nave that spans nearly 100 m (328 ft). Until the end of the 16th century most of the cathedral walls were covered with frescoes. During the Reformation these were whitewashed over, but many have since been restored. The five-panel altarpiece dates from 1479 and is the work of Bernt Notke of Lübeck. The Baroque pipe

organ dates from 1730, while the gilded baptismal font dates from the mid-15th century.

🏛 Kvindemuseet

Domkirkeplads 5. 📞 86 13 61 44. ◯ Sep–May: 10am–4pm Tue–Sun; Jun–Aug: 10am–5pm daily. 🖼 W www.kvindemuseet.dk

The Women's Museum, located in a former police station, has made a name for itself with its imaginative temporary exhibitions relating to women's issues – past and present. Since 1982 the museum has been collecting

Figure from Bernt Notke's altarpiece

objects, photographs and documents illustrating the many changes that have taken place over the centuries in the lives of women in Danish society.

🛕 Vor Frue Kirke

Frue Kirkeplads. 📞 86 12 12 43. ◯ May–Aug: 10am–4pm Mon–Sat; Sep–Apr: 10am–2pm Sun–Fri, 10am–noon Sat. W www.aarhusvorfrue.dk

This church consists of three parts. The oldest section is the 11th-century Romanesque stone crypt, which was

VISITORS' CHECKLIST

Road map D4. 🚶 255,000. 🚏 🚌 ℹ Rådhuset (1st floor). Park Allé, 86 12 16 00. 🎷 Århus International Jazz Festival (2nd half of Jul). W www.visitaarhus.com

discovered in the 1950s during restoration work. Its vault rests on a dozen or so stone arches. Built above it is the main church whose star adornment is a 16th-century wooden altarpiece carved by Claus Berg.

🏚 Den Gamle By

Viborgvej 2. 📞 86 12 31 88. ◯ Jan: 11am–3pm daily; Feb–Mar, Nov–Dec: 10am–4pm daily; Apr–May, Sep–Oct: 10am–5pm daily; Jun–Aug: 9am–4pm daily. 🖼 W www.dengamleby.dk

This open-air museum consists of 75 or so Danish buildings including shops, workshops, a mayor's house, a post office and a school as well as a theatre and a windmill. Covering the period from the Middle Ages to the 1900s, the overall effect is to recreate a typical Danish mercantile town and the way of life of its inhabitants.

The 11th-century crypt of Vor Frue Kirke

ÅRHUS CITY CENTRE

Domkirke ④
Kvindemuseet ⑤
Musikhuset ①
Rådhus ②
Vikingemuseet ③
Vor Frue Kirke ⑥

0 m   200
0 yards   200

KEY

ℹ Tourist information

🛕 Church

🅿 Parking

⊠ Post office

Harbour with Ringkøbing Fjord in the background

Ringkøbing Fjord ❽

Road map B4. 🚌 *Ringkøbing, Torvet, 70 22 70 01.*
W www.ringkobingfjord.dk

A THIN STRIP of land some 35 km (22 miles) long separates Ringkøbing Fjord from the North Sea. This sandy spit is about 1 km (half a mile) wide and has a large number of summer cottages tucked amongst the dunes. The only water access between the sea and Ringkøbing Fjord is through a channel and lock in the town of Hvide Sande. Ringkøbing Fjord is popular with windsurfers and the calm waters of the bay are suitable for novices; the North Sea on the other side of the spit offers more challenging conditions.

On the bay's northern shore is **Ringkøbing**, which is the largest town in this region. Ringkøbing was once a sea-port but over the centuries the entrance from the bay to the sea shifted southwards and the town became an inland harbour. Standing in Torvet, the town's main square, are some of the most historic buildings including Hotel Ringkøbing, a timbered building that dates from 1600. The local museum exhibits various objects that are associated with 20th-century explorations of Greenland.

The locality includes many attractions. **Fiskeriets Hus** (House of Fisheries) at Hvide Sande contains an aquarium with fish and shellfish from the North Sea and fjord waters as well as displays on the area's fishing industry. A paved footpath, suitable for wheelchair users, leads from the museum to **Troldbjerg**, Hvide Sande's main viewpoint. The mast at the top was once used by sailors to warn them about water levels. Another good view is from the 60-m (197-ft) high lighthouse on the Nøre Lyngvig dune, 5 km (3 miles) north of Hvide Sande.

A different kind of scenery can be found on the southern shores of Ringkøbing Fjord, where the marshes form **Tipperne Nature Reserve**, one of Denmark's most important sites for waterfowl. Access has been restricted to a few hours on Sunday mornings so as not to disturb the migrating birds. The reserve contains an observation tower and a small museum. Skjern-Egvad Museum on the eastern shores of the fjord can arrange visits.

Givskud Zoo ❾

Road map C4. Løveparken Givskud Zoo 📞 75 73 02 22.
⏰ *daily: mid-Apr–mid-Jun: 10am–6pm; mid-Jun–early Aug: 10am–8pm; mid-Aug–Sep: 10am–6pm; Oct–mid-Mar: 10am–5pm.* ♿
W www.givskudzoo.dk

A SHORT WAY north of Jelling is Givskud Zoo (sometimes referred to as Løveparken), home to the largest pride of lions in Scandinavia. When the park was established in 1969 the pride had 29 members; today it has over 40. In addition to the lions, Givskud has about 1,000 other animals representing 120 species. Givskud is part-zoo, part-safari park and many of the animals are left to wander freely within their allocated areas. Car drivers can travel along marked routes. Visitors on foot can enjoy a safari by bus. For obvious reasons, no one should step out of the car or bus while on safari.

Bust of Jacob Hansen, Givskud Zoo's founder

The lions are the most popular sight but there is no denying the appeal of the giraffes, zebras, buffalos, ostriches and other species that inhabit the park. One of the zoo's other attractions is the gorilla enclosure; the family of apes was brought over from Copenhagen's zoo in 2001.

Fenced-off areas provide children with the opportunity to stroke some of the park's

Small herd of zebra wandering freely in Givskud Zoo

Ancient burial mounds in Jelling

more domesticated animals or have fun feeding the camels.

Givskud Zoo is not only a family attraction but also a major scientific establishment. A third of the species at the park are endangered. One of Givskud's programmes resulted in deer and antelope reared at the park being re-introduced into the wilds of Pakistan in the late 1980s.

Jelling ❿

Road map C4. 👥 *2,500.* 🚌
ℹ️ *Gormsgade 23, 75 87 23 50.*
🎭 *Viking Fair (Aug).*
🌐 www.visitvejle.dk

FOR THE DANES Jelling is a special place: this unnassuming village served as the royal seat of Gorm the Old, a 10th-century Viking who conquered Jutland and then Funen and Zealand to create a new state. The dynasty he established has ruled Denmark continuously to this day.

Although no trace is left of the old royal castle, **Jelling Kirke** and the two burial mounds beyond it have revealed much of Denmark's ancient history. The church was built in about 1100, but it is now known that the site was occupied far earlier than this by at least three wooden churches. The first of these was, according to legend, built by Gorm's son, Harald I (Bluetooth) who came to the throne in 950 and adopted Christianity a short time afterwards. For a long time it was believed that the two knolls outside the church contained the remains of Denmark's first ruler but when they were excavated in

the 19th century nothing was found. In the late 1970s, however, archaeologists began a series of digs beneath Jelling Kirke and found the remains of the three earlier wooden churches, along with Viking jewellery and human bones. Forensic examinations, conducted at Copenhagen's Nationalmuseet, concluded that the bones were indeed those of Gorm and in the year 2000, in the presence of the current royal family, the remains were reburied under the floor of Jelling's church. It is likely that Gorm was moved by his son Harald I as an act of piety so that his remains might reside in a Christian shrine. Close to the church are two runic stones. The larger one, known as the "Danes' baptism certificate", was erected in 983 by Harald I, in memory of his parents – Gorm and Thyra. Still visible on the stone is a picture of

Runic stone in Jelling

Christ – the oldest representation of Christ in Scandinavia. The stone's inscription proclaims that "Harald king ordered this monument to be erected to Gorm his father and Thyra his mother for the glory of Denmark". This inscription is considered to be the first written record in which the word "Denmark" appears. In 1994 the entire complex was declared a UNESCO World Heritage Site.

Kongernes Jelling, an exhibition centre opposite the church is devoted to the history of the Vikings and the establishment of the Danish monarchy.

Jelling's atmosphere can best be enjoyed during the annual Viking Fair. This weekend-long event is popular with many Danes, some of whom take it as an opportunity to dress up as Vikings and parade through the streets of the town.

Another reminder of Denmark's past can be found at Fårup lake where a replica of a Viking ship takes visitors on cruises of the lake.

⛪ **Jelling Kirke**
🕐 *8am–5pm Mon–Fri, 8am–2pm Sat.*
🏛 **Kongernes Jelling**
🕐 *Jan, Oct–Dec: 1–4pm Tue–Fri; Feb–Apr: 1–4pm Tue–Sun; May–mid-Jun: 10am–4pm Tue–Sun; mid-Jun–end Aug: 10am–5pm daily; Sep: 10am–4pm Tue–Sun.* ♿

Runic writing including the oldest record of the name "Denmark"

LEGOLAND® ⑪

L EGO®, known and loved by children throughout the world, was invented in the 1930s by Ole Kirk Christensen. The amusement park was opened in 1968 and receives one and a half million visitors a year. Its attractions include amazingly detailed miniature versions of cities as well as famous landmarks constructed entirely from plastic LEGO® bricks. In addition there are thrilling rides, miniature trains and water chutes.

A LEGO® figure greets visitors

Imagination Zone
Hands-on fun is the main theme of this area. Among the activities are an interactive musical fountain and the chance to build a robot.

DUPLO® Land is for the youngest children.

★ **Miniland**
Over 20 million LEGO® bricks were used to construct famous buildings, airports, trains and even African animals. Each year new structures are added.

Entrance

LEGO® Train
Miniland can be explored aboard a train or viewed from a revolving platform that gradually ascends to the top of a tower.

Round the World Voyage
The famous LEGO® structures include the Statue of Liberty and can be seen while cruising in a miniature boat.

★ X-treme Racers
*This popular 400-m
(1,312-ft) roller coaster
negotiates bends at 60 km/h
(37 mph) and provides thrill
seekers with a hair-raising
experience.*

Jungle Rally
*Visitors who are too young
to try Adventure Land's more
breathtaking attractions can
race around in these small
electric cars.*

VISITORS' CHECKLIST

Road map C4. **☎** 75 33 13 33.
☐ Jul–mid-Aug: 10am–9pm
(rides until 8pm); Jun–early Jul,
2nd half Aug: 10am–8pm (rides
until 6pm); Mar–May, Sep–Oct:
10am–6pm daily. **⬤**
W www.legoland.dk

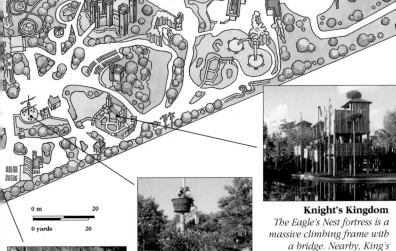

Knight's Kingdom
*The Eagle's Nest fortress is a
massive climbing frame with
a bridge. Nearby, King's
Castle offers a ride through
its medieval interior, complete
with sounds and smells.*

Merry-go-rounds
*Many rides in LEGOLAND®,
such as the merry-go-rounds
in Pirateland, are aimed at
younger children.*

0 m	20
0 yards	20

Pirateland
*The curious can meet LEGO®
pirates and make friends
with Captain Roger and his
talking parrot.*

STAR ATTRACTIONS

★ Miniland

★ X-treme Racers

Vindmølle, a Vejle landmark with a flour milling museum

Vejle ⑫

Road map B4. ⚄ 55. 🚊 🚌
🛈 Banegårdspladsen 6, 75 82 19 55.
ⓦ www.visitvejle.com

THE HARBOUR TOWN of Vejle makes a good base for visiting LEGOLAND® (see pp188–9) and the burial mounds at Jelling (see p187). Aside from these nearby attractions, its main point of interest is Sankt Nicolai Kirke, a Gothic church dating from the 13th century. Inside the church, resting in a glass-lidded coffin, is the mummified body of a woman. The body was discovered in 1835 in a nearby peat bog and nick-named Queen Gunhilde, the legendary queen of the Vikings. However, recent forensic examinations have revealed that the woman lived during the Iron Age around 450 BC. Another curiosity of the church, though they can't be seen, are the 23 skulls hidden in its walls, which belonged to 23 robbers executed in 1630.

Rådhustorvet, Vejle's main square, contains the town hall. It stands on the site of a Dominican monastery and its medieval bell can be heard ringing each day from the tower. The **Vejle Museum** is spread over a number of locations in town and beyond. The main venue is a short way northwest of Rådhustorvet housed in Den Smidtske Gard, an early 19th-century burgher's residence. The exhibition

covers 800 years of Vejle's history. On the edge of town, Vejle Vindmølle is also part of the museum. Built in 1890 and operational until 1960, the windmill houses an exhibition devoted to flour milling.

While in Vejle it is also possible to visit the Ecolarium. Set out over five floors, the centre aims to raise awareness of environmental issues and the potential of alternative energy.

🏛 **Vejle Museum**
Den Smidtske Gard. Søndergarde 14.
📞 75 82 43 22. 🕐 11am–4pm Tue–Sun. 🎫 ⓦ www.vejlemuseum.dk

Esbjerg ⑬

Road map B5. ⚄ 85,000. 🚊 🚢
🚌 🛈 Skolegade 33, 75 12 55 99.
🎪 Rock Festival (Jun); Esbjerg Festival Week (Aug), Chamber Music (Aug).
ⓦ www.visitesbjerg.com

WHEN Prussia invaded the southern part of Jutland in 1864 Denmark lost the regions of Schleswig and Holstein. As a result, the former fishing village of Esbjerg began to develop into a harbour from which Jutland's farmers and producers could export goods. Today it is Denmark's largest commercial port and a centre for North Sea oil operations.

Seals, a favourite sight at Esbjerg's aquarium

Because of its 19th-century origins, Esbjerg lacks a medieval district. Nevertheless, it has several places worth visiting. For years the town's main symbol was its **Vandtårnet** (Water Tower), which was erected in 1897. Today, it serves as an observation platform, from which there is a panoramic view of the town. Close to the tower is the Musikhuset (Concert Hall) designed by Jørn Utzon and built in 1997.

Esbjerg Museum presents an historical portrait of the town and also has a large collection of amber. The **Fiskeri-og Søfartsmuseet** (The Fisheries and Maritime Museum), 4 km (2 miles) northwest of Esbjerg's centre, contains a large aquarium and various marine-related displays. Most of the sea life in the aquarium comes from the North Sea. Its most popular inhabitants are the seals. This vast museum complex also features a collection of navigation instruments and model vessels, a number of fishing boats placed outside the building, a reconstructed coastal lifeboat station and an authentic World War II bunker.

Outside the museum grounds, on the seashore, are four 9-m (30-ft) tall snow-white stylised

Exhibition room in Esbjerg's Fiskeri-og Søfartsmuseet

figures of seated men, which were unveiled in 1995. The sculpture is entitled *Man Meets the Sea* and was created by Svend Wiig Hansen to mark the city's centennial. The maritime theme continues in Esbjerg harbour where the 20th-century **Horns Rev Lightship** is moored.

🏛 Vandtårnet
Havnegade 22. 【 75 12 78 11. ◯ Jun–mid-Sep: 10am–4pm daily. 🈂

🏛 Esbjerg Museum
Torvegade 45. 【 75 12 78 11. ◯ 10am–4pm. ⬤ Sep–May: Mon. 🈂

🏛 Fiskeri-og Søfartsmuseet
Saltvandsakvariet Tarphagevej 2–6.
【 76 12 20 00. ◯ Sep–Jun: 10am–5pm daily; Jul–Aug: 10am–6pm daily. 🈂

🏛 Horns Rev Lightship
◯ Jun–Aug: 10am–4pm Mon–Fri. 🈂

Ribe ⓮

Road map B5. 🏘 18,000. 🚉 🚌
🛈 Torvet 3, 75 42 15 00.
ⓦ www.visitribe.com

Scandinavia's oldest town is also one of the best preserved and contains many fine buildings including a medieval cathedral and a 16th-century schoolhouse. The medieval centre is beautifully preserved and features a maze of cobbled streets lined with crooked, half-timbered houses.

Ribe was once a seaport. With the passage of time the mouth of the river that flows through it became silted up, and now the town is quite a way from the seashore.

In 856 it was visited by the missionary Ansgar, known locally as the Apostle of Scandinavia. He built a small wooden church in Ribe, intending it to be a base for clergymen arriving here from Germany.

In the 10th century Ribe became a bishopric, and in the mid-12th century acquired an impressive cathedral, which still stands today. **Ribe**

Nave of Ribe Domkirke

Domkirke is built of a soft porous rock called tufa that was quarried near Cologne. The most prominent entrance, used by the bishops, is on the south side of the church. This entrance features a 13th-century "Cat's Head" doorway that got its name from the knocker made in the shape of a lion's head. Another feature of the portal is the pediment portraying Jesus and Mary – positioned at their feet are the images of Valdemar II and his wife Dagmar who died in childbirth in 1212. To this day at noon and 3pm the cathedral bells chime the tune of a folk song dedicated to the queen. The most notable features of the church's interior are the 16th-century frescoes and the modern mosaics created by Carl-Henning Pedersen. The left wing of the transept contains a marble floor slab from the tomb of Christoffer I, who died in 1259 and is laid in the adjacent sarcophagus. It is thought to be the oldest royal tombstone in Scandinavia. Stunning views can be obtained from the top of the 14th-century tower.

The night watchman in Ribe

Det Gamle Rådhus, opposite the cathedral's southeast corner, was built in 1496. The town hall's museum

has a small collection of medieval objects including some gruesome instruments of torture and executioners' swords. From here it is not far to the river, where the Stormflodssøjlen (Flood Column) indicates the floods that have submerged the town. Moored along the jetty is a replica of the *Johanne Dan*, a windjammer dating from 1867.

Ribe has two Viking museums. Standing opposite the railway station, on Odyna square, is **Ribes Vikinger** where the market-town atmosphere of late 8th-century Ribe is recreated. The **Vikingecenter**, 3 km (2 miles) south of the town centre, is an open-air museum that offers a portrait of Ribe during the Viking era.

⚓ Ribe Domkirke
Albert Skeelsgade 11. 【 75 42 02 48. ◯ Nov–Mar: 11am–3pm daily; Apr & Oct: 11am–4pm daily; May–Sep: 10am–5pm daily. 🈂

🏛 Det Gamle Rådhus
Von Støckens Plads. 【 76 88 11 22.
◯ Jun–Aug 1–3pm daily; May & Sep: 1–3pm Mon–Fri. 🈂

🏛 Ribes Vikinger
Odin Plads 1. 【 77 88 11 22.
◯ Jul–Aug: 10am–6pm daily; Sep–Oct & Apr–Jun: 10am–4pm daily; Nov–Mar: 10am–4pm Tue–Sun. 🈂

🏛 Ribe Vikingecenter
Lustrupvej 4. 【 75 41 16 11.
◯ May–Jun, Sep: 10am–3:30pm, Jul–Aug: 11am–5pm. 🈂

Half-timbered houses, adding to the charm of Ribe

Palisade by Rømø dyke

Rømø ⑮

Road map B5. 🏔 *850.* 🚌
🈁 *Tvismark, Havnebyvej 30, 74 75 51
30.* Ⓦ *www.romo.dk*

THE LARGEST Danish island
in the North Sea, Rømø
was a prosperous whaling
base in the 18th century. Its
western shores are fringed
with wide stretches of beach.
The island is connected to
Jutland by a causeway that
passes through marshland
rich in birdlife.

In the village of **Toftum** is
Komandørgaard (Captain's
House), which dates from
1748. The house, which now
serves as a museum, has a
thatched roof and some
original interior décor,
including wall coverings
consisting of 4,000 Dutch
tiles. Close by is an 18th-
century school. A short
distance further north, in the
hamlet of **Juvre**, is a
whale jawbone fence
constructed in 1772.
In **Kirkeby**, next to
the walls that
surround the Late-
Gothic church, are
whalers' gravestones
that were brought
back from Greenland.
The histories of
captains and their
families have been
carved by local artists.

The main point of
interest at the south
end of the island is
Havneby, which has
an amusement park
and a mechanical
dolls' museum. A ferry
goes from here to the
tranquil island of Sylt,
just to the southwest.

Tønder ⑯

Road map B5. 🏔 *8,200.* 🚃 🚌
🈁 *Torvet 1, 74 72 12 20.* 🎭 *Tønder
Festival (Aug).* Ⓦ *www.tdr-turist.dk
or www.visit-tonder.dk*

IN THE Middle Ages Tønder
was a major fishing port.
During subsequent centuries it
became the centre of a lace-
making industry, which is now
commemorated by a
lace-makers' festival
held every three
years. Examples of
fine lace and the
sophisticated tools
used in its production
are on display in the
Tønder Museum.
During the 17th and
18th centuries Tønder
also produced
ceramics that were
used as wall tiles.
Some of these can be seen in
the museum. Tønder's town

**Font in Haderslev
Domkirke**

centre is a pleasant place to
explore and the narrow streets
contain many houses with
decorative doorways and
picturesque gables and
window shutters. The best-
known house is Det Gamle
Apotek (The Old Pharmacy),
at Østergade 1, which has a
Baroque doorway dating from
1671. The market square
contains a 16th-century Rådhus
(town hall). Also in the square
is the 16th-century Kristkirken,
which has some fine paintings
and carvings.

🏛 **Tønder Museum**
Kongeveg 51. 🚹 *Jun–Aug:
10am–5pm daily; Sep–May:
10am–5pm Tue–Sun.* 🅿

Sønderborg ⑰

Road map C5. Als. 🏔 *30,000.* 🚃
🚌 🈁 *Rådhustorvet 7, 74 42 35 55.*
Ⓦ *www.sonderborg.dk*

SØNDERBORG,
meaning "South
Castle", is on the
island of Als. It owes
its name to a castle
fortress built by
Valdemar I in 1170.
Over the centuries
the castle served a
variety of purposes.
Christian II was held
prisoner here for 17
years in the early
16th century. Later on it was
used in turns as a warehouse,
a hospital, a prison and as a
military barracks. Today, it
houses the **Museum of
Southern Jutland** containing
exhibits on themes such as
the area's maritime history
and the German occupation
of Denmark.

The town's turbulent history
is brought to life at the
**Historiecenter Dybbøl
Banke** which is situated near
Sønderborg, close to the
village of Dybbøl. In the
spring of 1864 this area was
the scene of a fierce and
protracted battle between
Danish and Prussian forces.
Dybbøl Mølle, a windmill that
was damaged during the
fighting, is now regarded as
a national symbol. As a result
of Denmark's defeat
Sønderborg was destroyed

Doorway of a house in Østergade, Tønder

and southern Jutland was incorporated into Prussia and later into Germany (the territory was returned in 1920).

🏛 Museum of Southern Jutland
Slotsbakken. 📞 74 42 25 39.
🕙 10am–5pm daily. 📷
🏛 Historiecenter Dybbøl Banke
Dybbøl Banke 16. 📞 74 48 90 00.
🕙 mid-Apr–Sep: 10am–5pm daily. 📷

Haderslev ⑱

Road map C5. 🏠 25,000. 🚌
ℹ Honnørkajen 1, 74 52 55 50.
🌐 www.haderslev-turist.dk

THE PRESENT-DAY capital of southern Jutland is situated between a narrow fjord and a lake that was formed by the construction of a dam. In the 13th century Haderslev was a market town and its historic centre contains many period buildings.

During the Reformation Haderslev was a major centre of Protestantism and in 1526 it became the site of the first Protestant theological college. The town's main place of worship is Haderslev Domkirke. This cathedral was built in the 13th century but has been remodelled many times. It boasts a magnificent altarpiece featuring a 14th-century crucifix and alabaster statues of the apostles.

The most enchanting of the town's buildings are on Torvet, a square flanked by

Interior of the 13th-century cathedral in Haderslev

Courtyard at Koldinghus castle

half-timbered houses. From here it is easy to find the **Haderslev Museum**, which has exhibits on the archaeological history of the area, a local-history collection and a mini open-air museum.

🏛 Haderslev Museum
Dalgade 7. 📞 74 52 75 66. 🕙
Jun–Aug: 10am–4pm Tue–Sun;
Sep–May: 1–4pm Tue–Sun. 📷

Kolding ⑲

Road map C5. 🏠 59,000.
🚌 🚌 ℹ Akseltorv 8, 76 33 21 00.

KOLDING IS close to the bridge that links Jutland to Funen. The town's most important historic building is Koldinghus – a mighty castle that has a distinctive square tower with a flat roof (called the Heroes' Tower). The first fortress on this site was built in 1268 but the oldest surviving walls date from about 1440. More of the castle's history can be learned at the **Museet på Koldinghus**. Kolding's main square is Akseltorv, which contains one of the town's most beautiful buildings, the Renaissance Borchs Gård dating from 1595. The **Kunstmuseet Trapholt** on the town's eastern outskirts has a collection of Danish modern art.

🏛 Museet på Koldinghus
Adelgade 1. 📞 76 33 81 00.
🕙 10am–5pm daily. 📷
🏛 Kunstmuseet Trapholt
Æblehaven 23.
📞 76 33 81 00
🕙 10am–5pm daily. 📷

Fredericia ⑳

Road map C5. 🏠 36,000.
🚌 🚌 ℹ Danmarksgade 2A, 75 92 13 77.
🌐 www.visitfredericia.dk

FREDERIK III decided to build Fredericia on this strategic section of the Lille Bælt (Little Belt) in 1650. In 1657 the fortress town was captured by the Swedes who slaughtered the entire garrison stationed here. In 1849, during the Schleswig conflict, it was the scene of a battle fought by the Danes against the advancing Prussian army. Special ceremonies are held in Fredericia on the anniversary of that event; a daily reminder of it is the Landsoldaten monument by the Prince's Gate. The Danes killed in the battle were buried in a communal grave in the local cemetery. The town ramparts remain from the original fortress. The best section is by Danmarksgade, where the grassy embankments reach 15 m (49 ft) in height. The nearby water tower dates from 1909 and provides the best view of the surrounding area. **Fredericia Museum** has displays relating to the town's military and civilian history. Madsby Park, a short way outside the boundaries of the old town, contains a miniature version of Fredericia.

Coat of arms on gate in Fredericia

🏛 Fredericia Museum
Jernbengade 10. 📞 72 10 69 80.
🕙 May–Aug: 11am–4pm daily;
Sep–Apr: noon–4pm Tue–Sun. 📷

Man Meets the Sea, **sculpture outside Esbjerg** ▷

Northern Jutland

VISITORS TO NORTHERN JUTLAND *can enjoy beautiful scenery and peace. Remote from Denmark's main tourist attractions, this part of Jutland is sparsely populated. Aalborg is the area's only large city and for the most part the diverse landscape is made up of farmland and fields, heathland and dunes. There are a number of places to visit including a Viking burial ground at Lindholm Høje.*

The least populated and the wildest part of this region is its northern end where numerous coves make up the Limfjord straits. This part of the country provides excellent nesting grounds for a variety of birds. On the northwestern side, facing Skagerrak, the scenery is dominated by dunes, which display the clear effects of frequent sea breezes that shift the sand by up to 10 m (33 ft) each year.

Many visitors embark on trips to Grenen, Denmark's northernmost point, which is washed over by the waters of the Baltic and the North Sea. This area is sometimes referred to as the "Land of Light" and enjoys more hours of sunshine than anywhere else in Denmark. The extraordinary light has long been appreciated by artists, who came here in search of inspiration in the 19th century. Many settled around Skagen which became a magnet for prominent painters and writers who formed the Skagen School.

Another distinct feature of northern Jutland's landscape are its heathlands. As recently as the mid-19th century they covered one third of this region; now they can be seen only here and there. Northern Jutland also boasts Rold Skov, Denmark's largest forest, which forms part of Rebild Bakker, the country's only national park.

The most important of the area's historic sights are the Lindholm Høje prehistoric cemetery and the 1,000-year-old Viking fortress at Fyrkat, which has a replica Viking farmstead.

Some of Denmark's best beaches can also be found in northern Jutland and there are many holiday cottages and camp sites in the area.

Renaissance palace in Voergård

◁ **Lindholm Høje – the largest Viking burial ground in Scandinavia**

Exploring Northern Jutland

Aalborg makes a good base for exploring this part of the country, while smaller towns such as Thisted, Løgstør, Mariager or Skagen can also serve as good jumping-off points. When heading north, it is best to travel by car, since many of the most attractive areas are some distance from each other, and there may be problems with finding public transport. Even when travelling by car it pays to allow plenty of time as many roads are fairly minor and pass through villages. The advantage of travelling on these minor routes is that the scenery is varied and offers a portrait of Denmark quite different from any seen from motorways.

Viking enthusiast sharpening a blade in the village of Fyrkat

View of the cathedral from the shore of the lake in Viborg

SIGHTS AT A GLANCE

HANSTHOLM

FJERRITS

LØG

THISTED

LIMFJORDEN

Limfjorden **9**

NYKØBING
MORS

JESPERHUS

Nissum Bredning

SKIVE

LEMVIG

STRUER

HJERL HEDES FRILANDSMUSEUM **11**

MØNSTE **13**

Nissum Fjord

HOLSTEBRO **10**

KONGENSHUS MINDEPARK **12**

Herning

Herning

Esbjerg

Ringkøbing

0 km   20

0 miles   20

GETTING AROUND

The major transport artery of the region is the E45 motorway, running from the south of Jutland all the way to Frederikshavn. The larger towns of the region are all accessible by train. The main ferry harbours are in Frederikshavn and Hirtshals.

HIRTSHALS
2

Uggerbyå
40

55

FREDERIKSHAVN
4

HJØRRING
35

LØKKEN ●
55

E 39

SÆBY
5

ÅRUP 1

BRØNDERSLEV ●

VOERGÅRD SLOT
6

Læsø

VST
11

LINDHOLM
HØJE
7

8 *AALBORG*

E 45

187

595

E 45

507

541

13

REBILD
BAKKER
15

180

541

MARIAGER
16

HOBRO ●

FYRKAT
17

E 45

507

GAMMEL
ESTRUP
19

13

RANDERS
18

BORG

16

→ *Grenå*

Guden

26

46

↙ *Århus*   ↓ *Århus*

KEY

▨	Motorway
▨	Major road
▨	Scenic route
═	Other road
═	River
☀	Viewpoint

Former Carmelite monastery in Sæby

Fårup Sommerland, a vast amusement park

Fårup ❶

Road map C2. **ℹ** Pirupvejen 147,
98 88 16 00. **◐** mid-May–end of
Jun: 10am–6pm daily; Jul: 10am–8pm
daily; Aug: 10am–6pm daily. **[symbol]**
W www.faarupsommerland.dk

Fårup Sommerland is an amusement park set amid forests and heathlands, between Saltum and Blokhus. The park's history is linked with the Krageland family of merchants, who ran a wholesale business in Aalborg. When in the early 1970s the chain stores went into decline, the Kragelands switched their energy to creating a place that would combine relaxation with amusement. In June 1975 Fårup opened its doors for the first time. Among the thrills and spills on offer are water chutes, white-water rafting and roller-coasters. In addition, there are gentler attractions for younger visitors.

Hirtshals ❷

Road map C1. **[symbol]** 15,000. **[symbols]**
ℹ Nørregade 40, 98 94 22 20.

Towards the end of the 19th century Hirtshals was no more than a small fishing hamlet; now it is one of Jutland's major ports. Regular ferry links with the Norwegian towns of Kristiansand, Oslo and Moss make this small town an important bridge with Denmark's Scandinavian

neighbours on the other side of Kattegat. The town has a thriving fishing harbour and every day, at 7am, it becomes the venue for auctioning the night's catch.

The greatest attraction by far is the **Nordsømuseet**, a sea-life centre that is situated about 1 km (half a mile) east of the town centre. Since it's opened in 1984 the oceanarium has attracted thousands of visitors every year. Its vast tank contains 4.5 million litres (990,000 gallons) of water, making it one of Europe's biggest aquariums. The aquarium includes an amphitheatre that looks onto a huge glass pane that is 8 m (26 ft) high and 45 cm (18 inches) thick. The fish include schools of herring and mackerel as well as sharks. A diver enters the tank every day at 1pm to feed the fish.

As well as the aquarium, the Nordsømuseet has numerous displays that explain about the issues surrounding fishing in the North Sea and the ecology of the region. Outside is a seal pool, which has regular feed times at 11am and 3pm.

Huge aquarium at Nordsømuseet, Hirtshals

To keen ramblers and cyclists Hirtshals offers a network of walking and cycling trails, including one leading to a 57-m (187-ft) tall lighthouse and also to Husmoderstrand – a clean beach with many safe places for children to play and swim.

Hirtshals Museum is in a former fishermen's cottage that dates from 1880. This has an exhibition of everyday objects illustrating the lifestyle of the local population in the early 20th century.

➤ Nordsømuseet
Willemoesvej. **[** 98 94 44 44.
◐ Jul–Aug: 10am–8pm daily;
Sep–Jun: 10am–5pm daily. **[symbol]**
W www.nordsoe-museet.dk

Grenen, where the Baltic meets with the North Sea

Grenen ❸

Road map D1. **[symbols]** **ℹ** Sankt
Laurentii Vej, Skagen, 98 44 13 77.
W www.skagen-tourist.dk

Grenen is the northernmost point of Denmark. Standing by the car park, from which a 2-km (1-mile) trail leads to the point, is the Skagen Odde Naturcenter. Designed by the Danish architect Jørn Utzon, the centre aims to enable visitors to appreciate the natural environment of this region through a series of imaginative displays utilizing sand, water, wind and light.

The environs of Grenen consist of vast sand dunes, here and there overgrown with heather. This wild landscape captivated the Danish writer Holger Drachmann (1846–1908) to such an extent that he made it his wish to be buried in the sands of Grenen. His grave can be found on one of the nearby dunes.

Skagen

THE FORMER FISHING PORT of Skagen is now a fashionable resort, full of brightly painted yellow houses and a good number of local restaurants and shops. The town's character is accurately represented by its coat of arms, which features a painter's palette in the shape of a flounder. In the late 19th century many artists flocked here in order to "paint the light" and formed what is now known as the Skagen School. Its members included the writer Holger Drachmann, and painters Anna and Michael Ancher, Peder Severin Krøyer, Lautitz Tuxen, Carl Locher, Christian Krogh and Oskar Bjørck. The Skagens Museum exhibits many of their works and it is also possible to visit the former home of Michael and Anna Ancher.

The extraordinary light, produced by the reflection of the sun's rays in the waters surrounding Skagen and the dunes, was the inspiration for the 19th-century artists arriving here from all over Denmark, as well as from Sweden and Norway.

The Skagens Museum houses a huge collection of works. Most of the paintings are of local scenes and all of the Skagen School of artists are well represented.

The fishing harbour is crowded with cutters as Skagen is still one of the major centres of fishing in northern Denmark, although much of the town's income now derives from tourism.

Brøndums Hotel was founded by Erik Brøndums in 1859. Hans Christian Andersen once stayed here and the hotel was also popular with artists, who often met in the bar at night. The Skagens Museum is in the grounds.

The Skagen artists' work is often characterized by vibrant seascapes and naturalistic portraits. The painting above, by P.S. Krøyer, depicts Anna Ancher and the artist's wife, Marie.

Michael Ancher lived for four years in Brøndums Hotel. Ancher married Anna Brøndum, stepsister of the hotel's owner, who was herself a talented artist. This 1886 portrait of Ancher is by P.S. Krøyer.

Frederikshavn ❹

Road map D1. 🏛 *30,000.* 🚊 🚢
🚌 🛈 *Skandiatorv 1, 98 42 32 66.*
🎭 *Tordenskiold Festival.*
w̅ www.frederikshavn-tourist.dk

THE MAIN international ferry
port of Jutland has a
number of historical sights.
The Krudttårnet (Gunpowder
Tower) is all that remains of a
17th-century citadel that once
guarded the port. Today the
tower houses a small military
museum. Frederikshavn Kirke
dates from the 19th century
and contains a painting by
Michael Ancher, one of the
best-known of the Skagen
School *(see p201)*. The
Bangsbo-Museet is about
3 km (2 miles) south of the
centre. This 18th-century
manor house has an eclectic
collection that includes
objects relating to the town's
history and the Danish
Resistance during World War
II. There is also a display of
artifacts made from human
hair. Perhaps the best exhibit
is a reconstructed 12th-
century Viking merchant ship.

🏛 **Bangsbo-Museet**
Dronning Margrethesvej 1. 📞 *98 42
31 11.* ☐ *Jun–Aug: 10am–5pm;
Sep–May: 10am–5pm Tue–Sun.* 🎟

Sæby ❺

Road map D1. 🏛 *18,000.* 🚊 🚌
🛈 *Krystalgade 3, 98 46 12 44.*

THE TOWN skyline is
dominated by the tower of
Vor Frue Kirke (Church of
Our Lady), which once
formed part of a 15th-century
Carmelite monastery. The
church is richly decorated
with frescoes. Its beautiful
Late-Gothic altarpiece dates
from around 1520. Next to
the church is the grave of
Peter Jakob Larssøn, a 19th-
century buccaneer who went
on to become Sæby's mayor.

Sæby has a compact centre
with half-timbered houses
and an attractive harbour. In
summer a trumpeter heralds
the end of each day, which is
followed by the ceremonial
lowering of a flag. **Sæby
Museum**, housed in the
17th-century Ørums Consul's
House, contains a 1920s
schoolroom and a
violinmaker's workshop.

ENVIRONS: A short distance
north of town is **Sæbygård**,
a beautifully preserved and
picturesque 16th-century
manor house set in the midst
of a small beech forest.

🏛 **Sæby Museum**
Algade 1–3. 📞 *98 46 10 77.*
☐ *Jun–Aug: 10am–5pm Tue–Sun;
Sep–May: 10am–5pm Tue–Fri.* 🎟

Opulent dining room in Voesgård Slot

Voergård Slot ❻

Road map D2. Flauenskjold. 📞 *98
86 71 08.* ☐ *Easter, mid-Jun–mid-
Aug: 10am–5pm daily; May–mid-Jun:
2–5pm Sat & Sun; mid-Aug–mid-Oct:
2–5pm Sat, 10am–5pm Sun; late Oct:
2–5pm Mon–Sat, 10am–5pm Sun.*
🎟 🎦 w̅ www.voergaardslot.dk

THIS RENAISSANCE castle is
one of Denmark's most
stylish buildings. Its splendid
portal was intended originally
for the royal castle of
Fredensborg. Initially the
estate was part of a religious
complex but following the
Reformation it passed into
private hands. The parts open
to visitors include the main
wing, which has a large
collection of paintings and
antiques. The collection
includes works by Raphael,
Goya, Rubens and Fragonard.
Also on display are many fine
pieces of furniture and
porcelain (including a dinner
set made for Napoleon I).

Lindholm Høje ❼

Road map C2. **Cemetery** ☐ *until
dusk.* **Museum** *Vendilavej 11.* 📞 *96
31 04 28.* ☐ *Jan–mid-Mar: 10am–
4pm (11am Tue, Sun); mid-Mar–Oct:
10am–5pm daily; Nov–Dec: 10am–
4pm Tue, 11am–4pm Sun.* 🎟

DENMARK'S largest Iron Age
and Viking cemetery has
survived so well due to a thick
layer of sand that blew over
it, burying it for many
centuries. The 4-m (13 ft)
thick sand deposit kept the
site hidden until 1952, when
archaeologists happened upon

Half-timbered house in one of Sæby's picturesque streets

it and unearthed nearly 700 graves of various shapes. The oldest ones are triangular; others are circular. Some have even been made to resemble ships. Other finds discovered in the vicinity, including traces of houses and hearths, indicate that between the 7th and 11th centuries this was a trading settlement. Lindholm Høje comes to life each year during the last week of June, when a Viking festival is held here. Throughout the rest of the year it is possible to learn about the lives of its former inhabitants by visiting the small museum by the car park.

Aalborg **8**

See pp204–5.

Limfjorden **9**

See pp206–7.

Holstebro **10**

Road map B3. *31,000.* **Den Rode Plads 14, 97 42 57 00.**

THE EARLIEST records of Holstebro can be found in 13th-century documents. The town was often plagued by fire, however, and has few historic sights. Continuing a centuries-old tradition the town bells chime every day at 10pm reminding citizens to put out fires for the night.

The Rådhus (town hall) in the centre of town is mid-19th century. Standing in front of it is a sculpture by Alberto Giacometti. The nearby

Façade of the Holstebro Kunstmuseum

Village house in Hjerl Hedes Frilandsmuseum

Neo-Gothic church is 20th century and contains the remains of a 16th-century Dutch altar.

The **Holstebro Kunstmuseum** has a sizeable collection of paintings (including works by Picasso and Matisse) as well as sculpture and ceramics, which are mainly by contemporary Danish artists.

🏛 **Holstebro Kunstmuseum**
Museumsvej 2. 97 42 45 18. Jul–Aug: 11am–5pm Tue–Sun; Sep–Jun: noon–4pm Tue–Sun.

Hjerl Hedes Frilandsmuseum **11**

Road map B3. Hjerl Hedevej 14. 97 44 80 60. Apr–Oct: 10am–5pm daily.

A SHORT WAY northeast of Holstebro is a fascinating open-air museum that recreates the development of a Danish village from 1500 to 1900. The collection of buildings includes an inn, a school, a smithy and a dairy. In summer, men and women wear period clothes

and demonstrate traditional skills such as weaving and bread-making. Children can dress in Stone Age costumes and have a go at making flint tools and pottery. Older ones can try their hand at spear fishing from a dug-out canoe.

Kongenshus Mindepark heathland reserve

Kongenshus Mindepark **12**

Road map C3. Klostermarken 12, Viborg. 87 28 10 00. mid-May–mid-Sep: 10am–6pm (Fri 11am). www.kongenshus.dk

A SMALL SECTION of Demark's uncultivated heathland, of which just 800 sq km (309 sq miles) remains, can be explored at Kongenhus Mindepark. For many years early pioneers attempted to cultivate this windswept and inhospitable area. In the 18th century an army officer from Mecklenburg leased the land from Frederik V, intending it for cultivation. Assisted by the king's generosity he built a house, which he named Kongenshus (King's House). However, the German officer abandoned the project after 12 years and returned to his homeland. The house is now a visitor centre.

Aalborg

NORTH JUTLAND's capital city is situated on the south bank of the Limfordjen. It was founded by the Vikings in the 10th century and rapidly acquired a strategic significance as a hub of trade and transport. It prospered in the 17th century thanks to a thriving herring industry and many of its finest buildings date from this time. Aalborg remains a commercial centre and is the seat of the regional government and a university town. The local industry includes the country's leading producer of Danish schnapps, *akvavit*.

Satyr sticking out its tongue toward city hall

Panoramic view of Aalborg, capital of northern Jutland

Exploring Aalborg

Aalborg consists of two parts separated from each other by Limfjord. Most of the historic buildings are clustered around the compact medieval quarter. Jomfru Ane Gade has restaurants and bars and is the centre of the city's nightlife.

🔒 Vor Frue Kirke

Niels Ebbesens Gade. ⏰ *9am–2pm Mon–Fri, 9am–noon Sat.* 🌐 www.vorfrue.dk
The Church of Our Lady dates back to the 12th century. In the 16th and 17th centuries it was the main place of Christian worship in Aalborg. It has been remodelled many times, however, and all that remains of the original building is the Gothic portal decorated with stone reliefs depicting Christ and a number of biblical scenes. The wooden crucifix seen over the presbytery entrance is 15th century. In the vicinity of the church are some cobbled streets lined with half-timbered merchants' houses. Many have been turned into shops.

⚑ Aalborghus Slot

Slotspladsen. ⏰ *8am–9pm daily.* **Dungeons** ⏰ *May–Sep: 8am–3pm Mon–Fri.* **Underground passages** ⏰ *8am–9pm daily.*
This modestly-sized castle was built on the orders of Christian III and completed in 1555. It is surrounded by deep moats. The building was never used as a royal residence, however; instead it was the office of the king's functionaries. The dank castle dungeons and underground passages leading off them make for an eerie walk.

Coat of arms from Jens Bangs Stenhus

🏛 Jens Bangs Stenhus

Østergade 9. ● *to the public.*
A Dutch Renaissance-style house, this five-storey edifice, decorated with gargoyles and floral ornaments, was built in 1624 for Jens Bang, a wealthy merchant. Its façade facing the Rådhus (city hall) includes a stone figure of a satyr sticking its tongue out – this was intended to symbolize the owner's attitude towards the city's councillors who refused to admit him into their ranks. The cellars house a wine bar that has changed little over the years.

🏛 Rådhuset

Gammel Torv 2. ● *to the public.*
The yellow-painted Baroque city hall was completed in 1762 and stands on the site of a demolished Gothic town hall. The motto written above the main door translates as "Wisdom and Determination" and was used by Frederik V, who was on the throne when the city hall was built.

Soldiers preparing for a parade, Aalborghus Slot

🏛 Budolfi Domkirke

Algade 40. ◯ *Oct–Apr: 9am–3pm Mon–Fri, 9am–noon Sat; May–Sep: 9am–4pm Mon–Fri, 9am–2pm Sat.*

The Gothic cathedral's white plastered front was built around 1400, although some of its elements originate from an earlier church. Among the notable features of the interior are portraits of wealthy merchants, a gilded Baroque altarpiece and some 16th-century frescoes. The church's patron, St Budolfi, is the patron saint of sailors whose cult was propagated by English missionaries.

Delightfully simple interior of Budolfi Domkirke

🏛 Historiske Museum

Algade 48. 📞 *96 31 04 10.* ◯ *10am–5pm Tue–Sun.* 🏷 ⓦ www.aahm.dk

Just west of the cathedral is the local history museum. Its varied collection includes archaeological finds from Lindholm Høje *(see pp202–3)* and rare glassware and ancient coins. The museum's star exhibits include a reconstructed drawing room from an early 17th-century merchant's house. Most interesting of all, perhaps, is the skeleton of a 40-year-old female discovered in a peat bog who died around AD 400.

🏛 Helligåndsklostret

C.W. Obels Plads. 📅 *late Jun–mid-Aug: 2pm Mon–Fri.* 🏷

This convent was founded in 1431 and is one of the best preserved buildings of its type in Scandinavia. The only original part is the west wing; the north and the east wings are 16th century. Guided tours allow visitors to look at the frescoes in the hospital chapel, step into the refectory with its starry vault and listen to the story of an unfortunate nun who was buried alive for maintaining a relationship with one of the monks.

Helligåndsklostret

🏛 Nordjyllands Kunstmuseum

Kong Christians Allé 50. 📞 *98 13 80 88.* ◯ *10am–5pm Tue–Sun.* 🏷 ⓦ www.nordjyllandskunstmuseum.dk

Designed by the Finnish architect Alvar Aalto, this striking museum opened in 1972 and has a great collection of Danish and European modern art including works by Asger Jorn and Picasso.

AALBORG HISTORIC CENTRE

Aalborghus Slot ②
Budolfi Domkirke ⑤
Helligåndsklostret ⑦
Historiske Museum ⑥
Jens Bangs Stenhus ③
Rådhuset ④
Vor Frue Kirke ①

| 0 m | 200 |
| 0 yards | 200 |

KEY

ℹ Tourist information

P Parking

⊠ Post office

Limfjorden ●

L IMFJORDEN IS Denmark's largest body
of inland water. Although narrow
inlets connect it to both the Kattegat
and the North Sea, Limfjorden
resembles an inland lake. It has some
good beaches and is popular as a
holiday destination in summer. Just
how significant this area was at one
time can be deduced from the many
surviving churches and castles. In the
middle is the island of Mors, whose
aerial shape resembles Jutland.
According to legend, when God
created Jutland he first built a model.
It was so good that he decided to
place it at the centre of Limfjorden.

★ Jesperhus Park
*This park is planted
with half a million
flowers. Some are
planted to form
figures of animals
found in the park zoo,
such as a crocodile.*

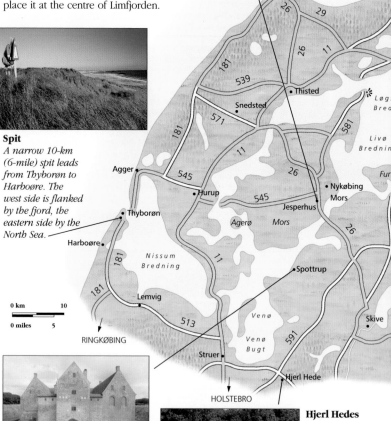

Spit
*A narrow 10-km
(6-mile) spit leads
from Thyborøn to
Harboøre. The
west side is flanked
by the fjord, the
eastern side by the
North Sea.*

★ Spøttrup Slot
*Protected against attack by a moat
and high ramparts, this medieval
castle has changed little since it
was built in 1500.*

**Hjerl Hedes
Frilandsmuseum**
*Among the many
historic buildings
at this open-air
museum are an
inn, a smithy, a
dairy, a school, a
vicarage and a
grocer's shop.*

Fjerritslev

Situated between the fjord and the North Sea, Fjerritslev is surrounded by beautiful scenery. The town brewery has been preserved as a museum.

VISITORS' CHECKLIST

Road map C2. **Aalborg** 🚆 🚌
🛈 Østergade 8, 99 30 60 90.
Nykøbing Mors 🚆 ⛴ 🚌
🛈 Havnen 4, 97 72 04 88.
W www.limfjorden.dk
W www.visitnord.dk
W www.turisme.mors.dk
W www.skive-egnen.dk

Aalborg

Northern Jutland's capital city has many interesting sights, including the superb Nordjyllands Kunstmuseum (see pp204–205).

Fjerritslev • Brovst • Aabybro
Vadum
gstør
Nibe
Aalborg
Svenstrup
Års
Farsø
Gedsted
Ålestrup
Møldrup
HOBRO
ÅRHUS
VIBORG

Nibe

For centuries this small town was associated with the herring industry and supplied fish for the royal table.

KEY

▬	Motorway
▬	Major road
▬	Other road
▬	River
⁎	Viewpoint

Lovns Bredning

This section of Limfjorden, which has some enchanting coves, is a protected area because of the rich diversity of birdlife found here.

STAR SIGHTS

★ **Jesperhus Park**

★ **Spøttrup Slot**

Mønsted's limestone mine

Mønsted ⑬

Road map C3. Mønsted Kalkgruber, Kalkværksvej 8. ☎ 86 64 60 11. ◯ Apr–Oct: 10am–5pm daily. 📷 Ⓦ www.monsted-kalkgruber.dk

AS FAR BACK as the 10th century the area around Mønsted was famous as a centre of limestone mining. The mine, which was still in operation in the 20th century, is now an unusual local attraction. Although only 2 km (1 mile) of the entire 60 km (37 miles) of its tunnels are open, a walk through the underground maze is an unforgettable experience. Visitors can wander at their own pace through the galleries, but they must wear safety helmets. In view of the mine's steady humidity and temperature, which stays at 8° C (46° C), some of the caves situated 35 m (115 ft) below the surface are used for ripening cheese.

Viborg ⑭

Road map C3. 🏘 30,000. 🚊 🚌
🛈 Nytorv 9, 87 25 30 75.
Ⓦ www.visitviborg.dk

VIBORG IS scenically located on the shores of two lakes. Its history dates back to the 8th century and it became one of Denmark's bishoprics in 1060. The 12th-century cathedral was used for

coronation ceremonies by the Danish monarchy until the 17th century. The present twin-towered Domkirke (cathedral) was completed in 1876. This huge granite building has some valuable relics as well as a crypt dating from 1130, which is all that remains of the original cathedral. Other features include a gilded altarpiece and a vast 15th-century candelabra. The cathedral's frescoes form an illustrated Bible and were created by the Danish artist Joakim Skovgaard (1901–06). Other works by the artist can be seen in the **Skovgaard Museet** next to the cathedral. The **Viborg Stiftsmuseum** (District Museum) contains exhibits relating to the town's history including some items from the Viking era.

Figures from Viborg Domkirke

🛕 Viborg Domkirke
Domkirkepladsen, Sankt Mogensgade 4. ☎ 87 25 52 50. ◯ Oct–Mar: 11am–3pm Mon–Sat, noon–3pm Sun; Apr–May, Sep: 11am–4pm Mon–Sat, noon–4pm Sun; Jun–Aug: 10am–5pm Mon–Sat, noon–5pm Sun.

🏛 Skovgaard Museet
Domkirkstræde 4. ☎ 86 62 39 75. ◯ May–Sep: 10am–12:30pm, 1:30–5pm daily; Oct–Apr: 1:30–5pm daily. 📷

🏛 Viborg Stiftsmuseum
Hjultorvet 9. ☎ 87 25 26 10. ◯ mid-Jun–Aug: 11am–5pm Tue–Sun; Sep–mid-Jun 1–4pm Tue–Fri, 11am–5pm Sat & Sun. 📷

Rebild Bakker ⑮

Map C3. 🛈 Rebild-Skørping Turistbureau, KulturStationen, 99 82 84 40. Ⓦ www.roldskovturist.dk

ROLD SKOV is the largest forest in Denmark. In 1912, after fund-raising among the Danish expatriate community in the USA, a section of it was purchased and turned into a national park covering 77 sq km (30 sq miles). An array of wildlife lives in the park, including foxes, deer, squirrels, wild boar, martens, badgers and numerous birds. The park contains a small museum and the **Lincoln Log Cabin**, which has photographs and other items relating to Danish emigration to America.

🏛 Lincoln Log Cabin
☎ 98 39 14 40. ◯ Jun: noon–4:30pm daily; Jul–Sep: 11am–5pm daily. 📷 Ⓦ www.rebild.org

Interior of the Lincoln Log Cabin, Rebild Bakker

Mariager ⑯

Road map D3. 🏘 2,500. 🚌
🛈 Torvet 18, 98 54 13 77.
Ⓦ www.visitmariager.dk

IN THE Middle Ages Mariager was a major centre of pilgrimages, owing to the nunnery that was established here in 1410. Today, it is a quiet fjord town, with cobbled streets and picturesque houses engulfed in roses. The main reminder of the convent is the church standing on a wooded hill. It is much smaller than the

**Banks of Limfjorden,
near Mariager**

original 14th-century building but it is possible to see what the convent was like from a model in **Mariager Museum**, which is housed in an 18th-century merchant's house.

At **Danmarks Saltcenter** visitors can learn about methods of salt production, produce their own crystals and take a bath in Denmark's version of the Dead Sea, which has pools filled with warm water so salty that it's quite impossible to dive beneath the surface.

🏛 **Mariager Museum**
Kirkegade 4A.
📞 98 54 12 87.
🕐 mid-May–mid-Sep: 1–5pm daily.
🏛 **Danmarks Saltcenter**
Ny Havnevej 6. 📞 98 54 18 16.
🕐 10am–6pm daily. ♿

**Small bag of salt from
Danmarks Saltcenter**

Fyrkat ⑰

Road map C3. Fyrkatvej 37B.
📞 98 51 19 27. 🕐 Easter–mid-Oct: 10am–4pm daily; Jun–Aug: 10am–5pm daily. ♿
W www.fyrkat.com
W www.vikingecenterfyrkat.com

IN 1950 the remains of a Viking settlement dating from around AD 980 were discovered in fields 3 km (2 miles) from the town of Hobro. A modern visitor centre has since been built around the site.

The entire settlement was surrounded by ramparts 120 m (394 ft) in diameter. The entry gates to the fortress, aligned strictly with the points of the compass, were linked with each other by two intersecting streets. An ancient cemetery containing 30 graves was discovered outside the main camp. One of the graves contained a skeleton of a woman buried together with her jewellery. A Viking-style farmstead north of the settlement recreates many aspects of Viking life.

Randers ⑱

Road map D3. 🏠 60,000. 🚉 🚌
ℹ Tørvebryggen 12, 86 42 44 77.
W www.visitranders.com

JUTLAND'S FOURTH largest city was already a major market town in the Middle Ages. Its most important historic sight is the 15th-century Sankt Morten's Kirke.

Hanging inside is a model of a ship dating from 1632. The three-storey Paaskesønnernes Gård nearby is late 15th century and one of the city's oldest houses. The most popular attraction is **Randers Regnskov**, an unusual tropical zoo that houses 200 animal species and 450 species of plants in a tropical rain forest environment. Here, regardless of the time of the year, the temperature remains at a constant 25° C (77° F), accompanied by very high humidity. Among the many animals kept at the zoo are crocodiles, gibbons, colourful butterflies, tapirs and snakes.

🦋 **Randers Regnskov**
Tørvebryggen 11. 📞 87 10 99 99.
🕐 Jun–mid-Aug: 10am–6pm daily; mid-Aug–May: 10am–4pm Mon–Fri, 10am–5pm Sat & Sun. ♿
W www.randers-regnskov.dk

Gammel Estrup ⑲

Road map C3. Randersvej 2. 📞 86 84 30 01. 🕐 Jan–Mar: 10am–3pm Tue–Sun; Apr–Jun, mid-Aug–Oct: 10am–5pm; Jul–mid-Aug: 10am–6pm; Nov–Dec: 10am–3pm Mon–Sat. ♿

ONE OF THE region's major attractions is the Gammel Estrup estate, near the village of Auning on the Djursland peninsula. The estate's 15th-century manor house is surrounded by a moat and provides an insight into Denmark's rural life. The house is now a museum and its interiors, complete with period furniture, paintings and tapestries, include reception rooms, bedrooms, a chapel and an alchemist's cellar. Some of the gardens and outbuildings form the Dansk Landbrugs-museum, which focuses on the estate's agricultural past and includes farm machinery and tools.

ENVIRONS: Rosenholm Slot, near Hornslet, is a 16th-century castle built on a small island in the middle of a lake. The house boasts one of Europe's largest collections of tapestries. The castle is said to be haunted by the ghost of an insane former owner.

Façade of Gammel Estrup's manor house

BORNHOLM

AR OUT IN THE BALTIC, *the idyllic island of Bornholm has an atmosphere all of its own. For years it remained relatively unknown to outsiders but the beauty of the island's sprawling beaches, its rugged coastal cliffs and distinctive architecture have made it a popular holiday destination. Tourism remains a low-key affair, however, and the villages and towns have changed little over the years.*

Bornholmers are proud of their ancestry and have their own flag and, among the older generation, a distinctive dialect that is as unique to the island as the *rundkirke* (round churches) that are found here.

The discovery of ancient burial mounds and engravings suggest that the island was inhabited by 3000 BC. At one time Bornholm was an important centre for trade, and coins have been unearthed from as far afield as Rome and the Near East. The name "Bornholm" appeared for the first time in AD 890 at a time when the island was inhabited by the Vikings.

From the mid-12th century much of Bornholm became the property of the Archbishop of the city of Lund, which at that time belonged to Denmark. For a period in the 17th century it was controlled by Sweden but the islanders' strong allegiance to Denmark resulted in a rapid withdrawal of Swedish forces. Following the surrender of Germany in May 1945 Bornholm was occupied by the Soviets until the Danish army established a permanent garrison.

Today, Bornholm has a thriving fishing industry and no visitor should leave without sampling its smoked herring, known as *bornholmers*.

A wide variety of natural habitats is found here ranging from secluded forests and pasture land to rugged cliffs and long, sandy beaches. Another of the island's assets is its climate, with mild winters and Denmark's highest percentage of sunny days. The local flora features many species typical of the Mediterranean, including orchids, figs, grapes and mulberry trees.

Svaneke's yacht marina

◁ Entrance to NaturBornholm in Åkirkeby, one of Bornholm's few modern landmarks

Exploring Bornholm

BORNHOLM HAS some good cycle paths and exploring by bicycle is both convenient and enjoyable. The northern shore is marked by steep cliffs while sandy beaches are the main feature of the south and southeast coasts. Bornholm is known for its round churches and for the atmospheric ruins at Hammershus Slot. Rønne, the island's main town, has some well-preserved quarters, as do many of the smaller harbour ports. Children will enjoy a visit to Joboland Park, which includes an aquapark and a small zoo, and Østerlars' history centre where they can see what life was like in a medieval village.

Modern power-generating windmills north of Hasle

SEE ALSO

- *Where to Stay* pp253–5.
- *Where to Eat* pp276–7.

SIGHTS AT A GLANCE

SANDVIG

HAMMERSHUS SLOT ❶ ❷ ALLINGE

TEJN

❸ OLSKER

159

158

❹ HASLE

KLEMENSKER

159

NYKER ❺

RØNNE ❻

38

❼ NYLARS

Læså

KEY

▦	Major road
▦	Scenic route
═	Other road
═	River
☀	Viewpoint

0 km   2

0 miles   2

Christiansø

The scenic coast of Bornholm

GUDHJEM
⑫

ØSTERLARS KIRKE
⑪

158

ØSTERMARIE

⑩   **SVANEKE**   ⑨

JOBOLAND

A L M I N D I N G E N   **IBSKER**

ØleÅ

158

38   **NEKSØ**

KEBY

BODILSKER

GETTING THERE

Bornholm's airport is
5 km (3 miles) southeast
of Rønne. A flight from
Copenhagen takes half an
hour. Many visitors arrive
by ferry. The journey from
Køge takes six to seven
hours (overnight ferries
are an option). As an
alternative, visitors can take
a train to Ystad in Sweden,
and pick up a ferry from
there to Rønne. Buses are
also available from Copenhagen to Ystad and cost a
little less.

One of Rønne's many colourful
half-timbered houses

Picturesque ruins of Hammershus Slot

Hammershus Slot ❶

Castle 🔲 *all year round.*
Hammershus Exhibition
Langebjergvej 26, Allinge. 🔲 *mid-Apr–mid-Oct: 10am–4pm daily;
Jun–Aug: 10am–5pm daily.* 📷

THE ATMOSPHERIC ruins of Hammershus Slot are the largest in northern Europe and stand on a 70-m (230-ft) high cliff. The castle was built in the 13th century on the orders of the Archbishop of Lund. Legend has it that Hammershus was originally to be built at a different site, but the walls erected during the day vanished each night. A change of location was thought necessary and horses were let loose; the spot where they finally stopped was chosen as the new site.

The entrance to the castle leads over a stone bridge that was once a draw-bridge. The ruins also include what remains of a brewery, a cistern, a granary and a bakery.

The impressive square tower, Manteltårnet, was used in the Middle Ages for storing the country's tax records and later served as the quarters of the castle commander and also as a prison. In 1660 Leonora Christina, daughter of Christian IV, and her husband were imprisoned in the tower, accused of collaboration with the Swedes.

Technological improvements in artillery eventually diminished Hammerhus Slot's defensive capabilities as its walls became vulnerable to attack from powerful cannons. The residing governor abandoned the castle in 1743 and much of the castle was used as building material for local homes. An exhibition includes a model of Hammerhus as it was at the peak of its might.

Allinge ❷

🏠 *2,000.* 🚌
ℹ️ *Kirkegade 4, 56 48 00 01.*

ALLINGE and nearby Sandvig, 2 km (1 mile) to the northwest, are treated as one town though the two have slightly different characters. Allinge has the majority of commercial facilities while Sandvig is quieter, with walking trails and neatly-tended gardens. Allinge's church is mostly 19th century, although the church itself grew out of a chapel erected five centuries earlier. Inside is a painting that once adorned the chapel in Hammershus Slot as well as tombstones of the castle's past commanders. On the outskirts of Allinge there is a well-kept cemetery for Russian soldiers, with a granite obelisk proudly displaying the Soviet star at the top. This is a

**Granite obelisk at
Allinge Cemetery**

reminder of the Red Army, who occupied Bornholm from the end of World War II until March 1946.

On the outskirts of Allinge is Madsebakke Helleristininger – the biggest and the most precious set of rock paintings to be found in Denmark. These simple Bronze Age drawings, depicting ships, boats and the outlines of feet, are thought to be 4,000 years old. Another local curiosity is the Moseløkken quarry, where between May and September visitors can learn all about the excavation of granite on Bornholm and even have a go at splitting a piece themselves.

12th-century three-storey round church in Olsker

Olsker ❸

🏠 *1,700.* 🚌

THE VILLAGE of Olsker, south of Allinge, has one of the best known of Bornholm's distinctive round churches. Historians once believed they were of pagan origin. This hypothesis has now been discarded and the current theory is that they were intended for defensive purposes, as well as being used for storage. This three-storey granite building is the slenderest of Bornholm's four round churches and has nine windows. It was erected in the mid-12th century in honour of St Olaf, a Norwegian king who died in 1031, and who is revered in Denmark. The hill on which the church stands affords a beautiful view of the surrounding countryside.

Round Churches

BORNHOLM'S four sparkling-white *rundkirke* (round churches) are each dedicated to a different saint. They were built between 1150 and 1200 at a time when pirate attacks were a constant threat to the island and have 2-m (7-ft) thick granite walls. Apart from the one at Nykirke, all are three-storey buildings. The bottom level was used mainly for worship.

The first floor served as a supply warehouse and also stored the church's valuables and donations received from the faithful. In times of danger the first floor also provided shelter for women and children, while the third, top level was used for surveillance and was an ideal place from which to shoot and throw stones at the advancing enemy.

Østerlars rundkirke has a central pillar 6 m (20 ft) in diameter. It is adorned with a 14th-century frieze depicting scenes from the life of Christ.

The churches are decorated with paintings dating from the 13th and 14th centuries. The most popular themes are biblical.

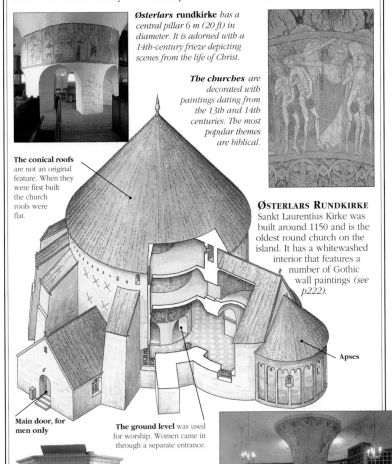

The conical roofs are not an original feature. When they were first built the church roofs were flat.

ØSTERLARS RUNDKIRKE
Sankt Laurentius Kirke was built around 1150 and is the oldest round church on the island. It has a whitewashed interior that features a number of Gothic wall paintings *(see p222)*.

Apses

Main door, for men only

The ground level was used for worship. Women came in through a separate entrance.

***Many elements of furnishing** are not as old as the churches themselves. A notable feature of Olsker's church is its richly ornamented 16th-century pulpit.*

***Top floors** were accessed by a stairway leading through narrow passages knocked out of the thick walls.*

Hasle ❹

🏃 1,800. 🚌 ℹ️ Havnegade 1, 56 96 44 81. Ⓦ www.hasle-turistbureau.dk

ONE OF Bornholm's oldest towns, Hasle is mentioned in records as early as 1149. The herring industry has long been the town's main source of revenue although many locals were once also employed in excavating brown coal until the mine closed in 1946. The town is popular with visitors, many of whom come to sample the herring from local smokehouses, which can easily be found thanks to their conspicuous chimneys. Many of the smokehouses also function as working museums, where visitors can watch the smoking process. The Silderogerierne Museum is probably the best of these and contains an exhibition illustrating the history of Hasle as well as the surrounding area.

In the centre of town stands an interesting 15th-century church with a lovely two-winged altarpiece made in Lübeck in 1520. According to one local story the altar was a gift from a sailor who miraculously escaped from a sinking ship.

A monument in the town square commemorates Peder Olsen, Jens Kofød and Porl Anker who became the local heroes of an uprising against the Swedes that erupted in Bornholm in 1658.

On the outskirts of the town, on the road leading towards Rønne, is a huge runic stone – the largest one on the island.

Nykirke's pillar with scenes from the Stations of the Cross

Nyker ❺

🏃 2,000. 🚌

THE SMALLEST of Bornholm's historic round churches (see p217) is in Nyker. It is only two storeys high and lacks external buttresses. In keeping with its name (Nykirke or New Church) it is also the most recently built of the churches. A Latin inscription found on the Late-Gothic chalice kept in the church proclaims that the church is dedicated to All Saints. Other items to look out for include the frescoes that decorate the main pillar of the church, which depict the Stations of the Cross, and a stone laid in the portico with a Resurrection scene that dates from 1648. Another interesting object is an 18th-century tablet carved with the names of the local inhabitants who died during two plagues that devastated the area in 1618 and 1654.

Rønne ❻

🏃 15,000. ✈️ 🚢 ℹ️ Nordre Kystvej 3, 56 95 95 00. 🛒 Wed, Sat. Ⓦ www.bornholm.info

ONE THIRD of Bornholm's population live in Rønne. The town has grown up around a natural harbour and two of the first buildings that can be seen when approaching from the sea are the 19th-century lighthouse and Sankt Nicolai Kirke.

Rønne has two main squares – Store Torv and Lille Torv (Big Market and Little Market). Store Torv was originally used for military parades but is now the venue for a twice-weekly market.

The Tinghus at Store Torv 1 dates from 1834 and was once used as the town hall, court-house and jail. A number of picturesque cobbled streets lead off from Store Torv and many of the early 19th-century houses are still standing, despite a series of bombing raids carried out by the Soviets in May 1945. One of Rønne's most unusual buildings is in Vimmelskaftet – its width allows for one window only. Standing at the corner of Østergade and Theaterstræde is the restored Rønne Theatre, one of the oldest theatres in Denmark, dating from 1823. **Bornholm Museum** has a good local-history section that includes archaeological finds, a small collection of paintings and a selection of 6th-century golden tablets known as *goldgubber*. Over 2,000 of these tablets engraved with small figures have been found on the island.

Distinctive white chimneys of a smokehouse in Hasle

Harbourside smithy in Rønne

The **Forsvarsmuseet** (Military Museum) is housed in a citadel south of the town centre that was built around 1650. The defensive tower houses a large collection that includes weapons, uniforms, ammunition and one of the oldest cannons in Denmark. The museum has a special section on the Soviet bombardment of Rønne in 1945.

🏛 **Bornholm Museum**
Sankt Mortensgade 29. ☎ 56 95 07 35. ◯ 10am–5pm Mon–Sat. 🌐
🏛 **Forsvarsmuseet**
Arsenalvej 8. ☎ 56 95 65 83. ◯ May: 11am–3pm Tue–Sat; Jun–Sep: 11am–5pm Tue–Sat. 🌐

Nylars ❼

SITUATED some 7 km (4 miles) east of Rønne, Nylars Rundkirke is one of Bornholm's four well-preserved round churches *(see p217)*. It was built in 1150 and is dedicated to St Nicholas, the patron saint of sailors. In order to climb the stairs to the upper levels it is necessary to squeeze through narrow passages knocked through thick walls. For invaders trying to reach the upper floor this presented a virtually insurmountable obstacle. The frescoes that adorn the distinctive pillar that rises through all three levels of the building depict biblical scenes including Adam and Eve's expulsion from the Garden of Eden.

Åkirkeby ❽

🏃 1,600. 🚍 ℹ Torvet 2, 56 97 45 20.

DURING THE Middle Ages this was the most important town on the island and the seat of Bornholm's church and the lay authorities. As a result, the 12th-century Åkirke is Bornholm's largest church. The Romanesque building contains a number of treasures including a 13th-century baptismal font and an early 17th-century pulpit. Climbing to the top of the church's 22-m (72-ft) high bell tower affords one of the best views of the town.
Åkirkeby's latest attraction is **NaturBornholm**, a state-of-the-art natural history museum situated on the southern outskirts of town. A trip to the museum takes visitors back

Denmark's national emblem, Åkirke

2,000 years and provides a fun way to learn about the flora and fauna of the island. Behind the centre is a gigantic natural fault created 400 million years ago, which marks the boundary between the continental plates of Europe and Scandinavia.

🏛 **NaturBornholm**
Grønningen 30. ☎ 56 94 04 00. ◯ mid-Mar–Oct: 10am–5pm. 🌐

Svaneke ❾

🏃 1,200. 🚍 ℹ Storegade 24, 56 49 70 79. 🚌 Sat.

IN THE 1970s this appealing town won the European Gold Medal preservation award and Svaneke continues to maintain its unspoilt historic character. A short distance south of the town centre is Svaneke Kirke. A majestic swan adorns the spire of this 14th-century church (Svaneke translates as "Swan Corner") and the image of a swan is also included in the town emblem.

In the local glass factory, Pernille Bulow, visitors can watch at close range as skilled workers produce a variety of glassware. As well as being known as one of the most photogenic towns on Bornholm, Svaneke is also famous for its windmills. These can be seen standing by each of the town's exit roads. The best preserved is the Årsdale Mølle (1877) on the road leading to Nexø. The mill is open to visitors and also sells its own flour.

Horse-drawn tram in Svaneke, a popular way to see the town

Joboland ⑩

3 km (2 miles) from Svaneke,
Højevejen 4. 📞 56 49 60 76.
🕐 May–23 Jun: 10am–6pm daily
(aquapark noon–4pm); 24 Jun–
mid-Aug: 10am–7pm daily
(aquapark noon–4pm). 📷
🔲 www.joboland.dk

THIS AMUSEMENT park has
enough entertainment to
last an entire day. Its greatest
attraction is the aquapark with
pools of water kept at a
constant 25° C (77° F). The
aquapark contains five slides
and a 125-m (410-ft) long
Wild River, which visitors can
ride on a rubber tyre. It is also
possible to sail a boat, whizz
down a "death slide" and
walk across a rope bridge.
During high season the park
lays on additional shows and
games for children, including
treasure hunts. As well as the
amusements, Joboland
also has a small zoo with a
variety of animals including
peacocks, goats, monkeys
and exotic birds.

Østerlars Kirke, the largest of the
island's round churches

Østerlars Kirke ⑪

Gudhjemvej 28. 📞 56 49 82 64.
🕐 mid-May–mid-Oct: 9am–5pm
Mon–Sat (Jul: 1–5pm Sun). 📷

THE LARGEST of Bornholm's
round churches (see p217)
is Østerlars Kirke, which is
scenically located in the
middle of wheat fields. The
church dates from 1150 and is
dedicated to Sankt Laurentius
(St Laurence). The sturdy
buttresses and conical roof
are later additions. Inside, the
central pillar is decorated with

Climbing frames at Joboland amusement park

14th-century frescoes. A rune
stone at the entrance dates
from 1070 and bears the
inscription: "Edmund and his
brother erected this stone to
the memory of their father
Sigmund. May Christ, St
Michael and St Mary help
his soul."

A short way from the
church is **Middelalder-
center**, a recreated village
where staff in medieval dress
work in the smithy, grind
corn and tend sheep. There
are daily demonstrations of
medieval skills such as
making clay pots and archery.

🏛 **Middelaldercenter**
Stangevej 1. 📞 56 49 83 19.
🕐 10am–4pm Mon–Sat. 📷
🔲 www.bornholms
middelaldercenter.dk

Gudhjem ⑫

🏠 900. 🚌 ℹ Åbogade 9,
56 48 52 10.

THE PRETTY village of
Gudhjem ("God's Home")
is built on a steep hill
overlooking the sea. The
picturesque harbour, cobbled

streets and brightly-painted
half-timbered houses with red-
tiled roofs make it a popular
spot with visitors in summer.

The village has long been
associated with the fishing
industry and in 1893 Gudhjem
acquired the first proper
smokehouse in Bornholm. The
famous "Sun over Gudhjem", a
herring smoked in its skin and
served with egg yolk, is well
worth trying.

In the centre of the village is
a late 19th-century church.
Close by are the remains of a
much older chapel dating from
the 13th century. The **Oluf
Høst Museet** has a large
selection of paintings by the
Bornholm artist Oluf Høst who
died in 1966. The collection is
housed in the artist's home,
which he built in 1929. An old
railway station houses the
Gudhjem Museum, which has
displays on local history.

🏛 **Oluf Høst Museet**
Løkkegade 35. 📞 56 48 50 38.
🕐 mid-May–end Sep: 11am–5pm. 📷
🏛 **Gudhjem Museum**
Stationsvej 1. 📞 56 48 54 62.
🕐 mid-May–mid-Sep: 10am–5pm
Mon–Sat, 2–5pm Sun. 📷

Half-timbered houses in Gudhjem

Cycling on Bornholm

THE BEST WAY to explore Bornholm is by bicycle and cycle groups are a common sight. The island has 235 km (146 miles) of well signposted cycling routes, many of which connect to the main towns. The routes provide an ideal way to enjoy Bornholm's meadows, fields and forests. Most are far away from busy roads. Rønne, Allinge, and Gudhjem are good places to start. An English language brochure entitled *Bicycle Routes on Bornholm* is available at tourist information centres. Be aware that cycling on Bornholm requires a reasonable level of fitness as there are numerous hills.

Åkirkeby's *church contains a 14th-century stone font created by Sigraf, a master stonemason from Gotland in Sweden.*

Gudhjem *is a pretty harbourside village. The Sankt Anna chapel dates from the 13th century.*

Rønne *is Bornholm's capital and an important port. The distinctive lighthouse is 19th century.*

Bornholm's harbours *are used by fishing boats throughout the year and by visiting yachts in summer.*

0 km   5

0 miles   5

KEY (KM/MILES)

- **···** 1. Rønne–Allinge (21/13)
- **···** 2. Rønne–Helligdommen (17/13)
- **···** 3. Rønne–Gudhjem (21/13)
- **···** 4. Rønne–Arsdale (31/19)
- **···** 5. Rønne–Neksø (26/16)
- **···** 6. Rønne–Svando (42/26)
- **···** 7. Allinge–Åkirkeby (28/17)
- **···** 8. Gudhjem–Helligdommen (21/13)

GREENLAND AND THE FAROE ISLANDS

T HESE TWO FAR-FLUNG *territories of Denmark offer spectacular adventure and some of the world's most stunning scenery. Greenland's vast frozen glaciers and wondrous northern lights, and the remote settlements and varied birdlife on the Faroe Islands, are ideal for visitors attracted by solitude and natural beauty.*

Denmark's two distant island territories enjoy a particular status. Greenland was granted home rule in 1979; the Faroe Islands in 1948. Both have their own government but due to the fact that Denmark retains responsibility for matters such as defence, both are represented in the Danish parliament.

Native Greenlanders share a common heritage with the Inuit of Alaska and northern Canada. Denmark's links with the island began in the 10th century when Viking settlers arrived here and began trading with the Greenlanders. The island was named by Erik the Red, a Viking chief who reached the southern end of Greenland around AD 985.

Early settlers on the Faroe Islands were from Norway. When Norway came under Danish rule in the 14th century the islands also became part of Denmark. Denmark ceded Norway to Sweden in 1814 under the Treaty of Kiel but the Faroes continued under the Danish crown until demands for independence led to eventual home rule. The local name for the Faroes is Føroyar, which translates as "sheep island". The Faroes are aptly named and there are currently almost twice as many sheep as people.

Both Greenland and the Faroe Islands are perfect for nature lovers. A boat tour through parts of Greenland, for instance, takes visitors through crystal-clear waters teeming with marine life including seals and whales. Dog-sled tours across frozen lakes are possible during the winter. The Faroe Islands are a paradise for hikers and ramblers and have a huge variety of birdlife.

Typical Faroe Islands scenery with rocky islets jutting out into the sea

◁ Distinctive houses in Qaqortoq's harbour, Greenland

Exploring Greenland

GREENLAND IS THE world's largest island (assuming Australia is a continent) and has a total area of 2,175,600 sq km (840,000 sq miles) and 40,000 km (25,000 miles) of coast. About 85 per cent of the land mass is covered by a huge ice-sheet that is up to 3 km (2 miles) thick. Despite its great size, the island has a population of just 55,000, the majority of whom are descended from a mixture of Inuits and European immigrants. For much of the year Greenland is a vast frozen wilderness. During spring and summer, however, the southern coastal regions thaw and the temperature can rise to as much as 26° C (70° F). Most of the towns and villages have both Inuit and Danish names.

Greenlander family in colourful
Inuit costumes

Midnight sun during summer months

LINCOLN SEA

KNUD RASMUSSEN LAND

6 QAANAAQ (THULE)

BAFFIN BAY

UPERNAVIK

Disko Øer

5 UUMMANN (UMANAK)

QEQERTARSUAQ (GODHAVN)

AASIAAT (EGEDESMINDE)

4 ILULISSAT (JAKOBSHA

SISIMIUT (HOLSTEINSBORG)

3 KANGERLUSSUAQ (SØNDRE STRØMFJORD)

NUUK **2** (GODTHÅB)

LABRADOR SEA

NARSARSUAQ

QAQORTOQ **1** (JULIANEHÅB)

Kap Farvel

ap Morris Jesup

PEARY
LAND

Greenland huskies, bred north of the Arctic Circle

FREDERIK VIII
LAND

GREENLAND SEA

DANMARKS HAVN

Ymers Øer

Traill Øer

KONG
CHRISTIAN X
LAND

ITTOQQORTOORMIIT
(SCORESBYSUND)

KONG
CHRISTIAN IX
LAND

Arctic Circle

ATLANTIC OCEAN

7
TASIILAQ
(AMMASSALIK)

GETTING THERE & AROUND

Kangerlussuaq, just north of the Arctic Circle, has Greenland's main international airport. It lies 370 km (230 miles) north of Nuuk and serves traffic from Copenhagen, Iceland and Canada. From Copenhagen and Keflavik in Iceland it is possible to fly to the southern town of Narsarsuaq.

All domestic inland services are handled by Greenlandair. These flights tend to be expensive. Travel by ferry is possible all year round, although sailing times are vulnerable to adverse weather conditions.

SIGHTS AT A GLANCE

Ilulissat (Jakobshavn) **4**
Kangerlussuaq (Søndre
    Strømfjord) **3**
Nuuk (Godthåb) **2**
Qaanaaq (Thule) **6**
Qaqortoq (Julianehåb) **1**
Tasiilaq (Ammassalik) **7**
Uummannaq **5**

KEY

▨	Green areas
☐	Permafrost

SEE ALSO

• *Where to Stay* p255.
• *Where to Eat* p277.

0 km   200

0 miles   200

Glacier near the small town of Ilulissat

The 19th-century church of St Saviour in Nuuk

Qaqortoq (Julianehåb) ❶

🏠 3,600. 📞 (+299) 64 24 44.
🌐 www.qaq.gl

THE TOWN of Qaqortoq was established in 1775. Traces of earlier, 10th-century Viking settlers can be seen in nearby Hvalsey where the remains of a local settlement and church are the best-preserved Nordic ruins in Greenland.

Other local attractions include the hot springs in Uunartoq and the research station in Upernaviarsuk which grows the only apple trees in Greenland.

Qaqortoq participates in Greenland's Stone and Man programme, an open-air sculpture project that uses natural rock formations as base material for a variety of abstract shapes and figures.

Nuuk (Godthåb) ❷

🏠 14,000. 🛈 Hans Egedesvej 29, P.O. Box 199, (+299) 32 27 00.
🌐 www.nuuk-tourism.gl

GREENLAND'S capital was founded in 1728 by Hans Egede, a Danish missionary who established a year-round trading post here. Nuuk is the largest and oldest town on the island and the seat of Greenland's government. Egede's monument is on a hill, close to the cathedral.

More information about the history of Nuuk can be found at the **National Museum**, which has a collection of Inuit costumes as well as other Greenland artifacts.

According to some traditions Santa Claus lives in Nuuk and even has his own box number (2412 Nuuk Post Office). Next to the post office is a huge letterbox for Santa's letters.

The best time to visit is summer – in June humpback whales can be seen in the bay.

🏛 **National Museum**
Hans Egedesvej 8.
📞 (+299) 32 26 11. 🕐 mid-May–mid-Sep: 11am–5pm. 🌀

Kangerlussuaq (Søndre Strømfjord) ❸

🏠 600. 🛈 Kangerlussuaq Tourism, P.O. Box 49. (+299) 84 10 98.

SITUATED NEAR the fjord of the same name, Kanger-lussuaq was until recently home to Blue West 8, a US base. A museum, located in the former HQ building, contains military memorabilia from the base's history including a replica of the commander's hut.

This area is an excellent venue for hiking, biking, camping and fishing and is inhabited by large herds of reindeer as well as musk ox, arctic foxes and polar hares. A popular day-trip destination

Gently sloping green coastline near Kangerlussuaq

is to Russells Glacier, an ice cap some 25 km (16 miles) away. Rising about 10 km (6 miles) from Kangerlussuaq is Sugarloaf Mountain, which has a wonderful view of the inland ice from its peak.

Ilulissat (Jakobshavn) ❹

🏠 4,600. Kussangajaannguaq 11, (+299) 94 43 22. W www.its.gl

T HE TOWN of Ilulissat looks out over Disko Bay, which is full of floating icebergs. It has been calculated that almost 10 per cent of the icebergs floating on Greenland's waters come from the nearby 40-km (25-mile) long glacial fjord, where the ice can be up to 1,100 m (3,600 ft) thick. The glacier can be reached by boat from Ilulissat.

The most famous inhabitant of Ilulissat was the polar explorer Knud Rasmussen (see p27). His former house contains objects associated with Inuit art and the everyday life of Greenlanders.

Other local museums include the Museum of Hunting and Fishing and the so-called Cold Museum (it has no heating), which has a selection of tools and machinery from a former trading settlement.

Uummannaq ❺

🏠 2,600. Trollep Aqqutaa B 1342, (+299) 95 15 18. W www.icecaphotels.gl

D ESPITE ITS location 600 km (373 miles) north of the Arctic Circle, this place enjoys more days of summer sunshine than anywhere else in Greenland. Such favourable conditions have for a long time been a magnet for hunters and whalers. The charm of this town, situated on a small island, is due in part to its colourful houses set on a rocky shore against the backdrop of the 1,175-m (3,855-ft) high Hjertetjeldet ("Heart Shaped") mountain. The old stone cottages with turf roofs date from 1925. The

Children dressed in traditional Inuit costumes

nearby museum, housed in a late 19th-century hospital, contains hunting implements, kayaks and a display devoted to German scientist Alfred Wegener's expedition across the inland ice in 1930 on propeller-driven sledges.

Nearby is the Inuit village of Qilaqitsoq, where some mummified bodies were discovered in a cave in 1972. The mummies can be seen in Nuuk's National Museum.

In winter it is possible to take a dog-sled trip across the frozen fjord.

Qaanaaq (Thule) ❻

🏠 800. P.O. Box 75, (+299) 97 14 73. W www.turistqaanaaq.gl

G REENLAND'S northernmost town was built in the 1950s. Its inhabitants follow a traditional way of life hunting for seals, walruses and polar bears. Visitors can participate in hunts, which involve sleeping in igloos and travelling by sled. Hunts such

as these are an important means of survival in this area and not for the squeamish.

About 500 km (311 miles) from Qaanaaq is the North and East Greenland National Park, covering an area of 1,000,000 sq km (386,000 sq miles). The park is mostly covered by an inland ice cap and contains musk ox, polar bears and, in summer, walruses. Permission to enter must be obtained from the Dansk Polarcenter in Copenhagen (www.dpc.dk).

Tasiilaq (Ammassalik) ❼

🏠 1,700. (+299) 98 15 43. W www.eastgreenland.com

S ITUATED ON the shores of a fjord, surrounded by high mountains, Tasiilaq is one of eastern Greenland's larger towns. The first Europeans arrived here about 100 years ago and tourism is becoming increasingly important to the region. From here, visitors can go whale watching, visit the nearby "Valley of Fowers" (in summer this is a splendid opportunity to enjoy the Arctic flora) or climb the mound that towers over the town (it was raised in 1944 to celebrate the 50th anniversary of Tasiilaq), from which there are some stunning views of the area.

The town's other points of interest include a modern church decorated with Greenland artifacts. The oldest of Tasiilaq's houses dates from 1894 and was built by a Danish missionary.

Uummannaq, built on the rocks of a small island

Exploring the Faroe Islands

THIS CLUSTER of 18 islands, sandwiched between the Atlantic and the Norwegian Sea, is home to about 48,000 people, almost half of whom live in the capital Tórshavn on Streymoy. The Faroes have a total area of 1,399 sq km (540 sq miles) and are 450 km (280 miles) from the Shetland Islands and 1,500 km (900 miles) from Copenhagen. Many of the islands are interlinked by a network of tunnels and causeways. The Faroes are perfect for ramblers, and marked trails cover many routes. This is rough terrain and the right equipment, including maps and a compass, should always be carried. The island's seafaring past is evident in the busy harbours, while the town museums have displays on island customs and folklore. Sea cruises are an ideal way to explore the Faroes.

Garden gate made from a ship's wheel

Rugged cliffs on the tiny island of Koltur

KEY

═══ Road

= = Tunnel

-- Ferry route

✈ Airport

VIÐAREIÐI
MÐLI
FUGLOY
ADALUR   VIÐOY   KIRKJA
UNOY   HVANNASUND
HARALDSSUND
SVINOY
SVINOY
ALSOY   KLAKSVÍK
LEIRVIK   BORÐOY

6 EYSTUROY

NORWEGIAN SEA

K
SHAVN
NÓLSOY
NÓLSOY
BØUR

O Y

SKÁLAVIK

DALUR

O Y

A DÍMUN

A DÍMUN

RI

UMBA

Steel sheep sculpture on the outskirts of Tórshavn

GETTING THERE & AROUND

The Faroe Islands Smyril Lane ferry service operates regularly between Tórshavn, the island's capital, and Hanstholm in northern Jutland. In summer there are additional services from Bergen in Norway, Lerwick on the Shetlands and Seyðisfjörður in Iceland. From April to September Atlantic Airlines serves routes from Billund and Copenhagen in Denmark, and also from Oslo in Norway. Twice-weekly routes operate from London and Aberdeen during these months. The Faroe Islands' international airport is near the town of Sørvágur, on the island of Vágar, about 70 km (43 miles) from Tórshavn. A bus connects the airport with Tórshavn. Most of the towns and villages are connected by road, while local ferries cater for the more outlying settlements.

SEE ALSO

- *Where to Stay* p255.

- *Where to Eat* p277.

0 km   10

0 miles   10

SIGHTS AT A GLANCE

Eysturoy **6**
Kalsoy **7**
Mykines **4**
Suðuroy **5**
Streymoy **2**
Tórshavn **1**
Vágar **3**

Fishing boats in Klaksvik's harbour

Brightly-coloured houses lining Tórshavn harbour

Tórshavn **❶**

🏠 19,000. ⛴ 🚌 ℹ *Undir Bryggjubakka 17, Tórshavn, (+298) 31 57 88.*

THE FAROE ISLANDS' capital is a lively and picturesque place with a well preserved old centre, although much of the town is fairly modern. Tórshavn was granted municipal status in 1909 but its history stretches back much further.

In the 11th century Tórshavn became a venue for annual Viking gatherings known as the Althings, an early form of the Faroese parliament. The meetings were held in summer and were used to settle quarrels and to trade. A permanent settlement developed around the annual event, and eventually became Tórshavn.

Some of the Faroes' earliest inhabitants were Irish friars, and Tórshavn's oldest building is the 15th-century Munkastovan or Monks' House, which is one of the few buildings to survive a fire in 1673.

The ruins of Skansin Fort, which was built in 1580 to defend the village from pirates, can still be seen. The fort aquired its present shape in 1780 and was used by British troops during World War II. Today, it provides a

good viewpoint for surveying the busy harbour, which is crammed with fishing boats, ferries and pleasure craft.

Føroya Fornminnissavn (Historical Museum) has a wide-ranging collection tracing the Faroes' seafaring history, including boats and fishing equipment, as well as religious artifacts and items dating back to the Viking era.

🏛 **Føroya Fornminnissavn** Kúrdalsvegur 2. 📞 *(+298) 31 07 00.* 🕐 *9am–noon, 1–3pm Mon–Fri.* 📷 🌐 *www.natmus.fo*

Streymoy **❷**

🏠 22,000. ⛴ 🚌

THE LARGEST of the Faroe Islands has a varied terrain and is criss-crossed by ancient paths that were used to travel between settlements. Some of these are now roads.

Saksun is a small village on the shores of an inlet that leads into Pollur lake – a fine spot to fish for trout and salmon.

The **Dúvuvardur Museum**, an old turf-roofed farmhouse, has exhibits on island life from medieval times to the 1800s.

Traces of a group of 8th-century Irish friars have been found in the village of Kirkjubøur, at the south end of Streymoy. Written records show that Kirkjubøur was a busy place in medieval times. A reminder of those days is the 12th-century church of St Olaf, the archipelago's oldest historic site.

Southwest from Tórshavn are the Vestmannabjørg (Bird Cliffs) where hundreds of sea birds inhabit the 640-m (2,100-ft) high cliff face.

🏛 **Dúvuvardur Museum** FO436, Saksun. 📞 *(+298) 42 23 03.* 🕐 *mid-Jun–mid-Aug: 2–5pm (or on request).* 📷

Vágar **❸**

🏠 2,800. ✈ 🚌 ℹ *At the airport, (+298) 35 33 00.*

THE FAROE ISLANDS' modern airport is on Vágar and was originally used as a landing strip by the RAF. This mountainous island has some of the region's most stunning sights including the 313-m (1,027-ft) tall needle rock called "Trollukonufingur" ("Troll Woman's Finger"). Lake Sorvagsvatn is a little way from Midvagur, Vágar's largest town, and is a great place for fishing. Sandavagur, a nearby village, is the birthplace of Venceslaus Ulricus Hammershaimb (b. 1819), creator of the Faroese alphabet.

House hugging the cliff on Streymoy

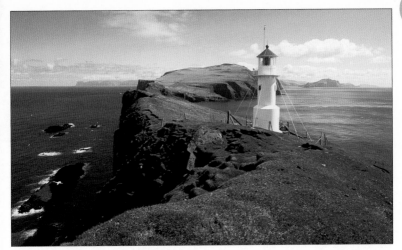

Lighthouse standing on the cliffs of Mykines

Mykines ❹

🚶 20. 🚢

ON THIS tiny island of only 10 sq km (4 sq miles), the inhabitants are vastly outnumbered by the birds, including thousands of puffins. All the islanders live in the same village, which is a pretty place with colourful houses topped by turf roofs. This is one of the hardest islands to reach but the trip is worth it, especially for keen hikers. Mykineshólmur, a tiny islet, is a good spot from which to view gannets, as well as large colonies of puffins. It is connected to the island by a footbridge that has been built 24-m (79-ft) above the sea.

Suðuroy ❺

🚶 5,000. 🚢 ℹ Suduroyar Kunningarstova, (+298) 37 24 80. @ sout-inf@post.olivant.fo

THE LARGEST town on Suðuroy, the Faroes' southernmost island, is Tvøroyri, which has a population of 1,800. The little village of Famjin, on the west coast, is more historically important, however, as its church contains the original Faroe Islands' flag. The red-and-blue cross on a white background was designed by two students and accepted as the national ensign in 1940. A short hike above the village is Kirkjuvatn ("Church Lake"), one of the Faroes' largest lakes.

The village of Sandvik, at the northern end of the island, has an isolated and expansive beach. In AD 1000 Sigmund Bresterson, an early Norwegian settler and hero of the Faroe Sagas, was murdered here while preaching Christianity. On the way from Sanvik to Hvalba are two stones that, according to legend, were brought here by Bresterson. Passing between them is believed to be unlucky and can spell misfortune or even death.

Goat on one of the islands' rural smallholdings

Eysturoy ❻

🚶 10,000. ℹ Fuglafjørdur á Bug, (+298) 44 48 60. 🌐 www.visiteysturoy.fo

THE SECOND LARGEST island of the archipelago is connected to Streymoy by a road bridge, which is often jokingly described by locals as the only bridge across the Atlantic.

Eysturoy has a number of unique features. At 882 m (2,894 ft), Slættaratindur is the Faroes' highest point. The summit can easily be reached by climbing the mountain's eastern ridge – the views from the peak are breathtaking.

Close to Fuglafjørdur are the Varmakelda hot springs. Their water remains at a constant 18° C (64.4° F) and is believed to have medicinal properties. Further north is the village of Oynadarfjordur. Just beyond its shore are the Rinkusteinar, or rocking stones, two huge blocks that constantly rock, moved by the motion of the sea. At nearby Gjøgv there is a 200-m (656-ft) long gorge that with time has eroded to become a sea-filled bay.

Kalsoy ❼

🚶 140. 🚢

NICKNAMED the "flute" because of its elongated shape, this rugged island is ideal for hikes. Many walkers head towards Kap Kallur, at the island's northern tip, where the lighthouse makes an excellent point from which to view the cliffs. Puffins are a frequent sight. The sea stacks at Eysturoy's northern tip can be seen on a clear day.

TRAVELLERS' NEEDS

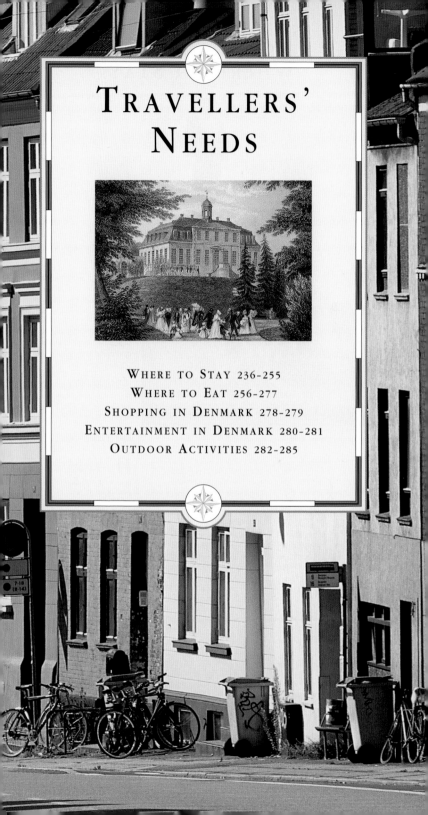

WHERE TO STAY

HOLIDAY accommodation in Denmark is of a high standard and provides visitors with plenty of options. The choice ranges from luxury hotels and apartments to roadside inns, budget hotels, family hostels, private homes and camp sites. Information is readily available from tourist offices and on the Internet. Some of Denmark's hotels can be expensive, however. For those on a tight budget,

Copenhagen hotel porter

staying on a camp site or in one of the country's well-run hostels provides a cheaper alternative. Those seeking something a little different might choose to stay in an historic castle or on one of the farms taking part in Denmark's agritourism scheme. Visitors to Greenland can even choose to stay in an igloo. Whatever your preference, Danish accommodation has a reputation for professionalism and a warm welcome is generally assured.

Main entrance to a hotel in Sandvig, Bornholm

CHOOSING A HOTEL

TRAVELLERS IN Denmark have a wide choice of hotel accommodation. Information is readily available and details of hotels found in brochures and on websites is generally both up to date and accurate. Many of Denmark's hotels are 3-star establishments, and are aimed at holiday-makers as well as business travellers. The majority of three-star hotels offer rooms with a private bathroom, telephone and TV. Be clear when booking a room if a bath

Pension sign in Elmehøj, Møn

is specifically required, as some hotels have showers rather than baths in rooms. Visitors may be able to use their laptops as rooms often have Internet access but it is wise to enquire. The cheaper hotels tend to be

rather plain but even these are generally clean and well run. An all-you-can-eat breakfast, consisting of pastries, bread, cereal, coffee/tea and fruit, is often included in the price of a room.

When planning a journey to Denmark by car, take into account the cost of parking in town centres. It is worth finding out in advance whether the hotel has its own car park or off-street parking. Hotels on Greenland and the Faroe Islands are not plentiful. Those that do exist can be fairly costly.

HOW TO BOOK

DURING PEAK season, hotels are often booked up in Denmark so it pays to reserve a room in advance. Hotel accommodation can be

booked via the Internet at *www.danishotels.dk* or *www.visitdenmark.dk*. Many individual hotels in Denmark also have their own websites. Alternatively, bookings can be made by telephone, fax or e-mail. It may also be worth contacting a travel agent, as they often have details about special offers or schemes. Local tourist offices can also provide accommodation lists in their towns.

HOTEL PRICES

HOTEL PRICES in Denmark can be rather high. There are many hotels at the lower end of the scale, however, which charge about 600 to 700 Dkr per night; the most expensive ones may quote up to 10,000 Dkr for a luxury suite. The majority of room prices fall into the 900–1,400 Dkr bracket. During summer and at weekends when business visitors are scarce, many hotels offer discounted rates. Another way to save money is by purchasing "Inn Cheques" from one of the tourist offices or online at *www.krohotel.dk*. More than 70 hotels belong to this scheme, which allows rooms to be booked in advance at a reduced price.

ADDITIONAL COSTS

SOME HOTELS and hostels belonging to the Green Key association add 35 Dkr "ecological tax" to the price of an overnight stay. This

◁ **Colourful houses lining a street in Århus, central Jutland**

A guest room in the Admiral Hotel, Copenhagen *(see p240)*

scheme, which began in 1994, ensures that the hotel has fulfilled certain ecological criteria such as using low-energy light bulbs, low-water consumption toilets and environmentally friendly cleaning products.

CHAIN HOTELS

THE MAJORITY of hotels in Denmark belong to large hotel chains including First & Clarion, Hilton, Radisson and Scandic. Some chains, such as Best Western, have their own schemes whereby visitors can get discounts at weekends or during the holiday period. It is best to book in advance for these, though deals can sometimes be struck on the spot.

HISTORIC HOUSES

A SMALL NUMBER of Denmark's manor houses and palaces offer accommodation. These historic buildings are run by **Danske Slotte & Herregaarde** (The Danish Association of Castles and Manor Houses), which can provide a brochure of the 60 or so historic houses available for overnight stays. The venues are undeniably romantic, although they can be rather epensive.

INNS

OUTSIDE LARGER towns, it is possible to stop for a night in an inn, known as *kro* in Denmark. The variety on offer ranges from modern roadside inns to meticulously restored period houses. Some country inns have retained much of their 18th or 19th-century rusticity; others are downright luxurious. Many *kro* offer a family atmosphere, and it is not unusual for inns to be used for family gatherings and big occasions.

Camp site on Hindsholm peninsula, Funen

CAMP SITES

DENMARK has over 550 camp sites. Of these, as many as 100 are open all year round. All are rated by the **Dansk Camping Union** using a system of stars from one to five. Prices depend on the number of stars, which reflect not only comfort and a site's attractiveness but also specific facilities, such as whether the site has a playground and the distance to the nearest grocery store. The cost generally includes a charge for pitching a tent or parking a caravan, plus a charge for each occupant. One-star sites will have little more than fresh drinking water and toilets. Three-star sights and above will have a TV room, on-site shop and a café or restaurant. Whatever the rating, it is rare to find a Danish camp site that is not well run. Roughly 400 of Denmark's camp sites feature chalet accommodation or cabins that can sleep four to six. Many cabins have cooking facilities but visitors usually have to supply their own linen and towels. Most cabins do not have private washing or toilet facilties.

A comprehensive database at *www.camping.dk* allows a search according to location and facilities. Tourist offices can provide a leaflet listing all the sites and the basic rules of camping in Denmark.

Anyone wishing to camp in Denmark will need a Visitor's Pass. These annual permits are readily available and can be bought on the spot at any of the official camp sites.

Pitching a tent in areas not designated as camp sites is not encouraged and anyone caught camping in a field or on the beach without permission may be fined.

Distinctive architecture of the Royal Holstebro, Jutland *(see p252)*

Historic hotel room in Liselund Slot, Møn

HOSTELS

ALL OF DENMARK'S 180 or so hostels or *vandrehjem* are incorporated into the **Danhostel** association, which registers its hostels in five categories marked (as in the case of hotels and camp sites) by stars. Along with communal dormitories, most hostels have private "family" rooms, which usually sleep four to six and must be booked well in advance. Blankets and pillows are usually provided, but it is generally the case that visitors supply their own bed linen and towels. In all hostels it is possible to buy breakfast; many also offer dinner, charging half-price for children up to the age of 12. Most hostels have kitchen facilities, where guests can prepare their own meals, although plates and cutlery are rarely provided.

The prices of family rooms can vary, but the maximum price of a bed in a communal dormitory is fixed each year for the entire country. Prices for an overnight stay vary between high and low seasons. From September until May a place in a provincial hostel must be booked at least three days in advance. During peak season all hostels should be booked as early as possible and couples wishing to rent a private room during this period may be asked to pay for all the beds in the room.

In order to stay at a hostel it is necessary to have a Youth Hostel Association (YHA) card. Holders of YHA cards pay the normal full price. Non-members can buy temporary membership for each night spent in the hostel, which may make sense if staying only one or two nights. For visits that exceed five days it is worthwhile buying a full membership.

Danhostel's website has telephone numbers and website addresses for all of its hostels, where additional information can be found.

BED & BREAKFASTS

DENMARK'S bed and breakfasts offer good quality and value, and usually charge about 150 Dkr per person per night. Many can be booked from local tourist offices. Alternatively, a list is available from **Dansk Bed & Breakfast**. Some Danish B&Bs quote a price that only includes accommodation. Breakfast may be at extra cost or may not be available at all.

DISABLED TRAVELLERS

MANY HOTELS can accommodate disabled guests. The majority of multi-storey hotels have lifts. VisitDenmark, the tourist board *(see p289)*, has a leaflet entitled *Access in Denmark – a travel guide*, which has information on disabled access to hotels.

TRAVELLING WITH CHILDREN

TAKING CHILDREN on holiday to Denmark is not a problem. Many hotels and hostels, particularly establishments aimed at holiday-makers, offer family rooms for three to four people. Hotels belonging to the Scandic group are also ready to receive young guests; many of these have playrooms. Hotel restaurants not only provide high chairs for babies and toddlers, but also offer special menus that will satisfy all but the most picky children.

Sign advertising one of Denmark's bed & breakfasts

COTTAGES AND HOLIDAY CENTRES

COTTAGES ARE available to rent for longer stays in a summer resort. Some summer cottages are let out by their owners, and are only available for the period when they are not using the house themselves. Others are run purely as commercial ventures. Both must be booked well

Entrance to one of Denmark's converted manor houses

Youth Hostel dormitory

in advance. Many companies are able to handle bookings nationwide.

Holiday centres, which have purpose-built accommodation, children's playgrounds, swimming pools and other family-friendly amenities, have lots of space for children to play. Prices vary widely.

FARM HOLIDAYS

SPENDING time on a farm is becoming an increasingly popular activity in Denmark. There are now more than 100 Danish farms where a stay is possible, and most are far away from busy resorts. Such rural retreats provide a chance to relax in pastoral surroundings and, in some cases, to muck in with the chores. An association called **Landsforeningen for Landboturisme** can book stays on farms and assist in selecting a farm for visitors depending on the facilities and location required.

A holiday of this sort can be arranged in several ways. It is possible to choose B&B or full-board accommodation. Cottages, a simple apartment with a kitchen, or a room can be rented. Alternatively, visitors can pitch a tent or park a caravan on farm land. Some farms offer theme holidays that may include angling, cookery courses or environmental studies.

Another possibility is to travel from farm to farm by bicycle or car. When travelling along well-marked routes this can provide an attractive alternative to camp sites and hostels. Regardless of what type of vacation is on offer, visitors can be sure of a clean room and warm rural atmosphere. Prices start from 200 Dkr per adult (for bed and breakfast).

Choosing a Hotel

Hotels in this guide have been chosen for their convenient location, high standard, good value and facilities on offer. The chart below first lists hotels in Copenhagen, which are then followed by places to stay in the rest of Denmark. Within each region, towns are listed alphabetically, and within each town the hotels are ordered by price.

	Number of Rooms	Restaurant	Garden or Terrace	Swimming Pool	Business Facilities
COPENHAGEN					
North Copenhagen: *Comfort Hotel Esplanaden* (Kr)(Kr)	117				■
North Copenhagen: *Copenhagen Admiral Hotel* (Kr)(Kr)	366	●			
North Copenhagen: *Hotel Østerport* (Kr)(Kr)	170				■
North Copenhagen: *Sophie Amalie* (Kr)(Kr)	134	●			■
North Copenhagen: *Christian IV* (Kr)(Kr)(Kr)	42				
North Copenhagen: *Clarion Hotel Neptun* (Kr)(Kr)(Kr)(Kr)	133	●			■
North Copenhagen: *Phoenix* (Kr)(Kr)(Kr)(Kr)(Kr)	213	●			■
Central Copenhagen: *Danhostel Copenhagen City* (Kr)	700				

North Copenhagen: *Comfort Hotel Esplanaden*
Bredgade 78. **Map** 2 E5. **☎** 33 48 10 00. **FAX** 33 48 10 66.
w www.choicehotels.dk **@** info.esplanaden@comfort.choicehotels.dk
One of Denmark's first completely non-smoking hotels, the Esplanaden is in an ornate, period building with lavish decorations. It is close to Churchillparken and the Little Mermaid statue.

North Copenhagen: *Copenhagen Admiral Hotel*
Toldbodgade 24–28. **Map** 2 E5. **☎** 33 74 14 14. **FAX** 33 74 14 16.
w www.admiralhotel.dk **@** admiral@admiralhotel.dk
This hotel occupies an 18th-century harbourside warehouse. The project of turning the warehouse into a hotel won a Europa Nostra award for the exceptional regard paid to the period features.

North Copenhagen: *Hotel Østerport*
Oslo Plads 5. **Map** 2 E3. **☎** 70 12 46 46. **FAX** 33 12 25 55.
w www.choicehotels.dk **@** booking.oesterport@comfort.choicehotels.dk
A modern hotel with bright, airy rooms. Although not strictly in the town centre, the hotel is situated close to public transport (both local and regional).

North Copenhagen: *Sophie Amalie*
Sankt Annæ Plads 21. **Map** 2 E5. **☎** 33 13 34 00. **FAX** 33 11 77 07.
w www.remmen.dk **@** sales@remmen.dk
Minimalist furnishing and a warm welcome are the key ingredients of this hotel's success. Located in a renovated period building, the hotel is named for Queen Sophie Amalie who won fame in the 17th century by refusing to quit the city when it was beleaguered by the Swedes.

North Copenhagen: *Christian IV*
Dr. Tværgade 45. **Map** 2 D5. **☎** 33 32 10 44. **FAX** 33 32 07 06.
w www.hotelchristianiv.dk **@** receptionen@hotelchristianiv.dk
A small, congenial hotel located in a trendy residential district, close to Rosenberg Slot. The rooms, some of which overlook a leafy garden, are furnished in a typical Danish minimalist style.

North Copenhagen: *Clarion Hotel Neptun*
Sankt Annæ Plads 18. **Map** 2 E5. **☎** 33 96 20 00. **FAX** 33 96 20 66.
w www.choicehotels.dk **@** info.neptun@clarion.choicehotels.dk
Attractively located close to the royal palace, this hotel is one of the oldest in town. The rooms have modern décor and many look onto a quiet, internal courtyard.

North Copenhagen: *Phoenix*
Bredgade 37. **Map** 2 E5. **☎** 33 95 95 00. **FAX** 33 33 98 33.
w www.phoenixcopenhagen.dk **@** phoenixcopenhagen@arp-hansen.dk
A luxurious hotel in a mid-19th-century building close to Amalienborg Slot and Nyhavn. This is an upmarket place with reproduction Louis XVI style antiques and gold fixtures in the bathrooms. The hotel is one of Copenhagen's best known and has been playing host to visiting royalty and Danish nobility for many years.

Central Copenhagen: *Danhostel Copenhagen City*
H.C. Andersens Boulevard 50. **Map** 3 A1. **☎** 33 11 85 85.
w www.danhostel.dk **@** copenhagencity@danhostel.dk
This new youth and family hostel opened in 2005 and is close to most of the main sights. Many of the comfortable rooms have superb city views.

Price categories are for a standard double room per night with bath or shower, including breakfast, service and tax.

Ⓚ up to 1,000 Dkr
ⓀⓀ 1,000–1,400 Dkr
ⓀⓀⓀ 1,400–1,800 Dkr
ⓀⓀⓀⓀ 1,800–2,200 Dkr
ⓀⓀⓀⓀⓀ over 2,200 Dkr

RESTAURANT
Restaurant is open to non-residents.

GARDEN OR TERRACE
Hotel has its own garden, a terrace or a courtyard with plants.

SWIMMING POOL
Hotel has a pool for the use of its guests.

BUSINESS FACILITIES
Hotel has Internet access and meeting room.

	NUMBER OF ROOMS	RESTAURANT	GARDEN OR TERRACE	SWIMMING POOL	BUSINESS FACILITIES
CENTRAL COPENHAGEN: Maritime Ⓚ	64		▪		▪
CENTRAL COPENHAGEN: Ascot ⓀⓀ	165				
CENTRAL COPENHAGEN: Opera ⓀⓀ	91				
CENTRAL COPENHAGEN: Skt Petri ⓀⓀ	270	●	▪		▪
CENTRAL COPENHAGEN: Sofitel Plaza Copenhagen ⓀⓀ	93	●			▪
CENTRAL COPENHAGEN: 71 Nyhavn ⓀⓀⓀ	150	●			
CENTRAL COPENHAGEN: Alexandra ⓀⓀⓀ	61				
CENTRAL COPENHAGEN: Copenhagen Strand ⓀⓀⓀ	174				

CENTRAL COPENHAGEN: Maritime Ⓚ
Peder Skrams Gade 19. **Map** 4 E1. 33 13 48 82. FAX 33 15 03 45.
w www.hotel-maritime.dk @ hotel@maritime.dk
This modern, attractively priced hotel owes much of its popularity to its close proximity to Nyhavn. Many of Copenhagen's attractions are within easy walking distance. The rooms are spacious and smartly furnished.

CENTRAL COPENHAGEN: Ascot ⓀⓀ
Studiestræde 61. **Map** 3 B1. 33 12 60 00. FAX 33 14 60 40.
w www.ascothotel.dk @ hotel@ascot-hotel.dk
The reliefs of men and women bathing are one of the few reminders that this was once a public baths. The hotel was recently renovated but has maintained its old-world atmosphere.

CENTRAL COPENHAGEN: Opera ⓀⓀ
Tordenskjoldsgade 15. **Map** 4 D1. 33 47 83 00. FAX 33 47 83 01.
w www.operahotelcopenhagen.dk @ hotelopera@arp-hansen.dk
A pleasant hotel with a wood-panelled restaurant and reception areas. The Opera is handy for Det Kongelige Teater (The Royal Theatre) and Strøget's shops and restaurants. A "Wall of Fame" in the lobby has photographs of famous actors and artists who have stayed here.

CENTRAL COPENHAGEN: Skt Petri ⓀⓀ
Krystalgade 22. **Map** 1 C5. 33 45 91 00. FAX 33 45 91 10.
w www.hotelsktpetri.com @ reservation@hotelsktpetri.com
Until recently this building served as a department store. It has now become one of the city's most popular hotels. The room furnishings were designed by Per Arnoldi, one of Denmark's top artists.

CENTRAL COPENHAGEN: Sofitel Plaza Copenhagen ⓀⓀ
Bernstorffsgade 4. **Map** 3 A2. 33 14 92 62. FAX 33 93 93 62.
w www.accorhotel.dk @ sofitel@accorhotel.dk
Just around the corner from the side entrance to Central Station, this recently renovated hotel is elegant and bright and has a contemporary ambience.

CENTRAL COPENHAGEN: 71 Nyhavn ⓀⓀⓀ
Nyhavn 71. **Map** 4 E1. 33 43 62 00. FAX 33 43 62 01.
w www.71nyhavnhotelcopenhagen.dk @ 71nyhavnhotel@arp-hansen.dk
In the 1970s this 19th-century harbour warehouse was converted into a hotel. The rooms are cosy and attempt to create a home-from-home ambience. Many have harbour or canal views.

CENTRAL COPENHAGEN: Alexandra ⓀⓀⓀ
H.C. Andersens Boulevard 8. **Map** 3 A1. 33 74 44 44. FAX 33 74 44 88.
w www.hotel-alexandra.dk @ reservations@hotel-alexandra.dk
Housed in what were once fashionable city apartments, the décor of this chic hotel is stylish and upmarket, with plenty of attention to detail. The walls are hung with original artworks and much of the furniture is original classic Danish design including pieces by Arne Jacobsen.

CENTRAL COPENHAGEN: Copenhagen Strand ⓀⓀⓀ
Havnegade 37. **Map** 4 D2. 33 48 99 00. FAX 33 48 99 01.
w www.Copenhagenstrand.dk @ copenhagenstrand@arp-hansen.dk
This hotel occupies a 19th-century harbour warehouse in a rapidly developing district of Copenhagen. The lobby area is cosy with leather sofas and a maritime theme. Many of the rooms have attractive harbour views.

For key to symbols see back flap

	NUMBER OF ROOMS	RESTAURANT	GARDEN OR TERRACE	SWIMMING POOL	BUSINESS FACILITIES

Price categories are for a standard double room per night with bath or shower, including breakfast, service and tax.
Ⓚ up to 1,000 Dkr
ⓀⓀ 1,000–1,400 Dkr
ⓀⓀⓀ 1,400–1,800 Dkr
ⓀⓀⓀⓀ 1,800–2,200 Dkr
ⓀⓀⓀⓀⓀ over 2,200 Dkr

RESTAURANT
Restaurant is open to non-residents.

GARDEN OR TERRACE
Hotel has its own garden, a terrace or a courtyard with plants.

SWIMMING POOL
Hotel has a pool for the use of its guests.

BUSINESS FACILITIES
Hotel has Internet access and meeting room.

CENTRAL COPENHAGEN: *Grand Hotel*   ⓀⓀⓀ
Vesterbrogade 9. **Map** 3 A1. ☎ *33 27 69 00.* 𝖥𝖠𝖷 *33 27 69 01.*
Ⓦ www.grandhotelcopenhagen.dk ⓐ grandhotel@arp-hansen.dk
Convenient for Tivoli Gardens, Central Station and the city centre, this hotel is one of Copenhagen's best known establishments. The building is large and well maintained, with superiour furnishings throughout. A small outdoor garden is open in summer. 🗓 🛏 📺 🌊 🍽 💆 🅿 🎧

| **161** | ● | ▨ | | |

CENTRAL COPENHAGEN: *Radisson SAS Royal*   ⓀⓀⓀ
Hammerichsgade 1. **Map** 3 A1. ☎ *33 42 60 00.* 𝖥𝖠𝖷 *33 42 61 00.*
Ⓦ www.radissonsas.com ⓐ copenhagen@radissonsas.com
Designed by Arne Jacobsen, this was the first skyscraper in Denmark. The deluxe interior includes classic Danish furniture. 🗓 🛏 📺 🌊 🏠 🍽 💆 🅿 🎧

| **260** | ● | | | ▨ |

CENTRAL COPENHAGEN: *The Square*   ⓀⓀⓀ
Rådhuspladsen 14. **Map** 3 B1. ☎ *33 38 12 00.* 𝖥𝖠𝖷 *33 38 12 01.*
Ⓦ www.thesquare.dk ⓐ thesquare@arp-hansen.dk
Breakfast is served on the sixth floor of this centrally-located hotel, which has wonderful views over Copenhagen. 🗓 🛏 📺 🏠 🍽 💆 ▤ 🎧

| **192** | | | | ▨ |

CENTRAL COPENHAGEN: *D'Angleterre*   ⓀⓀⓀⓀⓀ
Kongens Nytorv 34. **Map** 4 D1. ☎ *33 12 00 95.* 𝖥𝖠𝖷 *33 12 11 18.*
Ⓦ www.remmen.dk ⓐ sales@remmen.dk
One of Copenhagen's landmark hotels, the D'Angleterre dates back to 1755. The queen's official residence is just around the corner.
🗓 🛏 📺 🌊 🍽 💆 ▤ 🅿 🎧

| **123** | ● | | ● | ▨ |

SOUTH COPENHAGEN: *Danmark*   ⓀⓀ
Vester Voldgade 89. **Map** 3 B2. ☎ *33 11 48 06.* 𝖥𝖠𝖷 *33 14 36 30.*
Ⓦ www.hotel-danmark.dk ⓐ hotel@hotel-danmark.dk
Occupying a late 18th-century building, the rooms of this comfortable hotel have been furnished in a contemporary style. The hotel is popular with business travellers. 🗓 🛏 📺 🌊 🍽 💆 🅿 🎧

| **88** | | | | ▨ |

SOUTH COPENHAGEN: *Radisson SAS Scandinavia*   ⓀⓀ
Amager Boulevard 70. **Map** 4 E4. ☎ *33 96 50 00.* 𝖥𝖠𝖷 *33 96 55 00.*
Ⓦ www.radissonsas.com ⓐ copenhagen@radissonsas.com
Diners eating in the hotel restaurant on the 25th floor of this skyscraper hotel enjoy a breathtaking panorama of Copenhagen. The hotel's casino is very popular. 🗓 🛏 📺 🌊 🍽 💆 🅿 🎧

| **542** | ● | | ● | ▨ |

SOUTH COPENHAGEN: *Kong Frederik*   ⓀⓀⓀ
Vester Voldgade 25. **Map** 3 B2. ☎ *33 12 59 02.* 𝖥𝖠𝖷 *33 93 59 01.*
Ⓦ www.remmen.dk ⓐ sales@remmen.dk
Kong Frederik is a short way from Strøget and Tivoli Gardens. The hotel's history dates back to the 14th century, when an inn standing on this site offered accommodation to travellers. The comfortable communal areas and rooms are furnished in a colonial "English" style with plush carpets and wooden panelling. 🗓 🛏 📺 🌊 🍽 💆 🅿 🎧

| **110** | ● | ▨ | | ▨ |

FURTHER AFIELD: *Absalon Annex*   Ⓚ
Helgolandsgade 15. **Map** 3 A2. ☎ *33 24 22 11.* 𝖥𝖠𝖷 *33 24 34 11.*
Ⓦ www.absalon-hotel.dk ⓐ info@absalon-hotel.dk
An inexpensive no-frills hotel west of Tivoli, behind Central Station. 🗓 🌊 🎧

| **76** | ● | | | |

FURTHER AFIELD: *Cab Inn City*   Ⓚ
Mitchellsgade 14. **Map** 3 B3. ☎ *33 46 16 16.* 𝖥𝖠𝖷 *33 46 17 17.*
Ⓦ www.cabinn.com ⓐ city@cabinn.dk
This large hotel offers good value for money. The rooms are plain but the hotel has private underground parking. 🗓 🛏 🌊 📺 ♿ ▤ 🅿 🎧

| **350** | | | | |

FURTHER AFIELD: *Hotel 9 Smaa Hjem* (Kr) 13 ● ■
Classensgade 38–42. **(** 35 26 16 47. **FAX** 35 43 17 84.
W www.9smaahjem.dk @ salg@9smaahjem.dk
The prices quoted per week are very attractive at this hotel, which is ideal for
those wishing to stop in Copenhagen for an extended period. 1 🛏 TV 🛏 🖼

FURTHER AFIELD: *Ibis Copenhagen Crown Hotel* (Kr) 80
Vesterbrogade 41. **(** 33 21 21 66. **FAX** 33 21 00 66.
W www.accorhotel.dk @ crown@accorhotel.dk
A comfortable hotel; convenient for the attractions. 1 🛏 TV 🛏 🖼 🛏 🖼

FURTHER AFIELD: *Ansgar* (Kr)(Kr) 81 ● ■
Colbjørnsensgade 29. **(** 33 21 21 96. **FAX** 33 21 61 91.
W www.ansgar-hotel.dk @ ansgar@ansgar-hotel.dk
In summer guests can eat breakfast in the garden of this small hotel, which is
located in a quiet street west of Tivoli. 1 🛏 TV 🛏 🖼

FURTHER AFIELD: *Du Nord* (Kr)(Kr) 65 ■
Colbjørnsensgade 14. **(** 33 22 44 33. **FAX** 33 29 86 86.
W www.hoteldunord.dk @ reservations@hoteldunord.dk
This late 19th-century hotel has recently been renovated. All rooms are
elegantly furnished. The hotel is behind Central Station. 1 🛏 TV 🛏 🖼 🖼

FURTHER AFIELD: *Guldsmeden* (Kr)(Kr) 64 ■
Vesterbrogade 66. **(** 33 22 15 00. **FAX** 33 22 15 55. W www.hotelguldsmeden.dk
@ reception@hotelguldsmeden.dk
The lofty, elegant rooms of this well-regarded hotel are furnished in a French
colonial style. Most of the double beds have canopies, which give the rooms
a highly romantic feel. 1 🛏 TV 🛏 🖼 Y P 🖼

FURTHER AFIELD: *Ibsens Hotel* (Kr)(Kr) 118 ● ■
Vendersgade 23. **(** 33 13 19 13. **FAX** 33 13 19 16.
W www.ibsenshotel.dk @ hotel@ibsenshotel.dk
Each floor of the hotel has its own theme. Recently upgraded, the hotel is
hidden away in a narrow street lined with cafés and is within easy reach of
Nørreport station. 1 🛏 TV 🛏 🖼 🖼 🖼

FURTHER AFIELD: *Kong Arthur* (Kr)(Kr)(Kr) 107 ● ■
Nørre Søgade 11. **(** 33 11 12 12. **FAX** 33 32 61 30. W www.kongarthur.dk
@ hotel@kongarthur.dk
Standing close to the city lakes and Rosenborg Slot, this former orphanage has
a contemporary interior that includes a spacious modern wing. Breakfast is
served in the garden in summer. 1 🛏 TV 🛏 🖼 Y 🖼 P 🖼

FURTHER AFIELD: *Mayfair Hotel* (Kr)(Kr)(Kr) 106 ■
Helgolandsgade 3. **(** 33 31 48 01. **FAX** 33 23 96 86.
W www.choicehotels.dk @ info@themayfairhotel.dk
Tucked away behind Central Station and a short walk from Tivoli, this
English-style hotel has comfortable rooms decorated with Chinese antiques.
1 🛏 TV 🛏 Y 🖼 🖼

NORTHWESTERN ZEALAND

BIRKERØD: *Birkerød* (Kr) 29
Kongevejen 102, 3460 Birkerød. **Road map** F4. **(** 45 81 44 30. **FAX** 45 82 30 29.
W www.hotelbirkerod.dk @ mail@hotelbirkerod.dk
A good-value hotel that is convenient for Copenhagen and northwestern
Zealand. Facilities include tennis courts. 1 🛏 TV 🛏 Y 🖼 P 🖼

ESKEBJERG: *Myrebøj* (Kr) 10 ■
Vilhelmshøjvej 1, 4593 Eskebjerg. **Road map** E4. **(** 59 29 00 26.
FAX 59 29 00 28. W www.myre.homepage.dk @ myre@it.dk
The oldest buildings of this modest bed & breakfast are 17th century. The
beach is about 3 km (2 miles) away. TV 🛏 P

FREDENSBORG: *Danhostel Fredensborg* (Kr) 54 ■
Østrupvej 3, 3480 Fredensborg. **Road map** F4. **(** 48 48 03 15. **FAX** 48 48 16 56.
W www.fredensborghostel.dk @ danhostel@mail.dk
This hostel boasts a very attractive location. Its garden provides direct access
to Fredensborg Slot's park. Most of the beds are in double rooms.
1 🛏 TV 🛏 🖼 Y 🖼 🔲 P 🖼

Price categories are for a standard double room per night with bath or shower, including breakfast, service and tax.
Ⓚ up to 1,000 Dkr
ⓀⓀ 1,000–1,400 Dkr
ⓀⓀⓀ 1,400–1,800 Dkr
ⓀⓀⓀⓀ 1,800–2,200 Dkr
ⓀⓀⓀⓀⓀ over 2,200 Dkr

RESTAURANT
Restaurant is open to non-residents.

GARDEN OR TERRACE
Hotel has its own garden, a terrace or a courtyard with plants.

SWIMMING POOL
Hotel has a pool for the use of its guests.

BUSINESS FACILITIES
Hotel has Internet access and meeting room.

	NUMBER OF ROOMS	RESTAURANT	GARDEN OR TERRACE	SWIMMING POOL	BUSINESS FACILITIES
FREDENSBORG: *Pension Bondehuset* Ⓚ Sorupvej 14, 3480 Fredensborg. **Road map** F4. 📞 48 48 01 12. 📠 48 48 03 01. W www.bondehuset.dk @ info@bondehuset.dk On the edge of Lake Esrumset, this idyllic pension is in early 18th-century buildings that were originally used as a boatyard. It is a well-regarded hotel with plush communal areas and elegantly furnished rooms. 1 🛏 P 📧	15	●	■		
FREDENSBORG: *Fredensborg Store Kro* ⓀⓀ Slotsgade 6, 3480 Fredensborg. **Road map** F4. 📞 48 40 11 11. 📠 48 48 45 61. W www.storekro.dk @ info@storekro.dk One of Zealand's oldest inns, this was commissioned by Frederik IV in 1723. The rooms are furnished in a variety of styles, but always with taste. Some of the rooms have views of Fredensborg Slot. 1 🛏 TV P	49	●			■
HELSINGØR: *Danhostel Helsingør* Ⓚ Ndr. Strandvej 24, 3000 Helsingør. **Road map** F4. 📞 49 21 16 40. 📠 49 21 13 99. W www.helsingorhostel.dk @ helsingor@danhostel.dk Located between the sea and the forests, this hotel is situated in a renovated manor house. 1 🛏 TV 📧 P 📧	28		■		
HELSINGØR: *Hamlet* Ⓚ Bramstræde 5, 3000 Helsingør. **Road map** F4. 📞 49 21 05 91. 📠 49 26 01 30. The staff are pleasant and helpful at this hotel, which is close to the harbour. The rooms are clean and comfortable. 1 🛏 TV 📧 🛏 📧 📧	36	●			
HELSINGØR: *Marienlyst* ⓀⓀ Ndr. Strandvej 2, 3000 Helsingor. **Road map** F4. 📞 49 21 40 00. 📠 49 21 49 00. W www.marienlyst.dk @ hotel@marienlyst.dk This hotel enjoys panoramic views of Kronborg Slot and the Swedish coast. Many of the rooms have views of the beach. 1 🛏 TV 📧 📧 📧	225	●	■	●	■
HILLERØD: *Gilleleje Badehotel* ⓀⓀⓀ Hulsøvej 15, 3250 Gilleleje. **Road map** F4. 📞 48 30 13 47. 📠 48 30 04 69. W www.gillelejebadehotel.dk @ info@gillelejebadehotel.dk Housed in a luxurious late-19th-century beach house, the recently decorated rooms of this stylish hotel have a contemporary feel. 1 🛏 TV 📧 📧 P 📧	27	●	■		■
HORNBÆK: *Bretagne* Ⓚ Sauntevej 18, 3100 Hornbæk. **Road map** F4. 📞 49 70 16 66. 📠 49 25 65 04. W www.hotelbretagne.dk @ mail@hotelbretagne.dk A pleasant hotel with wonderful views of lake and forest areas. As well as a restaurant, there are cooking facilities in every room. 1 🛏 TV 📧 🛏 📧 P 📧	24	●	■		
HORNBÆK: *Havreholm Slot* ⓀⓀⓀ Klosterrisvej 4, 3100 Hornbæk. **Road map** F4. 📞 49 75 86 00. 📠 49 75 80 23. W www.havreholm.dk @ havreholm@havreholm.dk Surrounded by a lovely park, this manor house is just south of Hornbæk beach. A golf course is close by. TV 📧 P	31	●	■	■	
HUNDESTED: *Hundested Kro* ⓀⓀ Nørregade 10, 3390 Hundested. **Road map** F4. 📞 47 93 75 38. 📠 47 93 78 61. W www.hundested-kro.dk @ Hundested.kro@adr.dk Part of the Dansk Kroferie chain (the largest hotel group in Denmark), this hotel is a short way from the beach. Facilities include a gym. 1 🛏 TV 📧	40	●	■	●	
NYKØBING S: *Anneberg Vandrerhjem* Ⓚ Egebjergvej 162, 4500 Nykøbing S. **Road map** E4. 📞 59 93 00 62. 📠 59 93 01 62. W www.odsherred-naturskole.dk @ vandrerhjem@odsherred-naturskole.dk During high season this small, family-friendly hostel hosts themed activities, many of which take place in the surrounding countryside. 📧 📧	12		■		

ROSKILDE: *Comwell Roskilde* ⓚ ⓚ 104
Vestre Kirkevej 12, 4000 Roskilde. **Road map** F4.
(46 32 31 31. **FAX** 46 35 08 35.
W www.comwell.com **@** hotel.roskilde@comwell.com
Standing near the fjord and surrounded by greenery, this hotel is close to
Roskilde's main sights. Each of the rooms is provided with a working area that
includes a comfortable armchair and desk. 1 🛏 TV 🔁 🛏 🎑 P 🎴

ROSKILDE: *Prindsen* ⓚ ⓚ 76
Algade 13, 4000 Roskilde. **Road map** F4. **(** 46 30 91 00. **FAX** 46 30 91 50.
W www.prindsen.dk **@** info@hotelprindsen.dk
A very attractive and smartly furnished hotel, whose guests have included
Hans Christian Andersen and members of the Danish royal family. The rooms
are comfortable and warmly furnished. 1 🛏 TV 🔁 🛏 Y 🎑 P 🎴

ROSKILDE: *Scandic Hotel Roskilde* ⓚ ⓚ 98
Søndre Ringvej 33, 4000 Roskilde. **Road map** F4.
(46 32 46 32. **FAX** 46 32 02 32.
W www.scandic-hotels.com **@** roskilde@scandic-hotels.com
Situated near the park, this prestigious hotel has many facilities including
a sauna and solarium. The rooms are comfortable and furnished in a
traditional style. 1 🛏 TV 🔁 🛏 Y 🎑 P 🎴

TISVILDELEJE: *Sankt Helene Family Holiday & Conference Centre* ⓚ 68
Bygmarken 30, 3220 Tisvildeleje. **Road map** F4. **(** 48 70 98 50.
FAX 48 70 98 97. **W** www.helene.dk **@** info@helene.dk
This hostel is surrounded by greenery and close to sandy beaches. It is a
family-friendly place with a children's playground and areas for bonfires. The
grounds also include walking trails and sports fields. Each of the rooms has
four beds and a separate seating area. 1 🛏 🎑 & P

VEJBY: *Havgaarden* ⓚ 18
Strandlyvej 1, 3210 Vejby. **Road map** F4. **(** 48 70 57 30.
FAX 48 70 57 72. **W** www.havgaarden.dk **@** hotel@havgaarden.dk
Housed in a thatched farmhouse, this village hotel is an ideal place in which
to relax. In defiance of the modern world, none of the rooms have telephones
or televisions. A separate holiday cottage in the grounds is also available to
rent. 1 🛏 P 🎴

SOUTHERN ZEALAND AND THE ISLANDS

KØGE: *Danhostel Køge Vandrerhjem* ⓚ 26
Vamdrupvej 1, 4600 Køge. **Road map** F5. **(** 56 67 66 50. **FAX** 56 66 08 69.
@ koegedanhostel@koegekom.dk
Occupying a scenic spot northwest of the town centre, this hostel is close to a
children's playground and mini-market. 1 TV 🎑 P

KØGE: *Hvide Hus* ⓚ 126
Strandvejen 111, 4600 Køge. **Road map** F5. **(** 56 65 36 90. **FAX** 56 66 33 14.
W www.hotelhvidehus.dk **@** koge@hotelhvidehus.dk
A good-value hotel, situated a short way from the beach and offering a
pleasant and friendly atmosphere. 1 🛏 TV 🛏 Y 🎑 P 🎴

KØGE: *Niels Juel* ⓚ ⓚ 51
Toldbodvej 20, 4600 Køge. **Road map** F5. **(** 56 63 18 00. **FAX** 56 63 04 92.
W www.hotelnielsjuel.dk **@** hotelnielsjuel@post.tele.dk
The hotel affords a magnificent view of the harbour and the old part of town.
All rooms are furnished in a contemporary Danish style. The hotel is popular
with business travellers. 1 🛏 TV 🔁 🛏 Y 🎑 P 🎴

MARIBO: *Danhostel Maribo* ⓚ 24
Sdr. Boulevard 82B, 4930 Maribo. **Road map** E6. **(** 54 78 33 14.
FAX 54 78 32 65. **W** www.danhostel.dk/maribo **@** maribo@danhostel.dk
A clean, well-kept hostel close to an attractive woodland area. A lakeside path
leads to the centre of town. 1 TV 🛏 🎑 P 🎴

MARIBO: *Maribo Søpark* ⓚ 110
Vestergade 29, 4930 Maribo. **Road map** E6. **(** 54 78 10 11.
FAX 54 78 05 22. **W** www.maribo-soepark.dk **@** info@maribo-soepark.dk
This modern hotel enjoys an exceptionally lovely location. Its spacious rooms
are elegantly furnished; many have balconies with views of the lake.
1 🛏 TV 🔁 🛏 Y 🎑 P 🎴

For key to symbols see back flap

Price categories are for a standard double room per night with bath or shower, including breakfast, service and tax.

Ⓚ up to 1,000 Dkr
ⓀⓀ 1,000–1,400 Dkr
ⓀⓀⓀ 1,400–1,800 Dkr
ⓀⓀⓀⓀ 1,800–2,200 Dkr
ⓀⓀⓀⓀⓀ over 2,200 Dkr

RESTAURANT
Restaurant is open to non-residents.

GARDEN OR TERRACE
Hotel has its own garden, a terrace or a courtyard with plants.

SWIMMING POOL
Hotel has a pool for the use of its guests.

BUSINESS FACILITIES
Hotel has Internet access and meeting room.

		NUMBER OF ROOMS	RESTAURANT	GARDEN OR TERRACE	SWIMMING POOL	BUSINESS FACILITIES

NAKSKOV: *Harmonien*   Ⓚ | 28 | ● | | | |
Nybrogade 2, 4900 Nakskov. **Road map** E6. ☏ *54 95 91 90.*
FAX *54 95 91 30.* Ⓦ www.hotel-harmonien.dk @ hotel-harmonien@post.tele.dk
The Harmonien offers spacious, simply furnished rooms and is situated in the centre of Nakskov. A golf course is close by. 🔢 🛏 📺 🍴 🍷 P 🏌

NYKØBING F: *Danhostel Nykøbing F*   Ⓚ | 22 | ■ | | | ■ |
Østre Allé 110, 4800 Nykøbing F. **Road map** F6. ☏ *54 85 66 99.*
FAX *54 82 32 42.* @ nyk.f@danhostel.dk
A small seaside hostel opposite the zoo. 🔢 🛏 ♿ 🍷

NYKØBING F: *Falster*   Ⓚ | 68 | ● | | | ■ |
Stubbekøbingvej 150, 4800 Nykøbing F. **Road map** F6. ☏ *54 85 93 93.*
FAX *54 82 21 99.* Ⓦ www.hotel-falster.dk @ info@hotel-falster.dk
Opened in 1986, the Falster has spacious and comfortable rooms. The hotel has access to the nearby golf course. 🔢 🛏 📺 🍴 🍷 P 🏌

NYKØBING F: *Hotel Liselund*   Ⓚ | 24 | ● | | | |
Lundevej 22, 4800 Nykøbing F. **Road map** F6. ☏ *54 85 15 66.*
FAX *54 85 15 14.* Ⓦ www.motelliselund.dk @ liselund@post.tele.dk
A true American-style motel with cosy rooms and good food.
🔢 🛏 📺 🎿 🍴 🍷 🍷 🔳 P 🏌

PRÆSTØ: *Kirsebærkroen*   Ⓚ | 7 | ● | ■ | | |
Kirsebærvej 1, 4720 Præstø. **Road map** F5. ☏ *55 99 39 55.*
Ⓦ www.kirsebaerkroen.dk @ kroen@writeme.com
This modest hotel occupies a half-timbered late 18th-century building, a short distance from the fjords of Præstø. 🔢 🛏 P 🏌

RINGSTED: *Scandic Hotel Ringsted*   ⓀⓀ | 75 | ● | | | ■ |
Norretorv 57, 4100 Ringsted. **Road map** E5.
☏ *57 61 93 00.* FAX *57 67 02 07.*
Ⓦ www.scandic-hotels.com @ ringsted@scandic-hotels.com
A four-storey hotel south of the town centre. The rooms are comfortable and simply decorated. The hotel is popular with business travellers and makes a good base for exploring Zealand. 🔢 🛏 📺 🎿 🍴 🍷 🍷 P 🏌

RINGSTED: *Sørup Herregård*   ⓀⓀ | 102 | ● | ■ | ● | |
Sorupvej 26, 4100 Ringsted. **Road map** E5. ☏ *57 64 30 02.* FAX *57 64 31 73.*
Ⓦ www.sorup.dk @ info@sorup.dk
An ancient, red-brick manor house surrounded by acres of gardens and parkland. In the late 1980s the building was restored and converted into a modern hotel. Guests are offered numerous facilities including a swimming pool and solarium. 🔢 🛏 📺 🍴 🍷 🍷 P 🏌

RØDVIG STEVNS: *Rødvig Kro & Badehotel*   Ⓚ | 15 | ● | ■ | | |
Østersøvej 8, 4673 Rødvig Stevns. **Road map** F5. ☏ *56 50 60 98.*
FAX *56 52 80 14.* Ⓦ www.roedvigkro.dk @ info@roedvigkro.dk
In summer meals can be eaten in the garden of this small hotel, which overlooks the sea and attracts visitors with its warm atmosphere. 🔢 🍷 P 🏌

SAKSKØBING: *Våbensted Kro*   Ⓚ | 24 | ● | | | |
Kårup Møllevej 6, Våbensted, 4990 Sakskøbing. **Road map** E6.
☏ *54 70 63 63.* FAX *54 70 64 63.* Ⓦ www.hotel-vaabensted.dk
A pleasant hotel with a restaurant that serves excellent Thai dishes. 🔢 🛏 P

STEGE: *Præstekilde*   ⓀⓀ | 46 | ● | ■ | ● | |
Klintevej 116, 4780 Stege, Møn. **Road map** F6. ☏ *55 86 87 88.* FAX *55 81 36 34.*
Ⓦ www.praestekilde.dk @ info@praestekilde.dk
Located a short way from Møn cliffs, this hotel is in a pleasant rural farming area. A well-maintained golf course is nearby. 🔢 🛏 📺 🍴 🍷 🍷 P 🏌

FUNEN

ASSENS: *Marcussens* (Kr) | 33 | ●
Strandgade 22, 5610 Assens. **Road map** C5. ☎ 64 71 10 89.
FAX 64 71 41 75. W www.marcussens.dk @ info@marcussens.dk
This is an ideal place for those who wish to find small-town atmosphere on
Funen. Most of the rooms have a view of the coast. ⬛ 🛏 📺 🔄 🛏 🛗 🅿 🈸

FAABORG: *Færgegaarden* (Kr) | 15 | ●
Christian IX Vej 31, 5600 Faaborg. **Road map** D5. ☎ 62 61 11 15.
FAX 62 61 11 95. W www.hotelfg.dk @ kontakt@hotelfg.dk
A beautiful hotel with spacious and comfortable rooms. ⬛ 🛏 📺 🅿 🈸

FAABORG: *Mosegaard* (Kr) | 22 | ● ■ ■
Nabgyden 31, 5600 Faaborg. **Road map** D5. ☎ 62 61 56 91.
FAX 62 61 56 96. W www.hotelmosegaard.dk @ Post@hotelmosegaard.dk
A cosy hotel in a converted Funen farmhouse. ⬛ 🛏 📺 🅿 🈸

KERTEMINDE: *Danhostel Kerteminde* (Kr) | 30 | ■ ■
Skovvej 46, 5300 Kerteminde. **Road map** D5. ☎ 65 32 39 29.
FAX 65 32 39 24. W www.dkhostel.dk @ info@dkhostel.dk
An inexpensive hotel in a wooded area that is a short walk from the beach.
⬛ 🛏 📺 🔄 🛗 🅿 🈸

MARSTAL: *Ærø Strand* (Kr) | 100 | ● ●
Egehovedvej 4, 5960 Marstal. **Road map** D6. ☎ 62 53 33 20. FAX 62 53 31 50.
W www.hotel-aeroestrand.dk @ sales@hotel-aeroestrand.dk
Situated in an old harbour town the hotel has a range of facilities that include
a swimming pool, sauna, tennis court and nightclub. 🛏 📺 🔄 🔄 🅿 🈸

MIDDELFART: *Hindsgavl Slot* (Kr)(Kr) | 73 | ● ■
Hindsgavl Alle 7, 5500 Middelfart. **Road map** C5. ☎ 64 41 88 00.
FAX 64 41 88 11. W www.hindsgavl.dk @ hindsgavl@hindsgavl.dk
Occupying a medieval castle, this hotel enjoys a magnificent lakeside location.
⬛ 🛏 📺 🔄 🅿 🈸

MIDDELFART: *KongebroGaarden* (Kr)(Kr)(Kr) | 62 | ● ■ ● ■
Kongebrovej 63, 5500 Middelfart **Road map** C5. ☎ 63 41 63 41.
FAX 63 41 63 42. W www.kongebrogaarden.dk @ hotel@kongebro.dk
A luxurious hotel that is surrounded by forests and a deer park. Rooms and
suites are spacious and decorated in a modern style. One of the few hotels in
Denmark to be awarded five stars. 🛏 📺 🔄 🛏 🍽 📋 🅿 🈸

MUNKEBO: *Munkebo Kro* (Kr)(Kr) | 20 | ● ■
Fjordvej 56, 5330 Munkebo. **Road map** D5. ☎ 65 97 40 30.
FAX 65 97 55 64. W www.munkebo-kro.dk @ munkebo-kro@munkebo-kro.dk
This one-time country inn has been converted into a comfortable hotel and is
steeped in atmosphere. The rooms are attractively lit and tastefully furnished.
🛏 📺 🛏 🍽 🅿 🈸

NYBORG: *Nyborg Strand* (Kr)(Kr) | 284 | ● ● ■
Østerøvej 2, 5800 Nyborg. **Road map** D5. ☎ 65 31 31 31.
FAX 65 31 37 01. W www.nyborgstrand.dk @ nyborgstrand@nyborgstrand.dk
One of Funen's largest hotels with comfortable rooms. 🛏 📺 🔄 🔄 🅿 🈸

NYBORG: *Hesselet* (Kr)(Kr)(Kr) | 47 | ●
Christianslundskoven 119, 5800 Nyborg. **Road map** D5. ☎ 65 31 30 29.
FAX 65 31 29 58. W www.hesselet.dk @ hotel@hesselet.dk
Beautifully situated on the seashore and surrounded by a forest of beech
trees. The rooms are stylish and spacious. ⬛ 🛏 📺 🍽 🔄 🅿 🈸

ODENSE: *City Hotel Odense* (Kr) | 48 | ● ■ ■
Hans Mulesgade 5, 5000 Odense C. **Road map** D5. ☎ 66 12 12 58.
FAX 66 12 93 64. W www.city-hotel-odense.dk @ reception@city-hotel-odense.dk
Situated in the centre of Odense, this modern hotel was built in the 1980s.
The roof terrace affords panoramic views of Odense. ⬛ 🛏 📺 🔄 🔄 🅿 🈸

ODENSE: *Danhostel Odense City* (Kr) | 39 | ■
Østre Stationsvej 31, 5000 Odense C. **Road map** D5. ☎ 63 11 04 25.
FAX 63 11 35 20. W www.cityhostel.dk @ info@cityhostel.dk
This hostel is in the centre of Odense, next to the train station, and occupies a
19th-century building that was once a luxury hotel. ⬛ 🛏 📺 🔄 🔄 🛗 🅿 🈸

						NUMBER OF ROOMS	RESTAURANT	GARDEN OR TERRACE	SWIMMING POOL	BUSINESS FACILITIES

Price categories are for a standard double room per night with bath or shower, including breakfast, service and tax.
- Ⓚ up to 1,000 Dkr
- ⓀⓀ 1,000–1,400 Dkr
- ⓀⓀⓀ 1,400–1,800 Dkr
- ⓀⓀⓀⓀ 1,800–2,200 Dkr
- ⓀⓀⓀⓀⓀ over 2,200 Dkr

RESTAURANT
Restaurant is open to non-residents.

GARDEN OR TERRACE
Hotel has its own garden, a terrace or a courtyard with plants.

SWIMMING POOL
Hotel has a pool for the use of its guests.

BUSINESS FACILITIES
Hotel has Internet access and meeting room.

Entry	Rooms	Restaurant	Garden or Terrace	Swimming Pool	Business Facilities
ODENSE: *Domir* Ⓚ	35	●			▪
ODENSE: *First Hotel Grand* ⓀⓀ	138	●	▪	●	
ODENSE: *Clarion Hotel Plaza* ⓀⓀⓀ	68	●			
ODENSE: *Radisson SAS H.C. Andersen* ⓀⓀⓀ	145	●			▪
RINGE: *Ringe* Ⓚ	21	●			
SVENDBORG: *Svendborg* Ⓚ	133	●			▪
ÆRØSKØBING: *Danhostel Ærøskøbing* Ⓚ	27		▪		
BILLUND: *Legoland* ⓀⓀⓀ	154	●	▪		
EBELTOFT: *Ebeltoft Park* Ⓚ	74	●	▪	●	

ODENSE: *Domir*   Ⓚ
Hans Tausensgade 19, 5000 Odense C. **Road map** D5. 📞 66 12 14 27. **FAX** 66 12 14 13. 🗔 www.domir.dk @ booking@domir.dk
Located in a quiet street in the centre of Odense, the interior décor of this early 20th-century hotel is simple but elegant. 1 🛏 TV 📶 🛎 ⚡ P 🖂

ODENSE: *First Hotel Grand*   ⓀⓀ
Jernbanegade 18, 5100 Odense C. **Road map** D5. 📞 66 11 71 71. **FAX** 66 14 11 71. 🗔 www.firsthotels.com @ odense@firsthotels.dk
The air of traditional luxury in this century-old four-storey hotel is enhanced by the original chandeliers and plush marble bathrooms.
1 🛏 TV 📶 🛎 Y ⚡ P 🖂

ODENSE: *Clarion Hotel Plaza*   ⓀⓀⓀ
Østre Stationsvej 24, 5000 Odense C. **Road map** D5. 📞 66 11 77 45. **FAX** 66 14 41 45. 🗔 www.choicehotels.dk @ plaza@choicehotels.dk
A luxurious and elegant hotel situated close to the town centre. Non-smoking rooms are available on request. 1 🛏 TV 📶 🛎 ⚡ P 🖂

ODENSE: *Radisson SAS H.C. Andersen*   ⓀⓀⓀ
Claus Bergs Gade 7, 5000 Odense C. **Road map** D5. 📞 66 14 78 00. **FAX** 66 14 78 90. 🗔 www.radissonsas.com @ hcandersen@radissonsas.com
This luxurious hotel is situated a short way from the childhood home of Hans Christian Andersen. Some of the rooms look out onto a quiet inner courtyard. Visitors can try their luck in the hotel casino. 1 🛏 TV 📶 Y ⚡ P 🖂

RINGE: *Ringe*   Ⓚ
Algade 13, 5750 Ringe. **Road map** D5. 📞 62 62 12 00. **FAX** 62 62 55 55. 🗔 www.hotelringe.dk @ hotelringe@hotelringe.dk
About 20 km (12 miles) south of Odense, Hotel Ringe is a good alternative for visitors who cannot afford to stay in the city. Ringe is convenient for many of Funen's attractions. 1 TV 🛎 P 🖂

SVENDBORG: *Svendborg*   Ⓚ
Centrumpladsen 1, 5700 Svendborg. **Road map** D5. 📞 62 21 17 00. **FAX** 62 21 90 12. 🗔 www.hotel-svendborg.dk @ booking@hotel-svendborg.dk
The hotel stands in the heart of town and offers rooms furnished in a contemporary Danish style. 1 🛏 TV 📶 ⚡ ♿ P 🖂

ÆRØSKØBING: *Danhostel Ærøskøbing*   Ⓚ
Smedevejen 15, 5970 Ærøskøbing. **Road map** D6. 📞 62 52 10 44. **FAX** 62 52 16 44.
A pleasant hostel, close to the beach. Facilities include a children's playground and a picnic area with barbecues. 1 🛏 TV 📶 🛎 Y ⚡ ▤ P 🖂

SOUTHERN AND CENTRAL JUTLAND

BILLUND: *Legoland*   ⓀⓀⓀ
Aastvej 10, 7190 Billund. **Road map** C4. 📞 75 33 12 44. **FAX** 75 35 38 10. 🗔 www.hotellegoland.dk @ hotel@legoland.dk
As the name indicates, the hotel is intended mainly for visitors to LEGOLAND® and is connected to the park by an overhead walkway. Guests are offered discounted entry to the park. Children have at their disposal a playroom with thousands of LEGO® bricks. 1 🛏 TV 📶 🛎 Y ⚡ P 🖂

EBELTOFT: *Ebeltoft Park*   Ⓚ
Vibæk Strandvej 4, 8400 Ebeltoft. **Road map** D3. 📞 86 34 32 22. **FAX** 86 34 49 41. 🗔 www.ebeltoftparkhotel.dk @ mail@ebeltoftparkhotel.dk
The hotel stands on a white-sand beach. A heated swimming pool is available as an alternative in inclement weather. The nearby ferry terminal provides links with Zealand. 1 🛏 TV 🛎 ⚡ P 🖂

EBELTOFT: *Hvide Hus*   Ⓚ Ⓚ   **98**
Strandgårdshøj 1, 8400 Ebeltoft. **Road map** D3.
📞 86 34 14 66. **FAX** 86 34 49 69. **W** www.hhh-hotel.dk **@** hotel@hhh-hotel.dk
The hotel overlooks beautiful scenery, including the nearby beaches. Rooms are comfortable and well furnished. 1 🛏 TV 📶 🍴 Y 🔌 P 🐾

ESBJERG: *Scandic Olympic Esbjerg*   Ⓚ   **90**
Strandbygade 3, 6700 Esbjerg. **Road map** B5. 📞 75 18 11 88. **FAX** 75 18 11 08.
W www.scandic-hotels.com **@** esbjerg@scandic-hotels.com
This modern, four-storey hotel has recently been refurbished and offers clean, well-maintained accommodation. Numerous golf courses are nearby. The hotel is popular with business travellers and is convenient for Fanø and nearby attractions such as Ribe. 1 🛏 TV 📶 🍴 Y 🔌 P 🐾

ESBJERG: *Britannia*   Ⓚ Ⓚ   **79**
Torvegade 24, 6700 Esbjerg. **Road map** B5. 📞 75 13 01 11. **FAX** 75 45 20 85.
W www.britannia.dk **@** info@britannia.dk
An unremarkable exterior hides pleasant, functional rooms in this modern four-storey hotel. Close by is an architectural pearl – the Musikhus designed by Jørn Utzon. 1 🛏 TV 📶 🍴 Y 🔌 P 🐾

FANØ: *Sønderho Kro*   Ⓚ   **14**
Kropladsen 11, Sønderho, 6720 Fanø. **Road map** B5. 📞 75 16 40 09.
FAX 75 16 43 85. **W** www.sonderhokro.dk **@** sonderhokro@mail.dk
An 18th-century, thatched-roof inn with a pleasant atmosphere and many old-world features including beamed ceilings, antiques and four-poster beds. The French-Danish restaurant attracts gourmets. 1 🛏 TV P 🐾

FREDERICIA: *Kronprinds Frederik*   Ⓚ   **78**
Vestre Ringvej 96, 7000 Fredericia. **Road map** C5. 📞 75 91 00 00. **FAX** 75 91 19 99.
W www.kronprindsfrederik.dk **@** info@kronprindsfrederik.dk
As well as standard comforts and facilities this establishment offers ideal conditions for rest and relaxation amidst magnificent scenery.
1 🛏 TV 📶 🍴 Y 🔌 P 🐾

FREDERICIA: *Kryb-i-ly Kro*   Ⓚ Ⓚ   **77**
Kolding Landevej 160, Taulov, 7000 Fredericia. **Road map** C5. 📞 75 56 25 55.
FAX 75 56 45 14. **W** www.krybily.dk **@** krybily@krybily.dk
A cosy manor house with plenty of character. Facilities include a solarium and billiard room. The hotel's name means "take shelter". 1 🛏 TV 🍴 Y 🔌 P 🐾

GRENÅ: *Grenå Strand*   Ⓚ   **14**
Havneplads 1, 8500 Grenå. **Road map** D3. 📞 86 32 68 14. **FAX** 86 32 07 92.
W www.grenaastrand.dk **@** info@grenaastrand.dk
The hotel occupies a conspicuous early 20th-century yellow building. Next to it is a sailing jetty and a pleasant beach. Rooms are uncluttered and typically Danish in character. 1 🛏 TV P 🐾

HERNING: *Østergaards Hotel*   Ⓚ Ⓚ   **84**
Silkeborgvej 94, 7400 Herning. **Road map** C4. 📞 97 12 45 55. **FAX** 97 12 01 52.
W www.oestergaardshotel.dk **@** info@oestergaardshotel.dk
The hotel offers rooms with modern furnishings and is situated next to a golf course. 1 🛏 TV 📶 🍴 Y 🔌 P 🐾

HERNING: *Scandic Regina Herning*   Ⓚ Ⓚ   **142**
Fonnesbechsgade 20, 7400 Herning. **Road map** C4. 📞 97 21 15 00.
FAX 97 21 13 03. **W** www.scandic-hotels.dk **@** herning@scandic-hotels.com
Convenient for LEGOLAND® and the nearby golf courses, the facilities at this hotel include a children's playroom. 1 🛏 TV 📶 🍴 Y 🔌 P 🐾

HORSENS: *Best Western Hotel Danica*   Ⓚ   **39**
Ove Jensens Alle 28, 8700 Horsens. **Road map** C4.
📞 75 61 60 22. **FAX** 75 61 66 63. **W** www.hoteldanica.dk **@** info@hoteldanica.dk
A modern and comfortable hotel situated in the town centre.
1 🛏 TV 📶 Y 🔌 P 🐾

HORSENS: *Scandic Bygholm Park*   Ⓚ   **142**
Schüttesvej 6, 8700 Horsens. **Road map** C4. 📞 75 62 23 33. **FAX** 75 61 31 05.
W www.scandic-hotels.com **@** horsens@scandic-hotels.com
Occupying an old manor house surrounded by a park, this hotel is recommended to visitors seeking an alternative to a city atmosphere.
1 🛏 TV 📶 🍴 Y 🔌 P 🐾

For key to symbols see back flap

Price categories are for a standard double room per night with bath or shower, including breakfast, service and tax. ⓚ up to 1,000 Dkr ⓚⓚ 1,000–1,400 Dkr ⓚⓚⓚ 1,400–1,800 Dkr ⓚⓚⓚⓚ 1,800–2,200 Dkr ⓚⓚⓚⓚⓚ over 2,200 Dkr	**RESTAURANT** Restaurant is open to non-residents. **GARDEN OR TERRACE** Hotel has its own garden, a terrace or a courtyard with plants. **SWIMMING POOL** Hotel has a pool for the use of its guests. **BUSINESS FACILITIES** Hotel has Internet access and meeting room.	**NUMBER OF ROOMS**	**RESTAURANT**	**GARDEN OR TERRACE**	**SWIMMING POOL**	**BUSINESS FACILITIES**

	Rooms	Rest.	Garden	Pool	Business
KOLDING: *Comwell Kolding* ⓚⓚ Skovbrynet 1, 6000 Kolding. **Road map** C5. 76 34 11 00. **FAX** 76 34 12 00. ⓦ www.comwell.com @ hotel.kolding@comwell.com This modern hotel is a short way from Kolding's centre, next to a lake. The hotel is decorated in a contempory Danish style. ① 🔒 📺 🔧 🏠 🍴 🏊 🅿 🗐	180	●		●	▪
RIBE: *Dagmar* ⓚⓚ Torvet 1, 6760 Ribe. **Road map** B5. 75 42 00 33. **FAX** 75 42 36 52. ⓦ www.hoteldagmar.dk @ dagmar@hoteldagmar.dk A friendly hotel occupying a 16th-century, half-timbered building. The rooms are stylish with canopy beds and comfy armchairs. ① 🔒 📺 🏠 🍴 🅿 🗐	48	●	▪		
RIBE: *Weis Stue* ⓚⓚ Torvet 2, 6760 Ribe. **Road map** B5. 75 42 07 00. **FAX** 75 41 17 95. ⓦ www.weis-stue.dk @ info.esplanaden@comfort.choicehotels.dk An atmospheric old inn-style hotel that is situated in the heart of Ribe. ① 🔒 🏠 🏊 🅿 🗐	8	●			▪
RINGKØBING: *Fjordgarden* ⓚⓚ Vesterkær 28, 6950 Ringkøbing. **Road map** B4. 97 32 14 00. **FAX** 97 32 47 60. ⓦ www.hotelfjordgaarden.dk @ rec@fjordgaarden.dk A modern hotel a short distance from the town centre. The rooms are a good size with pleasant sea and country views. ① 🔒 📺 🏠 🍴 🏊 🅿 🗐	98	●		●	
RØMØ: *Færgegaarden* ⓚ Vestergade 1, Havneby, 6792 Rømø. **Road map** B5. 74 75 54 32. **FAX** 74 75 58 59. ⓦ www.faergegaarden.com @ info@faergegaarden.com A simple, thatched-roof hotel with an unpretentious atmosphere. The hotel is a short way from the island's best beaches. ① 🔒 📺 🏠 🏊 🅿 🗐	35	●	▪	●	
SILKEBORG: *Dania* ⓚⓚ Torvet 5, 8600 Silkeborg. **Road map** C4. 86 82 01 11. **FAX** 86 80 20 04. ⓦ www.hoteldania.dk @ info@hoteldania.dk Standing in the main square, this historic hotel is convenient for the train station. Rooms are uncluttered, with modern décor. ① 🔒 📺 🔧 🏊 🅿 🗐	48	●			
SILKEBORG: *Radisson SAS Hotel Silkeborg* ⓚⓚ Papirfabrikken 12, 8600 Silkeborg. **Road map** C4. 88 82 22 22. **FAX** 88 22 22 23. ⓦ www.radissonsas.com @ info.silkeborg@radissonsas.com Silkeborg's old paper mill was thoroughly refurbished and remodelled in 2002. The interior is bright and modern. ① 🔒 📺 🔧 🍴 🏊 🅿 🗐	86	●		●	
SKANDERBORG: *Skanderborghus* ⓚ Dyrehaven 3, 8660 Skanderborg. **Road map** C4. 86 52 09 55. **FAX** 86 52 18 01. ⓦ www.hotel-skanderborghus.dk @ post@hotelskanderborghus.dk This bright and airy lakeside hotel is surrounded by some breathtaking scenery. A golf course is nearby. ① 🔒 📺 🏠 🍴 🅿 🗐	45	●	▪	●	▪
SØNDERBORG: *Quality Hotel Sønderborg* ⓚⓚ Ellegårdvej 27, 6400 Sønderborg. **Road map** C6. 74 42 26 00. **FAX** 74 42 76 00. ⓦ www.qualityhotelsonderborg.dk @ Booking.Soenderborg@Quality.Choicehotels.dk An inexpensive hotel with excellent service. ① 🔒 📺 🔧 🏠 🍴 🏊 🅿 🗐	102	●		●	
TØNDER: *Schackenborg Slotskro* ⓚⓚ Slotsgaden 42, Møgeltønder, 6270 Tønder. **Road map** B6. 74 73 83 83. **FAX** 74 73 83 11. ⓦ www.slotskro.dk @ schackenborg@slotskro.dk An elegant hotel with an enchanting atmosphere. The hotel is situated in one of the most charming village streets in Denmark. The hotel stands close to the ducal palace of Schackenborg, and many of the hotel rooms were decorated under the supervision of Princess Alexandra. ① 🔒 📺 🏠 🏊 🅿 🗐	25	●	▪		

VEJLE: *Park*   Ⓚ   33
Orla Lehmannsgade 5, 7100 Vejle. **Road map** C4.
☎ 75 82 24 66. FAX 75 72 05 39. W www.park-hotel.dk @ park-hotel@mail.dk
Vejle's oldest hotel occupies a corner plot right in the town centre.
1 🛏 TV 📶 🛏 🍴

VEJLE: *Quality Hotel Australia*   ⓀⓀ   102
Dæmningen 6, 7100 Vejle. **Road map** C4. ☎ 76 40 60 00. FAX 76 40 60 01.
W www.choicehotels.dk @ booking.australia@quality.choicehotels.dk
A modern, 11-storey hotel with an impressive view of the town and the fjord.
The rooms are spacious and clean. 1 🛏 TV 📶 🛏 🍴 👶 P 🍴

ÅRHUS: *Cab Inn Århus*   Ⓚ   192
Kannikegade 14, 8000 Århus C. **Road map** D4. ☎ 86 75 70 00. FAX 86 75 71 00.
W www.cabinn.dk @ aarhus@cabinn.dk
A recently built, budget hotel with simple rooms, all of which have a private
bath. 1 🛏 TV 📶 📋 👶 P 🍴

ÅRHUS: *Guldsmeden*   Ⓚ   20
Guldsmedgade 40, 8000 Århus C. **Road map** D4. ☎ 86 13 45 50. FAX 86 13 76 76.
W www.hotelguldsmeden.dk @ aarhus@hotelguldsmeden.dk
A small hotel, situated just north of the centre, in a renovated 19th-century
town house. The hotel is furnished in a colonial style and emanates good
taste. Breakfast is served on the terrace in summer. 1 TV 🛏 🍴

ÅRHUS: *Best Western Hotel Ritz*   ⓀⓀ   67
Banegardspladsen 12, 8000 Århus C. **Road map** D4.
☎ 86 13 44 44. FAX 86 13 45 87. W www.hotelritz.dk @ hotel.ritz@image.dk
Smart and stylishly furnished, this hotel was built in 1932 and is situated at the
very heart of Århus, a short walk from the train station. The hotel restaurant is
one of the best in town; its exquisite wine cellar provides a further reason to
eat here. 1 🛏 TV 🛏 🍴 🍴

ÅRHUS: *Helnan Marselis*   ⓀⓀ   101
Strandvejen 25, 8000 Århus C. **Road map** D4. ☎ 86 14 44 11. FAX 86 14 44 20.
W www.marselis.dk @ booking@marselis.dk
The hotel is 3 km (2 miles) from the town centre and next to the beach. Built
in 1967 the hotel has been cleverly designed to offer a sea view from every
room. 1 🛏 TV 📶 🛏 🍴 🍴 P 🍴

NORTHERN JUTLAND

DRONNINGLUND: *Dronninglund*   Ⓚ   72
Slotsgade 78, 9330 Dronninglund. **Road map** D2. ☎ 98 84 15 33. FAX 98 84 40 50.
W www.dronninglundhotel.dk @ info@dronninglundhotel.dk
A simple, provincial hotel that offers comfortable surroundings and a family-
friendly atmosphere at a modest price. 🛏 TV 🍴 P 🍴

FREDERIKSHAVN: *Lisboa*   Ⓚ   32
Søndergade 248, 9900 Frederikshavn. **Road map** D1. ☎ 98 42 21 33.
FAX 98 43 80 11. W www.lisboa.dk @ info@lisboa.dk
A family-friendly hotel with a children's playground and a special children's
menu in the restaurant. 🛏 TV 🛏 🍴 P 🍴

FREDERIKSHAVN: *Scandic Stena Line Hotel Frederikshavn*   Ⓚ   213
Tordenskjoldsgade 14, 9900 Frederikshavn. **Road map** D1. ☎ 98 43 32 33.
FAX 98 43 33 11. W www.scandic-hotels.com @ info@scandic-hotels.com
A comfortable hotel with a heated swimming pool. The children's playground
has a jokey sign that reads "No Adults". 1 🛏 TV 📶 🛏 🍴 🍴 P 🍴

FREDERIKSHAVN: *Turisthotellet*   Ⓚ   23
Margrethevej 5–7, 9900 Frederikshavn. **Road map** D1. ☎ 98 42 90 55.
FAX 98 42 90 91. W www.turisthotellet.dk @ turisthotellet@1031.inord.dk
Simple and cosily furnished, this hotel is close to many of northern Jutland's
attractions. 1 🛏 TV 🛏 P 🍴

FREDERIKSHAVN: *Radisson SAS Jutlandia*   ⓀⓀ   95
Havnepladsen 1, Box 89, 9900 Frederikshavn. **Road map** D1. ☎ 98 42 42 00.
FAX 98 42 38 72. W www.radissonsas.com @ frost@hotel-jutlandia.dk
This large and elegant hotel is in the town centre and affords a beautiful view
of the harbour. The Danish royal family sometimes stay here.
1 🛏 TV 📶 🛏 🍴 🍴 P 🍴

Price categories are for a standard double room per night with bath or shower, including breakfast, service and tax.
Ⓚ up to 1,000 Dkr
ⓀⓀ 1,000–1,400 Dkr
ⓀⓀⓀ 1,400–1,800 Dkr
ⓀⓀⓀⓀ 1,800–2,200 Dkr
ⓀⓀⓀⓀⓀ over 2,200 Dkr

RESTAURANT
Restaurant is open to non-residents.

GARDEN OR TERRACE
Hotel has its own garden, a terrace or a courtyard with plants.

SWIMMING POOL
Hotel has a pool for the use of its guests.

BUSINESS FACILITIES
Hotel has Internet access and meeting room.

	NUMBER OF ROOMS	RESTAURANT	GARDEN OR TERRACE	SWIMMING POOL	BUSINESS FACILITIES
HOLSTEBRO: *Best Western Hotel Schaumburg* Ⓚ	57	●		●	

Nørregade 26, 7500 Holstebro. **Road map** B3.
📞 97 42 31 11. ℻ 97 42 72 82. 🌐 www.hotel-schaumburg.dk
@ mail@hotel-schaumburg.dk
An old and very beautiful hotel. The rooms are furnished in a modern style.
🔟 🛏 TV 📶 🐾 Y 🍴 P 🅿

HOLSTEBRO: *Royal Holstebro* ⓀⓀ	40				

Den Røde Plads 10, 7500 Holstebro. **Road map** B3. 📞 97 40 23 33.
℻ 97 40 30 87. 🌐 www.hotel-royal.dk @ hotelroyal@hotel-royal.dk
A strikingly modern hotel that includes a 27-m (88-ft) high glass prism. Close by is a golf course and a swimming pool complex; both offer reduced rates for the hotel's guests. 🔟 🛏 TV 📶 🐾 Y 🍴 🅿

NYKØBING M: *Pakhuset Hotel & Restaurant* Ⓚ	18	●			

Havnen 1, 7900 Nykøbing M. **Road map** B2. 📞 97 72 33 00. ℻ 97 72 52 33.
🌐 www.phr.dk @ phr@phr.dk
The thick walls of this former harbourside warehouse hide a pleasant hotel. The restaurant has an excellent menu and the wine cellar is well stocked.
🔟 🛏 TV 📶 🐾 Y P 🅿

RANDERS: *Randers* Ⓚ	79	●			▨

Torvegade 11, 8900 Randers. **Road map** D3. 📞 86 42 34 22. ℻ 86 40 15 86.
🌐 www.hotel-randers.dk @ hr@hotel-randers.dk
One of the town's best hotels, with spacious and stylish rooms. The public areas have recently been refurbished and are beautifully decorated. The hotel restaurant is well worth visiting. 🔟 🛏 TV 📶 🍴 🅿

RANDERS: *Scandic Hotel Kongens Ege* ⓀⓀ	130	●			▨

Gl. Hadsundvej 2, 8900 Randers. **Road map** D3. 📞 86 43 03 00. ℻ 86 43 22 73.
🌐 www.scandic-hotels.com @ Randers@scandic-hotels.com
A popular hotel standing on a hill amid ancient oak trees. The hotel overlooks both the town and the fjord. 🔟 🛏 TV 📶 🐾 Y 🍴 P 🅿

SKAGEN: *Color Hotel Skagen* Ⓚ	152	●	▨	●	

Gl. Landevej 39, 9990 Skagen. **Road map** D1. 📞 98 44 22 33. ℻ 98 44 21 34.
🌐 www.colorhotels.dk @ skagen@skagenhotel.dk
A modern hotel a little way from the main sights with an outdoor pool and a rather formal atmosphere. The rooms' large windows make the most of Skagen's famous light. 🛏 TV 🐾 P 🅿

SKAGEN: *Plesner* ⓀⓀ	16	●			

Holstvej 8, 9990 Skagen. **Road map** D1. 📞 98 44 68 44. ℻ 98 44 36 86.
🌐 www.hotelplesner.dk @ plesner@hotelplesner.dk
A good family-run hotel with a great atmosphere. The hotel is situated in the centre of town, within walking distance of Skagen's sights. 🔟 🛏 TV 🅿

SKAGEN: *Ruths Hotel* ⓀⓀ	26	●			▨

Hans Ruths Vej 1, DK-9900 Skagen. **Map** 2 F5. 📞 98 44 11 24. ℻ 98 45 08 75.
🌐 www.ruths-hotel.dk @ info@ruths-hotel.dk
An atmospheric hotel in the heart of the old part of Skagen. The excellent facilties include a gym and solarium. 🔟 🛏 TV 🅿

SKIVE: *Best Western Hotel Gl. Skivehus* Ⓚ	56	●	▨		

Sdr. Boulevard 1, 7800 Skive. **Road map** C3. 📞 97 52 11 44. ℻ 97 52 81 68.
🌐 www.skivehus.dk @ info@skivehus.dk
This modern, family-run hotel stands on a site previously occupied by a fort and later a manor house that provided the aristocracy with overnight accommodation. The rooms are clean, simple and uncluttered.
🔟 🛏 TV 📶 🐾 Y 🍴 P 🅿

SKØRPING: *Comwell Rebild Bakker* (K)
Rebildvej 36, 9520 Skørping. **Road map** C2. **[** 98 39 12 22. FAX 98 39 24 55.
W www.comwell.dk @ hotel.rebildbakker@comwell.com
This hotel is convenient for the rolling hills and forests of Denmark's only
national park. All rooms have balconies overlooking the countryside.

151

SÆBY: *Stibolt* (K)
Trafikcenter Sæby Syd 1, 9300 Sæby. **Road map** D1. **[** 96 89 66 69.
FAX 96 89 66 67. W www.tcss.dk @ hotel@tcss.dk
A modest and inexpensive hotel. It makes an excellent stopping-off place for
travellers on their way to Skagen.

10

VIBORG: *Best Western Palads* (K)(K)
Sct. Mathiasgade 5, 8800 Viborg. **Road map** C3.
[86 62 37 00. FAX 86 62 40 46. W www.hotelpalads.dk @ info@hotelpalads.dk
Right in the middle of town, this grand hotel combines tradition with comfort.
The rooms are pleasant and simply furnished. The hotel is a short way north
of the train station.

100

AALBORG: *First Hotel Aalborg* (K)
Rendsburggade 5, 9000 Aalborg. **Road map** D2.
[98 10 14 00. FAX 98 11 65 70. W www.firsthotels.dk @ aalborg@firsthotels.dk
A modern, pleasant hotel in the centre of Aalborg with views across
Limfjorden.

155

AALBORG: *Scandic Hotel Aalborg* (K)
Hadsundvej 200, 9220 Aalborg Øst. **Road map** D2. **[** 98 15 45 00.
FAX 98 15 55 88. W www.scandic-hotels.com @ Aalborg@scandic-hotels.com
The hotel specializes in golfing holidays and also sells golfing equipment. It is
some distance from the town centre. Among the facilities is a children's
playground.

101

AALBORG: *Radisson SAS Limfjord* (K)(K)(K)
Ved Stranden 14, 9000 Aalborg. **Road map** D2.
[98 16 43 33. FAX 98 16 17 47. W www.radissonsas.com
@ limfjord@radissonsas.com
This is one of the most luxurious hotels in northern Jutland. It has its own
casino and also offers comfortable rooms overlooking the fjord.

188

BORNHOLM

ALLINGE: *Abildgaard* (K)
Tejnvej 100, 3770 Allinge. **[** 56 48 09 55. FAX 56 48 08 35.
W www.hotel-abildgaard.dk @ mail@ hotel-abildgaard.dk
Situated on the shore, this hotel is an ideal place for summer holidays on
Bornholm. Facilities include a swimming pool.

83

ALLINGE: *Friheden* (K)
Tejnvej 80, 3770 Allinge. **[** 56 48 04 25. FAX 56 48 16 65.
W www.hotel-friheden.dk @ post@hotel-friheden.dk
With a terrace overlooking the Baltic, this hotel has a beautiful location. All
rooms have kitchenettes with refrigerators.

48

ALLINGE: *Klintely* (K)
Klinteløkken 9, 3770 Allinge. **[** 56 48 10 34. FAX 56 48 10 02.
W www.familieferiebornholm.dk @ info@familieferiebornholm.dk
The hotel consists of bungalows surrounding a pretty garden. The walking
and cycling trails nearby make it a good base for island forays.

24

ALLINGE: *Nordland* (K)
Strandpromenaden 5, 3770 Allinge. **[** 56 48 03 01. FAX 56 48 22 01.
W www.hotel-nordland.dk @ info@hotel-nordland.dk
Standing on a beach close to Sandvig's harbour, the hotel has a large terrace
where guests can take their meals in summer.

24

ALLINGE: *Pepita* (K)
Langebjergvej 1, 3770 Allinge. **[** 56 48 04 51. FAX 56 48 18 51.
W www.pepita.dk @ pepita@post5.tele.dk
The main building of this centrally-located hotel is 16th century. The pleasant
interiors have recently been refurbished.

36

For key to symbols see back flap

<table>
<tr><td colspan="2">

Price categories are for a standard double room per night with bath or shower, including breakfast, service and tax.

Ⓚ up to 1,000 Dkr
ⓀⓀ 1,000–1,400 Dkr
ⓀⓀⓀ 1,400–1,800 Dkr
ⓀⓀⓀⓀ 1,800–2,200 Dkr
ⓀⓀⓀⓀⓀ over 2,200 Dkr

</td><td>

RESTAURANT
Restaurant is open to non-residents.

GARDEN OR TERRACE
Hotel has its own garden, a terrace or a courtyard with plants.

SWIMMING POOL
Hotel has a pool for the use of its guests.

BUSINESS FACILITIES
Hotel has Internet access and meeting room.

</td></tr>
</table>

	NUMBER OF ROOMS	RESTAURANT	GARDEN OR TERRACE	SWIMMING POOL	BUSINESS FACILITIES
ALLINGE: *Sandkaas* Ⓚ Tejnvej 68–74, 3770 Allinge. ☎ 56 48 08 95. FAX 56 48 08 72. W www.hotelsandkaas.dk @ hotelsandkaas@mail.tele.dk This hotel has a lovely location, surrounded by greenery and close to the shore. All rooms have private entrances and a sea view. ① 🛏 TV 🔶 P 🖥	56	●	▪		
GUDHJEM: *Danhostel Gudhjem* Ⓚ Løkkegade 7, 3760 Gudhjem. ☎ 56 48 50 35. FAX 56 48 56 35. W www.danhostel-gudhjem.dk @ dgh@mail.tele.dk The hostel in Gudhjem is one of the oldest in Denmark. It stands close to the centre of town and occupies a pleasant building by the harbour. TV 🔶 P 🖥	37	●	▪		
GUDHJEM: *Jantzens Hotel* Ⓚ Brøddegade 33, 3760 Gudhjem. ☎ 56 48 50 17. FAX 56 48 57 15. W www.jantzenshotel.dk @ jantzenshotel@mail.dk Established in 1872, this hotel is one of the oldest on Bornholm. Many of its spacious rooms have balconies with sea views. At the back of the hotel is a sunny terrace and a rose garden. ① 🛏 TV 🔶 P 🖥	18	●	▪		
GUDHJEM: *Pension Koch* Ⓚ Melstedvej 15, 3760 Gudhjem. ☎ 56 48 50 72. FAX 56 95 34 66. W www.pensionkoch.dk @ info@pensionkoch.dk A comfortable, non-smoking hotel in the southern part of Gudhjem, a short way from the town centre. ① 🛏 TV 🔶 🔶 P 🖥	19		▪		
GUDHJEM: *Therns* Ⓚ Brøddegade 31, 3760 Gudhjem. ☎ 56 48 50 99. FAX 56 48 56 35. W www.therns-hotel.dk @ post@therns.dk This recently refurbished hotel is a short way from the shore. Some rooms have sea views, others overlook the sheltered garden. ① TV P 🖥	13	●	▪		
HASLE: *Danhostel Hasle* Ⓚ Falledvej 28, 3790 Hasle. ☎ 56 96 41 75. FAX 56 96 41 45. W www.dh-hasle.dk @ info@dh-hasle.dk A well-maintained hostel belonging to the Danhostel group. The hostel has an attractive location that is equally close to the beach and the woods. A well-developed network of cycling routes facilitates sightseeing. TV 🔶 🔶 P 🖥	22		▪		
NEXØ: *Balka Strand* Ⓚ Boulevarden 9A, 3730 Nexo. ☎ 56 49 49 49. FAX 56 49 49 48. W www.hotelbalkastrand.dk @ mail@hotelbalkastrand.dk A comfortable and well-appointed hotel. ① 🛏 TV 🔶 Y 🔶 ♿ P 🖥	95	●	▪	●	▪
NEXØ: *Strandhotel Balka Søbad* Ⓚ Vester Strandvej 25, 3730 Nexo. ☎ 56 49 22 25. FAX 56 49 22 33. W www.hotel-balkasoebad.dk @ mail@hotel-balkasoebad.dk A modern hotel standing by one of the island's best, family-friendly beaches. All rooms have a kitchenette and a balcony or terrace. 🛏 TV 🔶 P 🖥	106	●	▪	●	
RØNNE: *Danhostel Rønne Vandrerhjem* Ⓚ Arsenalvej 12, 3700 Rønne. ☎ 56 95 13 40. FAX 56 95 01 32. W www.danhostel-roenne.dk @ roenne@danhostel.dk A pleasant hostel in a neat and tidy area about 30 minutes' walk from the town centre. ① 🔶 P	26		▪		▪
RØNNE: *Skovly* Ⓚ Nyker Strandvej 40, Skovly, 3700 Rønne. ☎ 56 95 07 84. FAX 56 95 48 23. W www.hotel-skovly.dk @ skovly@bornholm.com This hotel stands right in the centre of a protected forest, with a long beach nearby. Every room has a private entrance and a terrace. The hotel restaurant serves delicious fish dishes. ① 🛏 TV 🔶 🚶 P 🖥	30	●	▪		

RØNNE: *Griffen* ⓀⓀ | 142

Nordre Kystvej 34, 3700 Rønne. 56 90 42 44. FAX 56 90 42 45.
Ⓦ www.bornholmhotels.dk ⓐ info@hotelgriffen.dk
This modern hotel is close to the centre and right by Rønne's harbour. The rooms are comfortable and well appointed. Many enjoy wonderful sea views.
1 ⬛ TV 📶 🔒 ⬛ P ⬛ ● *Jan–Mar.*

RØNNE: *Radisson SAS Fredensborg* ⓀⓀ | 72

Strandvejen 116, 3700 Rønne. 56 90 44 44. FAX 56 90 44 43.
Ⓦ www.radissonsas.com ⓐ info@hotelfredensborg.dk
A luxurious hotel that was built by the beach at Rønne's southern end in the 1960s. Rooms are decorated in a contemporary Danish style and all have a terrace or balcony. 1 ⬛ TV 📶 🔒 Y ⬛ P ⬛

SVANEKE: *Siemsens Gaard* ⓀⓀ | 51

Havnebryggen 9, 3740 Svaneke. 56 49 61 49. FAX 56 49 61 03.
Ⓦ www.siemsens.dk ⓐ hotel@siemsens.dk
The hotel, standing opposite the harbour, occupies a restored merchant's house that is 400 years old. Some of the cosy rooms have a sea view, others overlook the garden. 1 ⬛ TV 🔒 ⬛ P ⬛

ÅKIRKEBY: *Danhostel Boderne* Ⓚ | 86

Bodernevej 28, 3720 Åkirkeby. 56 97 49 50. FAX 56 97 49 48.
Ⓦ www.rosengaarden.dk ⓐ boderne@danhostel.dk
A variety of accommodation is on offer at this pleasant hostel, from singles to family rooms. It is located close to some of Bornholm's best beaches. Facilities include a playground and TV room. ⬛ TV 🔒 ⬛ P ⬛

GREENLAND

ILULISSAT: *Arctic* ⓀⓀⓀ | 65

Postbox 1501, DK-3952 Ilulissat, Greenland. (+299) 94 41 53.
FAX (+299) 94 40 49. ⓐ info@hotel-arctic.gl
A well-regarded hotel with breathtaking views of the fjord and icebergs. The view from the restaurant is hard to beat. From May to September guests can opt to stay in one of five aluminium igloos. Highly recommended.
1 ⬛ TV ⬛ ⬛

NUUK: *Seamans' Home* ⓀⓀ | 41

Postbox 1021, 3900 Nuuk, Greenland. (+299) 32 10 29. FAX (+299) 32 21 04.
Ⓦ www.greenland-guide.gl ⓐ nuuk@soemandshjem.gl
This hotel is a member of The Seamans' Home group, which has hotels in five towns on Greenland. The rooms are comfortable and clean; most have a view of Nuuk's harbour. 1 ⬛ TV ⬛ ⬛

UUMMANNAQ: *Hotel Uummannaq* ⓀⓀ | 40

3961 Uummannaq, Greenland. (+299) 95 15 18. FAX (+299) 95 12 62.
ⓐ uummannaq@icescaphotels.gl
A basic but comfortable hotel that is situated close to the shore. There is a wonderful view of Uummannaq fjord. 1 ⬛ TV ⬛ ⬛

THE FAROE ISLANDS

RUNAVIK: *Runavik* Ⓚ | 19

FO-620 Runavik, Heidavegur 6, Faroe Islands. (+298) 44 74 20. FAX (+298) 44 88 30.
Ⓦ www.hotel-runavik.fo ⓐ info@hotel-runavik.fo
A basic, old fashioned hotel that is situated in the centre of Runavik on the island of Eysturoy. The rooms have good harbour views. 1 ⬛ TV P ⬛

TÓRSHAVN: *Føroyar* ⓀⓀ | 108

FO-110 Tórshavn, Postbox 3303, Faroe Islands. (+298) 31 75 00.
FAX (+298) 31 60 19. Ⓦ www.hotelforoyar.com ⓐ hf@hotelforoyar.com
This good quality hotel on Streymoy offers single and double rooms. The hotel has splendid views of the town and fjord. 1 ⬛ TV ⬛ ⬛

TÓRSHAVN: *Hafnia* ⓀⓀⓀ | 56

FO-110 Tórshavn 4–10, Áarvegur, Postbox 107, Faroe Islands. (+298) 31 32 33.
FAX (+298) 31 52 50. Ⓦ www.hafnia.fo ⓐ hafnia@hafnia.fo
Hafnia is situated in the centre of Tórshavn, near the harbour and the historic part of town. The hotel's new owners are maintaining a high standard. The modern rooms are comfortable and warmly furnished. 1 ⬛ TV ⬛ P ⬛

WHERE TO EAT

ISITORS TO DENMARK can be assured of a good meal wherever they go. The choice ranges from city restaurants serving a fusion of Danish and French cuisine, to country inns catering for the lunchtime market with generous servings of *smørrebrød*. In small villages visitors can get a meal in a *kro* (inn), which often also provides overnight accommodation. Cafés are popular in Denmark.

Restaurant sign, Randers

As well as pastries and coffee, they often serve main meals and also beer and wine. Many cafés in Copenhagen open late into the night. At the bottom end of the spectrum are the street stalls selling *pølser*, a sausage or hot dog wrapped in a bun and served with onions and sauces. Spicier takeaway alternatives include Greek or Middle Eastern kebabs, which are in plentiful supply in larger towns.

Interior of the RizRaz restaurant in Copenhagen *(see p263)*

WHEN TO EAT

DANISH BREAKFAST tends to be a modest affair. It is usually eaten at home and apart from hotel restaurants there are few places that serve morning meals. As an alternative, many bakeries serve delicious bread, pastries and coffee and provide a table at which to sit.

Frokost (lunch) is the main meal of the day and is consumed between noon and 2pm. It can take various forms, from a light meal to a large banquet of open sandwiches and salads. At lunchtime many restaurants also serve hot main courses such as meatballs, but the helpings are smaller and prices lower than the same meal at dinnertime. *Aftensmad* (dinner) is from 6pm onwards and can be expensive. It is not unusual for prices to rise between lunch and dinner at the same establishment. At weekends many restaurants serve a brunch between 11am and 3pm. Late night snacks are generally limited to hot dogs or kebabs from a stall.

OPENING HOURS

BAKERIES OPEN EARLY; in some places it is enough to knock at the bakery door for the baker to open up and sell a loaf even before the shop is open. Fast-food restaurants that serve breakfast open at around 8 or 9am. Restaurants that cater for the lunchtime trade generally open around 10 or 11am. Pubs remain closed until early afternoon, except for the village *kros* (inns), which open earlier, especially during the holiday season. Most restaurants finish serving by 10pm, and restaurants that are not licensed to remain open all night close at 1am. Cafés tend to stay open all day and often late into the night.

MENU

MANY RESTAURANTS have menus written in English. In addition to the full menu, some offer a specially priced *dagens ret*, or "dish of the day", which is often written up on a board. Some restaurants serve good value fixed-price three-course lunches.

Entrance to a restaurant in Hammershusvej in Sandvig

Visitors at tables in front of a herring smokehouse in Svaneke

CHILDREN

MOST RESTAURANTS in Denmark offer high chairs and special "child-friendly" menus and activity packs. The best time to take children to a restaurant is late afternoon, when they are far less busy. This time of day is less stressful and generally means that no one need wait long to be served.

Café terraces lining one of Nykøbing F's little streets

PRICES AND TIPS

PRICES IN restaurants vary enormously. Many cheaper Danish establishments offer set-price all-you-can-eat buffets at lunchtime, as do some of the Thai and Indonesian restaurants. Some hostels also serve good value lunch and evening meals for about 60 Dkr. A three-course meal in a restaurant will cost about 100-150 Dkr not including alcohol. At an upmarket restaurant, diners

should be prepared to pay in excess of 800 Dkr.

Soft drinks, beer and *akvavit* (a kind of schnapps) cost about the same in most places. Prices for wines and liqueurs vary and tend to be steep in some of the upmarket restaurants.

Although a service charge and tax are included in the price, it is customary to tip in Danish restaurants (this can be as little as 5 per cent). In less prestigious places it is unusual to leave a tip, unless the service has been particularly good. Even then, simply rounding up the bill is sufficient. Leaving no tip is not considered bad manners in Denmark. Tipping is not practised in fast-food restaurants.

Most restaurants accept credit cards and display the appropriate signs at their entrance. It is unusual for there to be a minimum limit set for credit card payments.

RESERVATIONS

GUESTS ARE generally required to book well in advance at the most popular restauranst. Even in quieter restaurants it is advisable to make a booking at the weekend, especially for Sunday brunch, which is often a busy time.

If it is too late to book then the best option is to go some-where where there are clusters of restaurants. For small groups, there will normally be at least one restaurant that will have a table available after a short wait.

DRESS CODE

THE DANES ARE, for the most part, a relaxed people and do not attach too much importance to etiquette concerning their appearance. Nevertheless, it is customary to smarten up when visiting a restaurant. Dress requirements rise in step with the price of the menu; some upmarket restaurants expect diners to wear evening attire or at least a shirt and tie.

VEGETARIANS

THE DIET IN Denmark is based on meat and fish. However most restaurants have at least a few vegetarian dishes on their menus, as well as green salads. Restaurants that serve only vegetarian food are rare.

DISABLED GUESTS

AS ELSEWHERE in Europe, restaurants providing facilities for disabled people cannot be taken for granted. However, many restaurants in Denmark are accessible for disabled people, but it is advisable to check when making a reservation.

A Danish-language database, researched by Danish wheelchair users, lists all the restaurants (as well as attractions and cultural institutions) that are accessible to wheelchairs in Denmark. Local tourist offices can often help with this.

Interior of the Czarens Hus in Nykøbing F (see p270)

What to Eat in Denmark

D ANISH COOKING is largely based on meat and fish. Meats such as pork and beef are often roasted and served with vegetables. The most common form of fish is pickled herring. Alongside such hearty staples, Italian and Asian influences are gradually becoming more apparent in the Danish kitchen. *Smørrebrød* (literally "buttered bread") is one of the nation's most popular foods and generally consists of rye bread with a variety of toppings. Danish pastries are referred to as *wienerbrød* in Denmark. They are not overly sweet and quite delicious.

Prawns

Mayonnaise

Rejecocktail
A prawn cocktail served with a sauce consisting of mayonnaise, tomato ketchup, lemon juice and sherry. It is eaten with warm rundstykke (crispy rolls).

Stjerneskud
The Danes are famous for the variety of their smørrebrød. Stjerneskud ("shooting star")is bread with fried fish fillet and prawns, garnished with pieces of lemon and dill.

Pariserbøf
Brown bread and a minced beef steak are covered with a raw egg yolk, onion and capers. It tastes best when washed down with cold beer.

Bornholmer
Smoked herring topped with egg yolk, onion and chives. As the name suggests, this is a typical Bornholm dish.

Pickled herring   Capers and onion

Bread with dripping

Marineredesild
Herring marinated in vinegar and spices is served with onion and capers. It is particularly delicious when eaten with rye bread spread with dripping, and washed down with beer or akvavit.

Røget Fisk
Smoked fish is a major part of the Danish diet. Some of the best is from Bornholm, which has many smokehouses.

VEGETABLES
As well as green salads, the Danes eat a lot of cooked vegetables including potatoes, carrots, cauliflower and beetroot, which are served cold. Pickled vegetables including onions, cabbage, cucumbers or beetroot slices are also popular. These are often made at home and stored.

Rødkål
A common way of cooking rødkål (red cabbage) is to stew it for about 40 minutes with apples, vinegar and sugar.

Pickled beetroot slices

Rødbeder
Pickled beetroots are usually served with horseradish.

Flæskesteg
Joint of roasted pork with crackling served with cabbage and gravy; sometimes covered with slices of apple and a cream sauce.

Skipperlabsskovs
A stew consisting of beef, marinated for 24 hours in brine, which is then cooked with potatoes, black peppercorns and bay leaves.

Boller & Karry
Hybrid dish of meatballs with oat flakes, which are boiled in water until they float to the surface. Served with curry sauce and rice.

Stegt Flæsk
A classic Danish dish. Fried slices of pork on the bone are served with a creamy parsley sauce and potatoes.

Smørrebrødsmad
This Danish delicacy consists of pieces of roast beef fancifully arranged on rye bread and garnished with onion and grated horseradish.

Glaseret Skinke
Lightly salted ham is boiled for about two hours with pepper and then roasted in a marinade of mustard, sugar and honey. The ham is served with asparagus sauce.

Frikadeller
Meatballs made of a mixture of pork and veal, which are fried in olive oil and usually served with potatoes.

Boiled pork loin

Boiled vegetables

Horseradish sauce

Kogt Hamburgerryg
A classic Danish staple of pork loin cooked with thyme and parsley and usually served with boiled potatoes and vegetables. Horseradish or mustard sauce is often added to taste.

DESSERTS

Most Danes have a sweet tooth and the local cakes and pastries are particularly good. The most popular of these include *brune kager* (gingerbread with nuts), *kleiner* or tartlets, and *æbleskiver* (doughnut with blackcurrant jam). *Wienerbrød* (Danish pastries) are eaten at any time of day. Ice cream is another popular dessert and the Danish variety ranks with the best in the world.

Risalamande
A rice pudding with almonds, which is made at Christmas and served cold, topped with cherries.

Gulerodskage
A carrot cake made with walnuts and often served with whipped cream.

Cherry syrup

Rice with almonds

What to Drink in Denmark

As far as drinks are concerned the Danes have two passions – coffee and beer. They are also very attached to their liqueurs, which come in a variety of flavours and appear under the common name of *akvavit*. The beer market is dominated by a handful of companies, of which Carlsberg is the best known. Danish beer comes in a variety of strengths and colours, from fairly tame draught Pilsner through to stout with an alcohol content of about 10 per cent. Wine was not always so popular but is readily available in supermarkets and restaurants. Aside from coffee, non-alcoholic drinks include mineral water, as well as brand-name and locally produced soft drinks.

Drinkers enjoying the sun outside one of Denmark's extremely popular bars

LAGER

Faxe Royal lager

LAGER IS THE most popular Danish beverage. Most Danish beers are of the Pilsner type with an alcohol content of about 4.5 per cent. They include brands such as Carlsberg, Grøn Tuborg, Faxe and Star. Before Christmas and Easter the shops sell Julebryg and Påskebryg in standard and strong varieties. These beers are slightly sweet and make perfect additions to *akvavit*.

Bars and restaurants serve both draught beer (*fadøl*) and bottled beers. Sometimes draught beer is ordered in a jug. Beer is most often sold in bottles rather than cans. Carlsberg and Tuborg beers are also sold in plastic bottles.

Beer is consumed throughout the day. It is not uncommon, and perfectly respectable, for Danes to drink beer in the park at lunchtime. Drunkenness is rare and drink-driving is not tolerated.

Logo of the Carlsberg brewery

Carlsberg Pilsner

Tuborg lager

Carlsberg porter

Carlsberg stout

Carlsberg Elephant

BROWN ALE

THERE ARE ABOUT 150 varieties of beer produced in Denmark and among these are many fine brown ales. They generally have more flavour and are often stronger than Pilsner beers, with an alcoholic content of about 8 per cent or above. Some cafés and bars specialize in these dark beers, which tend to be slightly sweeter and less fizzy than lager. Among the popular brown ales are Carlsberg's Elephant and Sort Guld from the Tuborg brewery. The darkest beers are stouts and porters; these often have a higher percentage of alcohol.

WINE

T HE DANISH CLIMATE does not allow for the cultivation of grapes, although a few enthusiasts are trying to introduce the hardier varieties to southern Scandinavia. So far their efforts have not yielded any commercially viable vintages, and Danes, who are increasingly swapping a tankard of beer for a glass of wine, have to settle for imported wines. White wine is referred to as *hvidvin*, red wine is *rødvin* and sparkling wine is *mousserende-vin*. Hot mulled wine, or *gløgg*, is served with almonds and raisins in the run–up to Christmas and at New Year.

Gløgg – mulled wine

HOT DRINKS

T HE DANES ARE coffee connoisseurs and coffee is the most popular drink in the country. Roasted beans are freshly ground on café premises and brewed in special jugs. Strong Italian espressos are also available, as are cappuccinos and increasingly popular lattes. Caffeine-free coffee can also be found (ask for a a *koffeinfri*). For children there are delicious hot chocolates served with whipped cream. Tea is not as popular in Denmark as coffee and consists of no more than a tea bag placed in a cup. Caffeine-free herbal teas are available in some cafés.

An aromatic herbal tea

A cup of black coffee

LIQUEURS

T HE TRADITIONAL Christmas and New Year feasts are often accompanied in Denmark by chilled *akvavit*. This schnapps-like beverage comes in a variety of herbal flavours and often bears the name *akvavit* on the label. It is usually drunk in a single shot and is followed by a glass of beer. As well as schnapps, the Danes drink other strong alcoholic herb infusions. The most popular of these is Gammel Dansk, which is traditionally drunk early in the morning.

Many Danes regard a small glass of this bitter herbal preparation as a preventative medicine. Another popular drink is Peter Heering, a sweet liqueur made from cherries, which is sipped after meals.

Herb-flavoured Gammel Dansk

Akvavit – Danish schnapps

SOFT DRINKS

Sparkling mineral water

Fizzy soft drink

W HEN ORDERING a meal it is customary to ask for a bottle or jug of water. Danish tap water is completely safe – ask for *postevand* to be brought to your table. Still bottled water is *minaralvand;* the sparkling variety bears the proud name of *danskvand*. All restaurants, bars and pubs also serve low-alcohol beer, which is referred to as *let øl*. Soft drinks such as Coca-Cola are known as *sodavand*, while orange juice is *appelsinjuice*. Drinking chocolate is popular both hot *(varm chokolade)* and cold *(chokolademælk)*.

Bottle of chocolate milk

Choosing a Restaurant

THE RESTAURANTS LISTED below have been selected across a wide range of price categories, for their fine food, good value and interesting location. They are listed alphabetically according to area, beginning with Copenhagen and then the region as they appear in the guide. For more details on food and restaurants, see pages 256–61.

	CREDIT CARDS	GARDEN OR TERRACE	VEGETARIAN DISHES	CHILDREN'S MENU

COPENHAGEN

NORTH COPENHAGEN: *Eastern Corner* Ⓚ
Solvgade 85A, 1307 Copenhagen K. **Map 2 D4.** 【 33 11 58 35.
Ⓦ www.easterncorner.dk
A vast selection of Thai dishes are on offer here. The menu comes in two versions: European and Thai (the latter is more spicy).

| | ● | | ● | ■ |

NORTH COPENHAGEN: *Ida Davidsen* Ⓚ
Store Kongensgade 70, 1264 Copenhagen K. **Map 2 E5.** 【 33 91 36 55.
Ⓦ www.idadavidsen.dk @ ida.davidsen@cirque.dk
This family-run, cellar restaurant has been operating for over 100 years and serves some of the best *smørrebrød* in Copenhagen. Over 250 varieties are on offer; toppings include salmon, herring, shrimps, caviar and raw egg.

| | ● | | ● | ■ |

NORTH COPENHAGEN: *Sommersko* Ⓚ
Kronprinsensgade 8, 1114 Copenhagen K. **Map 2 E3.** 【 33 14 81 89.
Ⓦ www.sommersko.dk @ cafesommersko@sovino.dk
A lively café-restaurant with a pleasant French-style atmosphere and an eclectic menu that includes pesto French fries, oriental flat breads filled with meat or vegetables and a large range of fish dishes.

| | ● | | ● | |

NORTH COPENHAGEN: *SPQR* Ⓚ
Borgergade 17A, 1300 Copenhagen K. **Map 2 D5.** 【 33 12 20 06.
@ spqr@e-box.dk
A typical Roman *trattoria* transplanted to Copenhagen. SPQR serves delicious food and wine from various regions of Italy. 🅿

| | ● | | ● | |

NORTH COPENHAGEN: *Gendarmen* Ⓚ Ⓚ
Sankt Annæ Plads 16, 1250 Copenhagen K. **Map 2 E5.** 【 33 93 66 55.
Ⓦ www.gendarmen.dk @ restaurand@gendarmen.dk
The Gendarmen's *pièce de résistance* is its excellent choice of Danish cheeses; the long wine list is equally well chosen.

| | ● | | | |

NORTH COPENHAGEN: *Sushitarian* Ⓚ Ⓚ
Gothersgade 3, 1123 Copenhagen K. **Map 2 D5.** 【 33 93 30 54.
Ⓦ www.sushitarian.dk @ sushi@sushitarian.dk
A stylishly furnished restaurant offering a wide choice of Japanese sushi, soups and tempura. Here you can also take part in an eccentric Japanese tradition known as "Body Sushi" that involves eating sushi straight from the bodies of naked women or men.

| | ● | | ● | |

NORTH COPENHAGEN: *Salt* Ⓚ Ⓚ Ⓚ
Toldbodgade 24–28, 1253 Copenhagen K. **Map 4 E1.** 【 33 74 14 44.
Ⓦ www.saltrestaurant.dk @ info@saltrestaurant.dk
Salt is housed in a late 18th-century granary. The Parisian-style interior is in keeping with the upmarket menu that includes imaginative meat and fish dishes, such as fried fillet of pork with chick peas and pistachio-baked Norwegian haddock. The wine list is well chosen and extensive. 🅿

| | ● | ■ | ● | ■ |

CENTRAL COPENHAGEN: *Dubrovnik* Ⓚ
Studiestræde 32, Copenhagen K. **Map 3 B1.** 【 33 13 05 64.
Ⓦ www.restaurant-dubrovnik.dk
A convivial atmosphere and a menu that features a colourful and eclectic selection of Balkan cuisine. Dishes include grilled meat and fish.

| | ● | | | |

CENTRAL COPENHAGEN: *Grøften* Ⓚ
Vesterbrogade 3, 1620 Copenhagen V. **Map 3 A1.** 【 33 75 06 75.
Ⓦ www.groeften.dk @ info@groeften.dk
A reasonably priced and popular restaurant in Tivoli gardens, which has been in business for over 130 years. ◗ *mid-Apr–mid-Sep, Dec.*

| | ● | ■ | ● | |

| | | CREDIT CARDS | GARDEN OR TERRACE | VEGETARIAN DISHES | CHILDREN'S MENU |

Price per person for a three-course meal without alcohol, including tax (without tip).
Ⓚ up to 150 Dkr
ⓀⓀ 150–200 Dkr
ⓀⓀⓀ 200–300 Dkr
ⓀⓀⓀⓀ 300–350 Dkr
ⓀⓀⓀⓀⓀ over 350 Dkr

CREDIT CARDS
Eurocard, MasterCard, Visa, Diners Club all accepted.

GARDEN OR TERRACE
Meal can be served on a terrace, in a garden or courtyard.

VEGETARIAN DISHES
Good selection of vegetarian dishes available.

CHILDREN'S MENU
Simple food adapted to suit children's tastes.

	Credit Cards	Garden or Terrace	Vegetarian Dishes	Children's Menu
CENTRAL COPENHAGEN: *Jensens Bøfhus* Ⓚ Kultorvet 15, 1175 Copenhagen K. **Map 1** C5. 33 15 09 84. Ⓦ www.jensens.com One of a chain of Danish steakhouses with a meaty menu of steaks, chops and ribs. There is also an all-you-can-eat ice cream bar.	●			
CENTRAL COPENHAGEN: *Koh I Noor* Ⓚ Vesterbrogade 33, 1620 Copenhagen V. **Map 3** A1. 33 24 64 15. Ⓦ www.koh-i-noor.dk @ info@koh-i-noor.dk An interesting encounter with Pakistani cuisine. Among the culinary attractions are an exquisitely prepared pheasant and other wildfowl dishes.	●	●	●	
CENTRAL COPENHAGEN: *Nationalmuseet* Ⓚ Ny Vestergade 10, 1471 Copenhagen K. **Map 3** B2. 33 93 07 60. Ⓦ http://restaurant.natmus.dk @ restaurant@natmus.net An ideal place to stop for a meal after visiting the Nationalmuseet *(see pp84–5)*. On Sundays the restaurant serves a tasty brunch that combines elements of traditional Danish and international cuisine. **P**	●			
CENTRAL COPENHAGEN: *Nytorv* Ⓚ Nytorv 15, 1450 Copenhagen K. **Map 3** B1. 33 11 77 06. Ⓦ www.nytorv.dk A long-established restaurant housed in a former brothel. The tasty menu includes a wide selection of *smørrebrød*, plates of cheese, fish and other classic Danish lunches.	●			
CENTRAL COPENHAGEN: *RizRaz* Ⓚ Kompagnistræde 20, 1208 Copenhagen K. **Map 3** C1. 33 15 05 75. Ⓦ www.rizraz.dk @ rizraz@rizraz.dk This popular Copenhagen eatery specializes in spicy Mediterranean fare. The variety of dining areas includes a patio, which in summer fills with diners enjoying the all-you-can-eat buffet of pitta bread, salads and dips.	●	■	●	
CENTRAL COPENHAGEN: *Sushi Time* Ⓚ Grønnegade 28, 1208 Copenhagen K. **Map 3** C1. 33 11 88 99. Authentic sushi is available from this no-nonsense takeaway, which has an upstairs dining area. The price is extremely reasonable and the sushi is of a very high standard.	●	■	●	
CENTRAL COPENHAGEN: *Ultimo* Ⓚ Vesterbrogade 3, 1630 Copenhagen V. **Map 3** A1. 33 75 07 51. Ⓦ www.cafeultimotivoli.dk @ cafeultimotivoli@sovino.dk An Italian restaurant that serves particularly good *antipasti*.	●	■	●	
CENTRAL COPENHAGEN: *Victor* Ⓚ Ny Østergade 8, 1101 Copenhagen K. **Map 2** D5. 33 13 36 13. Ⓦ www.cafevictor.dk @ cafevictor@sovino.dk A Danish version of a Parisian bistro with some good daily specials.	●	■	●	
CENTRAL COPENHAGEN: *Anton* ⓀⓀ Østergade 52/54, 1001 Copenhagen K. **Map 4** D1. 33 18 28 00. Ⓦ www.anton-illum.dk @ restaurant@anton-illum.dk This café is part of the Illum department store. It is worth visiting not only after shopping but at any time to enjoy its famous *smørrebrød*. **P**	●	■	●	■
CENTRAL COPENHAGEN: *Azori* ⓀⓀ Højbro Plads 19, 1200 Copenhagen K. **Map 3** C1. 33 13 24 45. Ⓦ www.azori.dk A charming restaurant that serves luxury versions of Moldavan cuisine, which includes hearty marinated meat and fish stews. The restaurant also serves many Moldavan wines.	●			

For key to symbols see back flap

Price per person for a three-course meal without alcohol, including tax (without tip).
Ⓚ up to 150 Dkr
ⓀⓀ 150–200 Dkr
ⓀⓀⓀ 200–300 Dkr
ⓀⓀⓀⓀ 300–350 Dkr
ⓀⓀⓀⓀⓀ over 350 Dkr

CREDIT CARDS
Eurocard, MasterCard, Visa, Diners Club all accepted.

GARDEN OR TERRACE
Meal can be served on a terrace, in a garden or courtyard.

VEGETARIAN DISHES
Good selection of vegetarian dishes available.

CHILDREN'S MENU
Simple food adapted to suit children's tastes.

	Price	CREDIT CARDS	GARDEN OR TERRACE	VEGETARIAN DISHES	CHILDREN'S MENU
CENTRAL COPENHAGEN: *Baron von Dy* Frederiksborggade 5 (Strøget), 1360 Copenhagen K. **Map** 1 C5. ☎ *33 93 11 92.* ⓦ www.fondue.dk This restaurant specializes in fondue, allowing diners to choose what to dip into the cheese sauce. The salads are also worth recommending.	ⓀⓀ	●		●	
CENTRAL COPENHAGEN: *Det Lille Apotek* Store Kannikestræde 15, 1169 Copenhagen K. **Map** 1 C5. ☎ *33 12 56 06.* ⓦ www.det-lille-apotek.dk @ kontakt@det-lille-apotek.dk One of the oldest restaurants in Copenhagen, Det Lille Apotek specializes in Danish delicacies including a wide variety of pickled herring. The antique décor adds to the traditional ambience.	ⓀⓀ	●			
CENTRAL COPENHAGEN: *La Sirene* Nyhavn 51, 1051 Copenhagen K. **Map** 4 E1. ☎ *33 32 71 02.* ⓦ www.lasirene.dk @ capo@lasirene.dk A pleasant Italian restaurant that offers a bewildering choice of dishes far beyond simple pizza and pasta staples.	ⓀⓀ	●		●	
CENTRAL COPENHAGEN: *Philippe* Gråbrødretorv 2, 1154 Copenhagen K. **Map** 3 C1. ☎ *33 32 92 92.* ⓦ www.philippe.dk An upmarket brasserie serving beautifully presented French and Modern European dishes. A large selection of wines is also on offer.	ⓀⓀ	●	■	●	■
CENTRAL COPENHAGEN: *Piccadilly & Axelborg Bowling* Axeltorv 3A, 1609 Copenhagen V. **Map** 3 A1. ☎ *33 32 00 92.* ⓦ www.axelborg-bowling.dk @ info@axelborg.com A fun venue where it is possible to enjoy a good meal before having a go at 10-pin bowling or an evening of karaoke.	ⓀⓀ	●		●	■
CENTRAL COPENHAGEN: *Rosie McGee's* Vesterbrogade 2A, 1620 Copenhagen V. **Map** 3 A1. ☎ *33 32 19 23.* ⓦ www.rosiemcgee.dk A lively venue where guests can have a meal before shaking a leg on the dance floor. The restaurant's bar offers a good selection of cocktails. ♬	ⓀⓀ	●		●	
CENTRAL COPENHAGEN: *Zeleste* Store Strandstræde 6, 1255 Copenhagen K. **Map** 3 E1. ☎ *33 16 06 06.* ⓦ www.zeleste.dk @ restaurant@zeleste.dk This spacious restaurant and café offers a wide choice of hearty Mediterranean and Danish dishes, as well as a large selection of wines. Ⓟ	ⓀⓀ	●			
CENTRAL COPENHAGEN: *C-lounge* Klosterstrade 23, 1157 Copenhagen K. **Map** 3 C1. ☎ *33 13 84 14.* ⓦ www.clounge.dk @ info@clounge.dk A trendy bistro with classic Danish décor serving a menu consisting of sophisticated international cuisine.	ⓀⓀⓀ	●			
CENTRAL COPENHAGEN: *Copenhagen Corner* Rådhuspladsen, Vesterbrogade 1A, 1620 Copenhagen V. **Map** 3 A1. ☎ *33 91 45 45.* ⓦ www.remmen.dk/copenhagencorner A typically Scandinavian restaurant that enjoys a good view of the Rådhus (city hall). The menu is international in flavour.	ⓀⓀⓀ	●	■		●
CENTRAL COPENHAGEN: *Dansetten* Vesterbrogade 3, 1630 Copenhagen V. **Map** 3 A1. ☎ *33 75 06 80.* ⓦ www.dansetten.dk @ dansetten@dansetten.dk Part of the Tivoli complex, this restaurant serves a mixture of Danish and French food. A nightclub and concert venue is next door. ♬	ⓀⓀⓀ	●	■	●	■

CENTRAL COPENHAGEN: *Grønnegade* ⓀⓀⓀ
Grønnegade 39, 1107 Copenhagen K. **Map** 2 D5. 33 93 31 33.
ⓦ www.groennegade.dk @ mailtoulrik@groennegade.dk
This classy restaurant is housed in a 17th-century building. Its walls are decorated with paintings by Danish artists. The delicate French menu has subtle Danish twists and includes several kinds of caviar.

CENTRAL COPENHAGEN: *Ketchup* ⓀⓀⓀ
Pilestræde 19, 1112 Copenhagen K. **Map** 4 D1. 33 32 30 30.
ⓦ www.cafeketchup.dk @ cafeketchup@sovino.dk
A popular café-restaurant that opened in 2002. The feeling of space is emphasised by large windows looking out onto the street. The menu is a pleasant mixture of Asian, French and Danish dishes. A well-stocked bar is along one wall.

CENTRAL COPENHAGEN: *Leonore Christine* ⓀⓀⓀ
Nyhavn 9, 1051 Copenhagen K. **Map** 4 E1. 33 13 50 40.
ⓦ www.leonore-christine.dk
This tiny, 17th-century town house is now one of the best-known restaurants in Copenhagen. The French-inspired menu is delicious but fairly expensive. The *smørrebrød* makes a cheaper alternative.

CENTRAL COPENHAGEN: *Paafuglen* ⓀⓀⓀ
Vesterbrogade 3, 1630 Copenhagen V. **Map** 3 A1. 33 12 95 40.
ⓦ www.paafuglen.dk @ p@fuglen.dk
One of Tivoli's restaurants, this elegant establishment turns a visit to the gardens into an occasion to remember. It is not the cheapest of places, but the food is excellent and there is a good wine list.

CENTRAL COPENHAGEN: *Peder Oxe* ⓀⓀⓀ
Gråbrødretorv 11, 1154 Copenhagen K. **Map** 3 C1. 33 11 00 77.
ⓦ www.pederoxe.dk
A romantic Danish restaurant serving *smørrebrød* at lunch, and a wide-ranging menu that includes French- and Asian-influenced dishes in the evening. Steaks and organic beefburgers are popular choices.

CENTRAL COPENHAGEN: *l'Alsace* ⓀⓀⓀⓀ
Ny Østergade 9, 1101 Copenhagen K. **Map** 2 D5. 33 14 57 43.
ⓦ www.alsace.dk @ alsace@mail.dk
L'Alsace serves a blend of German and French cuisine, with a few Danish and Italian dishes on the menu for good measure. **P**

CENTRAL COPENHAGEN: *Reef N' Beef* ⓀⓀⓀⓀⓀ
Jarmers Plads 3, 1551 Copenhagen V. **Map** 3 B2. 33 33 00 30.
ⓦ www.reefnbeef.dk @ reef@reefnbeef.dk
This Australian restaurant claims to serve the wildest tasting food in town and it is not far wrong with a bushtucker menu that consists of such delicacies as crocodile salad and kangaroo fillets.

CENTRAL COPENHAGEN: *Divan 2* ⓀⓀⓀⓀⓀ
Vesterbrogade 3, 1620 Copenhagen V. **Map** 3 A1. 33 75 07 50.
ⓦ www.divan2.dk @ restaurant@divan2.dk
Situated on the Tivoli lakeshore, this oriental-style, garden restaurant opened in 1843. Exhibited to this day in the Tivoli Museum are the fabrics that once adorned the restaurant's walls. The menu consists mainly of classic Danish food, but there are also some French dishes and excellent wines.

CENTRAL COPENHAGEN: *Els* ⓀⓀⓀⓀⓀ
Store Strandstræde 3, 1255 Copenhagen K. **Map** 4 D1. 33 14 13 41.
ⓦ www.restaurant-els.dk
When Els opened as a café in 1853 it was popular with actors from the nearby Royal Theatre. Hans Christian Andersen was a frequent visitor and wrote a poem to celebrate its opening. Period furniture, original murals and antique wooden columns add to a sense of history, which is enlivened by a traditional menu of game, fish and fresh market produce.

CENTRAL COPENHAGEN: *Ensemble* ⓀⓀⓀⓀⓀ
Tordenskjoldsgade 11, 1055 Copenhagen K. **Map** 4 D1. 33 11 33 52.
ⓦ www.restaurantensemble.dk
This Michelin-starred restaurant has a fixed five-course menu featuring mouthwatering Danish and French food. A visit to Ensemble is a feast for both body and soul.

Price per person for a three-course meal without alcohol, including tax (without tip).
Ⓚ up to 150 Dkr
ⓀⓀ 150–200 Dkr
ⓀⓀⓀ 200–300 Dkr
ⓀⓀⓀⓀ 300–350 Dkr
ⓀⓀⓀⓀⓀ over 350 Dkr

CREDIT CARDS
Eurocard, MasterCard, Visa, Diners Club all accepted.

GARDEN OR TERRACE
Meal can be served on a terrace, in a garden or courtyard.

VEGETARIAN DISHES
Good selection of vegetarian dishes available.

CHILDREN'S MENU
Simple food adapted to suit children's tastes.

	CREDIT CARDS	GARDEN OR TERRACE	VEGETARIAN DISHES	CHILDREN'S MENU
CENTRAL COPENHAGEN: *Kommandanten* ⓀⓀⓀⓀⓀ	●			
CENTRAL COPENHAGEN: *Sankt Gertruds Kloster* ⓀⓀⓀⓀⓀ	●		●	
SOUTH COPENHAGEN: *Casa Mexico* Ⓚ	●			■
SOUTH COPENHAGEN: *Nemoland* Ⓚ	●	■	●	
SOUTH COPENHAGEN: *Ravelinen* ⓀⓀ	●	■	●	■*
SOUTH COPENHAGEN: *La Novo* ⓀⓀⓀ	●			
SOUTH COPENHAGEN: *Kanalen* ⓀⓀⓀⓀ	●	■	●	
SOUTH COPENHAGEN: *Era Ora* ⓀⓀⓀⓀⓀ	●			
FURTHER AFIELD: *Castro* Ⓚ	●	■	●	■

CENTRAL COPENHAGEN: *Kommandanten*   ⓀⓀⓀⓀⓀ
Ny Adelgade 7, 1104 Copenhagen K. **Map** 2 D5. ☎ *33 12 09 90.*
Ⓦ www.kommandanten.dk @ kommandanten@kommandanten.dk
Occupying the former residence of Copenhagen's 17th-century military commander, this chic restaurant has a menu that changes every two weeks. In its sublimely elegant rooms diners can enjoy Danish and French cuisine and sample wine selected from an impressively long list. The food is expensive but delicious.

CENTRAL COPENHAGEN: *Sankt Gertruds Kloster*   ⓀⓀⓀⓀⓀ
Hauser Plads 32, 1127 Copenhagen K. **Map** 1 C5. ☎ *33 14 66 30.*
Ⓦ www.sgk.as @ mail@sgk.as
The vaulted stone interior of this former monastery now houses one of the best restaurants in Copenhagen. The wines are sophisticated and the chefs' French-based menu superb. Sankt Gertruds Kloster is lit solely by candles and has a romantic ambience.

SOUTH COPENHAGEN: *Casa Mexico*   Ⓚ
Torvegade 64, 1400 Copenhagen K. **Map** 4 E3. ☎ *32 95 96 89.*
Ⓦ www.casamexico.dk
There are plenty of spicy meat dishes on the menu here. The *fajitas* are particularly good, allowing guests to sample a range of Mexican tastes. Live Mexican music adds to the atmosphere. 🎵

SOUTH COPENHAGEN: *Nemoland*   Ⓚ
Bådsmandsstrade 43, 1407 Copenhagen K. **Map** 4 E3. ☎ *32 95 89 31.*
Ⓦ www.nemoland.dk @ info@nemoland.dk
One of Christiana's best-known cafés and bistros, Nemoland emanates an easy-going and relaxed atmosphere. The food is simple and hearty, although the hippy ambience will not be to everyone's taste.

SOUTH COPENHAGEN: *Ravelinen*   ⓀⓀ
Torvegade 79, 1400 Copenhagen K. **Map** 4 E3. ☎ *32 96 20 45.*
Ⓦ www.ravelinen.dk
This garden restaurant is housed in a former toll-house and military guardroom, and serves classic Danish food including freshly smoked herring with egg yolk, various *smørrebrød* and filling meat stews.

SOUTH COPENHAGEN: *La Novo*   ⓀⓀⓀ
Torvegade 49–51, 1400 Copenhagen K. **Map** 4 E3. ☎ *32 57 75 10.*
Ⓦ www.lanovo.dk
Among the Italian cuisine on offer here are tasty pizza and pasta dishes.

SOUTH COPENHAGEN: *Kanalen*   ⓀⓀⓀⓀ
Wilders Plads 2, 1403 Copenhagen K. **Map** 4 E2. ☎ *32 95 13 30.*
Ⓦ www.restaurant-kanalen.dk
This cosy, candlelit restaurant offers diners a wide variety of herring and salmon dishes; the chef's special is a cucumber soup served with prawns.

SOUTH COPENHAGEN: *Era Ora*   ⓀⓀⓀⓀⓀ
Overgaden Neden Vandet 33B, 1414 Copenhagen K. **Map** 4 E3.
☎ *32 54 06 93.* Ⓦ www.era-ora.dk @ era-ora@era-ora.dk
A luxurious restaurant situated on one of Christianshavn's canals. Era Ora offers a vast wine list and excellent Italian food. The restaurant was recently awarded a Michelin star. Reservations necessary.

FURTHER AFIELD: *Castro*   Ⓚ
Nørrebrogade 209, 2200 Copenhagen N. **Map** 1 A3. ☎ *35 85 35 85.*
Ⓦ www.cafecastro.dk @ post@cafecastro.dk
The Cuban music, delicous coffee and pictures of Fidel Castro adorning the walls make this café-bistro a touch out of the ordinary. 🎵

FURTHER AFIELD: *Den Persiske Stue*
Nørrebrogade 102, 2200 Copenhagen N. **Map** 1 A3. 35 35 35 72.
www.persiskestue.dk
This cosy Persian restaurant has some good-value set menus that include
kebabs, yoghurt dips and some tasty vegetarian main courses.

FURTHER AFIELD: *Den Sorte Gryde*
Istedgade 108, 1650 Copenhagen V. 33 21 03 71. www.densortegryde.dk
Meaty barbecues and grills make this a good place to fill up.

FURTHER AFIELD: *Eugene*
Vesterbrogade 83, 1620 Copenhagen V. 33 25 13 19.
www.eugene.dk info@eugene.dk
A café-restaurant serving good-sized brunches and lunches during the day,
and hot meals at night. Among the evening meals are curries and salads.

FURTHER AFIELD: *Golden Bamboo*
Vesterbrogade 41, 1620 Copenhagen V. **Map** 3 A2. 33 21 71 58.
www.goldenbamboo.dk
One of the best Chinese restaurants in Copenhagen. The prices are reasonable
and the atmosphere is warm and inviting.

FURTHER AFIELD: *Govindas*
Nørre Farimagsgade 82, 1364 Copenhagen K. **Map** 1 B4. 33 33 74 44.
www.govindas.dk
This small inexpensive restaurant is run by members of the Hare Krishna
religious order. The menu is entirely vegetarian and no alchohol is served.

FURTHER AFIELD: *Hings Sushi & Cuisine*
Vesterbrogade 146A, 1620 Copenhagen K. 33 21 23 32. www.hing.dk
In Hings Sushi the guests are offered sushi in a large variety of
combinations. Of the Chinese food on offer the duck in sweet and sour
sauce is not to be missed.

FURTHER AFIELD: *Thai Pan*
Korsgade 1, 2200 Copenhagen N. 33 36 05 05. www.thaipan.dk
restaurant@thaipan.dk
A Thai restaurant offering an exotic atmosphere and an array of Asian
flavours at reasonable prices. P

FURTHER AFIELD: *Cassiopeia*
Gammel Kongevej 10, 1610 Copenhagen V. 33 15 09 33.
www.restaurant-cassiopeia.dk admin@restaurant-cassiopeia.dk
Cassiopeia's lunchtime menu is mainly *smørrebrød*. In the evening the food
takes on a French twist, with a reasonable selection of fish dishes available.

NORTHWESTERN ZEALAND

BIRKERØD: *P2*
Vasevej 115, 3460 Birkerød. **Road map** F4. 45 81 99 13.
www.restaurant-p2.dk mail@restaurant-p2.dk
The food on offer at this country restaurant is excellent. Good service and
attention to detail more than makes up for the high prices. P

FREDENSBORG: *Ciao*
Christopher Boecks Vej 1, 3480 Fredensborg. **Road map** F4. 48 48 23 24.
www.restaurantciao.dk
A classic Italian café-restaurant serving pizza, pasta and a variety of fish
and meat dinners. The wide range of prices will suit most budgets.

FREDERIKSSUND: *Regnbuen*
Ny Østergade 5C, 3600 Frederikssund. **Road map** F4. 47 38 58 10.
www.restaurantregnbuen.dk
The extensive menu at this bright and cheerful restaurant includes Italian,
Danish, Turkish and Kurdish food. P

FREDERIKSSUND: *Sukhumvit*
Havnegade 16, 3600 Frederikssund. **Road map** F4. 47 38 65 10.
www.sukhumvit.dk
Thai food is becoming increasingly popular in Denmark and this restaurant,
which offers tasty satays, aromatic red and green curries and other Thai
favourites, is one of the most authentic. P

	CREDIT CARDS	GARDEN OR TERRACE	VEGETARIAN DISHES	CHILDREN'S MENU

Price per person for a three-course meal without alcohol, including tax (without tip).
ⓚ up to 150 Dkr
ⓚⓚ 150–200 Dkr
ⓚⓚⓚ 200–300 Dkr
ⓚⓚⓚⓚ 300–350 Dkr
ⓚⓚⓚⓚⓚ over 350 Dkr

CREDIT CARDS
Eurocard, MasterCard, Visa, Diners Club all accepted.

GARDEN OR TERRACE
Meal can be served on a terrace, in a garden or courtyard.

VEGETARIAN DISHES
Good selection of vegetarian dishes available.

CHILDREN'S MENU
Simple food adapted to suit children's tastes.

HELSINGØR: *Konstantinopel*   ⓚ
Fenrisvej 27, 3000 Helsingør. **Road map** F4. ☎ 49 20 10 65.
🌐 www.konstantinopel.info
The Greek and Turkish cuisine on offer here is of a high standard. There is a belly dancing show at the weekend. 🎵

Vegetarian Dishes: ●

HELSINGØR: *Kronborg Havbad*   ⓚ
Strandpromenaden 6, 3000 Helsingør. **Road map** F4. ☎ 49 20 13 30.
🌐 www.kronborg-havbad.dk
A modern, harbourside restaurant with wonderful views over Kronborg Slot and a fish- and meat-based menu. There is a play area for children. 🅿 ♿

Garden or Terrace: ■   Children's Menu: ■

HELSINGØR: *Amici Miei*   ⓚⓚ
Stengade 15, 3000 Helsingør. **Road map** F4. ☎ 49 26 26 71.
An excellent Italian restaurant in a central location.

Credit Cards: ●   Vegetarian Dishes: ●   Children's Menu: ■

HELSINGØR: *Madam Sprunck*   ⓚⓚⓚ
Stengade 48, 3000 Helsingør. **Road map** F4. ☎ 49 26 48 49.
🌐 www.madamsprunck.dk 📧 restaurant@madamsprunck.dk
A good restaurant in an atmospheric old building with a mixture of Danish and international dishes on the menu.

Credit Cards: ●   Garden or Terrace: ■   Vegetarian Dishes: ●   Children's Menu: ■

HOLBÆK: *Nygade No 5*   ⓚ
Nygade 5, 4300 Holbæk. **Road map** E4. ☎ 59 44 25 11.
🌐 www.nygadeno5.dk
This café-restaurant has a good value à la carte menu. One option is to order a mini grill which is placed on the table allowing guests to cook their own meat. There is live music in the evenings. 🅿 🎵

Credit Cards: ●

HOLBÆK: *Linden*   ⓚⓚⓚⓚ
Markedspladsen 9, 4300 Holbæk. **Road map** E4.
☎ 59 43 04 18. 🌐 www.restaurantlinden.dk
📧 info@restaurantlinden.dk
The two young chefs operating from this stylish restaurant serve dishes that combine the best of Italian and French recipes. 🅿

Credit Cards: ●

HORNBÆK: *Søstrene Olsen*   ⓚⓚ
Øresundsvej 10, 3100 Hornbæk. **Road map** F4. ☎ 49 70 05 50.
🌐 www.sostreneolsen.dk
The "Olsen Sisters" restaurant occupies a late 19th-century summer house. The menu includes some fine seafood dishes and changes every two weeks. 🅿 ○ *Mar–Oct.*

Garden or Terrace: ■

HORNBÆK: *Oliva*   ⓚⓚⓚ
Havnevej 1, 3100 Hornbæk. **Road map** F4. ☎ 49 76 11 77.
🌐 www.oliva.dk 📧 oliva@mail.dk
A French restaurant with a menu that includes some quality fish dishes.

Garden or Terrace: ■

HUNDESTED: *Lynæs Kro*   ⓚⓚ
Frederiksværkvej 6, 3390 Hundested. **Road map** E4. ☎ 47 98 01 81.
🌐 www.lynaes-kro.dk 📧 info@lynaes-kro.dk
A traditional Danish inn serving a range of Danish favourites as well as a selection of international dishes including a tasty mulligatawny soup. The children's menu includes such perennial standbys as fish and chips and beef burgers. 🅿

Children's Menu: ■

KALUNDBORG: *Cafe Bogart*   ⓚⓚⓚ
Kordilgade 17, 4400 Kalundborg. **Road map** E4. ☎ 59 51 00 57.
🌐 www.cafe-bogart.dk 📧 bogart@post.tele.dk
Café Bogart owes its great popularity to its good food and its convenient location in the centre of town. 🎵

Credit Cards: ●   Garden or Terrace: ■   Vegetarian Dishes: ●   Children's Menu: ■

ROSKILDE: *Bryggergaarden*   Ⓚ
Algade 15, 4200 Roskilde. **Road map** F4. ☎ *46 35 01 03.*
🅆 www.rest-bryggergaarden.dk
This family-orientated restaurant combines French and Danish favourites. It
serves evening meals as well as brunches and lunches.

ROSKILDE: *Gringos*   Ⓚ
Hestetorvet 10, 4000 Roskilde. **Road map** F4. ☎ *46 36 14 47.*
🅆 www.gringos.dk
A Mexican-style restaurant that includes a wide variety of tacos on the
menu along with a range of spicy meat dishes.

ROSKILDE: *Store Børs*   ⓀⓀ
Havnevej 43, 4000 Roskilde. **Road map** F4. ☎ *46 32 50 45.*
🅆 www.store-bors.dk 🔼 info@store-bors.dk
A stylish restaurant that specializes in beautifully prepared fresh fish and
seafood dishes. Much of the fish is selected from the morning catch.

ROSKILDE: *Snekken*   ⓀⓀⓀ
Vindeboder 16, 4000 Roskilde. **Road map** F4. ☎ *46 35 98 16.*
🅆 www.snekken.dk 🔼 restaurant@snekken.dk
A bright and airy café enjoying uninterrupted views of the marina and
Roskilde Fjord. At night the café is transformed into a restaurant and the
metal-and-glass architecture is in perfect accord with the contemporary
menu on offer. 🅿

RUNGSTED KYST: *Nokken*   ⓀⓀⓀ
Rungsted Havn 44, 2960 Rungsted Kyst. **Road map** F4. ☎ *45 57 13 14.*
🅆 www.nokken.dk 🔼 nokken@nokken.dk
The fresh seafood and classic French meat dishes make this restaurant a
good option. The terrace with views of the harbour and the sound is an
added bonus. 🅿

SORØ: *Stovletkatrineshus*   ⓀⓀⓀⓀⓀ
Slagelsevej 63, 4180 Sorø. **Road map** E5. ☎ *57 83 50 80.*
🅆 www.stovletkatrineshus.dk 🔼 lars@stovletkatrineshus.dk
Located in a picturesque, half-timbered country house, this Danish *kro*
(inn) has plenty of character. The interior is equally traditional, as is the
menu, which features plenty of herring and fillets of fish.

TISVILDELEJE: *Sofie*   Ⓚ
Bygmarken 30, 3220 Tisvildeleje. **Road map** F4. ☎ *48 70 98 50.*
🅆 www.helene.dk
A spacious, modern restaurant that serves wholesome buffets and good-
sized fish dishes. The restaurant goes out of its way to welcome children. 🅿

TISVILDELEJE: *Tisvilde Bar and Bistro*   Ⓚ
Hovedgaden 38, 3220 Tisvildeleje. **Road map** F4. ☎ *48 70 41 91.*
🅆 www.tisvildebistro.dk 🔼 je.storgaard@mail.tele.dk
A French-style bistro next to a cinema that features a menu ranging from
hamburgers and steak to coq au vin and meaty Danish stews. 🎵

SOUTHERN ZEALAND AND THE ISLANDS

FAKSE: *Skovfogedstedet*   ⓀⓀⓀ
Ny Strandskov 4, 4640 Fakse. **Road map** F5. ☎ *56 71 02 27.*
🅆 www.skovfogedstedet.dk
A pleasant restaurant overlooking Fakse bay. It serves tasty hors d'oeuvres
including breast of duck with dried berries and raspberry vinegar. 🅿

KØGE: *Arken*   ⓀⓀ
Bådehavnen 21, 4600 Køge. **Road map** F5. ☎ *56 66 05 05.*
🅆 www.koege.net/arken
Built in 1979, the Arken (or "Ark") is a modern restaurant with a bright,
yacht-like interior. The menu includes Danish favourites such as meatballs.
Tables are laid on the restaurant's terrace in summer. 🅿

KØGE: *Casino*   ⓀⓀ
Torvet 17, 4600 Køge. **Road map** F5. ☎ *56 65 01 75.*
🅆 www.restaurantcasino.dk 🔼 post@restaurantcasino.dk
This smart restaurant occupies a 15th-century building. It serves food based
on Danish cookery, with French and Italian twists. The seafood is delicious.

<table>
<tr><td>

Price per person for a three-course meal without alcohol, including tax (without tip).
ⓚ up to 150 Dkr
ⓚⓚ 150–200 Dkr
ⓚⓚⓚ 200–300 Dkr
ⓚⓚⓚⓚ 300–350 Dkr
ⓚⓚⓚⓚⓚ over 350 Dkr

</td><td>

CREDIT CARDS
Eurocard, MasterCard, Visa, Diners Club all accepted.

GARDEN OR TERRACE
Meal can be served on a terrace, in a garden or courtyard.

VEGETARIAN DISHES
Good selection of vegetarian dishes available.

CHILDREN'S MENU
Simple food adapted to suit children's tastes.

</td></tr>
</table>

	CREDIT CARDS	GARDEN OR TERRACE	VEGETARIAN DISHES	CHILDREN'S MENU
NAKSKOV: *Lido* Søndergade 8–10, 4900 Nakskov. **Road map** E6. 【 *54 92 23 13.* ⓦ www.lido-nakskov.dk ⓐ lido@lido-nakskov.dk The Lido serves mainly meat dishes. Its Danish hors d'oeuvres, including the prawns with mayonnaise, are well worth trying. **P**	ⓚ			▦
NYKØBING F: *Czarens Hus* Langgade 2, 4800 Nykøbing F. **Road map** B2. 【 *54 85 28 29.* ⓦ www.czarenshus.dk A stylish restaurant that specializes in fish and Danish favourites. The restaurant's name harks back to a visit by Tsar Peter the Great in 1716.	ⓚⓚⓚ	●	●	
NYKØBING F: *Vinkælderen* Slotsgade 22, 4800 Nykøbing F. **Road map** B2. 【 *54 85 01 14.* ⓦ www.vinkaelderen.nu ⓐ vinkaelderen@mail.dk Danish and French food is on offer in this homely restaurant.	ⓚⓚⓚ	●		▦
NÆSTVED: *Mona Lisa* Sankt Jørgens Park 34, 4700 Næstved. **Road map** E5. 【 *55 73 41 92.* ⓦ www.restaurant-monalisa.dk ⓐ mona@restaurant-monalisa.dk Mona Lisa is a family-friendly restaurant. Children eat for free if their parents order the Colorado Steak. In the evenings the adults can take to the dance floor. **P** 🎵	ⓚ	●	▦	●	▦
RINGSTED: *Ernas Bøfhus* Vestervej 2, 4100 Ringsted. **Road map** E5. 【 *57 67 60 04.* ⓦ www.ernasboefhus.dk The meat-based menu at this Danish steakhouse is hearty and filling. It is an ideal place for large groups. **P**	ⓚ			
VORDINGBORG: *Vordingbowl* Næstvedvej 42, 4760 Vordingborg. **Road map** F6. 【 *55 34 20 95.* ⓦ www.vordingbowl.dk This bowling alley's restaurant serves surprisingly good food. Afterwards, diners can enjoy a round of 10-pin bowling. **P**	ⓚⓚ		▦	▦
VORDINGBORG: *Babette* Kildemarksvej 5, 4760 Vordingborg. **Road map** F6. 【 *55 34 30 30.* ⓦ www.babette.dk Inspired by the 1987 movie *Babette's Feast*, this stylish restaurant has an exquisite menu that includes locally sourced ingredients and a subtle blending of French and Danish cuisine. **P**	ⓚⓚⓚⓚ			
FUNEN				
FAABORG: *Ved Brønden* Torvet 5, 5600 Faaborg. **Road map** D5. 【 *62 61 11 35 .* ⓦ www.ved-bronden.dk ⓐ post@ved-bronden.dk A centrally-located inn serving a good variety of traditional Danish dishes.	ⓚⓚ	●	▦	
KERTEMINDE: *Café Daddy* Hans Schacksvej 5, 5300 Kerteminde. **Road map** D5. 【 *65 32 46 71.* ⓦ www.cafe-daddy.dk This pizza and burger restaurant is particularly worth recommending to young people who, after their meal, can work off some of the calories on the dance floor at the weekend. **P**	ⓚⓚ		▦	▦
KERTEMINDE: *Rudolf Mathis* Dosseringen 13, 5300 Kerteminde. **Road map** D5. 【 *65 32 32 33.* ⓦ www.rudolf-mathis.dk ⓐ bestilling@rudolf-mathis.dk This well-regarded fish restaurant stands right on the waterfront. **P**	ⓚⓚⓚ	●		

MIDDELFART: *Hindsgavl Slot* ⓀⓀⓀ
Hindsgavl Allé 7, 5500 Middelfart. **Road map** C5. **(** *64 41 88 00.*
w www.hindsgavl.dk @ hindsgavl@hindsgavl.dk
A good-value hotel restaurant serving well-prepared Danish food. Save
room for the desserts, which are especially good.

MUNKEBO: *Munkebo Kro* ⓀⓀⓀⓀ
Fjordvej 56, 5330 Munkebo. **Road map** D5. **(** *65 97 40 30.*
w www.munkebokro.dk @ munkebo-kro@munkebo-kro.dk
This charming Danish inn has been in business since the early 19th century,
and has played host to the Danish royal family. The menu is dominated by
excellent fish dishes. Booking is advisable. **P**

NYBORG: *Østervemb* ⓀⓀⓀ
Mellemgade 18, 5800 Nyborg. **Road map** D5. **(** *65 30 10 70.*
w www.ostervemb.dk @ info@ostervemb.dk
A wonderful restaurant with plenty of atmosphere. The seafood and
traditional dishes are cooked with great care and beautifully presented. **P**

ODENSE: *Capri* Ⓚ
Dronningensgade 2B, 5000 Odense C. **Road map** D5. **(** *66 12 37 18.*
w www.capri500.dk @ capri@capri500.dk
A traditional Italian restaurant serving pizza and pasta.

ODENSE: *Oriental Barbecue* Ⓚ
Slotsgade 20, 5000 Odense C. **Road map** D5. **(** *63 12 38 28.*
w www.orientalbarbecue.dk
Located in the town centre, this restaurant does a good line in inexpensive
Chinese and Japanese food. The sushi is well worth trying.

ODENSE: *Den Grimme Ælling* ⓀⓀ
Hans Jensens Stræde 1, 5000 Odense C. **Road map** D5. **(** *65 91 70 30.*
w www.grimme-aelling.dk
Situated close to Hans Christian Andersen's house, the restaurant's name
translates as "The Ugly Duckling". The menu is traditionally Danish and
includes a plentiful all-you-can-eat buffet at lunchtime.

ODENSE: *Djengis Khan* ⓀⓀ
Overgade 24–25, 5000 Odense C. **Road map** D5. **(** *66 12 88 38.*
w www.djengis-khan.dk
This exotic restaurant specializes in meat dishes including Mongolian-style
grills. The wine list includes French, Spanish and Californian vintages.

ODENSE: *Klos And's Spiseværts HUS* ⓀⓀ
Vindegade 76, 5000 Odense C. **Road map** D5. **(** *66 13 56 00.*
w www.klosands.dk @ info@klosands.dk
This informal restaurant is particularly popular with young people, who
often head down to the nightclub in the building's cellar after dinner.

ODENSE: *Vestergade 1* ⓀⓀ
Vestergade 1, 5000 Odense C. **Road map** D5. **(** *66 12 52 53.*
w www.vestergade1.dk
One of Odense's more elegant restaurants. Its fashionable "fusion" cuisine
combines Italian, French and Spanish culinary traditions.

ODENSE: *La Piazza* ⓀⓀⓀ
Brandts Passage 33–35, 5000 Odense C. **Road map** D5. **(** *66 14 60 70.*
w www.la-piazza.dk @ la.piazza@mail.dk
An authentic Italian restaurant with an extensive menu and wine list. The
dishes are appealing and lovingly presented.

ODENSE: *Klitgaard* ⓀⓀⓀⓀ
Gravene 4, 5000 Odense C. **Road map** D5. **(** *66 13 14 55.*
w www.restaurantklitgaard.dk
A sophisticated restaurant with a chic menu that fuses French and Italian
cookery. Much of the produce is fresh from the market.

SVENDBORG: *Pakhuset* ⓀⓀⓀ
Havnepladsen 3A, 5700 Svendborg. **Road map** D5. **(** *62 21 66 97.*
w www.restaurant-pakhuset.dk
This harbourside restaurant has a bright and airy ambience. Some Danish
favourites are included on the otherwise international menu.

Price per person for a three-course meal without alcohol, including tax (without tip).
ⓚ up to 150 Dkr
ⓚⓚ 150–200 Dkr
ⓚⓚⓚ 200–300 Dkr
ⓚⓚⓚⓚ 300–350 Dkr
ⓚⓚⓚⓚⓚ over 350 Dkr

CREDIT CARDS
Eurocard, MasterCard, Visa, Diners Club all accepted.

GARDEN OR TERRACE
Meal can be served on a terrace, in a garden or courtyard.

VEGETARIAN DISHES
Good selection of vegetarian dishes available.

CHILDREN'S MENU
Simple food adapted to suit children's tastes.

SOUTHERN AND CENTRAL JUTLAND

	CREDIT CARDS	GARDEN OR TERRACE	VEGETARIAN DISHES	CHILDREN'S MENU
EBELTOFT: *Molskroen* Hovedgaden 16, Femøller Strand, 8400 Ebeltoft. **Road map** D3. 📞 86 36 22 00. 🌐 www.molskroen.dk 📧 molskroen@molskroen.dk The restaurant occupies an early 20th-century, half-timbered manor house that also serves as a hotel. The chef has a good reputation and conjures up a range of French fare with imaginative Danish twists. 🅿 🎵 ⓚⓚ	●			
ESBJERG: *Jensens Bøfhus* Kongensgade 9, 6700 Esbjerg. **Road map** B5. 📞 75 18 18 70. 🌐 www.jensens.com This restaurant has its own courtyard, which is a pleasant place to enjoy the grilled meats in summer. ⓚ				
ESBJERG: *Den Røde Okse* Tarphagevej 9, 6710 Esbjerg V. **Road map** B5. 📞 75 15 15 00. 🌐 www.dro.dk 📧 kontakt@dro.dk One of the better restaurants in town, Den Røde Okse is known for its fish. Some excellent meat dishes are also on the menu. 🅿 ⓚⓚⓚ	●			▪
ESBJERG: *Pakhuset* Dokvej 3, 6700 Esbjerg. **Road map** B5. 📞 75 12 74 55. 🌐 www.pakhuset-esbjerg.dk 📧 info@pakhuset-esbjerg.dk Housed in an early 20th-century auction hall, this restaurant has plenty of atmosphere with a high ceiling and original paintings on the walls. The food is delicate and well prepared. A "tasting menu" is available, which consists of five mini portions of popular main dishes. 🅿 ⓚⓚⓚ	●			
FANØ: *Fanø Røgeri* Postvejen 16, Rindby, 6720 Fanø. **Road map** B5. 📞 75 16 34 36. 🌐 www.home19.inet.tele.dk/fanorog 📧 fanoe.roegeri@post.tele.dk This good-value restaurant specializes in fish. 🅿 ⓚ				▪
FREDERICIA: *Simon's* Torvegade 2, 7000 Fredericia. **Road map** C5. 📞 75 91 49 11. 🌐 www.simons-restaurant.dk The chef's concoctions are inspired by Italian and French cookery. ⓚⓚ	●	▪	●	
GRENÅ: *Det Gyldne Krus* Lillegade 18, 8500 Grenå. **Road map** D3. 📞 86 32 47 22. 🌐 www.kruset.dk This smart restaurant has some excellent meat dishes on the menu. Live music is often played in the evening. 🎵 ⓚ	●	▪	●	▪
HADERSLEV: *Dannevang* Kelstrupvej 73, 6100 Haderslev. **Road map** C5. 📞 74 58 29 75. 🌐 www.dannevang.com 📧 info@dannevang.com A pleasant hotel-restaurant set in a charming part of town that serves a mix of Danish and international cuisine. 🅿 ⓚⓚⓚⓚ	●	▪		
HERNING: *Hereford Beefstouw* Lundvej 16, 7400 Herning. **Road map** C4. 📞 97 12 35 44. 🌐 www.a-h-b.dk/dansk 📧 lund@a-h-b.dk One of Denmark's leading restaurant chains, this is the perfect place for all meat-lovers who dream of large, juicy steaks and spare ribs. 🅿 ⓚⓚⓚ				▪
HOLSTEBRO: *Cook's* Østergade 19, 7500 Holstebro. **Road map** B3. 📞 97 40 47 49. 🌐 www.restaurant-cooks.dk 📧 cooks@restaurant-cooks.dk The restaurant specializes in all kinds of pizza – Italian, Mexican and even Kurdish. Diners also have the opportunity to choose their own toppings. ⓚ	●		●	▪

HORSENS: *Lille Hejmdal*   ⓀⓀⓀ
Rædersgade 8, 8700 Horsens. **Road map** C4. **☎** *75 61 02 00.*
W www.lillehejmdal.dk
An old restaurant that opened as a café in 1888. The food is up-to-date,
however, and includes a fantastic selection of organic delicacies.

KOLDING: *Hereford Beefstouw*   ⓀⓀⓀ
Helligkorsgade 20, 6000 Kolding. **Road map** C5. **☎** *75 52 00 87.*
@ kolding@a-h-b.dk **W** www.a-h-b.dk/dansk/
A reliable chain restaurant serving meaty steaks in rich sauces. **P**

KOLDING: *Koldinghus*   ⓀⓀⓀⓀ
Markdannersgade 11, 6000 Kolding. **Road map** C5. **☎** *75 50 47 98.*
W www.koldinghus.dk **@** cafe.koldinghus@radissonsas.com
Delicious international cuisine is on offer in the 15th-century cellars of
Koldinghus Slot. In the 18th century the cellars housed the castle's bakery.

RANDERS: *Townhill*   Ⓚ
Dytmærsken 9, 8900 Randers. **Road map** D3. **☎** *86 43 02 03.*
W www.townhill.dk
This restaurant serves pizzas, pasta and grilled food.

RANDERS: *Slotskroen*   ⓀⓀⓀⓀ
Slotsgade, 8900 Randers. **Road map** D3. **☎** *86 43 56 64.*
W www.spiseguiden.dk/slotskroen **@** slotskroen@spiseguiden.dk
This stylishly furnished restaurant offers a variety of delicious dishes
prepared by the skilled Italian owners. **&**

RIBE: *Kammerslusen*   Ⓚ
Bjerrumvej 30, 6760 Ribe. **Road map** B5. **☎** *75 42 07 96.*
W www.kammerslusen.dk
Located opposite the cathedral, this hotel-restaurant has four dining rooms
that have bags of 19th-century character. The menu is international in
flavour and includes some good fish dishes. It is also possible to order take-
out lunch boxes, which can be eaten in the grounds, weather permitting. **P**

RIBE: *Sælhunden*   Ⓚ
Skibbrøn 13, 6760 Ribe. **Road map** B5. **☎** *75 42 09 46.*
W www.saelhunden.dk **@** saelhunden@stofanet.dk
The "seal tavern" is situated next to a river. The restaurant has an intimate
ambience and serves a variety of classic Danish dishes including meatballs
and strips of pork in cream. A terrace is open in summer.

RIBE: *Weis Stue*   Ⓚ
Torvet 2, 6760 Ribe. **Road map** B5. **☎** *75 42 07 00.* **W** www.weis-stue.dk
Housed in a 16th-century half-timbered house, this restaurant is in the
market square next to the cathedral. The restaurant's speciality is wild duck
served with roast potatoes and cream sauce. Definitely worth trying.

RY: *Julsø*   ⓀⓀ
Julsøvej 14–16, 8680 Ry. **Road map** C4. **☎** *86 89 80 40.*
W www.hotel-julso.dk
Julsø is housed in a former hotel in the heart of the Danish Lake District.
One of the star items on its international menu is the *gazpacho* soup. **P**

SILKEBORG: *Angus*   Ⓚ
Christian d.8 Vej 7, 8600 Silkeborg. **Road map** C4. **☎** *86 82 28 54.*
W www.angus.dk
A classic steakhouse serving a variety of grilled meat dishes as well as fish.
There is also a good selection of wines. **P**

SILKEBORG: *Zorba*   ⓀⓀ
Nygade 19, 8600 Silkeborg. **Road map** C4. **☎** *86 81 21 55.*
W www.restaurantzorba.dk **@** mail@restaurantzorba.dk
This spacious Greek restaurant has a good reputation. Chef Andreas
Fergadis returns each year to his home country to collect new recipes and
sample wines, which he later orders for his establishment. **P**

SILKEBORG: *Svostrup Kro*   ⓀⓀⓀ
Svostrupvej 58, 8600 Silkeborg. **Road map** C4. **☎** *86 87 70 04.*
W www.svostrup-kro.dk
Delicious country food in a beautiful setting just outside Silkeborg.

Price per person for a three-course meal without alcohol, including tax (without tip).
ⓚ up to 150 Dkr
ⓚⓚ 150–200 Dkr
ⓚⓚⓚ 200–300 Dkr
ⓚⓚⓚⓚ 300–350 Dkr
ⓚⓚⓚⓚⓚ over 350 Dkr

CREDIT CARDS
Eurocard, MasterCard, Visa, Diners Club all accepted.

GARDEN OR TERRACE
Meal can be served on a terrace, in a garden or courtyard.

VEGETARIAN DISHES
Good selection of vegetarian dishes available.

CHILDREN'S MENU
Simple food adapted to suit children's tastes.

	CREDIT CARDS	GARDEN OR TERRACE	VEGETARIAN DISHES	CHILDREN'S MENU
SILKEBORG: *Piaf* ⓚⓚⓚ Nygade 31, 8600 Silkeborg. **Road map** C4. 📞 *86 81 12 55.* 🔲 www.restaurant-piaf.dk So named because of the owner's resemblance to Edith Piaf, this restaurant strives to be a little different with paintings and posters on the walls, a mishmash of furniture and potted plants. The traditional smoked fish is outstanding as the restaurant has its own smoking oven.	●			
SØNDREBORG: *Jensens Bøfhus* ⓚ Perlegade 36, 6400 Søndreborg. **Road map** C6. 📞 *74 42 52 28.* 🔲 www.jensens.com A chain restaurant offering meat dishes served with a variety of sauces.				
TØNDER: *Torvets* ⓚⓚ Storegade 1, 6270 Tønder. **Road map** B6. 📞 *74 72 43 73.* 🔲 www.tonder-net.dk/torvet 📧 torvet@tonder-net.dk Situated in a former bank in the market square, this restaurant offers a large selection of dishes. The restaurant is more upmarket and consequently pricier, while the bistro offers a range of *smørrebrød*, pickled herring and pasta dishes. **P**	●		●	■
TØNDER: *Slotskro* ⓚⓚⓚⓚ Møgeltønder, 6270 Tønder. **Road map** B6. 📞 *45 74 83 83.* 🔲 www.slotskro.dk 📧 schackenborg@slotskro.dk This beautifully located hotel is the official royal inn for nearby Schackenborg Slot, home to Prince Joachim. The hotel's restaurant is highly regarded and serves a mix of French and Danish cuisine. **P**	●	■		
VEJLE: *Merlot* ⓚⓚⓚ Skyttehusgade 42, 7100 Vejle. **Road map** B4. 📞 *75 83 88 44.* 🔲 www.merlot-vejle.dk 📧 info@merlot-vejle.dk This intimate restaurant, situated in a historic building, serves French food and wines. Particularly fine are the *foie gras* and the delicious desserts. The restaurant also has a wine shop.		■	●	■
ÅBENRÅ: *Royal* ⓚ Nørretorv 1, 6200 Åbenrå. **Road map** C6. 📞 *74 62 03 30.* 🔲 www.royal.dk 📧 info@royal.dk Sumptuous roast beef, grilled meats and hamburgers are all on the menu at this good-value eatery. **P**	●			■
ÅBENRÅ: *Knapp* ⓚⓚⓚ Stennevej 79, Stollig, 6200 Åbenrå. **Road map** C6. 📞 *74 62 00 92.* 🔲 www.restaurant-hotel-knapp.dk 📧 info@restaurant-hotel-knapp.dk This smart hotel-restaurant, situated in an historic *kro* (inn), has an extensive menu and a pleasant, if formal, atmosphere. **P**	●			
ÅRHUS: *Italia* ⓚ Åboulevarden 9, 8000 Århus C. **Road map** D4. 📞 *86 19 80 22.* 🔲 www.italia-aarhus.dk The classic Italian cuisine on offer here includes pasta, grilled meat, and fish. The pizza from the wood-fired oven is especially good. What is more, the prices are low and the setting truly romantic.	●		●	
ÅRHUS: *Jacob's BarBQ* ⓚ Vestergade 3, 8000 Århus C. **Road map** D4. 📞 *87 32 24 20.* 🔲 www.jacobs-bar-bq.dk 📧 info@jacobs-bar-bq.dk The restaurant, situated in an 18th-century merchant's house, specializes in grilled meat and fish dishes. After a meal guests can move on to the bar where a pianist tickles the ivories Wednesday to Friday. 🎵	●	■	●	■

ÅRHUS: *Navigator* Ⓚ
Marselisborg Havnevej 46D, 8000 Århus C. **Road map** D4.
📞 86 20 20 58. 🔲 www.rest-navigator.dk
@ info@rest-navigator.dk
A lively restaurant serving well-cooked Danish staples that has dinner and
dance evenings on Saturdays. It is necessary to book in advance. 🅿 ♬

ÅRHUS: *Viggo* Ⓚ
Åboulevarden 52, 8000 Århus C. **Road map** D4. 📞 89 19 00 11.
🔲 www.cafeviggo.dk @ info@cafeviggo.dk
Viggo is more of a café than a restaurant, but in the evenings it also offers
hot meals such as Thai curry. On Monday, Tuesday and Saturday evenings
it serves Italian food.

ÅRHUS: *Olive* ⓀⓀ
Kaløgade 1, 8000 Århus C. **Road map** D4. 📞 86 12 95 61. 🔲 www.olive.dk
This cosy restaurant in the centre of town has a good quality meat- and
fish-based menu. The desserts are delicious. 🅿

ÅRHUS: *Dauphine* ⓀⓀⓀ
Frederiksgade 43, 8000 Århus C. **Road map** D4. 📞 86 19 39 22.
🔲 www.dauphine.dk
The Dauphine has an international menu and a comprehensive wine list.

ÅRHUS: *L'estragon* ⓀⓀⓀ
Klostergade 6, 8000 Århus C. **Road map** D4. 📞 86 12 40 66.
🔲 www.lestragon.dk
This tiny restaurant concentrates on producing good-quality French food
but makes maximum use of local Danish ingredients.

NORTHERN JUTLAND

AALBORG: *Duus Vinkælder* Ⓚ
Østerågade 9, 9000 Aalborg. **Road map** D2. 📞 98 12 50 56.
🔲 www.restaurant-merhaba.dk
A convivial eatery and bar that serves light lunches only. It is full of
character and makes a good stopping-off point when sightseeing.

AALBORG: *Fyrtøjet* Ⓚ
Jomfru Ane Gade 17, 9000 Aalborg. **Road map** D2. 📞 98 13 73 77.
🔲 www.fyrtoejet.dk @ info@fyrtoejet.dk
The oldest building on Jomfru Ane Gade houses a restaurant that serves a
good selection of classic Danish cuisine including some excellent fish. The
restaurant's glass-roofed courtyard is a pleasant place to dine.

AALBORG: *Layalina* Ⓚ
Ved Stranden 7–9, 9000 Aalborg. **Road map** D2. 📞 98 11 60 56.
This Lebanese restaurant serves a variety of spicy Middle Eastern meat
dishes in a warm and friendly atmosphere. The vegetarian plate filled with
roasted vegetables and Mediterranean delicacies is especially good, as are
the succulent kebabs. 🅿

AALBORG: *Provence* ⓀⓀ
Ved Stranden 11, 9000 Aalborg. **Road map** D2. 📞 98 13 51 33.
🔲 www.restaurant-provence.dk @ provence@email.dk
True to its name, this intimate restaurant serves mainly Provençal dishes
that include soufflés and *foie gras*. Several times a year Provence stages
exhibitions of works by Danish and international artists. 🅿

AALBORG: *Il Mulino* ⓀⓀⓀ
Bispensgade 31, 9000 Aalborg. **Road map** D2. 📞 98 12 39 99.
🔲 www.il-mulino.dk @ carlo@il-mulino.dk
Set in an 18th-century warehouse, this lively Italian restaurant has a menu
that includes wonderful pasta dishes and grilled meats. The pasta is
homemade and freshly rolled every day.

AALBORG: *Mortens Kro* ⓀⓀⓀⓀ
Mølleå 4–6, 9000 Aalborg. **Road map** D2. 📞 98 12 48 60.
🔲 www.mortenskro.dk @ info@mortenskro.dk
This restaurant's interior is sleek and upmarket. The owner and head chef,
Morten Nielsen, is something of a celebrity cook in Denmark and the wide-
ranging menu reflects his attention to detail.

Price per person for a three-course meal without alcohol, including tax (without tip).
Ⓚ up to 150 Dkr
ⓀⓀ 150–200 Dkr
ⓀⓀⓀ 200–300 Dkr
ⓀⓀⓀⓀ 300–350 Dkr
ⓀⓀⓀⓀⓀ over 350 Dkr

CREDIT CARDS
Eurocard, MasterCard, Visa, Diners Club all accepted.

GARDEN OR TERRACE
Meal can be served on a terrace, in a garden or courtyard.

VEGETARIAN DISHES
Good selection of vegetarian dishes available.

CHILDREN'S MENU
Simple food adapted to suit children's tastes.

	CREDIT CARDS	GARDEN OR TERRACE	VEGETARIAN DISHES	CHILDREN'S MENU
FREDERIKSHAVN: *Nikolines Cafeteria* Ⓚ	●	■	●	■

FREDERIKSHAVN: *Nikolines Cafeteria* Ⓚ
Nordvej 4, 9900 Frederikshavn. **Road map** D1. 📞 98 47 90 16.
🌐 www.nikolines.dk
This classic Danish café-restaurant offers a wide selection of fast and filling food. The menu is simple and unfussy and there are many dishes that will appeal to children. 🅿

HJØRRING: *Jensens Bøfhus* Ⓚ
Sankt Olai Plads 1, 9800 Hjørring. **Road map** D1. 📞 98 90 35 55.
🌐 www.jensens.com
One of the Bøfhus chain, this reliable restaurant serves tasty grilled meat and stews and a variety of tempting desserts.

SKAGEN: *Alfredo* Ⓚ ■ ● ■
Havnevej 13, 9990 Skagen. **Road map** D1. 📞 98 44 17 46. 🌐 www.alfredo.dk
This traditional Italian restaurant specializes in pizza and pasta, although the grilled meats are also worth trying. 🅿

SKAGEN: *Jacobs Cafe & Bar* ⓀⓀ ■
Havnevej 4, 9990 Skagen. **Road map** D1. 📞 98 44 16 90.
🌐 www.jakobscafe.dk
A popular Skagen eatery, this lively café-bar has good food and often hosts live music at the weekend. The varied menu is mainly Danish in character.
🅿 🎵

BORNHOLM

ALLINGE: *Nordbornholms Røgeri* Ⓚ ● ■
Kaempestrand 2, 3770 Allinge. 📞 56 48 07 30.
🌐 www.europage.dk/bornholm/roegerier
This is one of the best places to try smoked mackerel and herring on the northern coast. Eaten while still hot they are absolutely delicious. 🅿

ALLINGE: *Algarve* ⓀⓀ ● ●
Havnegade 9, 3770 Allinge. 📞 56 48 11 08.
🌐 www.oddfellowrestaurant.dk @ ofp@postkasse.com
A modest inn-style restaurant with a relaxed ambience and a good selection of beautifully prepared Danish favourites.

ALLINGE: *Toldkammeret* ⓀⓀⓀⓀ ● ■
Havnegade 19, 3770 Allinge. 📞 56 48 48 49.
🌐 www.restaurant-toldkammeret.dk @ timo@restaurant-toldkammeret.dk
A good modern restaurant with chic décor and some excellent fish dishes.

GUDHJEM: *Rø* Ⓚ ■
Røvej 51, 3760 Gudhjem. 📞 56 48 40 38. 🌐 www.bornholm-restaurant.dk
@ selskab@bornholm-restaurant.dk
The restaurant's menu bursts with classic Danish dishes. On chilly days guests can warm up by the restaurant's log fire. In summer, the garden makes a pleasant place to dine. 🅿

GUDHJEM: *PS* ⓀⓀ ● ■
Brøddegade 24, 3760 Gudhjem. 📞 56 48 53 56. 🌐 www.ps-gudhjem.dk
@ ps@ps-gudhjem.dk
The restaurant was once a local shop. It now serves a mix of pizza and steaks. The prices vary within a wide range.

HASLE: *Le Port* Ⓚ ● ■ ●
Vang 81, 3790 Hasle. 📞 56 96 92 01. 🌐 www.leport.dk
A traditional restaurant offering good-value, well-cooked food. The regional dishes are the restaurant's strong point. 🅿

HASLE: *Silderøgeriet i Hasle* ⓚ
Sdr Bæk 16–20, 3790 Hasle. ☎ 56 96 44 11. Ⓦ www.europage.dk/bornholm/roegerier
This is one of Bornholm's best smokehouses. Guests have the opportunity to watch the process of smoking the fish. 🅿 🎵

NEXØ: *Brasserie Truberg* ⓚ
Havnepromenaden 2, 3730 Nexø. ☎ 56 49 20 90. Ⓦ www.truberg.dk
@ brasserie@truberg.dk
This friendly restaurant serves a variety of Danish favourites. The restaurant owner considers it a point of honour to use as many locally sourced ingredients as possible. 🅿

RØNNE: *Fyrtøjet* ⓚⓚ
Store Torvegade 22, 3700 Rønne. ☎ 56 95 30 12. Ⓦ www.fyrtoejet.dk
This stylish and well-run restaurant serves Danish and international staples as well as many local specialities.

RØNNE: *Hansens Bøfhus* ⓚⓚ
Noerregade 2, 3700 Rønne. ☎ 56 95 00 69. Ⓦ www.hansens-beufhus.dk
Hansens Bøfhus offers a wide variety of steaks, many of them prepared according to traditional local recipes. It also offers a special children's menu.

SVANEKE: *Aarsdale Silderøgeri* ⓚ
Gaden 2, 3740 Svaneke. ☎ 56 49 65 08. Ⓦ www.dk-web.com/roegeri
@ roegeri@mail.tele.dk
Here, inside an atmospheric smokehouse, diners can enjoy some traditional smoked herring and mackerel. Guests can dine outside in summer. 🅿

SVANEKE: *Bryghuset* ⓚⓚ
Torvet 5, 3740 Svaneke. ☎ 56 49 73 21. Ⓦ www.bryghuset-svaneke.dk
@ mail@bryghuset-svaneke.dk
The restaurant's best dish is its marinated and grilled spare ribs. These can be washed down with a cold beer from the restaurant's own brewery. 🅿

GREENLAND

ILULISSAT: *Ulo* ⓚⓚⓚ
Postbox 1501, DK-3952 Ilulissat, Greenland. ☎ (+299) 94 41 53.
@ info@hotel-arctic.gl
This hotel restaurant enjoys a superb view. The menu includes international dishes as well as specialities of Greenland. Recommended.

NUUK: *Seamans' Home* ⓚⓚ
Postbox 1021, 3900 Nuuk, Greenland. ☎ (+299) 32 10 29.
@ nuuk@soemandshjem.gl
This hotel's informal cafeteria restaurant produces a good range of warming stews and desserts.

UUMMANNAQ: *Hotel Uummannaq* ⓚⓚ
3961 Uummannaq, Greenland. ☎ (+299) 95 15 18.
@ uummannaq@icescaphotels.gl
A hotel restaurant with some spectacular views of the sea.

THE FAROE ISLANDS

RUNAVIK: *Runavik* ⓚ
FO-620 Runavik, Heidavegur 6, Faroe Islands. ☎ (+298) 44 74 20.
Ⓦ www.hotel-runavik.fo @ info@hotel-runavik.fo
Attached to a hotel, this well-regarded restaurant on the island of Eysturoy is one of the best places to eat in the Faroe Islands.

TÓRSHAVN: *Glasstovan* ⓚⓚ
FO-110 Tórshavn, Postbox 3303, Faroe Islands. ☎ (+298) 31 75 00.
Ⓦ www.hotelforoyar.com @ hf@hotelforoyar.com
Hotel Foroyar's restaurant has a splendid view of the fjord and serves Faroe specialities as well as a range of international dishes.

TÓRSHAVN: *Hafnia* ⓚⓚⓚ
FO-110 Tórshavn, 4–10 Aarvegur, Postbox 107, Faroe Islands. ☎ (+298) 31 32 33.
Ⓦ www.hafnia.fo @ hafnia@hafnia.fo
Situated near the harbour, this hotel restaurant has some good fish dishes.

SHOPPING IN DENMARK

MOST MAJOR TOWNS in Denmark have large, shopping centres and department stores such as the country-wide chain Magasin du Nord. Prices can be high, however, especially in the more exclusive shops such as those found along Strøget in Copenhagen. Many bargains on clothes can be found, especially during the post-seasonal sales. Flea markets are widespread in Denmark. Much of what is on sale is tat but persistance and a keen eye can sometimes uncover real treasures. The many independently run shops selling beautiful household goods satisfy the Danes' love of good design. Jewellery made from Danish amber is also popular and relatively cheap. Danish herb-flavoured *akvavit* (a kind of schnapps) comes in a variety of flavours and colours and makes a good present.

Bearded Viking toy

Busy Saturday market in Svaneke, popular with Danes and visitors

OPENING HOURS

IN DENMARK shopping days and opening hours are highly regulated due to union demands for reasonable working hours. The regulated hours are, for the most part, rigorously adhered to, although during the Christmas season and around busy tourist centres longer openings are usual. Most shops open at 9 or 9:30am and remain open until 5:30pm Monday to Thursday. On Fridays many shops are open until 7 or 8pm. On Saturdays most shops close at about 2pm; some larger shops and department stores remain open until 4pm. Most shops are closed on Sundays.

Some smaller, independent shops keep longer opening hours. Stores attached to petrol stations and kiosks found in town centres remain open 24 hours but offer a limited choice of goods.

In the run-up to Christmas and other festivals many shops and department stores in the capital and in larger towns extend their opening hours and often trade on Sundays.

MARKETS

PRODUCE markets are becoming increasingly rare in Denmark and only occasionally will visitors stumble upon a fruit and vegetable market. On the other hand the Danes relish their flea markets, which are held periodically in many towns. Genuine antiques are mixed up with piles of bric à brac and a morning spent at a flea

Sign in Ærøskøbing

market offers a trip down memory lane for many Danes and also provides a good opportunity to munch on a hot sausage from one of the many snack bars.

Pre-Christmas fairs are also common. Seasonal fairs sell a variety of festive decorations including baubles, handmade wooden items, candles and colourful elves and gnomes fashioned from balls of bright wool.

VAT

THE RATE of VAT (locally known as MOMS) is 25 per cent in Denmark. Some goods, such as alcohol, tobacco and petrochemical products, carry an additional excise. Visitors from outside the EU can claim a tax refund of between 14 and 19 per

12th-century cellars being used for wine storage

Hvide Hus – a handicraft shop in Gudhjem on Bornholm

cent of the total price of an item on purchases over 300 Dkr. Shops operating this scheme carry a Tax Free logo. When making a purchase ask for a Global Refund certificate. The shopkeeper may ask to see a passport. On leaving the country the certificate must be stamped by a customs officer, who will need to see that the product is intact in its original packaging. The stamped certificate may be used when reclaiming VAT in allocated banks or border agencies. For more information visit *www.globalrefund.com.*

SEASONAL REDUCTIONS

REDUCTIONS ON many items can be obtained by shopping during the sales, which are known locally as "Tilbud" or "Udsalg". In Denmark, the traditional months for sales are January and July, although many stores shift their dates by one or two weeks either way. Sales are also held to mark the anniversary of a shop's opening or even the founding of a chain. One-off sales held at the start of the school year or before Easter are also common. As with most promotions, it pays to be cautious, however, as reductions can often be quite insignificant or apply only to a limited number of goods.

METHODS OF PAYMENT

CASH IS THE easiest form of payment but for larger sums it is safer to use credit cards, which are widely accepted throughout the country. Cards can be used in many shops, restaurants, hotels and museums. This method of payment does not carry any surcharge.

CONTEMPORARY DESIGN

DENMARK IS FAMOUS for its cutting edge design of ceramics, contemporary furniture and home accessories. Copenhagen has a wealth of independent outlets, but many brands are available throughout the country. The price of such merchandise can be high, especially for items by major designers, but smaller, less expensive items are available such as glasses by Bodum, silver Christmas tree decorations by Georg Jensen and "Olefant" bottle openers designed exclusively for the Carlsberg brewery.

FOOD PRODUCTS

MANY TYPES of cheese are produced in Denmark so there is no excuse for sticking to a simple Danish blue. Those who like sharp-tasting cheeses should go for "Gamle Ole". This strongly flavoured cheese goes particularly well with Danish rye bread, a dense loaf made with seeds and grains.

For those with a sweet tooth, chocolates and sweets are also well worth seeking out.

Often these are handmade, beautifully presented and far superior to the mass-produced variety. Handmade boiled sweets are also good quality.

One of the Danes' favourite foodstuffs is pickled herring, which is served on its own and often on bread as *smørrebrød.* Many different recipes are used when marinating the fish to produce a wide range of tastes. Smoked fish, especially from Bornholm, is also popular.

The southern region of Jutland is famous for its meat products, which include salamis of various flavours and seasonings, all of which are delicious.

Assorted coffee-related gadgets such as grinders and percolators are often on sale in coffee shops, which sell a bewildering range of roasted beans from around the world.

ALCOHOLIC DRINKS

WHILE IN Denmark it is worth sampling *akvavit* (a form of schnapps). Many regions, and even individual restaurants, have their own special recipes for these flavoursome drinks, which are then sold as *husets snaps.* Visitors can, for instance, savour an Aalborg Porse flavoured with Jutland herbs. As well as *akvavit,* Denmark produces some excellent beers (*see p260*). Some of the lesser known brands and dark beers are worth trying, and make a welcome alternative to the ubiquitous light Pilsners.

An antique shop in Copenhagen

ENTERTAINMENT IN DENMARK

D ENMARK IS A vibrant country with a wide range of culture and entertainment on offer. Clubs and bars promote all kinds of music from mainstream pop and jazz to the latest in alternative sounds, while venues such as Det Kongelige Teater (The Royal Theatre) put on world-class theatre and ballet. Summer time is the season for a number of high-profile festivals such as Roskilde's rock festival in

Viking Festival

June. Local festivals include recreations of Denmark's Viking past. Cinemas can be found in most towns and often screen English language films with Danish subtitles. Sport, too, is popular and Danish soccer clubs are among the best in the world. Children are sure to enjoy a visit to one of the country's amusement parks, including LEGOLAND®. For entertainment in Copenhagen see pages 100–101.

Pierrot, Harlequin and Columbine at Tivoli

THEATRE, MUSIC, DANCE AND CINEMA

V ISITS TO THE cinema or theatre are some of the most popular pastimes in Denmark. Cultural life blossoms not only in Copenhagen but throughout the country, and university towns, such as Århus and Odense, have much to offer.

Århus is probably the biggest cultural centre after Copenhagen and has the **Musikhuset Århus**, a modern venue that stages musical and dance performances, and is home to Den Jyske Opera (The Jutland Opera). Aalborg in northern Jutland has four cinemas, several theatres and a resident symphony orchestra, which often gives concerts in the Aalborg Kongres and Kultur Center.

Along with three cinemas, Funen's capital, Odense, has several theatres including **Mimeteatret**, which, as the

name suggests, is devoted to mime. The **Amfiscene** is a major venue that provides a platform for various kinds of live performance, including jazz and rock, and contemporary dance, while the **Odense Koncerthus** has a regular programme of classical music, which includes performances of music by Carl Nielsen (1865–1931), a native of Odense.

AMUSEMENT PARKS

D ENMARK'S amusement parks provide entertainment for children and adults alike. The parks are open mainly in summer, although some of them start their season earlier. The most famous park is

LEGOLAND in central Jutland (*see pp188–9*), which includes LEGO sculptures along with high-octane rides. As with many of Denmark's amusement parks, the admission price to LEGOLAND includes free use of all the attractions. Less high-profile amusement parks are dotted throughout the country and include fairgrounds, water parks and science centres. **BonBon-Land** in southern Zealand (*see p153*), for instance, is packed with rides and amusements as is **Fårup Sommerland** in northern Jutland (*see p200*).

In addition to its traditional zoos, Denmark has numerous safari parks and aquariums where visitors can see wild animals and aquatic creatures. Two of the best known are **Knuthenborg Safari Park** (*see pp156–7*) and Esbjerg's **Fiskeri-og Søfartsmuseet** aquarium (*see 190*).

Miniature buildings in LEGOLAND

Royal Theatre performance in Copenhagen *(see p69)*

NIGHTLIFE

THE BEST of Denmark's clubs are in university towns, such as Århus, Aalborg and Odense, where they cater for the exacting demands of the student population. Among the most popular places in Århus are **Train**, **VoxHall** and **Musikcafèen**, which play a mixture of rock and techno depending on the night. In Aalborg **Skråen** and **The Irish House** have a lively feel. Two of the best clubs in Odense are **Rytmeposten** and **Jazzhus Dexter**. The latter has live jazz at the weekend.

Performances in Danish music venues range from local bands to major acts from abroad. Many concerts are free although prices can be fairly steep for the biggest international names. Nightlubs are also popular and can be found even in some of the smaller towns. Clubwise, nothing really gets going until about 11pm in Denmark. Pubs and clubs usually stay open until 1am on weekdays. At weekends many of them don't close their doors until dawn.

SPECTATOR SPORTS

FOOTBALL (soccer) is a passion in Denmark and the Danish national side is one of the top teams in the world and achieved its greatest success when it defeated Germany in the final of Euro '92. Watching football is a popular pastime and many games are attended by entire families. Three of the best-known clubs are **Brøndby IF**, **FC København** and **Aalborg BK**. International matches are played at Parken, Denmark's national stadium and home ground of FC København.

Handball is another popular sport and has quite a high profile following the gold-medal success of the women's team at the 2000 Olympics. Other common sports include ice hockey, badminton, dirt-bike racing and cycling. Gymnastics clubs are also popular, and shows and competitions are frequently advertised in smaller towns.

Feeding the seals at the Fiskeri-og Søfartsmuseet, southern Jutland

---

DIRECTORY

THEATRE, MUSIC, DANCE AND CINEMA

Aalborg Teater
Jernbanegade 11,
9000 Aalborg.
℡ *96 31 60 20.*

Amfiscenen
Brandts Passage 37,
5000 Odense C.
℡ *66 13 78 97.*

GRAN teater for dans
Valdemarsgade 1,
8000 Århus C.
℡ *86 19 26 22.*

Mimeteatret
Vestergade 95B,
Odense C.

Musikhuset Århus
Thomas Jensens Allé,
8000 Århus C.
℡ *89 40 40 40.*

Odense Koncerthus
Claus Bergs Gade 9,
Odense C.
℡ *66 14 78 00.*

Odense Teater
Jernbanegade 21,
5100 Odense C.
℡ *89 40 40 40.*

Teatret Katakomben
Montergardens Have,
Overgade 48–50,
Odense C.
℡ *66 13 25 10.*

Århus Teater
Teatergaden, 8000 Århus C.
℡ *89 33 23 00 .*

NIGHTLIFE

Jazzhus Dexter
Vindegade 65,
5000 Odense C.

Musikcafèen
Mejlgade 53,
8000 Århus C.

Rytmeposten
Ostre Stationsvej 35,
5000 Odense C.

Skråen
Strandvejen 19,
9000 Aalborg.

The Irish House
Osteragade 25,
9000 Aalborg.

Train
Toldbodgade 6,
8000 Århus C.

VoxHall
Vester Allé 15,
8000 Århus C.

SPECTATOR SPORTS

Brøndby IF
Brøndby Stadion 30,
2605 Brøndby.
℡ *43 63 08 10.*
🖳 www.brondby.com

FC København
Parken, Øster Allé 50,
2110 Copenhagen.
℡ *35 26 85 61.*
🖳 www.fck.dk

Aalborg BK
Hornevej 2,
9220 Aalborg Øst.
℡ *96 35 59 00.*
🖳 www.aabsport.dk

OUTDOOR ACTIVITIES

THE DANES ARE keen on sport and fitness and many adults and most children participate in one sport or another. The country's gentle terrain and the many miles of well maintained cycle routes have helped to make cycling an integral part of Danish culture – it is not unusual for entire Danish families to embark on cycling holidays. Golfers are also well catered for and Denmark has over 100 courses, many of

A successful catch

which can be found close to hotels and camp sites. With its many fjords, protected waters and tiny islands to explore, Denmark is a good place for sailors. The country is also ideal for water sports such as windsurfing and canoeing. The same sheltered fjords are perfect for novice windsurfers and there are many companies near Danish holiday resorts that can arrange lessons. Horse riding is another popular activity.

HORSE RIDING

EQUESTRIAN PURSUITS are popular in Denmark and the country has a large number of riding stables. Some Danes have their own horses and keep them in community-style stables, where members are expected to make contributions both in cash and labour for the upkeep of the horses and ponies. Those who are unable to keep their own horses make use of the numerous riding clubs that offer riding lessons and provide horses for individual unsupervised rides. Prices vary widely though most clubs will expect a fee for the use of a horse and also for membership. A small number of clubs will accept riders paying an hourly rate. A good way for beginners to learn about riding and looking after horses is to sign up for a farm

Horse and driver on a carriage racetrack

holiday *(see p239)*, some of which include riding lessons and accompanied treks through the countryside.

For something a little different, it is possible to travel the country by wagon. Four to six people can usually be carried in the wagons, which are hired complete with horses from companies such as **Prærievognsferie Og Hesteudlejning** on Funen. Training is provided on the first day and the wagon is equipped with everything that travellers might need. A map is provided marking the route to the camp site, where there is pasture for horses and often a welcoming bonfire. Prairie wagon holidays can be great fun, particularly for children.

WATER SPORTS

THE MANY Danish lakes and some 7,300 km (4,536 miles) of coastline make Denmark a perfect location

for water sports enthusiasts. Equipment for windsurfing and water skiing can be readily hired in waterside resorts, as can jet skis and other related gear.

Visitors intending to take up some form of water sport should check in advance whether the region they plan to visit allows for such pursuits as certain water sports, such as water skiing, are prohibited in some ecologically sensitive areas.

FISHING

DENMARK IS an ideal destination for anglers. Its many streams and lakes are well maintained and have healthy stocks of fish including plentiful supplies of pike and trout both for coarse and fly-fishing. The long coastline is also good for saltwater fishing and anglers can realistically hope to catch sea trout, plaice, mackerel and cod.

Horse riding – a popular pastime in Denmark

Windsurfers making the most of Denmark's coastal waters

Anglers between the age of 18 and 67 must carry an appropriate licence. These are sold at post offices, tourist information offices and shops that sell angling equipment. Licences are issued for one day, one week or annually and cost 25, 75 and 100 Dkr respectively. Fishing in lakes and streams requires the permission of the owner, which very often is the local angling club. Tourist offices will have details of angling holidays and some camp sites are especially geared for anglers with rooms set aside for gutting and cleaning fish.

Anyone fishing in Denmark will be expected to know the regulations concerning the size and types of species that may be caught. Some clubs may impose restrictions concerning the number or the total weight of the catch.

Those keen on deep-sea fishing can join the crew of a

fishing vessel and head out to offshore fishing grounds where high-tech gadgetry, such as echo sounders, increases the likelihood of hauling in a big fish.

Anyone interested in a fishing holiday in Denmark should contact **Danmarks Sportsfiskerforbund** (The Danish Fishing Council).

MOTORCYCLE TOURS

T OURING AROUND Denmark by motorcycle is a pleasant way to get to know the country. Traffic is reasonably light and many Danes are themselves keen motorcyclists, and so visitors on motorbikes are unlikely to be treated with suspicion.

As a result of the popularity of riding motorbikes in Denmark there are many motorcycle rallies, known as *motorcykeltraft*, which are organized countrywide. The size of events varies from small weekly meetings to large rallies that feature live music and competitions for the most impressive bikes. Major events can last days and attract locals as well as foreign enthusiasts.

Denmark has a network of scenic roads known as the Marguerite Route, which takes in some of the most beautiful parts of the country. The route consists mostly of secondary and minor roads and is marked on road signs by a white daisy on a brown background *(see p300)*. Maps mark the route with green dots or a green line.

Anyone travelling in Denmark on a motorcycle should take into account the wind, which at times can be very strong and make riding difficult and sometimes even hazardous. When crossing bridges, particularly over some of the long straits, the wind can be especially strong and take the form of sudden and unexpected gusts. When strong winds prevail, motorcyclists may be banned from using these bridges.

Motorcyclists in Denmark must adhere to the highway code. Riders and passengers are required by law to wear helmets and carry the necessary documentation.

Cyclists on one of the country's many cycling routes

CYCLING

R IDING A BIKE is a hugely popular activity in Denmark and the lowland areas especially are excellent regions for a cycling holiday, as is the island of Bornholm *(see p223)*. The whole country is criss-crossed with an extensive network of cycling routes. It is easy to plan a journey and routes take in most of the big towns and cities as well as more rural parts of the country.

Organized cycle races are common in Denmark. Many cover short distances and are open to amateurs. Races for elite riders include the Grand Prix Aalborg and the prestigious CSC Classic, where teams compete to earn points for use on the world ranking list. Races such as the CSC Classic are for serious competitors only.

Bikers and bikes at an annual motorcycle rally

Playing the green at a golf club near Gilleleje, northwestern Zealand

CYCLING TOURS

CYCLING IS an excellent way to tour Denmark, and enthusiasts are very well catered for. Specialist bicycle shops are found throughout the country. Alongside traditional touring bikes, they sell the very latest in cycling equipment. Dedicated cycling maps make planning a cycling tour fairly straightforward. Maps are widely available and cover virtually every part of the country. The maps include not only cycle routes but all the major sights along the way such as museums and castles. In addition, they indicate which roads have cycle paths and on which roads it is forbidden or too dangerous to ride. Cycling maps are useful in a number of other ways. They often include details of camp sites and hostels, for instance, as well as grocery stores. Maps can be ordered from **Dansk Cyklist Forbund** (The Danish Cycling

Tandem bicycle, popular in Denmark

Federation) as well as from bookshops or tourist offices.

The Dansk Cyklist Forbund can also provide details of packaged cycling tours. Tours can be expensive but they have the advantage of providing suitable cycles and organizing the accommodation along the route. Tour operators often arrange for luggage to be carried, so that riders need not be weighed down by tents and other items.

There are numerous places in Denmark where visitors can hire a bicycle although many bikes will only be suitable for short distances. One company that hires good quality touring bikes is **Københavns Cykler** in Copenhagen.

Finding someone to fix a bike is easy. Most cycling maps include details of cycle workshops where minor repairs such as mending a punctured tyre or fixing a spoke can be carried out quickly and cheaply.

GOLF

DENMARK has over 100 golf courses. The majority of them will honour the membership card of your own club and most clubs admit novices as well as experienced players. Green fees vary but are fairly reasonable, averaging between 150 and 250 Dkr per day. Buying a package golfing holiday that also includes accommodation can work out cheaper. Golf clubs generally hire and sell golfing equipment and also run improvement courses for all levels. The **Dansk Golf Union** can provide information about the country's golf courses.

SAILING

THE WATERS around Denmark are dotted with islands, many of which have harbours in which to moor a boat. The coastline is highly diversified and there is plenty of scope for sailing at all levels of ability. Storms and gales are uncommon in bodies of water such as the sea between Zealand and Lolland as well as many of the fjords and these calm, forgiving conditions are perfect for less experienced sailors and novices.

A sailing boat can be hired in Denmark for about 4,500 Dkr per week, while larger motor-cruisers cost about 17,000 Dkr per week.

All craft intended for charter must carry a seaworthiness certificate issued by the State Inspectorate of Shipping. When chartering a boat it is important to ask to see this certificate before sailing.

Sailing boats, a common sight on Danish waters

Coastal dunes, an ideal area for walks

BOAT CRUISES

FOR VISITORS with little or no experience of sailing, boat cruises are the best option. Boat cruises are popular in Denmark and depart regularly from Nyhavn in Copenhagen, bound for the islands situated in the Øresund (Sound). It is even possible to book a cruise on a reconstructed Viking ship. Stationed in Roskilde harbour are several small ships that are faithful copies of 10th-century wooden Viking boats and these embark on regular cruises. Cruises of the lakes and rivers are another option. One popular jaunt is to jump aboard one of the small ships that depart from Ry harbour on a cruise along the Gudena river. Another alternative is to take a trip back in time on the *Hjejlen*, a paddle steamer that travels daily from Silkeborg to Himmelbjerget.

WALKING

WALKING TRAILS in Denmark are clearly signposted, with information boards giving the names of the destination points, the length of the route and – when applicable – the route number. These numbers correspond to those on local tourist maps. In Denmark the public have access to the coast even if the land is privately owned. Many signed walks follow the shoreline and are especially beautiful. The country's forests are also good for walking. Some marked trails lead across private land. When this is the case it is important to stick to the trail, otherwise walkers risk being arrested (although this is highly unlikely). Many routes are through nature reserves and are marked with the sign of a daisy. Tourist offices and libraries often have brochures listing some of Denmark's best walks.

Denmark's hostels and inns are used to catering for the needs of walkers, as are the country's camp sites. **Dansk Vandrelaug** (The Danish Ramblers Association) can provide a list of camp sites in Denmark that are open only to walkers and cyclists.

SWIMMING

DENMARK HAS many beautiful beaches. Most are ideal for swimming although the temperature can be on the chilly side. Even in summer, the water temperature rarely rises above 17° C (63° F). As an alternative, virtually all cities and major towns have swimming baths, which are well maintained.

Children, of course, are more likely to enjoy a visit to one of the water parks, such as **Fårup Sommerland** (*see p200*) and **Joboland** (*see p222*), which have splash pools and waterslides.

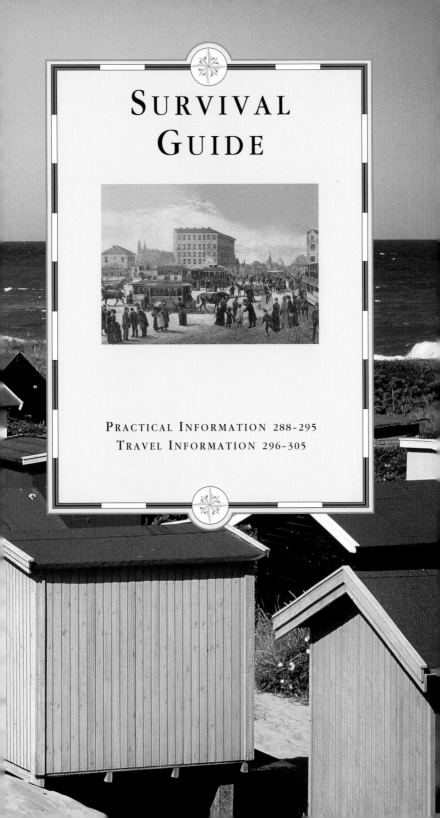

SURVIVAL
GUIDE

PRACTICAL INFORMATION

Tourist
information sign

Large numbers of holiday-makers arrive in Denmark each year, drawn by the wide range of attractions and accommodation on offer. The peak season is relatively short, however, as the winter months are cold and the daylight hours short. The country has a good tourism infrastructure with a network of efficient tourist offices. Information is easy to obtain, especially on the Internet, and planning a trip should be

a straightforward undertaking as most hotels and attractions have dedicated web sites, many of which have English versions. Denmark's hotels and inns are welcoming and clean, as are the many good-value camp sites and hostels. The major museums and galleries have world-class collections, and usually have English language displays and guidebooks to help visitors get the most from the exhibits.

WHEN TO VISIT

The best time to visit Denmark is the mild months between mid-April and mid-October, or in December, when most of the country's towns and villages sparkle with festive Christmas decorations.

For cycling holidays it is best to plan for the period between mid-June and late August. The Danes take their holidays mainly during the school vacations – from the third week in June to the end of the first week in August – and the peak holiday season is during the first three weeks of July, which are generally warm and dry. During this time the camp sites, beaches and resorts tend to be full. Children go back to school in mid-August in Denmark and this can be a good time to visit as the days are still warm, while the attractions and beaches are less busy.

TOURIST INFORMATION

Most towns and resorts throughout Denmark have well-run tourist information centres. The qualified staff can provide visitors with comprehensive details concerning the area including local attractions, festivals and events. Staff will also be pleased to give you free pamphlets containing a wealth of information about topics such as cycling routes, walking trails, fishing and disabled access to hotels and attractions. The personnel usually speak English and German. In smaller towns and villages, where there are no special tourist centres, visitors can usually get local information

Tourist
information logo

from their hotel. Visitors can also learn a great deal from the official website of VisitDenmark, the new name for the Danish Tourist Board.

CUSTOMS REGULATIONS

Duty-free goods were abolished in the EU in 1999. Nevertheless, Denmark continues to impose a limit on what can be brought into the country. Visitors arriving from EU countries are allowed to bring 300 cigarettes (or 75 cigars) and 1.5 litres of spirits or 90 litres of table wine; persons from outside the EU can bring 200 cigarettes (or 50 cigars) and 1 litre of spirits or 2 litres of table wine. Food articles that are not vacuum-packed by the manufacturer cannot be brought into Denmark. Articles imported in commercial quantities and presents of a value exceeding 1,350 Dkr are subject to customs duty. When bringing a large amount of cash (equivalent to over 40,000 Dkr) visitors must carry a certificate confirming the legality of its source.

There is no limit within reason on how much alcohol or tobacco EU citizens can take out of the country. US citizens are allowed to take home $400 worth of goods before duty must be paid.

Visitors enjoying a guided tour in Copenhagen

Tourist information office in Copenhagen

VISA REGULATIONS

CITIZENS OF the EU do not need a visa to enter Denmark; other visitors should check if their country has reciprocal agreements on waiving visa requirements. Visitors not obliged to have a visa are allowed to stay in Denmark for up to 90 days.

EMBASSIES

VISITORS TO Denmark should contact their embassy in an emergency if all other avenues of assistance have been exhausted. Emergencies might include the loss of a passport or a motoring accident. Embassies will expect you to have your own travel insurance, however, and are not likely to help if you been jailed or fined for committing a crime. Most embassies are in Copenhagen.

ADMISSION PRICES

THE COST OF admission to museums and historic attractions is not expensive in Denmark. In larger cities,

Copenhagen Card, entitling visitors to cut-price tickets

such as Copenhagen, Odense and Århus, visitors can purchase special weekly passes that combine reduced or free admission costs to museums, galleries and other attractions with unlimited use of public transport.

OPENING HOURS

OFFICE HOURS in Denmark are normally from 9am to 5pm. Once a week (usually on Thursday), the hours are from 9am until 6pm.

Shops open at about 9am, and remain open until 5:30pm. On Friday they close at 7 or 8pm; on Saturday at about 2 or 3pm. Most shops are closed on Sunday.

People interested in visiting churches should check their opening hours because Danish churches are only open on certain days and only between certain hours. Churches are closed to sightseers during services.

MUSEUMS AND HISTORIC SIGHTS

MANY TOURIST attractions make seasonal changes to their opening days and hours, reducing or extending them, as required. Some attractions and hotels close altogether during the darkest winter months.

Sightseeing is easiest in the period from April until the end of September, and also in the run-up to Christmas and the New Year. Tourist information centres provide current lists of museums, historic sights and attractions, including their opening hours.

PUBLIC TOILETS

PUBLIC TOILETS are generally free. In Copenhagen there are also automatic toilets which charge a small fee. Many public toilets are adapted for disabled users and also have baby-changing facilities. In larger railway stations, along with toilet facilities, there are often showers and sockets for electric shavers.

Personal Security and Health

Police sign

DENMARK IS A safe country with a low level of crime. Even in the larger cities there is little likelihood of visitors encountering problems. In the event of a crime or accident, the Danish police and emergency services work very efficiently. In case of any unpleasant incident it is worth asking passers-by or witnesses to the event for their help. As a rule, Danes will not refuse such a request. The chances of falling victim to crime can be further minimized by keeping credit cards, mobile phones and money hidden away and by not carrying excessive amounts of cash.

Sign outside a Copenhagen police station

the English language. In most cases they will be able to provide some assistance, such as getting in touch with a breakdown service.

AVOIDING THEFT

SUMMER AND the run-up to Christmas are the times when thieves are most likely to be operating, especially in busy places. Valuables should be deposited with the hotel reception or kept in the safe in your room; money and documents should be carried under clothing rather than in handbags or trouser pockets. Make sure all valuable items are out of sight if parking a car.

PERSONAL BELONGINGS AND LOST PROPERTY

ANY THEFT of money, travel documents, credit cards, as well as any theft from a car or hotel room should be reported immediately at the police station, where an officer will issue a note confirming that the crime has been reported. This note may well be required when filling out an insurance claim or visiting an embassy or consulate.

If documents or personal belongings have been lost you should enquire at the lost property office closest to the area in which the belongings went missing. Any items left behind on a railway train, S-tog or metro should be reported to the duty personnel at the station and, if lost on a bus, to the passenger service office of the appropriate bus company. Lost or stolen credit cards should be reported as soon as possible to the card issuer.

EMERGENCIES

IN CASE OF a road accident, a life-threatening situation, fire, attack or any other predicament that requires immediate intervention by the emergency services, visitors should telephone 112. This toll-free line is staffed by qualified operators who are able to speak foreign languages including English; they will decide which service should be sent to the scene of the incident.

Emergency telephones installed along the hard shoulders of motorways can be used to report a breakdown or accident. When in need, special telephones found on S-tog railway stations and on the metro lines enable people to contact railway duty officers.

An accident or mugging should be reported to the police. The victim and any witnesses to the incident are entitled to give evidence in their native language.

Consulates and embassies can help to contact a visitor's family in the event of an incident, and may also be able to provide financial help or advance the money for a ticket home.

POLICE

DURING THE summer season the police are dressed in blue shirts and black trousers; in winter they also wear black jackets. Road police generally wear all-in-one leather suits and ride large white motorcycles. Ordinary police patrol cars are white with the word-"POLITI" in blue lettering. Cars driven by the criminal division are dark blue. Criminal division police usually wear civilian clothes and will show their ID cards when required.

In Copenhagen visitors may encounter traffic wardens, sporting dark green jackets. Traffic wardens are not a part of the police force but are entitled to check if someone has a valid parking ticket and can impose a fine for illegal parking.

Most Danish policemen and policewomen will have at least a working knowledge of

Danish policeman

Navy blue police van

Red-and-white ambulance

MEDICAL ASSISTANCE

Aᴺʸᴼᴺᴱ ᴡɪᴛʜ a medical emergency is entitled to free treatment in hospitals and doctor's surgeries in Denmark, providing that the person has not arrived in the country for the sole purpose of obtaining medical treatment and is unfit to return home. Visitors from the EU are covered by Danish national health insurance but will need to present form E111. Non-EU citizens must have travel insurance.

For all visitors, travel insurance is advisable, however, as it can make it easier to get treated at a particular hospital and should cover the cost of an ambulance (which the patient is responsible for in Denmark) or an emergency flight home.

Addresses of doctors and hospitals can be obtained from hotel receptions or a camp site manager, and can also be found in a telephone directory. Most Danish doctors speak English.

PHARMACIES

Pʜᴀʀᴹᴀᴄɪᴇs display the word "Apotek" and a green logo in which the letter "A" is combined with the head of a snake. Pharmacies are usually open from 9:30am until 5:30pm on weekdays, and until 2pm on Saturdays. In larger towns there will be a

Danish pharmacy logo

small number of pharmacies open 24 hours a day. The addresses of 24-hour pharmacies can be found displayed on the doors or windows of any pharmacy. Controlled drugs require a doctor's prescription.

HEALTH

Tʀᴀᴠᴇʟʟᴇʀs ᴛᴼ Denmark do not require any special vaccinations. Visitors to the country should pack pain-killers, as well as antidiarrhoeal and travel sickness remedies. Anyone requiring constant medication should take an adequate supply with them as medicines can be very expensive in Denmark.

It is perfectly safe to drink the tap water in Denmark and stomach upsets are uncommon; any stomach problems that do occur are likely to be mild. In many shops and offices visitors should be able to get a free drink of water from one of the water dispensers.

Modern window of a pharmacy in Copenhagen

Banks and Local Currency

VISITORS ARRIVING in Denmark are obliged to have adequate means to pay for their food and accommodation for the duration of their stay. Immigration authorities are usually satisfied with a verbal assurance regarding a visitor's credit card limit. It is also worth having some Danish currency, although most places in Denmark accept credit cards as the Danes do not usually carry much cash. Most Danish banks have ATMs (cash machines) from which Danish kroner can easily be withdrawn by using a credit or debit card.

BANK OPENING HOURS

BANKS IN Denmark are usually open from 10am until 4pm, Monday to Wednesday and Fridays. On Thursdays banks remain open later, until 6pm. They are closed on Saturdays, Sundays and public holidays including, among others, Maunday Thursday, Good Friday, Christmas Day, Ascension Day and New Year's Day.

One of Denmark's many bureaux de change

EXCHANGING MONEY

FOREIGN CURRENCY can be exchanged in a wide variety of places in Denmark. Exhange booths are open most of the day at Copenhagen Airport. Hotels can also exchange money but offer the least favourable rates of exchange. Banks and special automatic money-exchange machines, available in some places, offer a slightly better rate, but also charge commission. The best deals can be

ATM (cash machine) of Nordea Bank

obtained at branches of Forex, Exchange or any other similar bureau de change, which do not charge a commission. In addition, their opening hours are usually more flexible than those of the banks. Exchange rates are usually displayed by the door.

Anyone who wishes to bring more than 40,000 Dkr into the country or make a deposit of a similar sum must have a certificate confirming the legality of the money's source.

CREDIT CARDS

THERE SHOULD be no problem with using credit cards such as Visa, Eurocard or MasterCard. American Express and Diners Club may be less readily accepted in Denmark. In many shops and restaurants staff will use a reader to enter a card's data and ask the customer to sign a receipt or key in the card's pin number.

Some shops may refuse to accept a card as payment for low-cost items.

DIRECTORY

BANKS

BG Bank
Højbro Plads 5,
1200 Copenhagen K.
Map 3 C1.
33 67 03 00.
www.bgbank.dk

Danske Bank
Holmens Kanal 2–12,
1200 Copenhagen.
Map 4 D1.
33 44 00 00.
www.danskebank.dk

Jyske Bank
Vesterbrogade 9,
1780 Copenhagen.
Map 3 A2.
33 78 75 76.
www.jyskebank.dk

Sydbank A/S
Kongens Nytorv 30,
1050 Copenhagen.
Map 4 D1.
33 69 78 00.
www.sydbank.dk

BUREAUX DE CHANGE

Copenhagen
Nørre Voldgade 90. **Map** 1 B5.
33 32 81 00.
Vesterbrogade 2B. **Map** 3 A2.
33 93 77 70.

Odense
Banegardscentret.
Østre Stationsvej 27.
66 11 66 18.

Århus
Ryesgade 28.
86 80 03 40.

A branch of Danske Bank

CURRENCY

Denmark is one of the few EU countries to reject joining the European monetary union. Therefore, on 1 January 2002 when most of Europe adopted the euro, Denmark kept the krone.

The Danish krone (or crown) is divided into 100 øre. The plural of krone is kroner. Coins come in denominations of 25 and 50 øre. There are also 1, 2, 5, 10 and 20 kroner coins. Notes come in denominations of 50, 100, 200, 500 and 1,000 kroner. In many places, especially large towns and tourist resorts, prices are often quoted in both kroner and euros.

The Danish krone is written as DKK in most international money markets but is written as Dkr in northern Europe and as kr in Denmark.

Banknotes

Danish banknotes differ from each other in terms of size and colour. The lowest denomination banknote in circulation is the violet-blue 50-kroner note. The largest denomination is the reddish-brown 1,000-kroner note.

50 kroner

100 kroner

200 kroner

500 kroner

1,000 kroner

20 kroner   **10 kroner**   **5 kroner**   **2 kroner**   **1 krone**

50 øre

25 øre

Coins

The 20 and 10 Dkr coins are golden in colour with the queen's image on the reverse. The 5, 2 and 1 Dkr coins are nickel with a hole in the centre. The 50 øre and 25 øre coins are copper-coloured.

Communications

Danish postal services' logo

Danish postal services are highly efficient. Letters and postcards take between two and four days to reach their destinations within Europe, and between one and two days within Denmark. Telephoning abroad from Denmark is straightforward, although there are fewer public telephones than there once were due to the popularity of mobile phones. Nevertheless, visitors should always be able to find a public telephone at any post office, railway station, camp site reception or hotel lobby. Before using the telephone in your hotel room it is best to check the price as hotels sometimes charge a premium rate for calls.

Entrance to a post office building in Copenhagen

USING THE TELEPHONE

Public telephone boxes have become an endangered species in Denmark, due to the prevalence of mobile phones. However, those public phones that do remain are well maintained. There are three types of phone booth: coin only, card only and phones that except both. Card phones can also accept credit cards. Phone cards can be purchased in about 1,500 outlets including post offices and many shops. Calling from a payphone is more expensive than using a private phone, but is cheaper than phoning from a hotel room. The minimum charge for a call from a public phone is 5 Dkr.

Public payphones in Denmark have clear instructions on how to make a call and usually have the dialling codes for many countries listed.

MOBILE TELEPHONES

Most subscription networks can provide the facilities for making international calls. You should check before departure whether your phone will work in Denmark on your current package. It is sometimes possible to get an upgrade for the duration of your holiday. When using a prepaid mobile phone in Denmark you should likewise check whether your package covers international roaming. The price of outgoing calls from Denmark will be higher than calls made at home and incoming calls will also be charged at an international rate. Receiving texts from abroad is free, but sending them is usually subject to a substantial charge.

Logo for Denmark's main phone company

DIALLING CODES

- Calling Denmark from abroad: 0045.
- From Denmark to the UK: 0044.
- From Denmark to the US/Canada: 001.
- Telephone services such as wake-up call: 80 20 00 49.

USING A CARD PHONE

1 Lift the receiver and wait for the dialling tone.

2 Insert the telephone card or credit card into the slot.

3 Key in the required number.

4 At the end of the call replace the receiver and withdraw the card.

Card-operated payphone of the type most frequently encountered in hotels and restaurants

USING A COIN-OPERATED PHONE

1 Lift the receiver and wait for the tone.

2 Insert coins (phones accept both euros and Danish kroner).

3 Key in the required number.

4 Replace the receiver at the end of the call.

All booths have a count down on the display so you can see how much the call costs

POSTAL SERVICES

DANISH POST offices are indicated by the word POST written in white letters on a red background. Most post offices are open Monday to Friday, from 9 or 10am to 5pm, until 6pm on Thursdays, and on Saturday from 10am until noon. From post offices you can make telephone calls, post parcels or registered letters and purchase stamps and envelopes. Poste restante mail can be collected from all of Denmark's post offices.

SENDING A LETTER

STAMPS can be purchased at post offices and in many souvenir shops. A small number of stamp-vending machines can also be found. A letter sent to a European country requires a "Europa" tariff postage stamp. Danish postboxes are painted red and feature the crown and trumpet insignia of the national postal service. They display information on the next collection time. Post offices have separate boxes for cheaper local mail (so-called B-post) and for fast delivery A-post or Prioritare mail, including international mail. International mail sent from Copenhagen should leave the country within 24 hours.

An address in Denmark should include the name of the addressee, street, house number, town and postcode. It is very important to include

Colourful examples of Danish postage stamps

the post code as many Danish towns, as well as streets within Copenhagen, have the same name.

Addresses for an apartment may sometimes include the floor and staircase as well as the number of a flat within the building itself. For example the address may be written as Bjergvej 20, 3.tv (3 stands for 3rd floor and tv stands for "til venstre", meaning "to the left".

INTERNET AND E-MAIL

MORE THAN half of Denmark's population has access to the Internet. The Internet is not regarded a luxury in Denmark, and it is easy to check for personal e-mail in many places, including Internet cafés. In some of the more upmarket hotels each room has an Internet link, while other hotels have special business rooms where visitors can plug in their laptops or use the hotel's computers. Most hotels in Denmark's holiday resorts can provide Internet access at reception. Many youth hostels and camp sites also have computers with broadband links to the Internet.

Copenhagen has quite a number of Internet cafés, as do many of the other large towns. These are ideal places to surf the net, send an e-mail or even download and print some documents. The cost is not prohibitive, although printing can add up, and the connection

speeds tend to be fast. Staff at Internet cafés are usually knowledgeable and generally willing to help.

MEDIA

MOST OF THE major foreign papers including US and UK dailies such as *The Times*, *Guardian* and the *Wall Street Journal* are on sale in Copenhagen and other large towns and can be picked up at train-station kiosks and from some of the larger newsagents. Magazines such as *Time* and the *Economist* are also readily available. Denmark's own press consists of about 50 daily newspapers. Of these, *Politiken* and *Jyllandsposten* have the largest circulation. The weekly *Copenhagen Post* has Danish news and a short listings section in English.

Denmark has three public-service television channels, DR1, DR2 and TV2. These screen news and current affairs along with light entertainment such as music and game shows. Other channels, such as TVDanmark 1, are more commercial in character with soaps and comedy. TV3 is aimed at families while TV3+ is the main sport channel. Many US and British shows appear on TV with Danish subtitles. English-language news is often available on cable and satellite. News in English is broadcast Mon–Fri at 10:30am, 5:10pm and 10pm by Radio Denmark International (1062 Mhz).

Easy to recognise Danish letterbox

Politiken and Copenhagen Post, two of Denmark's newspapers

TRAVEL INFORMATION

Flights to Denmark from most parts of northern Europe are fast and frequent. Planes land at Copenhagen from over 100 destinations worldwide and the airport receives over 18 million passengers every year. Fewer people arrive by train and ferry, although ferries are popular with visitors from elsewhere in Scandinavia. Ease of travel has been vastly improved with the construction

SAS aircraft

of the Store Bælt (Great Belt) bridge, linking Zealand and Funen, and the fixed-link Øresund bridge between Zealand and Sweden. Getting to the smaller Danish islands requires taking a ferry. Travelling on the mainland and around the major islands is fairly easy, thanks to a network of well-maintained motorways and railway lines, and the country's efficient coach service.

AIR TRAVEL

Most visitors to Denmark arrive at Copenhagen Airport (Kastrup), which is 12 km (7 miles) southeast of the city centre. **Scandinavian Airlines** (SAS) connects Copenhagen with most European capitals including Dublin and also has non-stop flights from New York, Chicago and Toronto. From Australasia the best connections are via Singapore and Bangkok. Billund (for LEGOLAND®) has flights from many European cities including Amsterdam, Frankfurt and London. **Ryanair** has daily low-cost flights from London Stansted to Århus and Esbjerg, and also to Malmø in Sweden with a special connecting coach to Copenhagen. Other airlines serving Copenhagen include **Aer Lingus**, **bmi** (British Midland), **British Airways**, **easyJet** (from London Stansted and Newcastle) and **Maersk Air**.

TARIFFS

Ticket prices charged by SAS are comparable with most airlines. However, intense competition means that airlines vary their prices continuously and it is difficult to be precise about tariffs. There are nevertheless certain set rules. Business class travel will always cost more than economy. The cheapest ticket will always be linked to some conditions, such as having to

	Terminal 3	
✈	Terminal	
🛬	Ankomsthal Arrival hall	
🛃	Told Customs	VAT · Tax free
💱	Valuta veksling Exchange	
✉	Postkontor Post office	
🧳	Garderobe Left luggage	

Information board at Copenhagen Airport

purchase it by a certain date and a limited period of validity. People who can afford to spend more on their tickets have more freedom to decide when to travel and to amend flight details if necessary. Visitors who book at short notice will inevitably pay higher prices.

A number of concessions are available from some airlines. SAS offer discounts to pensioners over 65 and also

to children and students. To get the best deal visitors should contact their local travel agent or browse the Internet for last-minute deals. Following the liberalization of the aviation market, many cheap, no-frills flights are now available within Europe.

DOMESTIC FLIGHTS

Air travel within Denmark is expensive. The major inland carriers are SAS, Cimber Air and Maersk Air. SAS flies from Copenhagen to Århus and Aalborg. Cimber Air flies from Copenhagen to Bornholm. Maersk Air links Copenhagen with Billund in Jutland and Rønne on Bornholm. If money is no object, the routes particularly worth recommending include Copenhagen to Aalborg (a six-hour journey by car) and Copenhagen to Bornholm.

General view of Copenhagen Airport

Modern entrance to Copenhagen Airport

AIRPORTS

THE COUNTRY'S main airport is Copenhagen Airport (formerly known as Kastrup). It has three terminals: two for international flights, and one for internal flights. The airport is situated on Amager Island, a short way from the city centre. Like many of the country's airports, it has helpful staff and excellent information services. The airport's facilities include shops and restaurants, cash machines (ATMs) and lockers. Rooms can be rented at the Transfer Hotel, located within the transit hall, for a minimum of four hours and a maximum stay of 16 hours. Cars can be hired at terminals 1 and 3.

A fast and economical train service runs every 10 minutes from the airport to Central Station in Copenhagen. Trains run throughout the day and most of the night (between 03:57am and 00:29am) and take 12 minutes. Local buses also make the journey and drop passengers off at Rådhuspladsen. The price of a bus ticket is much the same as the train, however, and the journey time is nearly three times as long. The taxi-rank immediately by the exit of Terminal 3 is a good option for visitors with a lot of heavy luggage. Billund international airport is served by

Logo of Scandinavian Airlines

buses running from Århus, Vejle, Horsens, Odense, Fredericia and LEGOLAND® as well as by long-distance buses from Kolding and Esbjerg. Car rental companies at Billund include Avis, Europcar and Hertz.

Århus airport is 40 km (25 miles) northeast of the city centre. Buses link the airport to the city and drop passengers off at Århus's railway station. The journey time is about 45 minutes.

Esbjerg's airport is 10 km (6 miles) east of the city centre. An hourly bus runs between the airport and the railway station.

An express bus links Aalborg's airport with the city centre. Parking around the airport is free, although drivers must pay if they wish to leave their car at the attended car park.

Check in at Copenhagen Airport

DIRECTORY

SAS

Denmark (3232 6800
Ireland (01 844 5440.
UK (0870 607 27727.
USA/Canada
(1800 221 2350 (toll free).
w www.scandinavian.net

OTHER AIRLINES

Aer Lingus
(01 818 365 5000 (Ireland).
w www.aerlingus.com

British Airways
(0870 607 0550 (UK).
w www.britishairways.com

bmi (British Midland)
(0870 6070 555 (UK).
w www.flybmi.com

easyJet
(0871 750 0100 (UK).
w www.easyjet.com

Maersk Air
(020 7333 0066 (UK)
or 7650 2650 (Denmark).
w www.maersk-air.com

Ryanair
(0871 246 0000 (UK).
w www.ryanair.com

DANISH AIRPORTS

Københavns Lufthavn (Copenhagen Airport)
Lufthavnsboulevarden 6,
2770 Kastrup.
(32 31 32 31.
w www.cph.dk

Billund Lufthavn
Postboks 10, 7190 Billund.
(76 50 50 50.
w www.bll.dk

Karup Lufthavn
N.O. Hansens Vej 4,
7470 Karup J.
(97 10 06 10.
w www.karup-airport.dk

Aalborg Lufthavn
Lufthavnsvej 100,
9400 Norresundby.
(98 17 11 44.
w www.aal.dk

Århus Lufthavn
Stabrandvej 24, 8560 Kolind.
(87 75 70 00.
w www.aar.dk

Travelling by Train and Ferry

Danish trains are not particularly cheap but are reliable, fast and extremely comfortable. The Danish railway system is currently undergoing a progamme of modernization on many lines, which should make journey times even faster in the future. Holders of an InterRail or similar pass are entitled to unlimited use of the extensive railway network throughout the country. A network of ferry links provides a convenient way to travel to some of Denmark's many islands as well as between Denmark and countries such as Germany, Sweden and Norway.

19th-century railway station building in Roskilde

DOMESTIC TRAINS

The DANISH state railway or DSB has an extensive network that covers both local and long-distance lines and, with an InterRail or similar pass, provides an extremely cheap and efficient way of seeing the country. Danish trains are modern and safe. The long-distance trains, such as those that run between Copenhagen and Aalborg, are stylish and sophisticated. Intercity trains have comfortable air-conditioned carriages. They

TICKET AND TRAVEL CARD DISPENSER FOR LOCAL TRAINS

are open-plan, with seating arranged in pairs facing each other. Above each seat is a reading light and, often, individual music jacks for head-phones and power supply sockets for laptops.

Information displayed on the back of each seat indicates whether a seat has been reserved and to which station. Intercity trains also contain payphones, baby-changing facilities, space for oversize luggage and even children's play areas. In some parts of the train dogs are not allowed; in others, known as rest sections, silence must be maintained and the use of mobile phones is prohibited. On some of the busiest routes DSB operate "business class" trains which, along with all the creature comforts of intercity trains, feature luxuries such as free drinks and snacks.

Local trains, many of which have double-decker carriages, are generally slower and have fewer facilities but are perfectly adequate.

Details of the network and main train schedules are available in a booklet from all DSB stations.

INTERNATIONAL RAIL SERVICES

DSB IS RESPONSIBLE for most of Denmark's internal railway system and some of the international routes. Train services operate to Denmark from most parts of northern Europe including Germany, Sweden and Norway. The most common route to Jutland is through Germany, while many people travel to Zealand by train from Sweden across the Øresund Bridge. Travel from the UK is generally via the Netherlands. Once in the country, Copenhagen's Central Station is the main point of arrival for international rail services and allows passengers to disembark in the centre of the capital.

The *Thomas Cook European Timetable*, available from Thomas Cook travel agents, gives a complete listing of train schedules in Europe.

Express train waiting at a platform in Copenhagen

TRAIN TICKETS

Tickets can be bought at stations or reserved by calling the DSB reservation line or logging onto the DSB website, which has an English language version.

Anyone wishing to travel extensively by train should consider one of the special passes. InterRail tickets are available to residents of European countries. Visitors from outside Europe can purchase a Eurail Pass. Both passes are available in a flexible range of options and give substantial discounts on travel in Europe.

Many other rail concessions are available within Denmark and you should always ask about discounts for off-peak travel, family tickets and discounted return fares. Children aged between 10 and 15 travel for half the adult fare in Denmark; children under 10 travel free. Further information can be obtained from DSB ticket offices.

A hydrofoil in Nexø, Bornholm

RAILWAY STATIONS

DANISH RAILWAY stations are clean and well maintained. Facilities include heated waiting rooms and snack bars. Copenhagen's Central Station is a major hub and has a small shopping centre with a variety of shops, and a supermarket, post office and police station.

DOMESTIC FERRIES

DENMARK'S TERRITORY covers a large number of populated islands. These islands are linked by an extensive domestic ferry service making ferry services an important element in the country's transport infrastructure. Some routes are very short, taking a matter of minutes. The longest route, from Copenhagen to Bornholm, takes seven hours.

Ferries in Denmark, especially the long-distance ones, are clean and comfortable with cafés, bars and passenger lounges. Some have casinos and nightclubs.

INTERNATIONAL FERRIES

MOST ferries are run by DFDS Seaways. The other major ferry company is Stena Line, which operates mainly between Denmark, Norway and Sweden.

The opening of the bridges spanning the Øresund (Sound) and the Store Bælt has to a degree reduced the demand for ferry travel between Denmark and Sweden, as well as between Zealand and Funen. Nevertheless, the Danes and visitors to the country continue to use many of the ferry services.

FERRY TICKETS

TICKETS FOR ferry services within Denmark as well as services between Denmark and other countries can usually be reserved using Internet websites. Fares can vary widely depending on the season or the time of day. Substantial discounts are often available for students and young people who have an international rail pass.

For many local routes it is not necessary to book a ticket and passengers need only arrive shortly before departure. Longer routes generally require a ticket to be purchased well in advance. Reservations should also be made in advance when travelling at busy times or if you are planning to bring a vehicle.

TRAVEL INFORMATION

DSB Train Tickets Reservation and Information
☎ 70 13 14 15.
🅦 www.dsb.dk

Train and Coach Service Information
🅦 www.rejseplanen.dk

DOMESTIC FERRY SERVICES

Scandlines
Dampfærgevej 10,
2100 Copenhagen Ø.
☎ 33 15 15 15.
🅦 www.scandlines.dk

Smyril Line
J. Broncksgøta 37, 100 Tórshavn,
Faroe Islands.
☎ (+298) 34 59 00.
🅦 www.smyril-line.com

DFDS Seaways (Denmark)
Sankt Annæ Plads 30, 1295
Copenhagen K.
☎ 43 73 86 58.
🅦 www.dfdsseaways.dk

INTERNATIONAL FERRY SERVICES

Color Line
Norgeskajen 2, 9850 Hirtshals.
☎ 99 56 20 00.
🅦 www.colorline.com

DFDS Seaways (UK)
Scananavia House, Parkeston
Quay, Harwich, Essex, CO12 4QG.
☎ 01 255 240 240.
🅦 www.dfdsseaways.co.uk

DFDS Seaways (USA)
Cypress Creek Business Park,
6555 NW 9th Ave, Suite 207,
Fort Lauderdale, Florida,
33309-2049.
☎ 1 800 533 3755 (ext 114).
🅦 www.dfdsseaways.com

Fjordline
Coastergade 10, DK - 7730
Hanstholm
☎ 97 96 30 00.
🅦 www.fjordline.dk.

Stena Line
Færgehavnsvej 10, 9900
Frederikshavn.
☎ 96 20 02 00.
🅦 www.stenaline.dk

International ferry docking in Copenhagen

Travelling by Car

Sign indicating scenic route

NOTWITHSTANDING Denmark's excellent public transport, a car can still be a convenient method of travel for visitors, particularly when travelling in groups of three or four. Using a car can reduce travel costs significantly and is good for visiting out-of-the-way places. Danish motorways are toll-free, the major roads are well signposted and of a good standard, and travelling over one of the new bridges, such as the Store Bælt Bridge between Zealand and Funen, can be a truly breathtaking experience on a clear day. Particularly scenic roads are signposted by a marguerite on a brown background.

Hertz Car Hire logo

the speed limit as well as for other motoring offences such as not wearing a seat belt or talking on a mobile phone while driving. Being caught driving under the influence of alcohol will incur even stiffer penalties and possibly imprisonment.

ARRIVING BY CAR

ANYONE DRIVING to Denmark must travel via Germany as this is the country's only land border. Following the implementation of the Schengen Treaty in 2001, immigration checkpoints between EU countries have been abolished. There are still customs checkpoints at sea and land borders with Germany and drivers may expect customs but generally you will not be required to stop and produce a passport. The main route into Denmark is the E45 which forms part of a European network and runs through Jutland, ending up at Frederikshavn.

Operating instruction

Fuel selector

Card slot

Banknote slot

Self-service Fuel Pump at a Petrol Station
Many stations in Denmark are equipped with special self-service fuel pumps. These are easy to use and accept both cash and credit cards.

Motorway road signs

RULES OF THE ROAD

AS IN ALL continental European countries, the Danes drive on the right. Cars from the UK will need to have their headlights adjusted. Both cars and motorcycles must have dipped headlights on during the day and seat belts must be worn at all times. Children under three must be in a child seat. When turning to the right, drivers must give way to cyclists on the inside. A warning triangle must be kept in the car in case of a breakdown.

The speed limit is usually 50 km/h (30 mph) in town, 80 km/h (50 mph) on most roads and up to 130 km/h (80 mph) on the motorways. Hefty fines may be charged on the spot for breaking

PARKING

TICKETS for parking are obtained from kerbside machines. Known as *billet-automat*, these accept most coins.

In many smaller towns, parking is free and is regulated by a parking disk available from all garages. The plastic disk has an hour hand that you leave on your dash board. Different zones are marked with a blue sign with the letter "P". Also on the sign is the time limit for parking. Signs marked as *1 time* mean you can stay for an hour; *2 timer* is two hours and so on. When parking within these time zones set the hour hand to indicate the time when you parked the car so that the wardens can check whether the limit has been exceeded.

In larger towns parking is often free between 6pm and 8am, after 2pm on Saturdays and all day Sundays. The Danish for no parking is *parkering forbudt*. For parking in towns, see page 303.

BREAKDOWNS

IN THE EVENT of a breakdown drivers should telephone the emergency number given by their hire company or breakdown organization. Phones on motorways are placed at 2-km (1-mile) intervals. For other emergencies dial 112 and ask for the relevant service.

CAR HIRE

REPRESENTATIVES of most major car hire firms can be found at airports, upmarket hotels and in city centres. Car hire tends to be expensive in Denmark; booking beforehand through an international firm can work out much cheaper. Three of the major firms in Denmark are **Avis**, **Europcar** and **Hertz**.

ROADS, MOTORWAYS AND BRIDGES

MOTORWAY signs in Denmark are colour coded and easy to understand. Exits are indicated by blue signs while green signs indicate cities that can be reached along the motorway.

There are five trans-European motorways in Denmark. The E20 runs west to east from Esbjerg though Kolding and Odense, across the Store Bælt and onto Køge and Copenhagen; the E29 links Hirtshals to Nørresundby; the E45 crosses the German border and links Kolding, Århus, Aalborg and Frederikshavn; the E47 links Helsingør, Copenhagen, Køge, Maribo and Rødbyhavn. The E55 runs between Helsingør, Copenhagen, Køge, Nykøbing F and Gedser.

Part of the E20 consists of

Caravans – a common sight on Denmark's roads

Danish motorway sign

bridges over the Store Bælt and Øresund (Sound). A toll is charged to cross and is collected at entry or exit points. The toll stations are equipped with card machines or are manned by staff at busier times.

The Store Bælt bridge toll charges are 125 Dkr for a motorcycle, 245 Dkr for cars up to 6 m (20 ft) and 370 Dkr for longer vehicles. The toll for the Øresund Bridge is 130 Dkr for a motorcycle, 250 Dkr for cars up to 6 m and 380 Dkr for vehicles over 6 m.

ROAD MANNERS

DANES ARE generally careful drivers and tend to observe the country's speed limits, both on motorways and local roads and when driving in town. On motorways cars often cruise along the middle lane, leaving the left one for faster traffic

and the right one for slower vehicles. A recent change in the law has made it compulsory to indicate when changing lane.

WHAT TO TAKE

ANYONE driving in Denmark must have all the relevant documents including insurance and an international driver's licence. Check that you have breakdown cover with a company that has reciprocal arrangements with Denmark. **FDM**, the Danish motoring organization, can provide further information.

It is not compulsory to carry a first-aid kit, but it is good to have one in the car, as well as a car fire extinguisher, a torch and a towrope.

DIRECTORY

INFORMATION

FDM
Vester Farimagsgade 1
45 27 07 07.
www.fdm.dk

TOLL CHARGES

Øresund Bridge
33 41 60 00.
www.oresundskonsortiet.dk

Store Bælt Bridge
70 15 10 15.
www.storebaelt.dk

CAR HIRE

AVIS
Avis Biludlejning,
Sjællandsbroen 1,
2450 Copenhagen SV.
33 26 80 00
www.avis.dk

Europcar
Gl Kongevej 13, Copenhagen.
70 11 66 99.
www.europcar.dk

Hertz
Vester Farimagsgade 1,
1606 Copenhagen V.
33 17 90 00.
www.hertzdk.dk

Motorway entrance

Getting Around Danish Towns

Sign indicating a cycle lane

MOST DANISH TOWNS and cities can easily be explored on foot. Cycling is widespread and all Danish towns, including the capital, have good cycle lane networks. On normal roads, drivers treat cyclists as they would any other legitimate road users. All this makes cycling an enjoyable way to explore a town. Public transport in most cities is efficient, safe and reasonably priced. Taxis are another good way to get around and are especially convenient for anyone that is carrying heavy luggage or large amounts of shopping.

Pedestrian crossing lights at a busy city intersection

ON FOOT

ALL OF DENMARK'S towns and cities are compact and most have pedestrianized areas. In addition, many sights tend to be closely grouped together and signposting is good, making getting around on foot a pleasurable experience.

Nevertheless, pedestrians should observe the traffic regulations. Care should be exercised when crossing the road, although Danish drivers are very attentive towards pedestrians and would never enter a crossing when there are people on it; nor would they force their right of way in any other situation.

Pedestrians who step onto the cycle lanes that run along beside the pavements are strongly frowned upon, however, especially during the busy rush hour. Danish cities such as Copenhagen, Århus and Odense often have walking tours, which offer an alternative way to explore the city.

BICYCLES

MOST DANES own and use bicycles – it has been estimated that Danes cycle, on average, over 600 km (373 miles) a year. Danish cities make many allowances for cyclists including numerous cycle paths and advantageous laws regarding right of way.

Copenhagen is especially cycle-friendly and even runs a scheme known as Bycykler, which allows anyone to borrow a bike for free. The scheme, which runs during summer, is aimed at reducing congestion in the city centre and provides over 2,000 bikes for anyone who wishes to use one. The bicycles have solid wheels and punctureless tyres and, to deter theft, are unsuitable for travelling long distances. They are available from 125 stands throughout the city. Many of the stands are located close to the main attractions and can also be found at some of the larger

S-tog stations. A 20 Dkr coin must be deposited in the Bycykler stand to release a bike. This deposit is returned once the bike is placed back in a stand.

Bikes and accessories such as helmets and child seats can be hired in many of Denmark's towns and cities from companies including **København Cykler** in Copenhagen, **City Cykler** in Odense or **Morten Mengel Cykelværksted** in Århus.

Although cycling can be a fun way to get around, there are a number of factors that should be taken into account. No bike should be left unlocked and expensive bikes should be avoided as they are highly desirable to thieves. In larger towns it is advisable to attach the bicycle to a cycle rack. On the busy streets of Copenhagen cyclists new to the city should exercise special care, as many of the city's native cyclists whizz around at an alarming pace and expect others to do the same.

When using cycle lanes cyclists must observe general traffic regulations, such as not jumping red lights. Bicycles must be equipped with lights after dark and have reflectors fitted at the back and front. Cyclists stopped under influence of alcohol may not only incur a hefty fine but also lose their driver's licence. Children are obliged by law to wear safety helmets when riding a bicycle.

Outside of peak hours, bicycles can be taken onto trains. Carrying a bicycle on

Bicycles, a popular form of transport in Danish towns and cities

City bus – tickets can be bought on board or in advance

the train or metro in the city requires a special bicycle ticket. The fee is minimal, however, and multiple-journey cards for transporting a bicycle are also available.

DRIVING IN TOWN

IN ACCORDANCE WITH their environmental concerns, the Danish government does its best to discourage people from using their car, and driving in the larger towns and cities is to be avoided if at all possible. Major cities are often congested and parking and fuel are very expensive, as is the cost of hiring a car. Pedestrians and cyclists take precedence on city roads and car drivers are obliged to give way when turning right to cyclists coming up on the inside and, even if there is a green light, to pedestrians crossing the road.

PARKING IN TOWN

A FEE IS charged for on-street parking in Denmark's city centres between 8am and 6pm Monday to Friday and from 8am–2pm on Saturdays. At all times it can be difficult to find a parking space, especially in the centre of towns and cities. It can also be expensive to park a car. Some Danish cities have parking zones, with zones closest to the centre costing the most. Non payment of parking charges or exceeding the permitted time limit incurs high fines. See page 300 for more on parking in Denmark.

PUBLIC TRANSPORT

MOST CITIES in Denmark have well run, modern systems of public transport and anyone planning to stay in the larger towns will have little need of a car. Many Danish cities, including Copenhagen, Odense and Århus, have their own travel cards, which entitle the user to unlimited use of local transport for a set period.

Maps and timetables are available from tourist offices in the major cities that list the main bus and rail routes as well as the main sights close to the stops. Central bus stations in towns and cities are usually situated next to the main train station or by the ferry terminal.

Books of tickets *(klip kort)* are readily available in the major cities, such as Århus, Copenhagen and Odense, which are valid on buses and local trains. Weekly or monthly passes such as the

Sign for a taxi rank

Århus Pass and Odense Eventrypas allow unlimited travel on public transport and include discounted or free admission to city attractions. Reduced-fare travel cards for children are available up to the age of 16 and are valid for the same periods and zones as adult travel cards.

For more detailed information on public transport in Copenhagen see pages 304–305.

TAXIS

IN DENMARK there is little problem with finding a taxi, although they can be rather expensive. Taxi ranks can be found in front of all railway stations, airports and ferry terminals, as well as in town centres and major shopping centres. Taxis can be booked by phone. Those with a lit sign saying *fri* can be flagged down in the street. Fares start at 24 Dkr and are then charged by the kilometre. A higher rate is levied at night. Most taxis in Denmark accept credit cards, and there is no need to offer a tip as these are included in the fare.

Parking Meter
Parking meters are found within all pay-zones. The driver has to estimate the parking time and pay the price. The meter then prints out a time-coded ticket.

Labels on parking meter:
- Information screen
- Coin slot
- Parking times and tariff information
- Change dispenser
- Ticket dispenser

DIRECTORY

BICYCLE HIRE

City Cykler
66 13 97 83.
www.citycykler.dk

København Cykler
33 33 86 13.
www.rentabike.dk

Morten Mengel Cykelværksted
86 19 29 27.
www.mmcykler.dk

TAXIS

Hovedstadens (Cph)
38 77 77 77.

Århus Taxa
89 48 48 48.

Odense Taxa
66 15 44 15.

Public Transport in Copenhagen

Logo of the S-tog train

COPENHAGEN IS AN easy city to explore thanks to its up-to-date system of public transport. The metro and the network of buses and trains run throughout the week and are cheap and efficient. Waterbuses make the most of Copenhagen's canals and provide an excellent means or getting around. The city's transport system has an integrated fare structure, which means that you can use *klippekort* (clip cards) and travel passes on the metro, buses and S-tog. Copenhagen is one of the safest cities in Europe and there should be no problem travelling alone, even at night.

BUSES

ONE OF THE easiest ways to get around in Copenhagen is by bus. Copenhagen's efficient HT bus network, run by **HUR**, has a common fare structure with the city's S-tog and metro trains. Bus stops are marked by posts carrying a yellow signboard with the letters BUS. Buses run according to a schedule displayed at the stop. When asked to stop at a particular stop the driver will announce its approach. Otherwise the driver is entitled to drive past the stop if no one is waiting. Tickets can be purchased at the time of boarding providing you have the correct change. Travel cards should be clipped by inserting them into the yellow time clock next to the driver. Disembarking takes place via the central or back doors.

Buses, like trains, begin operating at about 5am (6am on Sundays). Unlike trains, however, a number of buses run throughout the night and operate on special routes, according to a night timetable.

METRO

THE NEWEST form of transport in Copenhagen is the **Metro**, which is constantly being extended and has been designed to complement the S-tog network. Though operational, the network is not yet fully complete – an extension linking Lergravsparken to Copenhagen Airport is due to open in 2007. An additional route circling the city is still at the planning stage.

The bright, modern trains were produced in Italy and are fully in accord with the Danes' love of elegant design. Each train can hold up to 300 passengers, with seating for 96. Even at peak times they do not feel crowded and a journey through Copenhagen

in a light and spacious metro carriage is an enjoyable experience in itself.

Metro trains are fully automated and consist of single driverless carriages. The doors open automatically in line with the platform doors, making it impossible for anyone to fall onto the track. Call points by each of the carriage doors can be used in an emergency or by passengers in wheelchairs.

Tickets must be punched into the yellow time clocks on the platform before boarding. Metro stations are marked with the red letter "M" and can easily be spotted above ground by the 5-m (16-ft) high illuminated information posts outside them.

Board on platform showing S-tog departure information

S-TOG

COPENHAGEN'S rail system is known as **S-tog** and is run by DSB (Danish State Railways). This fast and convenient service consists of 10 lines that all pass through Central Station and run to the distant outskirts of the city. The DSB's website has a journey planner, allowing you to work out the best route from one part of Copenhagen to another.

Tickets can be bought at the station and must be punched into one of the yellow time clocks on the platform by inserting it with the magnetic strip facing downwards.

All trains are marked with with a red hexagon bearing a white letter "S". Those marked with an "x" are express trains with limited stops. Much of the system is adapted for disabled passengers, with lifts from street level to the platforms. Outside peak hours passengers are allowed to carry bicycles on the train. Trains begin operating from about 5am and run till about half past midnight.

Metro station in Copenhagen

Modern S-tog at the platform

TICKETS AND TRAVEL PASSES

COPENHAGEN'S public transport system has a common fare structure, which means that tickets are valid on trains, buses and the metro, and transferring from one mode of transport to another is possible on the same ticket. You can purchase tickets from ticket offices, vending machines at stations and bus drivers.

The metropolitan area is split into seven zones. Coloured zone maps can be found at information desks and are also on display at bus and train stations. The cheapest ticket *(billet)* allows you to travel within two zones. A *klippekort* is valid for 10 journeys within two zones. For travel between three or more zones you will need to buy the appropriate ticket or clip the appropriate number of tickets on your *klippekort*. Clipping stamps your ticket

with the date and time and the zone from which you are departing. Tickets clipped for journeys within the same zone or between two or three zones are valid for one hour. Four-, five- and six-zone tickets are valid for an hour and a half. Tickets and stamped 10-trip cards for all zones are valid for two hours. Travelling without a valid ticket carries a high penalty.

Between 1am and 5am fares double. If you are using a *klippekort*, you will need to clip an extra ticket. Special tickets are available which allow for unrestricted travel over a 24-hour period. Tourist passes, such as the Copenhagen Card, allow unlimited travel on public transport, as well as discounted admission to many of the city's attractions.

Two children up to the age of 12 travel free when accompanied by an adult carrying an appropriate ticket. Four children up to the age of 12 can travel on one ticket, or one clip of an adult *klippekort*. Children below the age of 16 pay a child's fare when travelling alone and may take another child up to the age of 12 at no extra cost.

WATERBUSES

CANAL BOATS are a popular form of transport in the city and are a particularly good way to avoid any traffic congestion. A trip aboard a waterbus is also a good way to see Copenhagen as the city's canals lead past many

of the major historic sights and attractions. One of the most popular tourist routes is the trip from Nyhavn, along Holmenskanal. Along the route the boat stops at the statue of the Little Mermaid, Amalienborg Slot, Christianshavn, Vor Frelsers Kirke, the Nationalmuseet, Christiansborg Slot, Holmens Kirke and back to Nyhavn.

Some trips on the canal are run privately by companies such as **DFDS** and are accompanied by a guide, who provides information about the sights. These are particularly appealing to families with small children as they keep the kids amused and avoid tired legs.

Cards can be purchased which allow unlimited travel on the yellow harbour bus network for a limited period. Holders of the Copenhagen Card and the weekly travel cards are also entitled to use the yellow harbour bus (guided tours must be paid for). Alternatively, it is possible to pay on the boat for a short ride from one stop to another. On some routes waterbuses run only at weekends; others operate only on weekdays.

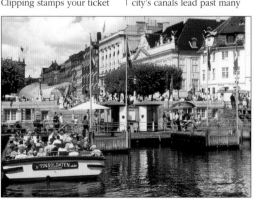

Waterbus departure point

Index

Acknowledgments

HACHETTE LIVRE POLSKA would like to thank the
following people whose contribution and assistance
have made the preparation of the book possible:

ADDITIONAL TEXT
Marek Pernal, Jakub Sito, Barbara Sudnik-Wójcikowska.

ADDITIONAL ILLUSTRATIONS
Dorota Jarymowicz, Paweł Pasternak.

ADDITIONAL PHOTOGRAPHS
Oldr˘ich Karasek, Jakub Sito, Barbara Sudnik-
Wójcikowska, Monika Witkowska, Andrzej
Zygmuntowicz and Ireneusz Winnicki, Juliusz
Żebrowski.

DORLING KINDERSLEY would like to thank the following
people whose contribution and assistance have made
the preparation of the book possible:

PUBLISHER
Douglas Amrine.

PUBLISHING MANAGERS
Anna Streiffert, Vicki Ingle.

MANAGING ART DIRECTOR
Kate Poole.

SENIOR EDITOR
Kathryn Lane.

EDITORIAL ASSISTANCE
Sam Fletcher, Anna Freiberger.

CARTOGRAPHY
Casper Morris.

DTP DESIGNER
Alistair Richardson.

FACTCHECKER
Britt Lightbody.

PROOFREADER
Stewart J. Wild.

INDEXER
Helen Peters.

JACKET DESIGN
Tessa Bindloss.

SPECIAL ASSISTANCE AND PERMISSIONS
The Publishers also wish to thank all persons and
institutions for their permission to reproduce
photographs of their property, for allowing us to
photograph inside the buildings and to use
photographs from their archives:

Amager Youth Hostel; Amalienborg, Copenhagen (S.
Haslund-Christensen, Lord Chamberlain and Colonel
Jens Greve, Palace Steward); Amber Museum,
Copenhagen; Aquarium, Charlottenlund;

Arbejdermuseet, Copenhagen (Peter Ludvigsen);
Bornholm Tourist Information Centre (Pernille Larsen);
Carlsberg Brewery; Ceramics Museum, Rønne;
Christiansborg, Copenhagen; Copenhagen Airports A/S
(Bente Schmidt – Event- and visitor department);
Copenhagen Town Hall (Allan Johansen); Corbis
(Łukasz Wyrzykowski); Danish Tourist Board Photo
Database (Christian Moritz – Area Sales Manager);
Dansk Moebelkunst (Dorte Slot) (Bredgade 32,
Copenhagen K) www.dmk.dk; Davids Samling,
Copenhagen; Danish Chamber of Tourism & SAS
Group PR (Agnieszka Blandzi, Director); Egeskov
Castle; Experimentarium, Copenhagen; H. Ch.
Andersen Museum, Odense; Holmegaard Glass Factory;
Jagna Noren – a guide to Bornholm; Jesper T. Møller
and other employees of the National Museum in
Copenhagen; Karen Blixen Museum; Knud Rasmussens
Haus; Kronborg castle; Legoland, Billund; Lene
Henrichsen – assistant to the director of the Louisiana
museum; Louisiana – Museum for Modern Kunst
(Susanne Hartz); The Museum of Holbæk and
Environs, Holbæk; Det Nationalhistoriske Museum på
Frederiksborg, Hillerød; Nationalmuseet, Copenhagen
(Heidi Lykke Petersen); The Nobel Foundation (Annika
Ekdahl); Ny Carlsberg Glyptotek in Copenhagen (Jan
Stubbe Østergaard); Palaces and Properties Agency,
Denmark (Peder Lind Pedersen); Pritzker Prize (Keith
Walker) for making available the photographs of the
interiors of Jørn Utzon's house; Ribe VikingeCenter
(Bjarne Clement – manager); Rosenborg Castle – The
Royal Danish Collection (Peter Kristiansen – curator);
Roskilde Cathedral; The Royal Library, Copenhagen
(Karsten Bundgaard – photographer); Royal Porcelain
Factory, Copenhagen; Skagens Museum (Mette Bøgh
Jensen – curator); Scandinavian Airlines SAS (Wanda
Brociek i Małgorzata Grążka); Statens Historiska
Museum, Stockholm; Statens Museum for Kunst: (Eva
Maria Gertung & Marianne Saederup); Stine Møller
Jensen (Press coordinator, Copenhagen Metro); Bo
Streiffert; Tivoli, Copenhagen – Stine Lolk;
Tobaksmuseet, Copenhagen (W.Ø. Larsens); Tycho
Brahe Planetarium, Copenhagen; Tønder Tourist Office
(Lis Langelund-Larsen – tourist officer); Voergård Slot;
Aalborg Symfoniorkester (Jan Bo Rasmussen); Østerlars
Kirke, Bornholm (Ernst A Grunwald).

201cr; © Stefan Lindblom 28tclb, 45br ; © Massimo Listri 25b, 50; © Wally McNamee 45c; © Adam Woolfitt 54br, 168.

DANSK MOEBELKUNST; 22clb, 23cla.
NIELS JAKOB DARGER; 89b.
DAVIDS SAMLING: 58cra.

FREDENSBORG; 125tr, 127ca.
FREDERIKSBORG; Hans Petersen 39t, 40c, 41t, 41crb; Larsen, Lennart 27bl, 38clb, 40t; Ole Haupt 36t.

JAKUB SITO: 20t, 21tc, 21ca, 25tr, 25cl.

OLDR˜ICH KARASEK: 48t, 48b, 49b, 57b, 224, 226t, 229t, 282t.

LOUISIANA – MUSEUM FOR MODERNE KUNST: Asger Jorn, Dead Drunk Danes (1960) © DACS 24b; Cesar, Big Thumb (1968) © DACS 118g; Pablo Picasso, Breakfast on the Grass (1961) © DACS 118 cra; Jean Arp, Venus de Meudon (1956) © DACS 118clb; Louise Bourgeois, Eyes (1997) © DACS 118b; Andy Warhol, Marilyn Monroe (1967) © DACS 119cra; Henry Moore, Semi-reclining figure No.5 (1969–1970) © DACS 119clb.

MEPL: 9c, 34clb, 36cr, 37t, 37bra, 38t, 39bl, 42bl, 43t, 44t, 44bla, 44brb, 47c, 109c, 235c, 287c.

NATIONALMUSEET: 33bl, 84t, 84cra, 84clb, 84b, 85cla.
THE NOBEL FOUNDATION: 27cb.

B. V. PETERSEN; 18cl, 18clb, 18cra, 18c, 19cla, 19clb, 19cra, 19ca, 19crb

RIBE VIKINGE CENTER: 28b
ROSENBORG CASTLE: 60b, 61ca, 61b
ROYAL LIBRARY: (Karsten Bundgaard) 117br

SAFARI PARK: (Finn Brasen) 156t, 156b, 157cra, 157crb
SKAGENS MUSEUM P. S. Krøyer, Michael Ancher (1886) phot. Esben Thorning 201br
ANNA AND JANUSZ STAROSCIK: 5t

STATENS MUSEUM FOR KUNST (COPENHAGEN): 24tra, 24tlb, 32, 42cl, 42br, 42–43c, Henry Matisse, Portrait of Mrs Matisse (1905) © DACS 62b; Emil Nolde, Last supper (1909) © DACS 63cra.
BARBARA SUDNIK-WÓJCIKOWSKA; 18bla, 19cl.

TIVOLI: 64; Henrik Stenberg 76cla, 77t, 77bl.
TØNDER TOURIST OFFICE: 30t.

JØRN UTZON: 22–23c.

VISITDENMARK: 59b, 83c; Aalborg Tourist- og Kongressbureau 207ca; Bent Næsly 29c, 113, 201cl; Bob Krist 280c; Cees van Roeden 2–3, 34cra, 100t, 170b, 179b, 206bla, 283cr; Danmarks Turistråd 121cl, 212; Dorte Krogh 279b, 300tr; Henrik Steberg 160–161; Ireneusz Cyranek 90; Jan Kofoed Winther 96b; Jette Jørs 100c; John Sommer 38b, 58clb, 197d, 284c, 301t; Jørgen Schytte 260t; Juliusz Żebrowski 225b, 230t, 230b, 231t; Klaus Bentzen 132–133, 286–287; Peter Søllner 33t; Strüwing 23br; Ted Fahn 46–47, 108–109; Thomas Nykrog 234–235; ukendt 1, 281t; Wedigo Ferchland 208–209; WoCo 6b.

MONIKA WITKOWSKA: 226b, 227t, 227b, 228t, 228b.

AALBORG OPERA: 31t.

JACKET
Front: ALAMY IMAGES: Gavin Hellier main image; CORBIS: Werner Forman Archive crb; DK IMAGES: Dorota & Mariuz Jarymowicz clb; GETTY IMAGES: Stone/Rex Ziak bc. Back - ALAMY IMAGES: Robert Harding World Imagery tl; DK IMAGES: Dorota & Mariuz Jarymowicz br. Spine - ALAMY IMAGES: Gavin Hellier.

All other images Dorling Kindersley
For further information see
www.dkimages.com

Phrasebook

IN AN EMERGENCY

Can you call an ambulance?	Kan du tilkalde en ambulance?
Can you call the police?	Kan du tilkalde politiet?
Can you call the fire brigade?	Kan du tilkalde brandvæsenet?
Is there a telephone here?	Er der en telefon i narheden?
Where is the nearest hospital?	Hvor er det narmeste hospital?

USEFUL PHRASES

Goodnight	God nat
Goodbye	Farvel
Good evening	God aften
Good morning	God morgen (mornings), God dag (after about 9am)
yes	ja
no	nej
please (when serving food)	varsgo/velbekomme
Thank you	Tak
How are you?	Hvordan har du det? /Hvordan går det?
Pleased to have met you	Det var rart at mode dig
See you!	Vi ses!
I understand	Jeg forstår
I don't understand	Jeg forstår ikke
Does anyone speak English?	Er der nogen, der kan tale engelsk?

USEFUL WORDS

near	tat pa
far	langt fra
to the left/on the left	til venstre
to the right/on the right	til højre
open	åben
closed	lukket
warm	varm
cold	kold
big	stor
little	lille

MAKING A TELEPHONE CALL

I would like to call…	Jeg vil gerne ringe til…
I will telephone again	Jeg ringer en gang til

IN A HOTEL

Do you have double rooms?	Findes her dobbeltværelser?
With bathroom	Med badeværelse
With washbasin	Med håndvask
key	nøgle
I have a reservation	Jeg har en reservation

SIGHTSEEING

railway station	banegard
cathedral	domkirke
church	kirke
airport	lufthavn
museum	museum
train	tog
ferry terminal	færgehavn
bus stop	busstoppested
a public toilet	et offentligt toilet

SHOPPING

I wish to buy…	Jeg vil gerne købe…
Do you have…?	Findes der…?
How much does it cost?	Hvad koster det?
expensive	dyr
cheap	billig
size	størrelse
grocery store	supermarked
market	marked

EATING OUT

Do you have a table for…people?	Har I et bord til… personer?
I wish to order…	Jeg vil gerne bestille…
I am a vegetarian	Jeg er vegetar
children's menu	børnemenu
starter (appetizer)	forret
main course	hovedret
dessert	dessert
wine list	vinkort
May I have the bill?	Ma jeg bede om regningen?

MENU

brød	bread
danskvand	mineral water
fisk	fish
fløde	cream
grøntsager	vegetables
is	ice cream
kaffe	coffee
kartofler	potatoes
kød	meat
kylling	chicken
laks	salmon
lam	lamb
leverpostej	liver paté
mælk	milk
oksekød	beef
ost	cheese
pølse	sausage
rejer	shrimps
rødspætte	plaice
røget fisk	smoked fish
saftevand	squash
salat	salad
sild	herring
skaldyr	shellfish
skinke	ham
smør	butter
sodavand	fizzy drink
svinekød	pork
te	tea
torsk	cod
vand	water
wienerbrød	Danish pastry
æg	egg
øl	beer

TIME

today	i dag
tomorrow	i morgen
yesterday	i går
before noon	om formiddagen
afternoon	om eftermiddagen
evening	om aftenen
night	en nat
minute	et minut
hour	en time
week	en uge
month	en måned
year	et år

DAYS OF THE WEEK

Monday	Mandag
Tuesday	Tirsdag
Wednesday	Onsdag
Thursday	Torsdag
Friday	Fredag
Saturday	Lørdag
Sunday	Søndag

MONTHS

January	Januar
February	Februar
March	Marts
April	April
May	Maj
June	Juni
July	Juli
August	August
September	September
October	Oktober
November	November
December	December

NUMBERS

0	nul		20	tyve
1	en		30	tredive
2	to		40	fyrre
3	tre		50	halvtreds
4	fire		60	tres
5	fem		70	halvfjerds
6	seks		80	firs
7	syv		90	halvfems
8	otte		100	hundrede
9	ni		1,000	tusind
10	ti		2,000	totusinde

EYEWITNESS TRAVEL INSURANCE

FOR PEACE OF MIND ABROAD,
WE'VE GOT IT COVERED

DK INSURANCE PROVIDES YOU
WITH QUALITY WORLDWIDE
INSURANCE COVER

For an instant quote
go to **www.dk.com/travel-insurance**

Organised by Columbus Travel Insurance Services Ltd, 17 Devonshire Square, London EC2M 4SQ, UK.
Underwritten by certain underwriters at Lloyd's and Professional Travel Insurance Company Ltd.